ONE & ALL

A HISTORY OF POLICING IN CORNWALL

THE CORNWALL CONSTABULARY 1857–1967

ONE & ALL

A HISTORY OF POLICING IN CORNWALL

THE CORNWALL CONSTABULARY 1857–1967

KEN SEARLE

HALSGROVE

First published in Great Britain in 2005

British Library Cataloguing-in-Publication Data
A CIP record for this title is available from the British Library

ISBN 1 84114 451 7

HALSGROVE
Halsgrove House
Lower Moor Way
Tiverton, Devon EX16 6SS
Tel: 01884 243242
Fax: 01884 243325
email: sales@halsgrove.com
website: www.halsgrove.com

Printed and bound by CPI Bath Press, Bath.

CONTENTS

The Oath*

I, ——— do swear that I will well and truly serve our

Sovereign Lady the Queen, in the office of Constable for the

County of Cornwall, without favour or affection, malice or ill will;

and that I will, to the best of my power, cause the peace to be

kept and preserved and prevent all offences against the persons

and properties of Her Majesty's subjects; and that while I

continue to hold the said office, I will, to the best of my skill and

knowledge, discharge all the duties thereof faithfully, according to

the law, So help me God.

*Sworn by Officers on joining the Police Force

INTRODUCTION

The Cornwall Constabulary was formed in February 1857 following the passing of the County & Borough Police Act 1856 and remained as a separate Force until the amalgamation into the Devon and Cornwall Constabulary in 1967. Throughout its history the Force was generally held in high esteem by the public and adjoining Forces. Ken Searle has carried out a thorough research into the history of the Force and compiled an excellent summary and display of photographs together with a detailed record of the personnel who served during its existence. The information provides a snapshot of part of the history of Cornwall and should be of great interest to many, in particular to ex-members, their families and historians.

In many of the Police Forces formed throughout the 1800s the various Committees looked to the military for leaders and this was the case in Cornwall resulting in the appointment of Col. W.R. Gilbert as Chief Constable. It is not surprising therefore that a military-orientated approach ensued with a Sergeant Major, strict discipline, and police stations with rooms defined as guardrooms etc.

A major stage in the administration of the Force followed the appointment of R. Middleton Hill as Chief Constable in 1896. He was instrumental in producing a book of instructions for the Force entitled *Rules and Regulations for the Guidance of the Cornwall Constabulary*. The book published in 1900 became known as the 'Black Book' and was issued to each member of the Force. For many years the instructions contained in the book were strictly enforced and it is interesting to have a brief examination of some of the requirements, a few extracts are set out below.

In the book there is a heading 'Beat Duty' and one must bear in mind that at the time patrols were on foot, although there were concessions for the use of bicycles, where directed, on a Route Sheet, or with express permission from a senior officer:

> *(Beat Duty – para 3) 'The night duty is to be arranged in such a manner that as much ground as possible may be covered by the Constables, and each Constable on most nights should make two points, (meeting places known as Conference Points) these points should never be at the village in which they are stationed, but at a distance of two or three miles, so that an hour or so will be required to go to the first, and the same to come home to the last; the point respectively to one another should be considerable distances, and the Constables instructed not always to go the same way. Twelve miles is not too great a distance for a night's patrol but this is for the discretion of the Superintendents, who must be guided by the state of the roads and weather, and other circumstances. Churches and villages (except where a particular reason to the contrary exists) should be avoided as places of meeting, and cross roads, lone farms, or houses, near wayside beer-shops or woods, chosen, with such places as maybe resorted to at night by poachers, thieves and marauders generally'. Etc. etc.*

(Beat duty – Para8) Whenever the unfortunate necessity arises for the use of a truncheon, the Constable should secure it to his hand by the thong, or it may be (as it often has been) snatched from him and used against him. Constables compelled to use their truncheons must not strike on the head, unless in danger of death or grievous bodily harm. A blow to the head may have far more serious effect than the striker intends, the result depending as much on the thickness of the skull struck as on the force used.

(Beat Duty – Para 13) Every Constable, when his usual hours of patrol are over, will return to his home and remain therein, taking necessary rest, and unless called out to perform some serious service (the nature of which must be reported by him) it is expected that he will be found at his lodgings until the hour of again going on duty. No Constable is permitted to be absent from his beat except on duty, or by permission of the Superintendent.

Beat Duty – Para 15) Constables are not to leave their Stations except in the performance of their duties, without permission. On arrival at a new Station they are to report themselves to all Justices residing on their beat.

Under the heading 'Conditions of Service' appears the following:

(Para 18) Any Constable who shall marry without first obtaining the permission of the Chief Constable will be liable to dismissal.

Many of the rules and regulations in the 'Black Book' appear to have been draconian in their severity but they worked and many were maintained up to relatively recent times. I recall in my early years of service being required to remain in the Station between tours of duty (to gain experience! This often meant looking after the telephone or cleaning duties). Time off was one rest day (8am to midnight), pay was £3.46 per week, paid monthly in arrears at a pay-parade where you were frequently subjected to an interrogation on the law and procedures by the Superintendent, these were at times intimidating experiences. During the war, whilst I was serving in the RAF, I married my wife, Daphne, but the 1900 rule applied and I was required to produce evidence as to my prospective wife's character for approval.

The Cornwall Constabulary had a 'police family' tradition whereby several generations followed each other into the Service. A remarkable case is that of P.C.243 John Pomeroy, his great grandfather P.C.30 William Pomeroy joined in 1857, his grandfather John Pomeroy (joined the Metropolitan Force) but John's father P.C.154 John Pomeroy returned to the fold joining on the 1 June 1919; his son P.C.243 John Pomeroy joined on the 1 June 1939, exactly 20 years after his father's enlistment, and retired in 1966. There is also the case of the Hugo family where Constable Mathias Hugo joined in 1865, followed by his son Ernest Garibaldi Hugo in 1883, then his son Claude Hugo and finally his two sons, Douglas Roy Hugo and Ernest Henry Guy Hugo respectively in 1935 and 1938. There are several other cases of family lineage within the Force records.

Following the end of the 1939–1945 war things started to improve in the Force, pay increased, restrictions were relaxed slightly in connection with off duty attendance at Police Stations, but the monthly pay parade continued, still in arrears.

This winter helmet displaying the 'garter' badge was issued in 1872. With only a few minor changes it was worn continually to 1936.

I took early release from the RAF and after a short period at St Ives I was posted to St Erth, a country station near Hayle. Daphne and I moved into the police house in 1946, a fine granite-built house. St Erth was a grand little village with friendly and generally law-abiding parishioners. The beat covered a rather large area with many farms and a few hamlets.

On arrival our main problem was we had very little furniture. War-time rationing was still in force and we did not have enough coupons to put curtains on all the windows. The front room was left empty, not even a floor covering, and for curtains we obtained some broccoli netting to give some semblance of occupation. There was no electricity upstairs, no bathroom or indoor toilet, in fact there was no running water. There was a Cornish range which belched smoke and soot with every change of the wind. Water was obtained from a well (20 turns on the windlass to raise the bucket) and a worrying point was the well was only a matter of yards from a burial ground. There was an earthen closet at the bottom of a forty-yard garden path, of a type known locally as a 'thunderbox'. It took a brave or desperate person to use it in the dark.

After a while we were supplied with an electric cooker and the closet was upgraded to an 'Elsan' chemical toilet. We thought we were going up in the world, and we very nearly did! The chemical provided was war surplus and very strong; the vapour was overpowering, and there was no secret where you had been when you re-entered the house. A sprig of ivy which grew through a crack in the back of the closet wilted and died and pigeons which roosted on the roof left and never returned. Great care was needed in using the toilet as you could get more shocks from chemical droplets than you would ever get from an electric cooker.

We eventually got more furniture and managed to get our curtains. I bought a new bike (no car in those days) and we felt quite posh. We had some happy years at St Erth and maintained friendly contact with a few of the residents for years after we left.

I have diverted from the more formal 'Introduction' but please excuse my digression, I am sure several of my old colleagues and their wives will have experienced similar moves, or know of someone who has, and after all we are dealing with the history of the Cornwall Constabulary of which these experiences all form a part.

I served in the police for over 35 years with periods in every rank from Constable to Detective Superintendent, and on to Chief Superintendent, and I do not regret a moment. There were difficult and stressful times, in particular in the investigation of a serious crime, but there is more to policing than murder and mayhem, there is the element of public service. Throughout my service I experienced a high level of co-operation with official bodies, also goodwill and close relationships with the public. I have no doubt that this was the experience of the majority of my contemporaries.

The level of understanding and co-operation with the public at large was a great help to law enforcement but I have doubts if it exists to the same extent today. This is not intended as a criticism of the modern force as they have serious problems to face. Society has changed, family influence does not seem to have the authority it once had. There was a time when a word from a police officer with the mother or father of a wayward child would assist in the child's correction, these days there is a real possibility the parents would turn on the officer. Further the sight of a uniformed officer on foot patrol was a reassuring presence, it instilled confidence and deterred wrongdoers, also respect and trust was built up from personal contact. These days there is clearly a serious increase in the lack of respect for people and property particularly amongst the young, this notwithstanding the fact that much effort has gone into Community Policing.

The drug problem was growing before I retired and now, coupled with the increase in alcohol abuse and the resulting resort to violence and possible crime, there is a great drain on resources. One must also consider the effect of the media and peer pressure on the young; of a multi-cultural society from various ethnic backgrounds; the massive increase in vehicular traffic and the problems it creates, the increased mobility of criminals, some of whom travel in groups and operate in rural and urban areas well away from their home territory, and many are accomplished and ruthless in their nefarious deeds; there is no easy answer.

Policing today is light years away from the days of the fatherly figure of the 'Country Bobby' but let us give credit where credit is due. These men and women and their urban colleagues laid the foundation for a fine police force forming part of what was considered by many to be the finest police service in the world. The Cornwall Constabulary played its part and those members still surviving, their wives and their families can be proud of their achievements. This book will help to preserve the memory of their legacy and that of their predecessors.

Ex Chief Superintendent A.T.Jenkin.
Former Det/Supt Cornwall CID
and Deputy District Commander,
No1 District Cornwall,
Devon & Cornwall Constabulary.

ACKNOWLEDGEMENTS

I would like to dedicate this book to all who have helped in its compiling, particularly those listed below:

The Chief Constable of the Devon and Cornwall Constabulary.

The Archivist of the Devon and Cornwall Constabulary Museum at Exeter.

Chief Inspector Phillip John Hutchings.

The Chief Archivist at the Cornwall County Record Office and staff.

To all the staff at the various town museums in Cornwall, especially The Bodmin Town Museum, The Liskeard and District Museum and The Lostwithiel Museum.

Alan Sanders, Chairman, Cornwall Branch, National Association of Retired Police Officers.

Alfred Trahair Jenkin. The most senior surviving Officer of the Cornwall County Constabulary for his help and encouragement.

To my Family for their help and encouragement and especially to my wife Vera for all her help.

THE BEGINNINGS

A Chronological History of Police Forces in Cornwall

The Municipal Corporations Act, 1835, led to the establishment of the first real police forces in the County. The following lists give details of the separate forces that existed in Cornwall some twenty-two years before the Cornwall County Constabulary was set up.

BODMIN BOROUGH POLICE;
1836	Established.	
	H.M.I.C. Report 29.9.1856	One Officer.
22.10.1865	Merged with Cornwall County	One Officer.

LISKEARD BOROUGH POLICE;
1836	Established.	
	H.M.I.C. Report 29.09.1856	Two Officers.
16.07.1877	Merged with Cornwall County	Three Officers.

LAUNCESTON BOROUGH POLICE;
1836	Established.	
	H.M.I.C. Report 29.09.1856	One Officer.
Jan. 1883	Merged with Cornwall County	One Officer.

FALMOUTH BOROUGH POLICE;
1836	Established.	
	H.M.I.C. Report 29.09.1856	Three Officers.
01.04.1889	Merged with Cornwall County	Four Officers.

HELSTON BOROUGH POLICE;
1836	Established.	
	H.M.I.C. Report 29.09.1856	One Officer.
01.04.1889	Merged with Cornwall County	One Officer.

PENRYN BOROUGH POLICE;
1836	Established.	
	H.M.I.C. Report 29.09.1856	Two Officers.
01.04.1889	Merged with Cornwall County	Two Officers.

ST IVES BOROUGH POLICE;
1836	Established.	
	H.M.I.C. Report 29.09.1856	One Officer.
01.04.1889	Merged with Cornwall County	One Officer.

TRURO BOROUGH POLICE;
1836	Established.	
	H.M.I.C. Report 29.09.1856	Six Officers.
01.03.1921	Merged with Cornwall County	Thirteen Officers.

PENZANCE BOROUGH POLICE;

1836	Established.	
	H.M.I.C. Report 29.09.1856	Seven Officers.
	Merged with Cornwall County under defence regulations.	
01.04.1947	Merger ratified	Twenty four Officers.

The County and Borough Police Act, 1856, directed the Justices in every County to establish an efficient Police Force.

CORNWALL COUNTY CONSTABULARY;

06.01.1857	Established	179 Officers.
01.06.1967	Amalgamated with Devon & Exeter and Plymouth City Police Force	478 Officers.

There were only six men who held the office of Chief Constable of The Cornwall County Constabulary:

Colonel Walter Raleigh Gilbert. C.B.	1857–1896
R.Middleton Hill Esq.	1896–1909
Lt.Col. Sir Hugh Protheroe-Smith O.B.E.	1909–1935
Major Edgar Hare, M.C.	1935–1956
Richard Bonar Matthews	1956–1964
Kenneth Mortimore Wherly. Q.P.M.	1964–1967

DEPUTY CHIEF CONSTABLES:

Superintendent John G.Vincent	1857–1890
Superintendent Henry Miller	1890–1894
Superintendent George Barnes	1894–1902
Superintendent William H.Beare	1902–1910
Superintendent Richard Banfield	1910–1927
Superintendent Albert J.Davies.M.B.E.	1927–1935
Superintendent William J.Matthews.	1935–1939
Superintendent Ernest J.Hosking.	1939–1942

ASSISTANT CHIEF CONSTABLES:

Ernest John Hosking	1943–1948
Reginald Roland	1948–1956
Kenneth George Julian. Q.P.M.	1956–1965
James Arthur Henry Pill	1965–1967

THE POLICE DISTRICTS:

Launceston with headquarters at Camelford.
Liskeard with headquarters at St.Germans.
Bodmin with headquarters at Bodmin.
Truro with headquarters at Truro.
Helston with headquarters at Helston.
Penzance with headquarters at Camborne.

The Chief Constable had his office at Bodmin, that being the County Town, and the Districts were to be commanded by a Superintendent, the Divisions by an Inspector and the Subdivisions by a Sergeant.

The first Constable was appointed to the Cornwall Constabulary on the 23rd., February, 1857. He was Charles Blake Bray.

The last Constable was appointed to the Cornwall Constabulary on the 30th., May, 1967. He was David Henry Cann who transferred from the Metropolitan Police.

The Police in the Cornish Boroughs were quite well established by 1857 but there was some serious opposition to the establishment of a County Force by some of the local councils who wrote to the Houses of Parliament to object.

THE FOOD RIOTS

A Brief Note on One the County's Most Turbulent Events

The 1840s had seen a decade of terrible suffering and strife in the county and this period has become known as the hungry forties. On the 21 May, 1847 the *West Briton* newspaper reported as follows:

Food Riots at Wadebridge
Early on Thursday morning the owners of the corn in the cellars proceeded to ship it on board a vessel, when, information was received that a large body of men from the Delabole Quarries were approaching. Soon after about four hundred men entered the town, and went at once to the Quay. It appeared that no outrage was likely to be committed, and that a great portion of the men were really in want of food, the Magistrates and others purchased all the bread procurable in the town, and distributed it amongst them, each receiving a part of a loaf on his passing over the Bridge on his way home. Most of them had crossed the bridge when a rumour was spread that the party of the preceding day were again at hand. This rumour was soon realised, and between three and four hundred men entered the town, each armed with a bludgeon, and marched onto the Quay, cheering as they proceeded. The quarrymen, or most of them, then returned, and mixed with others (streamers, china clay men, and tinners from Roche, Luxulyan, St.Austell, etc.) and when gathered together, they presented a most formidable appearance, and created great consternation. The vessel, which was partly laden with corn, was by this time afloat, and it moved down the river, the rioters being assembled around the cellars, and threatening their destruction; but the coast guard being placed within, seemed to deter them. The men were assured that very little corn remained in the cellars, but this did not satisfy them, and some of them were allowed to enter and judge for themselves.

The Royal Cornwall Polytechnic Report, 1941, contained a report by Ashley Rowe about the Food Riots of the 'forties' in Cornwall.

There was no scarcity of work in Cornwall, but the price of the bare necessities of life was not only soaring but food itself was almost unobtainable. In February at Redruth, one family was found frying turnips in a baker with a little salt only, many had no other food than turnips fried with tallow from miners candles. One family was found to have no other food for some days than the draff from the brewery.

On Thursday, June 3rd., Redruth started to take precautions, the magistrates, Stephen Davey and J.P.Magor, commenced swearing in Special Constables and application was made for military assistance. The work of swearing in Constables continued on the Friday and 100 soldiers arrived That Friday, June 4th 1847 was a memorable day for Redruth. The disturbances commenced at Pool where a flour warehouse was pillaged, later the rioters took possession of Redruth Market, and then broke into a flour store in the town. At 11 am a great crowd, estimated at over 2000 attacked the stores of Joel Blamey, a flour merchant at Pool. The most active of the mob were women, who beat on the door with large stones; one woman fetched a sledge hammer from a smithy and the door soon fell. The mob rushed in, and women came rushing back covered with flour. Tea, coffee, pins and saffron were all mixed up in their aprons. But few of these were local women. Prudence Thomas, a woman of 47, was waving a paddle above her head(it was explained at the trial, that a paddle was a tool used for cutting weeds). One of the constables told her to put it down and she said she " would stick it in his mouth if he did not hold his tongue". A young woman , Mary Ann Craze, was seen with various goods she told the crowd that Mrs Mildren, who was there, was Blamey's servant and would inform against them. Mrs Mildren, in her evidence, said "than a great many came around me and asked if I was Mr.Blamey's servant, the mob said if I was a spy they would beat my brains against the wall". This is very clear proof that they were not local people, or from any near parts . There had been a conference between Blamey and the crowd: he spoke to them from an upper window and told them he could not sell flour at the price they wanted. He said he could not do it - " I have fallen (reduced) the flour now more that I can afford to do it, and if you don't believe me you can see my invoices". He then tied some invoices to a cord and let them down to be shown to the people. When the magistrates arrived from Redruth, with a military force, the riot act was read and the crown dispersed.

The news of the riot at Pool had caused great excitement at Redruth. Shops were closed and special constables paraded, their badge of office being a bit of white tape tied on the breast of each man. The magistrates ordered public houses and beer shops to close and the Bell-man (Town Crier) to announce that the Cornish Bank would be kept open until six o'clock to accommodate miners with change who were accustomed to get it from the publicans. It is clear that they had considerable faith in the honesty of the rioters! By one o'clock Redruth Streets were full, when two market gardeners, with a large stock of cabbage, were required by one or two women to sell at a lower price. The noise with which this demand was made drew a large crowd and the market was soon in uproar. The farmers agreed to sell at any price if only they could have protection from violence.

Mr Stephen Davey, a magistrate, was soon there and offered to compensate the growers for their loss. The mob then cried, "Now for the meat market". There would have been no trouble there but for the boasting a silly young butcher who was heard to say "that if any man touched anything belonging to him, he would put a knife into him". It took all the very active interference of the constables to stem the rush. The boaster and his unlucky neighbour were glad to sell at any price. Other butchers took the opportunity to pack up.

Mr Pendarves and Mr Magor, supported by other magistrates addressed the crowd from a porch of Andrew's Hotel (later Tabbs Hotel). There were nearly 5000 people there. Mr. Magor proposed that the crowd sent a deputation into them. After some hesitation, Trevethen of Chacewater, and Williams, a cattle jobber, of Gwennap, were pushed forward. Being asked their demand, Williams said that they required to have meat sold to them at 4d per pound, Mr Magor , who happened to know him immediately asked, "will you sell your cattle at that price?" "No" said he, " nor yet for 5d nor yet for 6d" Needless to say the conference was fruitless.

Word them came that a mob was attacking Warmingtons flour store, behind the Association Chapel (the Chapel is now part of Jims Cash and Carry). Three of the magistrates, the Rev. Thomas Pascoe and Messrs Magor and Richard Davey with a party of Constables, unarmed, went to the store and found that the mob had broken in and were making off with the flour. The Magistrates and the constables went in and cleared the house. They were then forced to barricade themselves in, while the mob threw stones at the door. Eventually, a violent fellow of great strength broke in the door with a grinding stone which he wielded by the iron handle. The constables being unfurnished with staves, escaped through the back window of an upper room. Mr. Magor went off to fetch the military; when the soldiers were announced " there must have been two or three hundred people in the yard stealing and wasting flour" but when the soldiers actually came in every creature had disappeared, some escaping over the walls and houses which at any other time would have thought perfectly impracticable". The mob was still in the street and the riot act was read repeatedly. At length the mob agreed to disperse if the prisoners were liberated – names and addresses were taken and the men set free. By ten o'clock at night the streets were unusually quiet.

These were the lawless and frightening days from which, ten years later, Col. W.R. Gilbert was going to have to start a Police Force from scratch. Prior to this there were no police houses and no police stations, while opposition to a force was considerable.

In 1967 at the time of the amalgamation, the following places had Police Stations:

Camborne, Pool, Troon, Praze, Isles of Scilly, Redruth, St.Day, Illogan, Penzance, Newlyn, Mousehole, Heamoor, Marazion, Goldsithney, St.Just, Pendeen , St.Buryan, Sennen, St.Ives, Carbis Bay, Nancledra, Hayle, Copperhouse, St.Erth, Crowlas, Helston, Ashton, Rame, Porthleven, Mullion, Mawgan-in-Meneague, The Lizard, St.Keverne, Constantine, Truro, Higher Town, Devoran, Perranporth, Chacewater, St.Agnes, Blackwater, Tregoney, Veryan, Portscatho, Probus, St.Mawes, Falmouth, Penryn, Mawnan Smith, Mylor Bridge, Ponsanooth, Newquay, St.Columb, Indian Queens, Mawgan in Pydar, Wadebridge, Port Isaac, St.Kew, St.Minver, Padstow, St.Merryn, Liskeard, Menheniot, St.Neot, Dobwalls, Looe, Pelynt, Duloe, Lerryn, Polperro, Polruan, Callington, Pensilva, Stoke Climsland, Gunnislake, St.Mellion, St.Austell, Bugle, St.Stephens, Mevagissey, Roche, Sticker, St.Dennis, Lanivet, Lostwithiel, Blisland, Fowey, Tywardreath, St.Blazey, Torpoint, Anthony, Kingsand, Millbrook, Seaton, St.Germans, Saltash, Burraton, Launceston, Five Lanes, Coads Green, Egloskerry, Bude, Kilkhampton, Jacobstow, Whitstone, Boscastle, Tintagel.

THE PHOTOGRAPHS

A very early photo of a constable wearing a high hat. Believed to be dated c.1860 and taken outside Callistick Mill near Truro.

P.C. 82 Frederick John Julian. Appointed 20.3.1860.

P.C. 121 Robert Pill with his wife Mary Elizabeth Rose. Appointed 7.9.1868.

First issue of helmets 1871.

The St Columb Road Horse Bus being used to transport a prisoner to Bodmin Gaol. From the background it looks like St Columb Major. There appears to be one police officer, immediately to the rear of the bus, the bus driver, the prisoner, and two prison officers. Thought to date from the 1880s.

P.C. 72 Maurice Light. Appointed 25.2.1893.

Cornwall County Constabulary Headquarters (now demolished), built in 1867 in the County Town of Bodmin. The building at the rear is the old Bodmin Borough Police Station which was taken over by the County on the amalgamation of the Borough Force on the 22.10.1865.

A Falmouth Borough Constable watching the Falmouth Packet leaving harbour.

This is purported to be the Bodmin Borough Constable.

The one-and-only St Ives Borough Constable.

Truro City Police pictured with the Town Crier who was on the Police strength. Note that the Sergeants have nickel helmet plates and, at the time of the amalgamation in 1921, the men broke the crowns off their badges in protest against the change.

Penzance Borough Police with their Chief Officer Harry Kenyon. They are wearing what they referred to as their bandsman uniform, so called because of the white piping. Penzance was one of only two forces in the UK who issued straw helmets for use during the summer months. They were not that successful as when it rained the top collapsed and the author was told that the only way to keep it up was to stuff it full of newspaper.

The building of Falmouth Police Station in 1899. The Falmouth Borough Police Station was in the main street at the shop which was once occupied by the Cornish Stone Company, and is now a card shop.

The completed Falmouth Police Station. Occupied in 1901. On the left is the station and on the right the Superintendent's house with the Super and his wife in the gateway and the maids looking out of the upstairs windows. A familiar 'blue' lamp hangs over the station doorway marked 'COUNTY POLICE STATION'.

Right: *Constable Horatio Nelson; the one-man Police Force of the Isles of Scilly in the 1890s.*

The men of the new Police Station, Falmouth. The Inspector, with the large crowns on his collar stands next to the Superintendent in the centre. Note the belted frock tunics. The nickel buckle of the belt was surmounted by the Victorian crown, fifteen bezants in the centre and 'ONE AND ALL' around the outside. The Sergeants have stripes below the elbow. Inverted strips on the Constables' tunics denote years of service.

Another photograph of the Force in Falmouth: Second left back row: P.C.163 George Strike, P.C. 17 William John Osborne, P.C. 90 Edwin Lemin, P.C. 74 William Osborne, P.C. 114 William John Keast, P.C. 115, P.C. 39 John Roberts, P.C. 68. Middle row: P.C.26, P.C. 174, Sergeant, Superintendent, Sergeant, P.C. 106. Front row: P.C. 5 John William Matthews, P.C. 178, P.C. 57 William John Ough.

Opening of the Prince of Wales Pier at Falmouth.

Left: *Portrait photograph of Inspector Ernest Garibaldi Hugo, appointed 26.3.1883. One of the Hugo family, almost all of whom were in the County Police.*

Cottage Fire at Bugle c.1901.

The Sergeant Major with his class. 1904. Back row: P.C. unknown, P.C. 168 Ernest Sampson White (appointed 7.11.1903), P.C. 19 William Henry Morgan. Front row: Sergeant Major, P.C. 54 James Ball (appointed 15.02.1904), P.C. 184 William John Osborne (appointed 21.12.1903), P.C. 120 William Henry Eddyvean, P.C. 44 William Wilton (appointed 26.11.1903)

R. Middleton Hill Esq., Chief Constable, 1896–1909.

Superintendent William H. Beare (circa 1900)

P.C. Ough on duty at St Day with some residents.

Superintendent William H. Beare after his promotion to Deputy Chief Constable 1902–910. Photographed outside his house at Bodmin HQ.

P.C.108 Edwin French, appointed 11.11.1895.

The newly built Redruth Police Station in Chapel Street.

A search party, 1904, at the time of the murder of Miss Jessie Rickard.

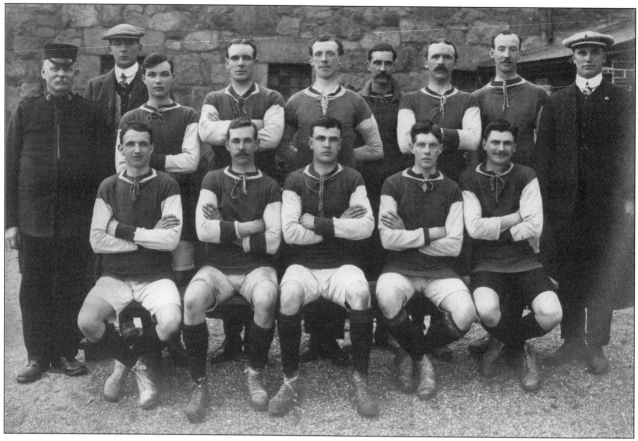

Soccer team including two Hugo's 1907–1908.

P.C.89 Thomas Lee (in centre), appointed 23.3.1899.

P.C.60 William Henry Eade, appointed 01.01.1906. P.C. Eade is wearing his summer-issue helmet identified by a cloth-covered top cap.

Left: P.C.50 William Charles Hill, appointed 01.01.1920.

Escort for the officers of the Assize, the Judge and the Sheriff of Cornwall. The escorts were originally armed and were called the 'javelin men', their staves representing javelins.

This photograph was taken outside what is now Gladys Holman House in Camborne. It was taken to celebrate the retirement of Superintendent Vercoe who was the subject of an article in the main Police magazine of the time The Police Review and Parade Room Gossip. Vercoe was one of the policemen who had been on duty in Camborne at the time of the Camborne Riots.

Claude Hugo, appointed 02.06.1909.

Right: P.C.59 Ernest Edwin Steer, appointed 08.09.1902. He retired to Devoran and after he and his wife died his son secured the house with everything in it left exactly as it was while his parents were alive. Sadly, in the later part of the last century the house was broken into and as a result all this came to light. Inside was found all his uniforms and police equipment etc.

Soccer team with Claude Hugo, second right front row.

Inspector Miller and P.C. Pomeroy attend what is said to be the first ever road traffic accident in Cornwall, in which a car collided with, and killed, a bullock.

P.C. Pomeroy is seen here resting in the back of the car while Inspector Miller, posing for the camera, make notes about the constable being asleep.

Chief Constable Lt-Col. Sir Hugh Protheroe-Smith OBE, 1909–1935.

Group in Moor Street Police Station, Camborne. Some of the faces from Superintendent Vercoe's retirement photo can be recogised as being still in service six years later. Front row second left P.C. Ayers, third left Sgt. Cornelius, fifth left Inspector W.Wright. Third row fifth left P.C. Hambly, seventh left P.C. Phillips. Back row fifth left P.C. Crocker.

Location unknown but it would appear to be Bodmin. The Sergeant Major is sitting beside the Superintendent.

The infamous summer clay strike, 1913. Centre is P.C.163 George Strike, appointed 17.09.1900, pictured with the Glamorgan Constabulary cycle contingent. Note the spectacular helmet with the nickel retainer chain. This was one of the forces who were drafted into Cornwall to help during this turbulent time.

Above: *This is the Slades Road–Clifton Road junction at Mount Charles, St Austell. The picture shows just Cornish policemen. Many of the clay workers had been to the USA gold mining and had returned home with 'souvenirs'. In consequence the Constable from Lerryn who was on duty at Halviggan works was shot in the thigh with a revolver.*

Left: *An officer at Charlestown harbour on strike duty.*

Below: *Cycle contingent at the clay strike, 1913. Fifth from left P.C.1 Samuel Ley, appointed 29.07.1989. Second from right P.C.111 John Andrew, appointed 25.01.1900.*

Left: *Glamorgan County Police tea break.*

Below: *Also at tea break but with a Cornish minder on the far right. Note the Glamorgan Sergeant in the centre of the group with the Prince of Wales' feathers over his stripes.*

Below: *Glamorgan cycle contingent and their coach. These were specially chosen men who arrived in Cornwall immediately after dealing with striking coal miners at Tonypandy in South Wales.*

Devon County Constabulary called in for the strike.

A group photo taken when a change of uniform was underway. The Sergeant, fourth from left sitting, has the new seven-button tunic. The man fourth from right middle row is also wearing the new uniform.

Escort for German prisoners of war 11.08.1914 in Blowing House Hill, Redruth

The Moor, Falmouth. Though the occasion is unknown, it appears that the Mayor is reading a proclamation. The photograph is known to pre-date 1904 as the policemen are not wearing the belted uniform. Note the seamen are wearing traditional white headgear while the naval officers have fore-and-aft hats. The helmets seen lower left are military and could be the Duke of Cornwall's Light Infantry. In the centre behind the Mayor is a military officer, and on the far left there are two Policemen with their backs to the camera and the uniformed officer standing next to them appears to be the Fire Chief. The building on the right is the fire station.

Unknown group photograph taken with the Chief Constable. Unusual photograph in as much as there are five officers, all Inspectors, four Sergeants and just four Constables: Back row. P.C.182 Reginald Terrill Darlington, appointed 24.08.1925. Middle row first left. P.C.98 Ernest Charles Menear, appointed 01.11.1912, second left. P.C.94 Arthur George Passmore, appointed 01.02.1926. Front row left. P.C.57 William John Ough, appointed 24.10.1898, third left. P.C.90 Kenneth James Dunstan, appointed 01.07.1924.

Front from left: P.C.72 Harry Hambly, appointed 07.09.1919, P.C.51 William John Babbage, appointed 01.111912, P.C. 26 William Tamblin, appointed 01.03.1919. Back row: P.C.179 Sidney Valentine Rose, appointed 06.05.1907, P.C.56 William Pearce, appointed 09.09.1907, P.C.159 Richard Curgenven, appointed 01.01.1913.

Pictured outside Tehidy Mansion in Camborne following the fire which took place after the building had been given to the people of Cornwall as a sanatorium in 1918. It shows officers of the Redruth Fire Brigade led by the Fire Chief who is wearing his german-silver helmet. The Police presence includes an Inspector, a Sergeant and four Constables. Front right is P.C. Phillips of Portreath and second left is P.C. Ayers.

Peace Sunday at Falmouth in 1919, with the Mayor, Corporation and dignitaries. Superintendent Nicholls is on duty at the roadside and two Constables heading up the parade. They are wearing summer-weight helmets.

Left: Left: P.C.108 Edwin French, appointed 11.11.1895. Centre: Inspector Miller. Right: P.C.94 Edgar Brown, appointed 15.11.1898.

A photograph taken c.1921–1925. Back row: P.C.73 Titus Hambly, unknown, P.C. 112 Arthur John Kitt., P.C.223 John Balment, P.C.214 Richard Henry Palmer, unknown, unknown, P.C.6 Mark Prust. Middle row; P.C.221 Frank Sloman, P.C.152 Elford Neil Hoskin, P.C.119 Nicholas Mayne, P.C. Frank Redvers Ebbett, P.C.128 Robert Matthews, P.C.192 Ernest Wheay, P.C.185 Sidney Beswetherick, P.C.66 Thomas Tonkin. Front row: P.C. 116 James Arthur Stephens, P.C.108 Edwin French, Sergeant, Superintendent, Sergeant, Sergeant, P.C.219 Tom Julyan. Sitting. P.C.88 Phillip Richard Martin Scantlebury, P.C.62 Fred Barrett.

P.C.194 Andrew Angwin French, appointed 01.10.1925. Note cut-away pocket flaps and the St Johns Ambulance badge on the sleeve indicating expertise in First Aid, black tunic buttons and the crown on his collar which was issued for a limited period.

Dedication of the Cornwall Constabulary War Memorial at Bodmin.

Joining picture 1926. P.C.133 G.W.Kersey, P.C.62 G.A.Clarke, Inspector F.T. Basher, P.C.23 C.J.J. Carrivick, P.C.66 W.W. Wright.

Believed to be Newquay. P.C.182 Drew, appointed 01.10.1921, P.C.9 Brooker, appointed 01.09.1928, P.C.189 Greet, appointed 01.04.1912, P.C.40 Trewella, appointed 04.02.1920, P.C.222 Sercombe, appointed 17.05.1913, P.C.103 Johns, appointed 01.02.1924, P.C.217 Tabb, appointed 01.01.1921, P.C.61 Clark, appointed 27.08.1902, Inspector, Sergeant Peters, appointed 09.09.1907, P.C.170 Dann, appointed 15.09.1911.

The first Representative Board, 1919. This marked the beginning of the Police Federation in Cornwall. Before this came the Police Union and the Police strike. P.C.94 Brown, appointed 15.11.1898, P.C.98 Peters, appointed 09.09.1907, P.C.57 Ough, appointed 24.10.1898, P.C.90 Lemin, appointed 13.06.1898, Sergeant Crocker, appointed 24.02.1899, Sergeant Patrick, appointed 29.09.1897.

Joining photograph, 1928: P.C.33 Nicholls, P.C.150 Harry, P.C.219 Williams, P.C.39 Holman, P.C.9 Brooker (all were appointed 01.03.1928).

Joining Photograph 1926: P.C.111 Dale, P.C. Passmore, P.C.220 Williams, P.C.218 Harding, P.C.247 Pollard, P.C.107 Dyer (all appointed 01.04.1926).

Falmouth District with the Chief Constable. The P.C.67 Crocker in this photograph is the Sergeant Crocker in the First Representative Board photograph shown earlier. P.C. Crocker was a fluent French speaker and was the obvious choice when it came to police being employed in the Carrick Roads during furore in Monte Carlo when a man supposedly broke the bank. Constable Crocker arrested him on his boat in Falmouth.

A group photograph, location unknown. Back row: P.C.2 Banfield, appointed 09.07.1889, P.C.199 Penrose, appointed 15.07.1912, P.C.1 Ley, appointed 29.07.1889, P.C.15 Hoskin, appointed 18.09.1909, P.C.206 Bastion, appointed 12.08.1913, P.C.60 Eade, appointed 01.01.1906, P.C.107 Dyer, appointed 01.02.1926, P.C.19 Wherry, appointed 01.02.1921, P.C.107 Cowling, appointed 15.01.1900, P.C.101 Harris, appointed 01.07.1923, P.C.121 Mitchell, appointed 01.11.1919, P.C.12 Teague, appointed 01.12.1922, Third row: unknown, P.C.184 Toy, appointed 31.10.1904, P.C.136 Wherry, appointed 01.06.1924, P.C.215 Langdon, appointed 01.11.1920, P.C.25 Bray, appointed 31.08.1914, P.C.203 Pooley, appointed 01.05.1919, P.C.65 Rowland, appointed 14.09.1914, P.C.129 Harfoot, appointed 01.06.1898, P.C.135 Sloman, appointed 01.04.1901, P.C.207 Dawe, appointed 01.05.1919, P.C.106 Bulford, appointed 01.11.1906, unknown. Second row: P.C.123 Basher, appointed 22.01.1900, P.C.118 Colwill, appointed 16.03.1914, P.C.185 Jago, appointed 10.09.1900, P.C.69 Cobbledick, appointed 01.01.1920, P.C.79 Goble, appointed 01.11.1919, P.C. 93 Gomm, appointed 04.07.1896, P.C.163 Hoskin appointed 01.06.1919, P.C. 48 Dyer appointed 01.04.1920, P.C. 27 Badcock appointed 01.07.1912, P.C.171 Hicks, appointed 26.05.1913, P.C.125 Dines, appointed 01.01.1923, P.C.18 Brooking, appointed 06.10.1913, P.C.204 Rogers, appointed 03.07.1913. Front row: P.C.202 Doney, appointed 01.10.1912, P.C.5 Matthews, appointed 26.11.1895, Sergeant, Sergeant, Inspector, Superintendent Nicholls, Inspector, Sergeant, Sergeant, P.C.84 Prout, appointed 17.02.1905. P.C.186 Dustow, appointed 16.04.1908, P.C.49 Jago, appointed 06.01.1911.

Joining Photograph: P.C.12 Teague, P.C.117 Endean, P.C.137 Dyer, P.C.30 Pearce, P.C.10 Butterall, P.C.93 Allen, P.C.43 Miller, P.C.36 Tippett, P.C.125 Dines.

Unknown group with the Chief Constable - possibly Bodmin.

Joining Photograph 17.08.1925: P.C.181 Soloman, P.C.124 James, P.C.73 Dunstan, P.C.182 Darlington, P.C.194 French.

Joining Photograph 01.01.1922: P.C.141 Sambells, P.C.82 French, P.C.56 Bennetts, P.C.169 Brooks, P.C.177 Stephens, Inspector Basher, P.C.155 Thomas.

Scantlebury's butchers, unknown location. P.C. Keast.

Left: *P.C.50 William Charles Hill, appointed 01.01.1920.*

Unknown group.

Claude Hugo in soccer team 1907–1908.

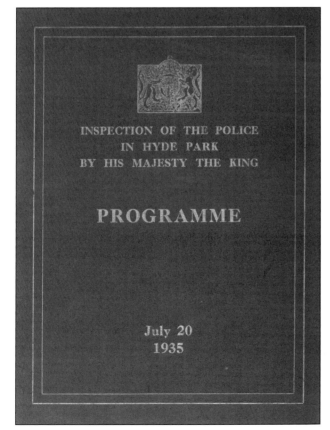

P.C.167 William Thomas Walke, appointed 01.11.1933, Inspector Horace Osborne KPM, appointed P.C.122 01.09.1920.

Left: *Programme for the* Royal Review of the Police, *20 July 1935.*

Judges escort at the Assizes with Inspector Basher. Far left: P.C.140 John Burrough, appointed 05.02.1906, third from left P.C.31 Charles Cory, appointed 01.11.1906, P.C.35 Edward Henry Stevens, appointed 28.12.1907.

Informal group – St Ives – P.C. Wilfred Kersey, seated far left.   The officer, Centre, appears to be Inspector Horace Osborne K.P.M.

Unknown group.

Group taken in Camborne Police Station 1935 to celebrate the promotion of Superintendent William John Matthews to Deputy Chief Constable. Some well known younger faces can be seen. Back row first left P.C. Keast (later Superintendent), fourth row no.4 P.C. Timmins (later Sergeant), fourth row no.5 P.C. Kersey (Illogan), fourth row no.10 P.C. Cock (Illogan), second row no.1 P.C. Pill (later Assistant Chief Constable), second row no.6 P.C. Roberts (later Detective Superintendent).

Group attending the 1935 Royal Review in London. Front row: P.C.63 Bennetts, appointed 02.06.1913, P.C.11 Dickenson, appointed 01.02.1913, P.C.27 Badcock, appointed 01.07.1912, P.C.221 Sloman, appointed 23.08.1911, the Chief Constable, P.C.65 Rowland, appointed 14.09.1914, P.C.165 Masters, appointed 01.10.1919, P.C.203 Pooley, appointed 01.05.1919, P.C.208 Prince appointed 01.07.1931. Middle row: P.C.53 Woolcock, appointed 12.07.1919, P.C. 50 Hill, appointed 01.01.1920, P.C.40 Trewella, appointed 04.02.1920, P.C.98 Menear, appointed 01.11.1921, P.C.128 Matthews, appointed 15.08.1911, P.C.99 Clark, appointed 01.09.1920, P.C.205 Pearce, appointed 01.03.1919, P.C.224 Moon, appointed 26.06.1914, P.C.93 Allen, appointed 01.12.1922. Back row: P.C.49 Jago, appointed 06.01.1911, P.C.7 Coombe, appointed 16.09.1914, P.C.185 Beswetherick, appointed 01.10.1919, P.C.65 Roberts, appointed 01.02.1927, P.C.84 Juleff, appointed 01.02.1924, P.C.170 Dann, appointed 15.09.1911, P.C.78 Worboys, appointed 18.05.1931.

Tug of War Team. The Constable in uniform on left is P.C.79 William Herbert Doble, appointed 01.11.1919.

New Motor cycles. ERL 425 P.C.116 Ewart Claude Pearce, appointed 01.11.1924, later to be awarded the Military Medal for 'devotion to duty on July 21st, 22 and 23, 1918 in Russia, when he continually drove his Drury Car, bringing up working parties and tools for 60 hours as well as assisting in the fighting.' ERL 423 P.C.69 Sidney Norman Roberts, appointed 01.10.1931, later Detective Superintendent Queens Police Medal. ERL 426 P.C.1 William James Martin Lamerton, appointed 01.10.1923.

Police Station, Moor Street, Camborne, now demolished.

Left: P.C.197 Richard James Kersey, appointed 16.02.1927.

Believed to be the Coronation parade from St Euny Church, Redruth, for King George VI.

On the night of the 31 January 1938 the Hungarian ship S.S. Alba was wrecked off the Island at St Ives when four men were awarded the King's Police Medal for gallantry. Sergeant Horace Osborne, P.C.28 Leslie Jones, P.C.40 Noel Wilkinson, P.C.214 Edgar George Appleton. Sergeant Osborne was awarded the Gold Cross of Merit and Constables Appleton and Jones the Silver Cross of Merit by his Serene Highness the Regent of the Kingdom of Hungary. The photograph shows them with Superintendent William John Matthews outside Buckingham Palace where they received their medals. Mr Matthews was awarded the the Kings Police Medal for meritorous service.

Chief Constable Edgar Hare M.C. 1935–1966.

P.C.138 Bertie Hancock Leading the Judges Escort at the Assizes, Bodmin, c.1940.

Judge and Escort leaving St Petroc's Church in Bodmin: From left no.1 P.C.10 Treloar, P.C.145 Taylor, P.C. Tippett. Right no.1 P.C.138 Hancock, P.C. Hugo, P.C. Stothers, Sgt A.V. Clark.

P.C.191 Vaskaby Lester, appointed 13.01.1947.

Helicopter Rescue at Tintagel 25 May 1956. Sergeant Brooker and P.C.14 Corin attended this rescue of a man and his dog from the rock. The photo of the incident, involving an early Sikorski helicopter, was taken by a Mr Youlton of Tintagel and published all over the world. It was believed to be the first such rescue by helicopter.

Cornwall Constabulary Choir.

P.C.151 Douglas Frederick Simmonds, appointed 30.10.1950.

Joining Photograph of P.C.4 Searle and P.C.245 Gregor. There were many different Police Forces at this time. This photo was taken at Glamorgan County Police Headquarters, Glamorgan being the host force which had most recruits. When out on duty at this time policemen still wore the helmet as pictured in the clay strike photos. Clearly seen are the helmets of Swansea Borough Police who are wearing the combed helmet with the Swansea Borough coat of arms as their helmet plate.

The new Police Station at Penzance, 1950s.

P.C.51 May, appointed 01.03.1937, P.C.43 Bulford, appointed 01.06.1939, P.C.287 Watmore, appointed 23.08.1948, P.C.314 Boyling, appointed 28.07.1952.

Judges Escort, Bodmin. P.C.247 Robins, appointed 17.11.1947 (left), and P.C.310 Deal (right), appointed 03.07.1950.

P.C.314 Boyling, appointed 28.07.1952.

Foxhole Police Station in the 1950s.

Right: *The Centenary Review Programme.*

1857　　1957

Cornwall County Constabulary

CENTENARY REVIEW

Tuesday, 2nd July, 1957

at

The Depot of the Duke of Cornwall's Light Infantry

BODMIN

(By kind permission of the Colonel of the Regiment)

INSPECTION BY

Lt. Col. Sir E. H. W. Bolitho, K.B.E., C.B., D.S.O.

LORD LIEUTENANT FOR THE COUNTY OF CORNWALL

at 3.15 p.m.

P.C. Delmas Wilcox, appointed 31.3.1949.

P.C. Tonkin and his class of cadets.

Informal group of Wilfred Kersey, Arthur Bray, Owen Bulford, Ira Barrett, Dave Boyling, George Smitheram, Eric Botheras and Doug Simmons.

This group photograph appears to have been taken at Bodmin.

Redruth Special Constabulary 1950s.

From an original album of photos taken at the Centenary Review on the 2 July 1957, on Bodmin Barracks Square. Chief Constable Matthews greeting the Lord Lieutenant Sir Edward Bolitho on his arrival to inspect the force on its hundredth birthday.

Panorama of the whole parade.

Traffic Department.

Inspection being followed by Her Majesty's Inspector of Constabulary Mr Johnston.

Inspector W.G.T. Cock and squad.

The front of the main parade.

Cornwall Cadets with W.P.C. Vicky Staddon as right-hand marker.

Motorcycle contingent.

Taking the salute at the march past.

Assistant Chief Constable Julian and squad.

Superintendent Brown and squad.

Heading the left hand column Chief Inspector Pill.

Pensioners. Leading the on left is former Sergeant Oatey, and on the right former Superintendent Leach.

P.C.4 Searle with one of the many John O'Groats-to-Land's End runners of the time on the steps of Penzance Police Station, 1959.

Centenary Parade presentation.

Left: P.C.4 Searle inside the Police Station at Penzance in 1962.

Joining photo taken at Bridgend. P.C.s Simmons and Trounce from Cornwall.

The Buxton Trophy (first aid competition). Sergeant H.F. Short P.C.103, appointed 01.03.1939, and Sergeant G.K. Richards P.C.85, appointed 24.03.1946, P.C.246 G.Cowling, appointed 23.04.1956, P.C.308 J.Radley, appointed 25.03.1957, Chief Inspector O. Sivell, P.C.175 appointed 01.12.1933, P.C.83 A. Floyd, appointed 24.03.1946.

Bravery Award Presentation.

Ladycross Police Station 31.03.1966, transferred to Cornwall from Devon.

P.C. 239 Cedric Vokes at Ladycross.

Egloskerry Police Station.

P.C.4 Searle at the rear of the Police Station, Egloskerry, 1963.

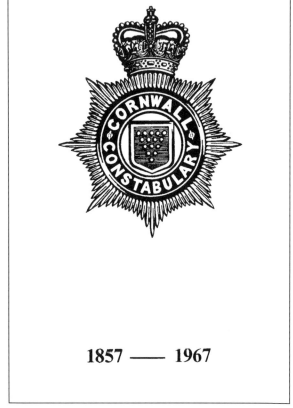

1857 —— 1967

Progamme for the laying up of the Cornwall County Constabulary Badge in the Cathedral.

Parade starting from Lemon Quay en route to the Cathedral.

The last meeting of the Cornwall Branch Board.

Chief Inspector A. Jenkin at Penzance Promenade after the great storm of 1963.

THOSE WHO SERVED

A Complete Listing of Serving Officers, Men and Woman

1857-1967

CORNWALL CONSTABULARY
14.2.1857

Superintendent Clerk John George Vincent
Police Officer transferred from Hertfordshire.
Aged 28 years, married.
Appointed: 14.2.1857.
H.Q. Grade One 8.4.1857.
Removal: 27.10.1890. Died 5.1.1891.

Superintendent Alfred Stephens
Police Officer from Newport, Isle of White.
Aged 30 years, married.
Appointed: 14.2.1857.
Grade Two 16.4.1858.
Stationed at: Liskeard 31.10.1857.
Penzance 15.9.1868.
Removal: 12.10.1873.

Sergeant Major George Piddick
A 29 year old single man from Ramsgate.
Public Service: Royal Artillery.
Appointed: 14.2.1857.
Removal: 2.5.1858. **Reappointed:** 3.8.1858.
Removal: 19.4.1888.
Died from stomach cancer.

P.C. 1 Charles Blake Bray
A 21 year old carpenter/farrier from Bodmin.
Appointed: 23.2.1857.
Stationed at: Launceston 7.5.1857.
Removal: 19.5.1857. Resigned.

P.C. John Stephens Lucas
A mason from Bodmin aged 32 years, married.
Appointed: 23.2.1857.
Stationed at: Launceston 7.5.1857. Bodmin
4.8.1858.
Removal: 17.5.1860. Dismissed.

P.C. 3 James Couch
A 23 year old married labourer from
Barnstaple.
Appointed: 23.2.1857.
Stationed at: H.Q.
Removal: 23.2.1857. Resigned.

P.C. 3 Joseph Opie
A 23 year old miner from Tywardreath,
single.
Appointed: 23.2.1857.
Promotion: 1.6.1857 to 1st class Constable.
15.1.1859 to Sergeant. 6.5.1867 to
Inspector. 23.2.1877 to Superintendent
Stationed at: Launceston 7.5.1857. Bodmin
15.11.1857. Truro 2.2.1858. Launceston
1.1.1859. Bodmin 10.2.1859. Launceston
16.9.1860. Liskeard 25.5.1862. Bodmin
11.5.1867. Helston 18.5.1876. Bodmin

28.2.1877. Truro 1.2.1883.
Removal: 6.1.1891. Retired.

P.C. 4 Samuel Osborne
A shoe maker from Little Petherick, aged 19
years, single.
Appointed: 23.2.1857.
Stationed at: Launceston 14.5.1857.
Removal: 23.6.1857. Resigned.

P.C. 5 Henry James James
A boot maker from Manaccan, aged 24
years, married.
Appointed: 25.2.1857.
Promotion:
14.6.1857 to 1st class constable. 15.8.1857
to Sergeant. 30.3.1862 to Inspector.
Stationed at: Liskeard 15.5.1857. Penzance
17.11.1857. Liskeard 13.3.1862. Bodmin
17.7.1864. Liskeard 19.5.1867. Bodmin
26.9.1870. Truro 19.7.1871. Launceston
18.5.1876. Helston 23.2.1877. Penzance
8.8.1878.
Removal: 14.10.1883. Retired.

Inspector John Harris
A gardener from Veryan aged 31 years,
married.
Appointed: 2.3.1857.
Stationed at: Truro 16.2.1858.
Removal: 15.11.1858. Resigned.

P.C. 7 James Martin
A engine driver from Marazion, aged 22
years, married.
Appointed: 2.3.1857.
Stationed at: Liskeard 15.5.1857. Helston
9.6.1857.
Removal: 7.11.1861. Resigned.

P.C. 8 James Benoy
A single labourer from St Stephens by
Launceston, aged 23 years.
Appointed: 2.3.1858.
Promotion: 15.11.1857 to 1st Class
Constable. 10.8.1891 to Merit Class
Constable.
Stationed at: Launceston 7.5.1857.
Removal: 29.8.1893. Retired.

P.C. 9 Samuel James Williams
A painter from Padstow aged 23 years, single.
Appointed: 2.3.1857.
Stationed at: Liskeard 15.5.1857.
Removal: 17.7.1857. Resigned.

P.C. 10 John Buckingham
A 21 year old Miner from North Hill,
Launceston.
Appointed: 2.3.1857.

Promotion: 1.6.1857 to 1st class Constable.
Stationed at: Launceston 7.5.1857. Truro
29.4.1858. Penzance 1.7.1858.
Removal: 13.4.1859. Resigned 6.8.1857.
Fined 2/6 for neglecting to report a robbery
to Superintendent. 2.5.1858 reduced to 2nd
class Constable for being the worse for drink
in North Tamerton. 9.7.1858 fined 10/- for
being the worse for liquor.

P.C. 11 John Sambells
A 22 year old single labourer from
Lewannick.
Appointed: 2.3.1857.
Promotion: 14.6.1857 to 1st Class
Constable.
26.6.1859 reduced to 2nd class Constable.
For being drunk and quarrelling with P.C.
Bone. 16.9.1860 to 1st Class Constable.
27.3.1863 to sergeant. 25.9.1870 to
Inspector.
Stationed at: Liskeard 15.5.1857.
Launceston 27.1.1858. Liskeard 26.6.1859.
Penzance 17.7.1864. Launceston
26.9.1870. Bodmin 29.10.1888.
Removal: 1.1.1894. Retired.

P.C. 12 Laity
A 27 year old farmer from Marazion,
married.
Appointed: 2.3.1857.
Station at: Liskeard 15.5.1857.
Removal: 22.3.1859. Dismissed the force
with forfeiture of pay for having improper
connections with a married woman at St
Day.

P.C. 13 Mitchell
A 29 year old labourer from Lewannick,
single.
Appointed: 2.3.1857.
Stationed at: Liskeard 15.5.1857.
Removal: 11.12.1860.
21.3.1858 Fined 2/6 for being dirty.
18.4.1858 Reduced to 2nd class Constable
for general inefficiency. 14.10.1860 fined
10/- and removed to Dobwalls at his own
expense for breach of article 122 page 141
of the book of instructions. 11.12.1860.
Dismissed the Force with forfeiture of a
week's pay for drinking in a public house
when he should have been out on duty.

P.C. 14 William J.Heart
A 25 year old miner from St Austell, married.
Appointed: 2.3.1857.
Promotion: 1.6.1857 to 1st class Constable
Stationed at: Launceston 7.5.1857.
Removal: Dec 1858. Resigned.

P.C. 15 John Hawke
A miner from St Ive, married aged 26.
Appointed: 2.3.1857.
Stationed at: Launceston 7.5.1857.
Removal: 16.10.1857.
Dismissed the force with forfeiture of pay for being absent from his station and drunk at a fair.

P.C. 16 John Penhall
A married carpenter from St Austell aged 23 years.
Appointed: 2.3.1857.
Stationed at: Liskeard 10.5.1857.
Removal: 2.11.1857.
Dismissed the force for ill treating his wife and other disgraceful conduct.

P.C. 17 John Houghton
A 31 year old miller from St Columb Major. Married.
Appointed: 2.3.1857.
Stationed at: Liskeard 15.5.1857.
Removal: 23.2.1859. Called on to resign for inefficiency. 4.4.1858 Fined 5/- for telling a falsehood to his Superintendent.

P.C. 18 John Francis Ellis
A 25 year old labourer from the Isles of Scilly.
Appointed: 2.3.1857.
Promotion: 6.9.1857 to 1st class Constable. 4.9.1859 reduced to 2nd class Constable for drinking in a public house at the Lelant fair and using disgraceful language. 16.9.1860 to 1st class Constable. 4.12.1864 to Sergeant.
Stationed at: Bodmin 2.3.1857. Truro 4.4.1858. Penzance 24.7.1859. Bodmin 4.9.1859. Truro 4.12.1864. Bodmin 28.4.1867.
Removal: 5.11.1868. Called on to resign for using his staff improperly on a prisoner 13.11.1859 Fined 2/6 for neglecting to right up his journal daily in accordance with G.O.

P.C. 19 Walter Gartrell
A single shoemaker from Stoke Climsland aged 21 years.
Appointed: 2.3.1857.
Removal: 16.3.57.
Dismissed the force for drinking in a public house at St Ives on 7.3.1857.

P.C. 20 John Endean
A labourer from Launceston, aged 27 years single.
Appointed: 2.3.1857.
Removal: 24.4.1857.
On the 24.4.1857 reported for being the worse for liquor when on parade and being found in the tap room of the Fifteen Balls the same evening, for which he was dismissed the force with forfeiture of pay.

P.C. 21 Samuel Dawe
A single shoemaker from Bodmin aged 22 years.
Appointed: 2.3.1857.
Stationed at: Launceston 7.5.1857.
Removal: 28.5.1857. Resigned.

P.C. 22 Alfred Stripling
A 19 year old single carpenter from Launceston.

Appointed: 2.3.1857.
Promotion: 14.6.1857 to 1st class Constable. 15.11.1857 to Sergeant.
Stationed at: Liskeard 15.5.1857. Truro 16.11.1857. Penzance 20.7.1857.
Removal: 25.11.1859. Resigned.

P.C. 23 Edward Blewett
A 21 year old single miner from St Ives.
Appointed: 2.5.1857.
Promotion: 14.6.1857 to 1st class Constable. 15.11.1857 to Sergeant.
Stationed at: Liskeard 15.5.1857. Helston 17.11.1857. Launceston 20.7.1858.
Removal: 1.1.1859. Dismissed with forfeiture of pay for neglect of duty and drinking with P.C. Barrett in a public house at Camelford.

P.C. 24 Arscott Ward
A labourer from Holsworthy, married aged 23 years.
Appointed: 2.3.1857.
Promotion: 1.6.1857 to 1st class Constable. 5.9.1857. Reduced to 2nd class Constable.
Stationed at: Launceston 7.5.1857. Liskeard 18.10.1857.
Removal: 3.3.1858. Dismissed the force for apprehending a man, not having any charge against him and after allowing him to escape from his custody.

Superintendent William Gifford
Aged 30 years, transferred from Metropolitan Police.
Appointed: 2.3.1857.
Stationed at: Liskeard 17.5.1857.
Removal: 30.10.1857. Called upon to resign.

P.C. 25 Joseph Short
A single farmer from Launceston, aged 21 years.
Appointed: 3.3.1857.
Stationed at: Launceston 17.5.1857. Helston 9.6.1857.
Removal: 30.6.1857. Dismissed, was found drunk on duty at Helston by Sergeant Stevens.

P.C. 26 William Grieve
A single farmer from Probus, aged 26 years.
Appointed: 3.3.1857.
Promotion: 25.7.1858 to 1st class Constable. 17.8.1862 to Sergeant. 24.12.1865 to Inspector.
Stationed at: Liskeard 15.5.1857. Bodmin 27.1.1858 Helston 4.8.1858. Truro 22.6.1862. Bodmin 17.8.1862 Launceston 19.6.1864. Bodmin 31.12.1865. Liskeard 13.7.1872.
Removal: 3.11.1872.

P.C. William Wallace Opie
A married mason from Tywardreath aged 29 years.
Appointed: 3.3.1857.
Removal: 20.3.1857.

Superintendent Alfred Hipwood Jarrett
A 33 year old married bookbinder from Bristol.

Transferred from the Penryn Borough Police.
Stationed at: Launceston 7.5.1857. Truro 18.10.1857. Helston 23.10.1860.
Removal: 8.10.1861 Called on to resign for being drunk.

Sergeant Henry Coomb
A 39 year old married labourer from Okehampton.
Appointed: 17.3.1857, transferred from the Plymouth Police.
Promotion: 17.3.1857 to Inspector.
Stationed at: Launceston 14.5.1857. Penzance 17.8.1857. Helston 14.10.1858. Liskeard 17.7.1864.
Removal: 3.12.1865. Called upon to resign: He cut his throat and the Chief Constable would not keep him.

Sergeant George Pappin
A 29 year old married labourer from St Austell.
Appointed: 7.4.1857.
Promotion: 10.11.1861 to Inspector.
Stationed at: Liskeard 5.5.1857 Launceston 10.11.1861 Truro 21.6.1863. Penzance 5.11.1867 Helston 8.8.1878.
Removal: 10.10.1886. Pension.

P.C. 143 John Westlake
A 34 year old married mason from Okehampton.
Appointed: 16.3.1857. From St Austell Police.
Promotion: 11.11.1860. Reduced to 1st class Constable from Sergeant for allowing a prisoner to escape
Stationed at: Launceston 7.5.1857. Bodmin 18.10.1857 Launceston 30.11.1857. Bodmin 16.9.1860. Truro 11.11.60. Helston 20.7.1862. Truro 4.12.1864. Liskeard 6.7.1867.
Removal: Resigned on Pension £36.7.6. P.a. 28.1.1899 Died at Hatherleigh, Devon.

P.C. 28 Edward Currah
A single miner from Mawgan in Pydar. Aged 29 years.
Appointed: 9.3.1857.
Promotion: 18.10.1857 to 1st class Constable. 11.12.1859 to Sergeant. 26.10.1873 to Inspector.
Stationed at: Liskeard 5.5.1857. Penzance 3.12.1859. Helston 10.11.1861. Penzance 7.6.1866. Liskeard 31.10.1873.
Removal: 14.10.1889. Pension £70.18.4.

P.C. 66 John Bone
A 22 year old labourer from Jacobstow, married.
Appointed: 6.4.1857.
Promotion: 6.3.1859 to 1st class Constable. 26.6.1859 reduced to 2nd class Constable. For being drunk and quarrelling with P.C. Sambells. 22.5.1864 reduced to 2nd class Constable for playing skittles at a public house with P.C. Parkyn who was drunk.
Stationed at: Launceston 7.5.1857. Liskeard 26.6.1859. Bodmin 15.9.1861
Removal: 14.8.1864. Resigned.

P.C. 20 Philip Gilbert
A mason from Phillack, married, aged 35 years.
Appointed: 9.3.1857.
Stationed at: Launceston 7.5.1857.
Removal: 31.5.1857. Dismissed for being drunk on the 26.5.1857.

P.C. 36 William Hill
A 32 year old tailor from Helston. Married man.
Appointed: 9.3.1857.
Promotion:
10.1.1858 to 1st class Constable.
Stationed at: Launceston 7.5.1857. Helston 9.5.1858.
4.4.1857 Fined 2/6 for being the worse for liquor when on parade and for being in a public house drinking with others the same evening. 17.5.1859 Dismissed the force.

P.C. 64 Samuel Pengelly
A 22 year old married farmer from Helston.
Appointment 9.3.1857.
Promotion: 27.4.1862 to 1st Class Constable.
Stationed at: Liskeard 15.5.1857. Penzance 24 .1.1858.
15.11.1857 Fined 10/- for being away from his station without leave for three days.
Pension £39.11.9.
Died 22.4.1902.

P.C. 132 William Currah
A single 24 year old miner from Mawgan-in-Pydar.
Appointment 9.3.1857.
Promotion: 2.5.1858 to 1st class Constable. 30.3.1862 to Sergeant. 7.7.1872 to Inspector.
Stationed at: Liskeard 17.5.1857. Truro 30.3.1862. Penzance 14.9.1862. Liskeard 31.1.1864. Bodmin 13.7.1872. Launceston 22.2.1877.
Removal: 8.7.1885. Pension £70.19.4.

P.C. 29 Francis Dreadon
A 29 year old married labourer from Helland.
Appointed: 9.3.1857
Promotion: 1.6.1857 to 1st class Constable. 7.2.1858 to Sergeant.
Stationed at: Launceston 7.5.1857. Liskeard 2.2.1861. Truro 6.9.1866. Penzance 31.1.1868. Launceston 1.12.1874.
Removal: 6.4.1884. Pension £46.10.8.
Died 6.8.1887.

P.C. William Exelby
A 32 year old married labourer from St Keverne.

P.C. 19 Thomas Martin
A 22 year old married miner from St Austell.
Appointed: 9.3.1857.
Promotion: 16.4.1858 to 1st class Constable. 10.7.1859 to Sergeant. 14.9.1857 Reduced to 2nd class Constable for accepting two glasses of gin without paying for same.
Stationed at: Launceston 7.5.1857. Helston 9.6.1857. Penzance 14.11.1858. Bodmin 10.7.1859.

Removal: 14.5.1860. Dismissed the force for being drunk with forfeiture of pay.

Sergeant **John Caddy**
A 33 year old married labourer from North Petherwin. Was in the Metropolitan Police and Falmouth Borough Police.
Appointed: 9.3.1857.
Removal: 11.5.1857. Ordered to resign.

P.C. William Perry
A 25 year old single tailor from Helland.
Appointed: 9.3.1857.

P.C. 27 Edward Stacey
A 23 year old single farmer from Stratton.
Appointed: 9.3.1857.
Stationed at: Launceston 7.5.1857. Penzance 2.1.1858.
Removal: 20.5.1858. Called upon to resign for making a false entry in his journal.

P.C. 35 John Rich
A 22 year old labourer from Bodmin, single man.
Appointed: 9.3.1857.
Stationed at: Liskeard 15.5.1857.
Removal: 30.6.1857. Resigned.

P.C. 133 Amos Hugo
A 24 year old single labourer from Probus.
Appointed: 10.3.1857.
Stationed at: Launceston 7.5.1857.
Removal: 17.8.1861. Resigned.

P.C. 69 William Tucker
A labourer from St Cleer, aged 21 years, single.
Appointed: 10.3.1857.
Stationed at: Liskeard 15.5.1857. Bodmin 7.2.1858. Truro 5.6.1860.
7.1.1858 Fined 2/6 for being absent from his conference point. 21.2.1858 Fined 5/- for being absent from his station without leave. 29.6.1860 Resigned.

P.C. 52 Andrew Stephens
A 35 year old labourer from St Ives.
Appointed: 16.3.1857.
Stationed at: Helston 9.6.1857.
Removal: 5.12.1858. Dismissed the force being absent from his conference point and telling the Chief Constable a falsehood, when questioned relating to this.

Superintendent **Henry Brice**
A 31 year old married labourer from Okehampton.
Appointed: 16.3.1857.
Stationed at: Helston 9.6.1857. Launceston 23.10.1860.
Removal: 28.6.1864. Resigned through ill-health. Granted a gratuity of £60.0.0. At the midsummer sessions of 1864.

P.C. 73 Cyrus Tippett
A 30 year old married shoe maker from Truro.
Appointed: 16.3.1857.
Stationed at: Helston 9.6.1857.
Removal: 10.8.1857. Fined 2/6 for neglecting to report a death and inquest, also for taking a fee and not reporting it. Resigned by order of the Chief Constable.

P.C. John Johns
A 22 year old single farmer from St Germans.

Inspector **Joseph Ward**
A 34 year old married labourer from Gerrans. Served in the London Police, Truro and Camborne.
Stationed at: Liskeard 16.5.1857. Penzance 17.8.1857.
Removal: 19.10.1869. Resigned through ill-health. Gratuity £105.1.3.

P.C. 32 Samuel Lobb
A 21 year old single labourer from St Teath.
Appointed: 11.3.1857.
Stationed at: Liskeard 8.5.1857.
12.1.1858 Fined 5/- for leaving his station whilst on the sick list.
Removal: 4.2.1858. Dismissed the force for repeatedly leaving his station without leave.

P.C. 71 Samuel Mildern
A single miner from St Ives aged 23 years.
Appointed: 16.3.1857.
Stationed at: Liskeard 15.5.1857. Helston 9.6.1857.
Removal: 15.8.1857. Resigned.

P.C. 34 Edward Barrett
A married sawyer from St Mellion. Aged 32 years.
Appointed: 16.3.1857.
Stationed at: Launceston 17.5.1857.
19.1.1858. Reduced to 2nd class Constable for disgraceful conduct in a public house.
1.1.1859. Dismissed the force for drinking in a public house at Camelford and neglecting his duty.

P.C. 37 William Burnman
A 20 year old single engine man from Calstock.
Appointed: 16.3.1857.
Stationed at: Liskeard 15.5.1857.
Removal: 5.9.1857 Resigned.

P.C. 30 William Pomeroy
A single tailor from St Pinnock.
Appointed: 16.3.1857.
Promotion: 14.6.1857 to 1st Class Constable
Stationed at: Liskeard 15.5.1857.
26.6.1859. Fined 5/- for being absent from his conference point. Resigned.
5.5.1862. **Reappointed:** as P.C. 40.
Promotion:
21.5.1865. To 1st Class Constable.
Stationed at:
Liskeard 10.6.1862.
Dismissed for being drunk.

Inspector **William Fleet**
A married gardener from Worcester aged 33 years. From Worcestershire and Folkstone Police.
Appointed: 30.3.1857.
Stationed at: Launceston 7.5.1857. Bodmin 11.11.1861. Launceston 21 6.1863. Bodmin 18.5.1876.
Removal: 31.1.1886. Pension of £70.19.5.
Died at Fowey 20.5.1899.

P.C. 130 John Sleeman
A farmer from St Tudy. Aged 29 year
married.
Appointed: 23.3.1857.
Promotion:
16.10.1859 to 1st class Constable.
Stationed at: Liskeard 15.5.1857.
Fined 2/7 for being absent from his station
without leave.
Removal: 14.3.1866. Resigned.

P.C. 83 William Barnes
A 25 year old married engraver from
Penzance.
Appointed: 4.4.1857.
Promotion: 25.7.1858 to 1st class Constable.
Stationed at: Penzance Sept. 1857. Helston
25.4.1861.
Removal: 31.5.1862. Resigned by order of
the Chief Constable as his wife was
constantly abusing Sergeant Currah.

P.C. 67 William Davys
From St Neot, a married miner aged 28
years.
Appointed: 6,4,1857.
Promotion: 10.5.1858 to 1st Class
Constable.
Stationed at: Helston 9.6.1857.
Removal: 21.12.1858. Dismissed the force
for being absent from his station without
leave and telling his Sergeant a falsehood
when questioned on the Subject.

Sergeant Frederick Wreford
A former farmer from Crediton married aged
25 years. From Hampshire Constabulary.
Appointed: 6.4.1857.
Promotion: 15.11.1857 to Inspector.
Stationed at: Liskeard 15.5.1857.
30.10.1860. Resigned and reappointed:
Truro 10.11.1861. Bodmin 30.3.1862.
Removal: 7.3.1863. Resigned.

P.C. 65 Joshua Osborne
A married labourer from St Columb aged 24
years.
Appointed: 6.4.1857.
Stationed at: Liskeard 15.5.1857.
Removal: 6.12.1857. Dismissed the force
for inefficiency.

P.C. 53 Robert Crispin
A 30 year old married stable keeper from
London.
Appointed: 6.4.1857.
Public Service: Royal Cornwall Rangers
Militia.
Stationed at: Launceston 7.5.1857. Helston
9.6.1857.
1.6.1857 Reduced from Sergeant to 2nd
class Constable for drinking in a public house
in Camelford on 26.5.1857.
Removal: 23.11.1857. Dismissed the force
for drunkenness.

P.C. 45 William Lobb
A quarryman from St Teath. Aged 20 years
single.
Appointed: 6.4.1857.
Stationed at: Helston 9.6.1857. Liskeard
18.4.1858. Penzance 5.2.1860.

15.11.1857. Fined 5/- for being absent from
his conference point and telling a falsehood
to his Superintendent. 18.4.1858. Fined 5/-
for having his lantern dirty when inspected
by Sergeant Brice. 5.4.1860 Fined 5/- for
neglect of duty.
Removal: 18.4.1860. Resigned.

P.C. 51 Samuel Sawry
A single miner from St Mabyn, aged 27 years.
Appointed: 6.4.1857.
Stationed at: Launceston 26.5.1857.
25.5.1857 Fined 2/6 for drinking in a low
beer house in Bodmin. 7.6.1857 Dismissed
the force with forfeiture of pay for being
drunk on duty.

P.C. 62 James William Thomas
A single labourer from Veryan, aged 20 years.
Appointed: 6.4.1857.
Promotion: 16.10.1859 to 1st class
Constable.
Stationed at: Helston 9.6.1857.
25.9.1857. Fined 5/- for receiving liquor
from persons assembled in a public house,
and 5/- for remaining in the house from 1am
to 2 am.
Removal: 8.5.1862. Resigned.

P.C. 14 Thomas Sambells
A married labourer from Tavistock, aged 38
years.
Appointed: 16.5.1857. From the Plymouth
and St Austell Police.
Stationed at: Launceston 9.6.1857.
Penzance 17.8.1857. Helston 10.2.1859.
Penzance 25.2.1866.
10.2.1866. Reduced to 1st class Constable.
For neglecting to report a Constable for being
drunk.
Removal: 30.6.1879. Called to resign.
Pension £29.0.0 p.a.

Sergeant John Stevens
A 30 year old married engraver from
London.
Appointed: 30.4.1857.
Promotion: 9.7.1864 to Inspector.
Stationed at: Helston 9.6.1857. Bodmin
10.7.1859. Penzance 30.3.1862. Helston
17.7.1864.
Removal: 24.11.1864. Dismissed for being
drunk.

P.C. 50 James Cornish
A 33 year old married wheelwright from St
Columb.
Appointed: 13.4.1857.
Promotion: 7.10.1858 to 1st class Constable.
Stationed at: Helston 9.6.1857.
15.11.1857 Fined 2/6 for being dirty at the
petty sessions at Helston.
2.4.1861 Fined 10/- and reduced to 2nd
class Constable, for smoking when out on
duty, and for having his clothing and appoint-
ments in a very dirty state.
Removal: 14.4.1861 dismissed the force for
telling a falsehood.

P.C. 58 George Staple Luxon
A single mason from St Enoder, aged 24
years.

Appointed: 17.4.1857.
Promotion: 18.10.1857 to 1st class
Constable. 24.1.1858 to Sergeant.
Stationed at: Launceston 14.5.1857. Bodmin
27.1.1858.
Removal: 13.7.1862. Resigned.

P.C. 75 James King
A 21 year old single miner from St Hilary.
Appointed: 13.4.1857.
Promotion: 2.5.1858 to 1st class Constable.
29.4.1860 reduced to 2nd class Constable
for being the worse for liquor.
Stationed at: Liskeard May 1858.
Launceston 17.8.1862. Truro 15.4.1881.
Helston 17.7.1884.
Removal: 5.11.1891. Pension £51.11.4pa.

P.C. 33 Nicholas Higman
A former miner from Roche, married aged 30
years. Transferred from the London Police.
Appointed: 13.4.1857.
Promotion: 6.9.1857. To 1st class Constable.
29.5.1859 Fined 2/6 for riding in a public
conveyance without leave.
Stationed at: Helston 9.6.1857.
Removal: 22.5.1864. Ill-health.

P.C. 6 Richard Harris
A tailor from Bodmin, married aged 30 years.
Appointed: 20.4.1857.
Stationed at: Launceston 20.5.1857.
31.8.1857 Fined 2/6 for being absent from
his conference point and 2/6 for making a
false entry in his journal. 18.4.1858. Fined
5/- for being absent from his conference
point. 29.1.1859 Dismissed the force for
general inefficiency.

Superintendent Henry Miller
A former labourer from Christchurch,
married and aged 33 years. Transferred from
the Hampshire Constabulary.
Appointed: 27.4.1857.
Promotion: 16.4.1858 to 1st class
Superintendent. 1.12.1880 to Chief
Superintendent and D.C.C.
Stationed at: Penzance 17.8.1857.
Launceston 15.9.1868. Penzance
31.10.1973. H.Q. 9.12.1880
Removal: 19.5.1894. Died. Gratuity of
£608.9.8.

Inspector James Brazier
A former labourer from Warnford,
Hampshire, aged 36 years.
Appointed: 27.4.1857.
Promotion: 2.11.1857. To Superintendent.
26.10.1873 to 1st Class Superintendent.
Stationed at: Liskeard 15.5.1857. Bodmin
2.11.1857. Helston 8.10.1861. Truro
13.8.1869. Launceston 31.10.1873.
Removal: 8.2.1877. Died.

Sergeant George Bond
Former labourer from Malmsbury aged 25
years and married.
Appointed: 27.4.1857.
Stationed at: Liskeard 18.5.1857.
Launceston 2.6.1862.
Removal: 18.9.1864. Resigned.

P.C. 61 Samuel Chammingo
A labourer from Jacobstow, married aged 22 years.
Appointed: 27.4.1875.
Promotion: 18.4.1858 to 1st class Constable. 21.10.1858 reduced to 2nd class Constable for being absent from his conference point. 11.12.1859 to 1st class Constable.
Stationed at: Launceston 1.6.1857. Bodmin 14.10.1858. Liskeard 15.9.1861.
4.1.1863. Fined 5/- for being absent from his conference point.
7.2.1871.
Removal: Resigned for swearing and falsehoods.

P.C. 74 Samual Venner
A married miner from Calstock aged 25 years.
Appointed: 24.8.1857.
22.8.1857 Fined 5/- for being in the tap room of the Sportsman's Arms.
Removal: November 1857 Resigned.

P.C. 131 William Rice
A single labourer from Botus Flemming, aged 30 years. Transferred from Plymouth Police.
Appointed: 27.4.1857.
Stationed at: Liskeard 30.5.1857.
Removal: 13.7.1857 Resigned.

P.C. Hoar
A married horse breaker from St Columb Minor.

P.C. 70 Frederick William West
A former miner from St Austell, single aged 20. Transferred from the Metropolitan Police.
Appointed: 27.4.1857.
Promotion: 10.1.1858 to 1st class Constable. 1.1.1859 to Sergeant.
Stationed at: Launceston 21.5.1857. Truro 1.1.1858. Penzance 10.1.1861. Helston 2.7.1866. Called to resign for being drunk on more that one occasion.

P.C. 48 Abraham Whiting
A 25 year old single miller from St Breward.
Appointed: 27.4.1857.
Promotion: 10.1.1858 to 1st class Constable.
Stationed at: Launceston 30.6.1857.
Removal: 16.11.1891. Pension £41.9.1.

P.C. 48 William Worth
A single miner from Calstock aged 22.
Appointed: 27.4.1857.
Stationed at: Launceston 2.6.1857.
Removal: 13.7.1857. Resigned.

Inspector John Barry Wood
A former boot and shoe maker from Lyme Regis, 28 years and married.
Transferred from Hampshire Police.
Appointed: 28.4.1857.
Stationed at: Launceston 7.5.1857. Liskeard 13.12.1865.
Removal: 28.2.1872. Called to resign for neglect of duty.

P.C. 56 William Hutchings
A single blacksmith from Truro.
Appointed: 28.4.1857.
Promotion:
6.12.1863. To 1st class Constable.
Stationed at: Helston 9.6.1857. Penzance 23.4.1870.
13.6.1858. Fined 5/- for being absent from his conference point, and being in plain clothes. 5.12.1858. Fined 2/6 for breach of Article 122 Page 41 of the book on instructions. 30.1.1871 Reduced to 2nd class Constable. For disobedience of orders and making a false entry in his journal. 2.6.1871 Dismissed for being drunk on duty.

P.C. George Trebilcock
A shoe maker from St Columb, aged 23 years single.
Appointed: 28,4,1857,
Removal: 28.4.1857.

P.C. 60 Joseph Biscombe
A miner from Calstock, married aged 28 years.
Appointed: 4.5.1857
Stationed at: Liskeard 30.5.1857.
Removal: 5.9.1857 Resigned.

P.C. 78 William Hitchens
A 29 year old married mariner from Newlyn.
Appointed: 11.5.1857.
Promotion: 18.4.1858. To 1st class Constable.
Stationed at: Helston 9.6.1857. Truro 7.8.1858.
Removal: 12.11.1861. Died.

P.C. 83 John Johns
A 26 year old married tin streamer from Mevagissey.
Appointed: 11.5.1857.
Removal: 15.8.1857. Dismissed the force with forfeiture of pay for being found asleep on duty and appearing in plain clothes.

P.C. 1 James Varcoe
A single mason from St Enoder, aged 22 years.
Appointed: 8.5.1861.
Promotion: 6.10.1867 to 1st class Constable. 5.11.1877 to Sergeant.
Stationed at: Launceston 15.7.1857. Liskeard 5.7.1861. Helston 11.10.1863. Truro 22.8.1864. Penzance 6.11.1877. Bodmin 23.10.1882.
Removal: 1.1.1884. Pension £41 .16. 0.

Sergeant Thomas Sherstone
A former labourer from Yeovil, aged 24 years. Transferred from Somerset.
Appointed: 14.5.1857.
Promotion: 15.11.1857. To Inspector. 26.10.1873. To Superintendent 2nd class. 22.2.1891 to Superintendent 1st Class.
Stationed at: Launceston 1.6.1857. Helston 11.6.1857. Bodmin 16.11.1857 Helston 6.12.1864. Liskeard 26.9.1870 Bodmin 31.10.1873. Launceston 3.2.1877.
Removal: 21.5.1894. Died.

Sergeant Joseph Harris
A former tailor from Bodmin, married aged 28 years.
Appointed: 18.5.1857.
Promotion: 4.12.1864 to Inspector.
Stationed at: Bodmin 2.6.1857. Launceston 15.7.1857. Helston 20.7.1858. Penzance 3.7.1861. Truro 14.9.1862. Liskeard 4.12.1864.
Removal: 1.5.1867. Dismissed the force for getting his niece in the family way.

P.C. 31 Charles Broad
A labourer from Redruth, aged 28 single.
Appointed: 18.5.1857.
Stationed at: Helston 9.6.1857.
Removal: 12.8.1857. Resigned.

P.C. 57 Luke Mitchell
A miner from Truro. A married 25 year old.
Appointed: 18,5,1857,
Stationed at: Penzance 17.8.1857.
Removal: 12.10.1858. Dismissed for being drunk on duty.

P.C. 76 William Coomb
A single mariner from St Germans, single aged 23.
Appointed: 18.5.1857.
Stationed at: Helston 9.6.1857. Truro 3.2.1861.
13.10.1861. Fined 2/6 for being absent from his conference point and 2/6 for filling in P.C. Dyers journal. 16.10.1861. Dismissed with forfeiture of one weeks pay for being absent from his station without leave and other misconduct.

P.C. 82 William Tamlin
A married labourer from Plymouth aged 30 years.
Appointed: 18.5.1857.
Stationed at: Liskeard 30.5.1857.
Removal: 19.3.1858. Dismissed the force for having tried to appropriate money (awarded by the Magistrates for the repair of his clothing) to his own use.

Inspector George Barnes
A Married Police Officer from Christchurch, Hampshire.
Appointed: 19.5.1857.
Promotion: 9.10.1861. To Superintendent 3rd class. 19.2.1871 to Superintendent 1st class 22.5.1894 to D.C.C.
Removal: 30.11.03. Pension £140.0.0 pa

P.C. 46 James Matthews
A farmer from Zennor, aged 25 years single.
Appointed: 20.5.1857.
Promotion: 13.6.1858. To 1st class constable. 10.11.1861. To Sergeant. 19.6.1865. Reduced to 1st class Constable for neglecting to report and pay over 2/6 received as fees.
Stationed at: Penzance 17.8.1857. Liskeard 10.11.1861. Launceston 25.5.1862. Liskeard 19.6.1864.
Removal: 9.3.1866. Resigned.

Inspector William Laughton
A former painter from Bechampstead. Married aged 34 years. Transferred.

Appointed: 20.5.1857.
Stationed at: Helston 9.6.1857.
Removal: 19.9.1858. Resigned.

P.C. 68 William Strike
A 25 year old married carpenter from Linkinhorne.
Appointed: 25.5.1857.
Stationed at: 15.7.1857 Liskeard.
17.6.1859 Called upon to resign for inefficiency.

P.C. 49 William Bassett
A 41 year old single farmer from Bridgerule.
Appointed: 28.5.1857.
Stationed at: 28.6.1857 Bodmin.
11.8.1857. Liskeard.
21.7.1857 Fined 5/- for allowing a prisoner to smoke when marching him to St Austell and for having his coat hat and smock off.
12.9.1857 Fined 2/6 for allowing Hugh Littlejon to take him by the collar without the P.C. Apprehending him. 18.10.1857 Dismissed the force for inefficiency.

P.C. 80 James Rickard
A tailor from Saltash aged 21 .
Appointed: 2.6.1857.
Promotion: 27.4.1862 to 1st class Constable.
Stationed at: Penzance 17.8.1867. Truro 7.10.1866.
Removal: 3.8.1891. Pension £41.9.1.

P.C. 21 Stephen Garrish
A farmer from Truro, single aged 25.
Appointed: 2.6.1857.
Promotion: 1.4.1860 to 1st class Constable
Stationed at: Penzance 17.8.1857.
Launceston 3.3.1861.
3/3/1861. Reduced to 2nd class Constable.
For drunkenness and 5/- for absence from conference point.
Removal: 12.6.1862. Dismissed for contracting debts with publicans.

P.C. 85 Henry Burnard
A 22 year old single carpenter from Alternun.
Appointed: 3.6.1857.
Promotion: 15.11.1857. To 1st class Constable.
30.7.1858 reduced to 2nd class Constable for making a false entry in his journal and bringing a false charge against Inspector Harris.
Stationed at: Bodmin 29.7.1857. Truro 6.11.1857. Helston 1.8.1858.
Removal: 5.11.1859. Resigned.

P.C. 72 John Doidge
A miner from Stoke Climsland, single aged 24 years.
Appointed: 3.6.1857.
Promotion: 25.7.1858 to 1st class Constable. 10.8.1891 to merit class Constable.
Stationed at: Launceston 15.7.1857. Bodmin 9.9.1866. Liskeard 19.6.1868.
Removal: 18.11.1892. Pension £43.9.6.

P.C. Samuel Christopher
A married labourer from Mawnan, aged 28 years.
Appointed: 3.6.1857 Resigned. 17.6.1857.

P.C. 77 Joseph Saunders
A single labourer from St Neot, aged 20 years.
Appointed: 7.6.1857
Stationed at: Penzance 17.8.1857.
3.4.1858. Fined 2/6 for neglecting to fill in his journal. 16.10.1859 Fined 10/- for being absent from his conference point.
Removal: 25 .10.1859 Resigned.

P.C. 35 Joseph Loady
A 25 year old mason from St Germans, married.
Appointed: 15.6.1858.
Promotion: 14.9.1862. To 1st class Constable. 20.1.1866 to Sergeant.
Stationed at: Liskeard 18.7.1857. Bodmin 10.11.1861. Penzance 31.10.1873. Launceston 17.7.1884.
Removal: 6.4.1891. Pension £51.11.4. Died 7.11.1898.

P.C. 54 John Bice
A 19 year old single miner from St Austell.
Appointed: 15.6.1857.
Stationed at: Penzance 17.8.1857.
15.9.1857. Fined 2/6 for disobedience to order and remaining in a public house when on duty, called upon to resign at once for having tendered his resignation when he had only been in the force a short time.

P.C. 136 Mark Benny
A 20 year old married miner from St Cleer.
Appointed: 15.6.1857.
Stationed at: Penzance 9.9.1857.
5.11.1857 Dismissed the force for being drunk when on duty.

P.C. 44 William Neal
A labourer from North Petherwin, single aged 23.
Appointed: 15.6.1857.
Stationed at: Penzance 9.9.1857.
Removal: 19.8.1858. Resigned.

P.C. 84 Robert Lamerton
A 22 year old single labourer from Landrake.
Appointed: 22.7.1857.
Stationed at: Penzance 17.8.1857. Liskeard 2.4.1858.
30.12.1857 Fined 5/- for allowing a prisoner to go at large after he had taken him into custody without any order from a Magistrate so to do. 8.1.1860. Fined 5/- for quitting his station without leave when sick.
Removal: 16.1.1860 called upon to resign through ill-health.

P.C. 48 Charles Grigg
A labourer from Marlborough, Wiltshire, aged 23 single.
Appointed: 22.6.1857.
Promotion: 15.11.1857 to 1st class Constable.
Stationed at: Bodmin 28.6.1857. Helston 7.7.1857. Penzance 26.4.1863.
21.2.1858 Fined 2/6 for being in his lodgings when he should have been on duty.
30.10.1868 Fined 5/- for neglect of duty in allowing a prisoner to escape.
Removal: 5.8.1891. Pension £41.9.1.

P.C. 59 James Williams
A married labourer from St Austell aged 21 years.
Appointed: 25.6.1857.
Promotion: 25.7.1858 to 1st class Constable
Stationed at: Penzance 17.8.1857.
Removal: 9.5.1875. Resigned.

P.C. 20 John Brown Foot
A married labourer from North Hill, aged 31.
Appointed: 2.7.1857.
Promotion: 16.11.1857 to sergeant.
Stationed at: Penzance 17.8.1857.
Removal: 24.4.1862. Resigned.

Inspector William Ward
Former labourer from South Hampton, married aged 28 years.
Transferred from Hampshire Police.
Appointed: 4.7.1857.
Stationed at: Liskeard 31.7.1857.
Bodmin 5.2.1859.
Removal: 19.8.1859. Called upon to resign for getting into debt and other impropriety of conduct.

P.C. 47 Thomas Letcher Ham
A single miner from St Cleer, aged 18 years.
Appointed: 6.7.1857.
Promotion: 6.3.1858 to 1st class Constable. 13.6.1858 reduced to 2nd class Constable for highly improper conduct with a prostitute on the night of 9.6.1858.
Stationed at: Bodmin 13.6.1858. Liskeard 4.8.1858.
Removal: 11.9.1858. Dismissed the force for being in plain clothes and other misconduct.

P.C. 79 Richard Plint
A miner from Newlyn East married aged 25 years.
Appointed: 13.7.1857.
Promotion: 25.7.1858 to 1st class Constable.
Stationed at: Penzance 9.9.1857.
15.9.1861 Fined 5/- for being absent from his station without leave.
Removal: 12.7.1862. Resigned.

P.C. 51 John Harris
A miner from St Agnes aged 24 married.
Appointed: 13.7.1857.
Promotion: 3.5.1859 to 1st class Constable.
Stationed at: Penzance 9.9.1857. Helston 17.10.1873.
Removal: 25.8.1880. Pension £31.12.8.

P.C. 63 James Merrifield
A 25 year old miner from Newlyn, married.
Appointed: 7.7.1857.
Promotion: 18.9.1859 to 1st class Constable.
Stationed at: Penzance 9.9.1857.
Helston 23.4.1870.
Removal: 9.6.1871. Resigned.

P.C. 38 John Williams
A single shoemaker from Calstock aged 22 years.
Appointed: 13.7.1857.
Promotion: 2.5.1858 to 1st class Constable.
Stationed at: Penzance 17.8.1857.
Bodmin 8.12.1861.

Removal: 1.12.1865. Died 10.1.1866. Widow received £40.0.0. Gratuity from superannuating fund.

P.C. 42 Thomas Cook
A 28 year old miner from St Cleer, married.
Appointed: 13.7.1857.
Stationed at: Liskeard 9.9.1857.
Removal: 23.9.1857. Dismissed for having (after being thoroughly instructed in his duties and drill) sent in his resignation after being only one week at his station.

P.C. 9 John Barnfield
A married tailor from Veryan, aged 30 years.
Appointed: 21.7.1857.
Stationed at: Penzance 17.8.1857.
Removal: 14.6.1861. Dismissed for indecently assaulting a female prisoner.

P.C. 4 Simon Hermisman
A 28 year old married miner from St Agnes.
Appointed: 22.7.1857.
Stationed at: Penzance 17.8 1857.
Removal: 3.9.1860 Resigned.

P.C. 31 Samuel Painter
A 25 year old married man from Boyton.
Appointed: 22.7.1857.
Stationed at: Penzance 17.8.1857.
Removal: 14.7.1858. Resigned.

P.C. 131 Abraham Dunstan
A miner from Stithians. Married aged 25 years.
Appointed: 22.7.1857.
Stationed at: Penzance 15.11.1857.
Removal: 21.4.1859. Dismissed the force for general inefficiency.

P.C. 71 William Shave
A labourer from Christchurch, single aged 21 years.
Appointed: 1.8.1857.
Stationed at: Liskeard 2.9.1857.
12.4.1858 Removed from the force through ill-health.

P.C. 95 George Reed
A labourer from Christchurch, single aged 20.
Appointed: 5.8.1857.
Promotion: 25.7.1858 to 1st Class Constable
Stationed at: Penzance Sept.1857. Helston 14.11.1857.
29.5.1859 Fined 10/- for remaining 3 hours in a public house. 9.6.1860 Dismissed the force with forfeiture of pay and imprisoned for one month for drunkenness and assaulting a civilian.

P.C. 115 Nicholas Trenarry
A single miner from Cubert aged 25 years.
Appointed: 17.8.1857.
Promotion: 8.12.1861 to 1st class Constable. 19.6.1864 to Sergeant.
Stationed at: Bodmin Sept 1857. Truro 28.1.1858. Liskeard 5.2.1859. Launceston 19.6.1864. Penzance 26.9.1870. Helston 25.10.1873. Bodmin 24.11.1883. Truro 16.9.1886.
1.5.1859 Fined 10/- for allowing a prisoner

to get drunk whilst in his custody.
Removal: 4.8.1891. Pension £51.11.4.

P.C. 112 John Searle
A 36 year old married tailor from Helston.
Appointed: 19.8.1857.
Stationed at: Penzance 9.9.1857.
29.6.1859 Removed from the force in consequence of being permanently disabled by a kick in his thigh whilst in the execution of his duty. A gratuity of £60.0.0.

P.C. 119 Joseph Higman
A 31 year old married labourer from Roche.
Appointed: 19.8.1857.
Stationed at: Bodmin Sept 1857. Truro 16.1/1858.
28.3.1860. Died.

Sergeant George Pardy
A former shoemaker from Wimborne, aged 27 single.
Transferred from Hampshire Police.
Appointed: 31.8.1857.
Stationed at: Bodmin Sept. 1857. Launceston 18.10.1857. Bodmin Dec 1858. Launceston 10.7.1859.
Removal: March 1860. Resigned.

P.C. 41 Joseph Plowman
A 24 year old single labourer from Christchurch.
Appointed: 7.9.1857.
Stationed at: Liskeard 29.10.1857.
Removal: 17.12.1859. Dismissed for running up bills in public houses.

P.C. 89 William Lamerton
A single labourer from Landrake, aged 28 years.
Appointed: 8.9.1857.
Promotion: 6.7.1859 to 1st class Constable.
Stationed at: Bodmin Oct 1857.
13.12.1857 Fined 5/- for liberating a prisoner without going before a Magistrate.
Removal: 20.2.1860. Dismissed with forfeiture of a weeks pay for disobedience of orders.

P.C. 94 Sampson Lucas
A married labourer from Pillaton, aged 23 years.
Appointed: 10.9.1857.
Stationed at: Bodmin Oct 1857.
Removal: 8.12.1857. Dismissed for drinking at a Public House on a Sunday with a man recently liberated from gaol.

Superintendent Henry Complin
A former coach maker from Hampshire married aged 30 years.
Transferred from Hampshire Police.
Appointed: 11.9.1857.
Promotion: 6.4.1858 to 1st class Superintendent.
Stationed at: Truro Sept 1857. Launceston 9.10.1857. Truro 23.10.1860. Helston 13.8.1869.
7.9.1870. Called on to resign for gravely deceiving the Chief Constable with reference to a matter which took place at Penryn and making a false return thereon.

P.C. 129 Nicholas Lawry
A single miner from St Just, aged 20 years.
Appointed: 16.9.1857.
Stationed at: Bodmin 15.11.1857.
Removal: 21.2.1858. Resigned.

P.C. 86 John Screech
A 28 year old married labourer from Crediton.
Appointed: 16.9.1857.
Stationed at: Truro 15.12.1857. Launceston 6.3.1859.
Removal: 14.5.1859 Requested by the Chief Constable to resign.

Sergeant Edward Marshall
A former farm labourer from Christchurch, aged 25 single. Transferred from Hampshire Police.
Appointed: 18.9.1857.
Promotion: 24.1.1858 to Inspector, 8.9.1870 to Superintendent.
Stationed at: Bodmin Oct 1857. Liskeard 5.7.1859. Bodmin 4.12.1864. Truro 31.10.1873.
!0.1.1883. Accidentally killed by the upsetting of his trap at Higgen Bridge near Truro. Mrs Marshall received a gratuity of £150.1.3.

P.C. 88 William Palmer
A yeoman from St Germans Creek, married aged 33.
Appointed: 21.9.1857.
Stationed at: Launceston 10.11.1857.
20.12.1857. Fined 5/- for being absent from his conference point and for being in plain clothes. 6.4.1860 Dismissed for insubordination.

P.C. 96 John Ward Badcock
A married farm labourer from Holsworthy.
Appointed: 21.9.1857.
Stationed at: Liskeard 15.11.1857.
Removal: 12.4.1858. Resigned.

P.C. 90 John Roberts
A 28 year old married miner from St Just.
Appointed: 22.9.1857.
Stationed at: Penzance 15.11.1857.
26.5.1863 Dismissed for being the worse for liquor and behaving in a disgraceful manner in a railway carriage.

P.C. 87 Joseph Voss
A 23 year old married labourer from Cardinham.
Appointed: 24.9.1857.
Promotion: 22.8.1858 to 1st class Constable. 21.5.1865 to sergeant. 11.10.1886 to Inspector.
Stationed at: Liskeard 29.10.1857. Launceston 21.5.1865. Liskeard 8.6.1871. Truro (St Columb) 22.10.1886.
Removal: 24.9.1894. Pension £70.19.5.

P.C. 118 George Wearne
A 20 year old single carpenter from Gwithian.
Appointed: 1.10.1857.
Stationed at: Bodmin 4.11.1857. Liskeard Feb 1858.
Removal: 18.6.1858 Resigned.

P.C. 116 Robert Edwards
A 20 year old single man from St Ives, Miner.
Appointed: 1.10.1857.
Stationed at: Helston 15.11.1857.
Bodmin 27.5.1860. Liskeard 30.3.1863.
11.11.1860. Fined 2/6 for being in a public
house when he should have been on duty.
Removal: 14.6.1863. Resigned.

P.C. 92 Zacharia Williams
A 21 year old single miner from Ludgvan.
Appointed: 1.10.1857.
Stationed at: Liskeard 16.11.1857.
Helston 23.12.1857. 29.12.1857. Fined 2/6
for not going direct to his station when
ordered to by the Chief Constable.
21.8.1858. Fined 2/6 for being absent from
his conference point.
17.5.1859 Dismissed the force for drunkenness.

P.C. 113 Jeremiah Dailey
A 20 year old single miner from Redruth.
Appointed: 1.10.1857.
Stationed at: Penzance 1.11.1857.
Truro 21.2.1858. Bodmin 18.4.1858.
13.6.1858 Dismissed with forfeiture of pay
for being drunk and in plain clothes.

P.C. 109 James Vingoe
A single miner from Sancreed, aged 20.
Appointed: 1.10.1857.
Promotion: 24.6.1860 to 1st class
Constable.
Stationed at: Bodmin 18.12.1857.
Helston 10.11.1861.
Removal: 4.1.1863. Resigned.

P.C. 114 William Davey Williams
A 28 year old miner from St Just. Married.
Appointed: 5.10.1857.
Stationed at: Truro 4.11.1857.
Helston 26.6.1859. Penzance 12.2.1866.
Helston 17.6.1866. Penzance 25.10.1872.
Removal: 8.8.1892. Pension £51.11.4.
Died 6.2.1898.

P.C. 104 James Warne
A single tailor from Liskeard, aged 20.
Appointed: 12.10.1857.
Stationed at: Liskeard 15.11.1857.
Helston 18.4.1858. 24.7.1859
Fined 5/- for being absent from his confer-
ence point.
Removal: 15.1.1860. Resigned as he was
suffering from a disease of the heart.

P.C. 93 William Glendenning
A 20 year old single miner from St Mawes.
Appointed: 14.10.1857.
Stationed at: Bodmin 5.11.1857. Penzance
5.2.1858.
Removal: 7.7.1863. Resigned.

P.C. 105 George Dreadon
A 21 year old single sawyer from Bodmin.
Appointed: 17.10.1857.
Promotion: 18.10.1861 to 1st class
Constable.
Stationed at: Liskeard 15.11.1857.
Removal: 27.9.1862. Resigned.

P.C. 129 John Coppin
A labourer from Blisland, single aged 20.
Appointed: 20.10.1857.
Promotion: 17.10.1858 to 1st class
Constable.
Stationed at: Bodmin 10.11.1857.
Launceston 20.5.1859. Liskeard 17.8.1862,
Removal: 16.3.1863. Dismissed for having
charged a prisoner 1/6 more than he ought
to have done.

P.C. 55 Charles Williams
A 20 year old single miner from St Dennis.
Appointed: 20.10.1857.
Stationed at: Bodmin 18.11.1857.
Helston 9.5.1858.
Removal: 10.4.1861 Resigned.

P.C. 98 William Rodda
A 23 year old single mason from St Blazey.
Appointed: 2.11.1857.
Promotion: 24.7.1859 to 1st class Constable.
Stationed at: Bodmin 19.11.1857.
Removal: 18.7.1861. Resigned.

P.C. 81 William James Richards
A miner from Sancreed, single aged 20.
Appointed: 5.11.1857.
Stationed at: Bodmin 20.12.1857.
Penzance 10.7.1858. Helston 27.5.1860.
26.6.1859 Fined 7/6 for being absent from
his conference point and making a false entry
in his journal.
Removal: 23.3.1862 Resigned.

P.C. 103 John Thomas
A miner from Sennen, single aged 20.
Appointed: 5.11.1857.
Stationed at: Truro 15.1.1858. Helston
4.9.1873. Bodmin 31.10.1873. Launceston
24.11.1883. Truro 17.1.1887. Liskeard Oct
1889. Penzance 9.12.1890.
Removal: 7.9.1891. Pension £51 .11.4.

P.C. 106 William Santo
A 27 year old single butcher from Lostwithiel.
Appointed: 10.11.1857.
Stationed at: Bodmin 19.12.1857.
17.10.1858 Fined 5/- for liberating a prisoner without taking him before a Magistrate.
4.2.1860. Fined 2/6 for being absent from
his conference point.
Removal: 23.2.1860. Dismissed with forfeiture of pay for being the worse for liquor.

P.C. 110 John Rodd
A miller from Holsworthy, aged 25 married.
Appointed: 9.11.1857.
Stationed at: Liskeard 10.12.1857.
Bodmin 10.11.1861 Launceston 9.10.1864.
Removal: 6.5.1865. Dismissed for gross
neglect of duty.

P.C. 125 John Williams
A 31 year old married labourer from St
Keverne.
Appointed: 9.11.1857.
Stationed at: Truro 15.1.1858. Bodmin
26.4.1863.
Removal: 29.7.1864. Dismissed for insubor-
dination

P.C. 108 John Paul
A carpenter from Mevagissey, aged 21 single.
Appointed: 9.11.1857.
Stationed at: Truro Jan 1858.
Removal: 1.3.1858. Dismissed.

P.C. 107 John Body
A 24 year old married labourer from St Cleer.
Appointed: 10.11.1857.
Stationed at: Liskeard 15.1.1858.
6.3.1858. Fined 2/6 for being absent from
his conference point.
4.4.1858 Fined 5/- for being absent from
his conference point.
Removal: 4.5.1859. Dismissed for being
absent from his conference point.

P.C. 134 John LeWarne
A 28 year old married miner from
Perranzubuloe.
Appointed: 17.11.1857.
Stationed at: Truro 15.1.1858. H.Q.
2.6.1858.
Removal:. 12.10.1873. Pension £30.8.4.

P.C. 101 James Penberthy
A 21 year old married miner from Ludgvan.
Appointed: 17.11.1857.
Promotion: 24.6.1860 to 1st Class
Constable. 21.5.1865 to Sergeant.
11.1.1887 Reduced to 1st class Constable,
for gross irregularities of duty now P.C. 37.
Stationed at: Truro 15.1.1858. Bodmin
21.5.1865. Launceston 28.1.1866. Truro
1.12.1874. Launceston 1.5.1884. Truro
17.7.1884. Liskeard 17.1.1887.
Removal: 13.7.1891. Pension £41.9.1.

P.C. 40 Elijah Roseveor
A single carpenter from St Ewe, aged 22 years.
Appointed: 16.11.1857.
Promotion: 5.7.1860 to 1st class constable.
27.4.1862 to Sergeant. 11.11.1886 to
Inspector.
Stationed at: Truro 15.1.1858.
Liskeard 27.4.1862. Bodmin 7.10.1870.
Launceston 8.6.1871. Helston 24.11.1883.
Penzance 17.7.1884. Truro 11.1.1886.
Helston 20.10.1886. 26.6.1859.
Fined 5/- for leaving his station and appear-
ing in plain clothes in another district.
Removal: 4.12.1891 Died. Widow
received a gratuity of £277.13.4.

P.C. 124 Joseph Bawden
A 39 year old married labourer from Duloe.
Appointed: 17.11.1857.
Promotion: 16.5.1858 to 1st class Constable.
14.11.1858 to Sergeant.
Stationed at: Bodmin Nov 1857.
Truro 24.7.1859. Penzance 6.9.1868.
Removal: 13.11.1876. Died.

P.C. John Watters
A 26 year old married mason from Falmouth.
Appointed: 23.11.1857.
The Chief Constable discovered he had
enlisted in the Militia.

P.C. William Cock
A 20 year old single plumber from Kenwyn.
Appointed: 23.11.1857. Left the same day.

P.C. 94 Azariah Carpenter
A 21 year old single labourer from St
Germans.
Appointed: 23.11.1857.
Stationed at: Truro 15.1.1858.
Removal: 2.5.1858. Dismissed for being
dirty.

P.C. 53 Thomas Stephens
A labourer from St Austell, aged 20 years,
single.
Appointed: 23.11.1857.
Stationed at: Truro 15.1.1858.
Launceston 12.10.1858.
Removal: 7.1.1860. Dismissed for commit-
ting an indecent assault on a girl.

P.C. 3 Peter Semens
A tin dresser from Ludgvan, married aged 22
years.
Appointed: 23.11.1857.
Promotion: 29.5.1859. To 1st class
Constable.
Stationed at: Truro 18.1.1858.
Removal: 19.1.1861. Dismissed for gross
immorality of conduct.

P.C. 16 Richard May
A married labourer from Duloe, aged 24 years.
Appointed: 24.11.1857.
Stationed at: Launceston 15.1.1858.
Removal: 21.2.1860. Dismissed with forfeiture
of a weeks pay for being drunk, absent from his
conference point and telling a falsehood.

P.C. 22 John Tonkyn
A 24 year old single shoemaker from
Liskeard.
Appointed: 30.11.1857.
Stationed at: Truro 27.1.1858. Launceston
29.4.1858. Bodmin 14.7.1853. Truro
5.11.1865. Liskeard 9.5.1867.
29.5.1858 Fined 2/6 for having his clothes
dirty.
Removal: 29.8.1888. Dismissed for dishon-
esty.

P.C. 25 John Oliver
A 24 year old single labourer from
Boconnoc.
Appointed: 30.11.1857.
Stationed at: Truro 27.1.1858. Bodmin
10.2.1858. Truro 4.8.1858.
Removal: 23.11.1858 Dismissed for being
the worse for liquor when on duty.

P.C. 42 James Burgoyne
A labourer from Poundstock, married aged
34 years.
Appointed: 30.11.1857.
Stationed at: Bodmin 27.1.1858.
Removal: 9.5.1858. Called upon to resign
for having tendered his resignation after
being in the force only a few months.

P.C. 20 Melchizeder Tremayne
A single labourer from Constantine aged 31
years.
Appointed: 1.12.1857.
Stationed at: Bodmin 27.1.1858.
Removal: 18.4.1858. Called upon to resign
for inefficiency.

P.C. 68 William Parkyn
A 25 year old married sawyer from St
Columb.
Appointed: 1.12.1857.
Stationed at: Truro 15.1.1858.
13.11.1859 Fined 5/- for being absent from
his conference point.
Removal: 5.9.1860. Dismissed for running
into debt.

P.C. 26 John Trethewey
A single labourer from Probus aged 20 years.
Appointed: 7.12.1857.
Stationed at: Launceston 15.1.1858.
Removal: 14.7.1858. Dismissed the force
with forfeiture of pay for insubordination.

P.C. 74 Richard Hobbs
A footman from Jacobstowe, 34 years,
widower.
Appointed: 12.12.1857.
Stationed at: Truro 27.1.1858. Liskeard
24.3.1858. Bodmin 1.4.1858.
21.3.1858. Fined 5/- for being the worse for
liquor and 5/- for being at St Columb in plain
clothes.
Removal: 10.5.1858 Dismissed the force
with forfeiture of pay for being drunk on
duty and in addition to the punishment he
was fined £1.0.0. And in default of payment
was committed to gaol for seven days by the
magistrates for neglect of duty.

P.C. 23 Abel Paul
A 23 married miner from Perranzabloe.
Appointed: 10.12.1857
Stationed at: Bodmin 27,1.1858
Removal: 1.7.1858. Resigned.

P.C. 15 Charles Hoare
A 26 year old sailor from St Columb, single.
Appointed: 10.12.1857.
Stationed at: Bodmin 27.1.1858.
Removal: 30.3.1858. Dismissed the force
with forfeiture of pay for being drunk and
telling a falsehood to the Chief Constable.

P.C. 37 Thomas Carlyon
A shoemaker from Helston, single aged 23.
Appointed: 7.12.1857.
Promotion: 16.5.1858 to 1st class Constable.
Stationed at: Bodmin 27.1.1858.
Removal: 16.5.1861. Dismissed for gross
immorality of conduct.

P.C. 122 Martin Jelbert
A miner from Gulval, married aged 28.
Appointed: 14.12.1857.
Promotion: 16.10.1859 to 1st class
Constable.
Stationed at: Truro 27.1.1858. Helston
3.4.1859. Truro 10.11.1861.
29.9.1858 Fined 5/- for having liberated a
prisoner without taking him before the
magistrate.
Removal: 11.6.1862. Dismissed for neglect
of duty.

P.C. 128 Philip John Michell
A married hairdresser from St Austell, aged
28 years.
Appointed: 14.12.1857.

Stationed at: Bodmin 10.2.1858.
4.4.1858 Fined 2/6 for being absent from his
conference point.
Removal: 5.7.1858 Dismissed the force for
being the worse for liquor.

P.C. 123 John Beer
A miner from Barnstaple, aged 33 married.
Appointed: 22.12.1857.
Promotion: 22.8.1858 to 1st class Constable.
14.8.1859 reduced to 2nd class Constable
for getting drunk.
Stationed at: Liskeard 10.2.1858.
Removal: 30.8.1859. Dismissed for drunk-
enness.

P.C. 111 Richard Brooks
A 29 year old married labourer from
Tavistock.
Appointed: 21.12.1857.
Promotion: 25.5.1862 to 1st Class
Constable. 9.7.1864 to Sergeant.
Stationed at: Launceston 10.2.1858 Bodmin
9.7.1864. Truro 21.4.1867. Bodmin
16.9.1886.
Removal: 12.10.1890. Retired. Pension
£48.13.4.

P.C. 97 Samuel Sowden
A married miner from Roche aged 27 years.
Appointed: 21.12.1857.
Stationed at: Bodmin 10.2.1858. Liskeard
9.1.1859.
26.6.1859 Fined 5/- for being absent from
his conference point.
Removal: 21.7.1860. Resigned.

P.C. 120 Henry Thomas Bevercomb
A shoe maker from Blanford, married aged
32 years.
Appointed: 22.12.1857.
Stationed at: Liskeard 27,1.1858.
Removal: 18.6.1858. Dismissed the force
with forfeiture of pay having been convicted
and sentenced to two months imprisonment
for an indecent assault on a child.

P.C. 49 Richard Nicholls
A miner from Gulval, married aged 24 years.
Appointed: 22.12.1857.
Promotion: 17.8.1862 to 1st class Constable.
1.11.1869 to Sergeant. 26.2.1877 to
Inspector.
Stationed at: Truro 10.2.1858. Bodmin
5.11.1869. Launceston 29.10.1888.
1.5.1859 Fined 2/6 for allowing a prisoner
to have a pint and half of beer whilst in his
custody. 5.2.1860 Fined 2/6 for carrying a
bucket of onions which he had purchased for
his own consumption.
Removal: 26.2.1894. Retired Pension
£70.19.5.

P.C. 39 Joseph Rice
A 22 year old single carpenter from
Bridgewater.
Appointed: 28.12.1857.
Promotion: 16.9.1860 to 1st class Constable.
Stationed at: Bodmin 10.2.1858.
3.2.1862 Reduced to 2nd class Constable
for telling a falsehood and then allowed to
resign.

P.C. 91 Henry Pellow
A 25 year old single labourer from Crantock.
Appointed: 28.12.1857.
Stationed at: Bodmin 10.2.1858. Penzance 18.12.1859.
Removal: 22.1.1860. Resigned.

P.C. 117 Henry Trythall
A 34 year old married miner from Ludgvan.
Appointed: 28.12.1857.
Stationed at: Truro 10.2.1858. Helston 18.12.1861.
Removal: 23.8.1866. Dismissed for drunkenness.

P.C. 102 John Hitchens
A seaman from Paul, aged 34 married.
Appointed: 28.12.1857.
Stationed at: Penzance 10.2.1858. Helston 3.12.1866.
Removal: 25.5.1867   Resigned.

P.C. 137 Bernard Carpenter
A 23 year old married labourer from St Germans.
Appointed: 29,12.1857.
Stationed at: Bodmin 10.2.1858. Launceston 4.8.1858.
25.7.1858 Fined 2/6 for being absent from his conference point. 1.5.1859 Fined 5/- for neglect of duty in not bringing a letter to H.Q. Of which he had the charge.
Removal: 9.11.1864.   Resigned

P.C. 135 John Jenkin
A 27 year old married mason from Madron.
Appointed: 29,12.1857.
Stationed at: Helston 10.2.1858.
Removal: 8.5.1858. Dismissed the force with forfeiture of pay for being drunk on duty.

P.C. 100 William Henry Blewett
A 22 year old married labourer from St Buryan.
Appointed: 30.12.1857.
Promotion: 18.8.1861 to 1st class Constable.
Stationed at: Truro 10.2.1858. Bodmin 16.9.1860.
Removal: 28.12.1866. Called upon to resign for liberating a prisoner without taking him before a magistrate and for making a false entry in his journal.

P.C. 114 James Paddock
A 20 year old butcher from Blanford, single.
Appointed: 4.1.1858.
Promotion: 3.12.1865 to 1st class Constable. 30.9.70. to Sergeant 6.1.1891 to Inspector.
Stationed at: Penzance 2.6.1858. Helston 26.9.1870. Bodmin 12.12.1872. Helston 11.4.1881. Bodmin 13.1.1891.
Removal: 20.4.1894. Pension £70.19.5.

P.C. William Thomas
A 30 year old woolcomber from Callington, married.
Appointed: 4.1.1858.
Absented himself giving as a reason that he did not like to be drilled and could not refrain from going into a public house after a glass of ale.

P.C. 126 John Leigh
A married labourer from Lawhitton, married aged 31 years.
Appointed: 4.1.1858.
Promotion:
31.10.1869 to 1st class Constable.
Stationed at: Launceston 10.2.1858. Liskeard 16.9.1860. Bodmin 17.5.1868. Penzance 13.10.1873.
21.8.1859 Ordered into drill for impropriety of conduct.
Removal: 20.7.1891.   Pension £41.9.1.

P.C. 136 John Guy
A 22 year old single labourer from St Tudy.
Appointed:. 4.1.1858.
Promotion: 13.11.1859 to 1st class Constable. 10.5.1867 to Sergeant.
Stationed at: Launceston 10.2.1858. Liskeard 10.11.1861.
Removal: 12.9.1875. Resigned.

P.C. 60 Joseph Sleeman
A 19 year old single shoemaker from St Tudy.
Appointed: 4.1.1858.
Stationed at: Liskeard 10.2.1858. Bodmin July 1858.
29.5.1859 Fined 10/- for allowing a prisoner to get drunk. 4.8.1860. Dismissed for drinking in a public house when he should have been on duty and giving evidence before the bench in the most improper manner.

P.C. 14 Andrew Borlase
A 22 year old single labourer from St Austell.
Appointed: 5.1.1858.
Stationed at: Penzance 10.2.1858.
Removal: 16.5.1859 Resigned.

P.C. 5 John Penrose
A miner from St Blazey, aged 19 single.
Appointed: 12.1.1858.
Stationed at: Bodmin 23.3.1858. Liskeard 2.4.1858.
Removal: 26.7.1862. Resigned.

P.C. 99 William Parsons
A 32 year old quarryman from Tavistock, single.
Appointed: 12.1.1858.
Stationed at: Bodmin March 1858.
4.4.1858. Fined 5/- for being in a tap room the worse for liquor. 5.2.1860   Fined 5/- for being the worse for liquor. 23.9.1860. Dismissed the force with forfeiture of pay for drunkenness.

P.C. 142 William Robins
A miner from Bere Alston, married aged 30 years.
Appointed: 9.1.1858.
Stationed at: Bodmin 24.3.1858.
22.8.1858 Resigned by order of the Chief Constable.

P.C. 143 Richard Pearce
A 21 year old married farmer from St Buryan.
Appointed: 18.1.1858.
Promotion: 14.11.1859 to 1st class Constable. 11.11.1860 to Sergeant.
Stationed at: Camborne 24.3.1858. Helston

3.2.1861.
20.10.1861 Dismissed the force for drinking in a public house with a prostitute.

P.C. 138 John Bishop Cole
A 30 year old married labourer from Dartmouth.
Appointed: 22.1.1858.
Promotion: 21.8.1859 to 1st class Constable.
Stationed at: Bodmin 24.3.1858. Liskeard 27.7.1860. Bodmin 26.3.1865. Launceston 9.9.1866. Liskeard 3.12.1875.
Removal: 27.6.1881. Retired through ill-health. Pension £31.10.6.

P.C. 139 Mark Davey
A single miner from St Breward aged 25 years.
Appointed: 25.1.1858.
Stationed at: Truro 20.3.1858.
Removal: 21.9.1860 Resigned.

P.C. 140 John Clogg
A labourer from East Looe, single aged 33.
Appointed: 28.1.1858.
Stationed at: Truro 24.3.1858. Bodmin April 1860. 24.5.1863. Fined 5/- for having his uniform in a dirty state.
29.11.1863. Dismissed for being asleep and being the worse for liquor at a Conference Point.

P.C. 141 Stephen Hawke
A married labourer from St Clether, aged 28 years.
Appointed: 1.2.1858.
Promotion: 11.12.1859 to 1st class Constable.
Stationed at: Bodmin May 1858. Truro 21.5.1865. Penzance 5.12.1884.
21.5.1865 Fined 2/6 for drinking in a public house when he should have been out on duty.
Removal: 30.11.1891. Pension £41.9.1.

P.C. 32 William Hunkin
A 33 year old married mason from Torrington.
Appointed: 6.2.1858.
Stationed at: Liskeard 24.3.1858.
7.6.1858 Dismissed the force with forfeiture of pay for keeping money belonging to his Superintendent and refusing to give it up. This P.C. Afterwards summoned the Chief Constable to the County Court for the pay forfeited but was non suited.

P.C. 29 John Evans Palmer
A carpenter from Lezant, aged 29 married.
Appointed: 15.2.1858.
Stationed at: Bodmin May 1858.
9.5.1858. Called upon to resign for tendering his resignation when he had been in the force for a few months.

P.C. 24 Syrus Cundy
A single labourer from St Stephens-in-Brannel, aged 23yrs.
Appointed: 22.3.1858.
Stationed at: Bodmin 15.5.1858. Penzance 26.6.1859.
26.6.1859. Fined 5/- for being absent from

his conference point. 16.8.1859 Dismissed for getting into debt.

P.C. 108 George Martin
A 30 year old single miller from Holsworthy.
Appointed: 1.3.1858.
Promotion: 11.12.1859. To 1st class Constable. 15.1.1861 to Sergeant.
Stationed at: Bodmin 10.5.1858. Liskeard 5.2.1860. Bodmin 3.2.1861. Liskeard 11.10.1870.
29.5.1871. Dismissed for being drunk on duty.

P.C. 129 John Hancock Symons
A butcher from St Cleer, aged 21 single.
Appointed: 11.3.1858.
Stationed at: Bodmin May 1858. Launceston 16.10.1859. Penzance 5.2.1860.
3.3.1860 Dismissed with forfeiture of pay for being the worse for liquor. And for drinking in a public house when he should have been on duty.

P.C. 82 Thomas Anneford
A married farm labourer from Ashburton, aged 24 years.
Appointed: 30.3.1858.
Stationed at: Bodmin 13.8.1858.
13.3.1860 Resigned.

P.C. 96 George Lucas
A single shoemaker from Fowey aged 25 years.
Appointed: 12.4.1858.
Stationed at: Bodmin 28.12.1859.
Dismissed for highly improper conduct for a Police Officer.

P.C. 94 James Tait
A 21 year old married labourer from Saltash.
Appointed: 19.4.1858.
Stationed at: Launceston 2.6.1858.
14.7.1859. Ordered to H.Q. At his own expense for drill for being absent from his conference point. 3.10.1859. Called upon to resign for being generally dissatisfied.

P.C. 42 Richard Barber
A streamer from Alternun, married aged 25 years.
Appointed: 26.4.1858.
Stationed at: Truro 2.6.1858. Helston 3.7.61.
9.1.59. Fined 2/6 for not keeping his journal filled in daily. 25.8.1868 Fined 10/- and moved at his own expense for being drunk on duty. 27.8.1868 Resigned.

P.C. 29 John Cruett
A labourer from Menheniott, married aged 25 years.
Appointed: 27.4.1858.
Stationed at: Cawsand 2.6.1858.
Removal: 4.10.1858.

P.C. Reubin Trevail
A 27 year old streamer from Luxulyan.
Appointed: 12.5.1858.
Removal:. Cried to go home and the Chief Constable sent him away.

P.C. 74 Caleb Wakely
A 26 year old blacksmith from Bideford.
Appointed: 6.5.1858.
Stationed at: Liskeard 25.5.1858.
23.10.1858. Resigned.

Sergeant Major David Cockrane
A 39 year old married baker from Midlothian.
Appointed: 10.5.1858.
2.8.1858 Resigned.

P.C. 73 Samuel Saltern
A 22 year old single miner from St Cleer.
Appointed: 24.5.1858.
Stationed at: Bodmin 3.9.1858. Penzance 19.8.1860. Truro 4.1.1863.
12.11.1863. Resigned.

P.C. 54 William Saltern
A married miller from St Cleer, aged 25.
Appointed: 24.5.1858.
Reappointed: 11.7.1859.
Stationed at: Bodmin 3.7.1858. Launceston 16.9.1860.
6.11.1864. Fined 5/- for allowing P.C. Truscott to book himself in P.C. Saltern's journal and for not obeying the order of his Superintendent. 26.2.1865 Resigned.

P.C. 135 John Curnow
A single miner from Penzance aged 20.
Appointed: 17.5.1858.
Stationed at: Bodmin 3.7.1858.
2.5.1860 Resigned.

P.C. 118 John Rundle
A 20 year old single labourer from Camelford.
Appointed: 1.6.1858.
Stationed at: Penzance 2.7.1858.
7.5.1860 Resigned.

P.C. 113 Robert Truscott.
A Millwright from St Stephens-in-Brannel. Aged 20.
Appointed: 31.5.1858.
Promotion: 16.10.1859 to 1st class Constable.
Stationed at: Liskeard 3.7.1858. Launceston 3.7.1860.
30.10.1860 Resigned.

P.C. 22 Edward Stephens
A single 23 year old tailor from Tintagel.
Appointed: 10.6.1858.
Promotion: 29.5.1859. To 1st class Constable.
Stationed at: Bodmin 6.8.1858.
25.1.1860 Resigned.

P.C. 107 Richard Ham
A married labourer from St Issey, aged 27 years.
Appointed: 10.6.1858.
Promotion: 22.6.1863 to 1st Class Constable. 30.9.1877 reduced to 3rd class constable for refusing to take any steps to trace a felony because he was on leave at the time.
Stationed at: Bodmin 6.8.1858. Liskeard 5.2.1860. Bodmin 21.3.1869. Launceston

29.4.1880.
Removal: 10.1.1891 Pension £35.7.9.

P.C. 26 Richard Bassett
A 22 year old single bookmaker from Launceston.
Appointed: 14.6.1858.
Stationed at: Bodmin 6.8.1858. Bodmin 9.4.1860. Penzance 12.10.1862.
1.5.1859 Fined 2/6 for being absent from his conference point. 14.9.1862 Fined 10/- for being asleep when on duty. 18.9.1864. Resigned.

P.C. 120 John Oates
A single 20 year old blacksmith from Gunwalloe.
Appointed: 14.6.1858.
Stationed at: Bodmin 6.8.1858.
18.8.1858 Resigned.

P.C. 128 William Pearce
A shipwright from St Columb Minor. Aged 25. Married.
Appointed: 5.7.1858.
Stationed at: Bodmin 6.8.1858. Truro 16.9.1860.
12.4.1861 Resigned.

P.C. 31 William Heller
A boat maker from Fowey, aged 23 married.
Appointed: 13.7.1858.
Promotion: 6.12.1863 to 1st class Constable.
Stationed at: Truro 6.8.1858. Bodmin 17.6.1866 Liskeard 8.6.1871.
25.8.1858. Fined 2/6 for being absent from his conference point and 2/6 for making a false entry in his journal. 10.2.1867 Fined £1.0.0. For allowing a prisoner to escape thereby losing his good conduct pay for two years. 23.2.1872 Fined 10/- for not entering in his journal money he had received. 2.10.1874. Dismissed for stealing a tree.

P.C. Nathaniel Guard
A 20 year old single blacksmith from Roche.
Appointed: 15.7.1858.
Removal: 17.7.1858 Resigned.

P.C. 15 Samuel Bullock
A labourer from St Enador, aged 20 single.
Appointed: 20.7.1858.
Stationed at: Liskeard 8.9.1858.
22.3.1860 Resigned.

P.C. 23 Edward Plaister
A 24 year old married footman from Oxford.
Appointed: 10.8.1858.
Stationed at: Bodmin 9.9.1858.
10.2.1859 Dismissed for appearing at the Petty Sessions in a disgracefully dirty state.

P.C. 132 John Dustow
A 22 year old single wheelwright from Devonport.
Appointed: 31.8.1858.
9.9.1858. Dismissed the force for having produced a false Certificate of Character, and afterwards committed for trial for having committed a similar offence at Devonport.

P.C. 142 Joshua Arthur
A single labourer from Roche, aged 22.
Appointed: 6.9.1858.
Stationed at: Penzance 21.10.1858.
6.9.1869. Dismissed for making false statements to a Magistrate and also for telling the Chief Constable a falsehood.

P.C. 44 Thomas Rickard
A married labourer from Egloshayle aged 25.
Appointed: 8.9.1858.
Stationed at: Bodmin 18.10.1858.
Launceston 29.4.1860.
14.10.1860 Fined 10/- for gross neglect of duty. 26.9.1870 Dismissed for drinking and associating with low characters.

P.C. 71 William Scoble
A 23 year old married porter from St Keverne.
Appointed: 2.9.1858.
Stationed at: Penzance 18.10.1858. Bodmin 1.4.1860.
11.10.1860. Dismissed the force with forfeiture of a weeks pay for drunkenness.

P.C. 32 Thomas Burton
A single labourer from St Columb Major, aged 28.
Appointed: 13.9.1858.
Stationed at: Liskeard 18.10.1858. Bodmin 5.2.1860.
9.3.1860   Resigned.

P.C. 47 John Veal
A 23 year old single labourer from St Columb.
Appointed: 9.9.1858.
Stationed at: Penzance 18.10.1858.
19.5.1860 Dismissed the force with forfeiture of a weeks pay for drunkenness.

P.C. 120 George King
A married labourer from Southhampton aged 29.
Appointed: 21.9.1858.
Stationed at: Launceston 29.9.1858. Bodmin 21.7.1861.
30.8.1861 Dismissed for riding in his donkey cart.

P.C. 124 William White
A 25 year old married labourer from St Keverne.
Appointed: 18.9.1858.

P.C. 57 William Mitchell
A married miner from Alternun aged 23 years.
Appointed: 6.10.1858.
Stationed at: Liskeard 15.12.1858.
18.2.1869 Dismissed the force with forfeiture of pay for highly improper conduct and general inefficiency.

Sergeant John Bray
A farmer carpenter/joiner from Crediton, married aged 25.
Transferred from Hampshire Police.
Appointed: 6 .10.1858.
Promotion: 11.11.1860 to Inspector.
Stationed at: Penzance Oct. 1858. Liskeard

11.11.1860.
18.3.1862 Dismissed the force for falsely accusing his Superintendent of drunkenness.

P.C. 20 Richard Bone
A labourer fro m Jacobstow, single aged 21.
Appointed: 13.10.1858.
Promotion: 24.4.1864. To 1st class Constable.
Stationed at: Launceston 15.12.1858. Liskeard 21.6.1861.
4.12.1864 Fined 5/- for telling his Superintendent a falsehood. 5.8.1867 Dismissed having been convicted and sentenced to four months imprisonment with hard labour at the Assizes for causing Actual Bodily Harm to a farmer named Richards of Landrake.

P.C. 35 John Quarm
A shoe maker from Laneast, aged 30 years single.
Appointed: 26.10.1858.
Promotion: 12.10.1862 to 1st class Constable.
Stationed at: Bodmin 15.12.1858 Truro 2.4.1860.
Removal: 3.7.1888.   Pension £40.8.10.

P.C. 74 Samuel Boucher
A 21 year old single labourer from Helston.
Appointed: 28.10.1858.
Stationed at: Penzance 15.12.1858. Bodmin 14.10.1860. Truro 17.8.1862.
20.11.1862. Called upon to resign being slightly deranged in his mind.

P.C. 29 William Yelland
A 21 year old single labourer from St Stephen-in-Brannel.
Appointed: 1.11.1858.
Stationed at: Truro 15.12.1858.
1.5.1859 Dismissed for general inefficiency.

P.C. 142 Richard Merefield
A single miner from St Enodor aged 20 years.
Appointed: 2.11.1858.
Stationed at: Launceston 10.1.1859.
23.11.1859 Dismissed the force for being absent from his conference point and bringing a false charge against his Sergeant.

P.C. 145 Richard Bettison
A wool sorter from St Columb, aged 26 and married.
Appointed: 3.11.1858.
Stationed at: Liskeard 10.1.1859. Launceston 26.6.1859. Bodmin 21.5.1865.
29.4.1866 Dismissed the force with a forfeiture of a weeks pay for being drunk.

P.C. 146 William H.Tregonning
A 20 year old single miner from Perranzubaloe.
Appointed: 9.11.1858.
Stationed at: Bodmin 21.1.1859. Truro 18.4.1861.
2.10.1862   Resigned.

P.C. 148 John Stacey
A married labourer from Pleynt, aged 26 years.

Appointed: 9.11.1858.
Stationed at: Bodmin 10.2.1859.
10.5.1863 Dismissed for being drunk.

P.C. 150 George James Vosper
A single carpenter from Swansea aged 20 years.
Appointed: 19.11.1858.
Stationed at: Liskeard 10.7.1859 Penzance 13.11.1859. Bodmin 2.2.1860.
5.2.1860 Fined 10/- for being absent from his conference point and making a false entry in his journal. 11.11.1860 Fined 5/- for leaving his station contrary to orders. 26.11.1860 Dismissed for neglect of duty.

P.C. 150 William Wherry
A 27 year old widower from Lanlivery, a miner.
Appointed: 27.11.1858.
Stationed at: Bodmin 10.2.1859. Bodmin 4.3.1862.
14.8.1864. Resigned.

P.C. 152 Abraham Andrews
A single blacksmith from Stithians, aged 21.
Appointed: 30.11.1858.
Stationed at: Helston 10.2.1859.
11.3.1861 Resigned.

Inspector Arthur Thomas Grant
A former grocer from Wiltshire, married aged 28 years.
Transferred from Hampshire Police.
Appointed: 4.12.1858.
Promotion: 1.7.1864 to Superintendent. 8.11.1877 to 1st class Superintendent.
Stationed at: Truro 5.12.1858. Bodmin 21.6.1861. Launceston 1.7.1864. Bodmin 15.9.1868. Helston 10.9.1870.
Removal: 10.10.1892. Pension £106.9.2. Died at 2 am on 9.8.1900.

P.C. 151 John Maynard
A 25 year old single miller from Lanlivery.
Appointed: 9.12.1858.
Stationed at: Helston 10.2.1859.
16.4.1859 Dismissed the force with forfeiture of pay for being drunk on duty and afterwards committed to one months imprisonment for neglecting to bring his clothing and accoutrements to H.Q.

P.C. 155 Richard Dawe
A labourer from North Hill, single aged 27.
Appointed: 13.12.1858.
Promotion: 31.3.1861 to 1st class Constable.
Stationed at: Truro 10.2.1859. Bodmin 21.5.1865.
Removal: 5.8.1891   Pension £41.9.1. Died 14.12. 1900 at 6pm.

P.C. 154 William Jonas
A labourer from Alternun married aged 26 years.
Appointed: 13.12.1858.
Promotion: 22.7.1860. To 1st class Constable.
Stationed at: Launceston 24.1.1859.
29.11.1863 Dismissed the force with forfeiture of a weeks pay for falsely stating that he

had paid a bill and borrowing money from a beer house keeper.

P.C. 153 Thomas Williams
A single engine man from Menheniott, aged 21.
Appointed: 14.12.1858.
Stationed at: Helston 10.2.1859.
11.7.1859 Dismissed the force for drinking at a public house at the expense of the land-lord.

P.C. 67 Richard Bunt
A 23 year old single farmer from Warleggan.
Appointed: 27.12.1858.
Stationed at: Liskeard 10.3.1859. Helston 14.10.1860.
10.6.1861 Resigned.

P.C. 70 Peter Parkyn
A labourer from Ruan Highlanes, aged 20 single.
Appointed: 27,12.1858.
Stationed at: Truro 10.3.1859. Bodmin 22.6.1861.
1.5.1864 Dismissed the force with forfeiture of a weeks pay for being drunk and playing skittles at Tywardreath.

P.C. 6 William I.Harris
A 20 year old single sailor from Paul.
Appointed: 11.1.1859.
Stationed at: Truro 10.3.1859. Bodmin 1.5.1859.
15.1.1861 Resigned.

P.C. 52 Thomas Henry Hosken
A tailor from Week St Mary single aged 19 years.
Appointed: 15.1.1859.
Stationed at: Bodmin 10.3.1859.
16.4.1859. Dismissed the force with forfeiture of pay for having tendered his resignation within two months after he had joined the force.

P.C. 34 James Stephens
A 21 year old single labourer from North Hill.
Appointed: 19.1.1859.
Stationed at: Truro 10.3.1859.
10.5.1859. Dismissed for inefficiency.

P.C. 156 William Downing
A 21 year old married labourer from Launceston.
Appointed: 15.2.1859.
Stationed at: Liskeard 13.4.1859.
6.1.1863 Fined 5/- for not going on duty at the hour fixed on his route. 28.2.1867 Resigned. Considerably in debt at this time which was supposed to be the reason for his leaving.

P.C. 23 John Richards
A single miner from Sancreed aged 20.
Appointed: 24,2.1859.
Stationed at: Helston 16.4.1859.
24.3.1861 Resigned.

P.C. 57 George Guy
A 29 year old married sail maker from

Madron.
Appointed: 3.3.1859.
Promotion: 27.4.1862 to 1st class Constable. 5.11.1877 to Sergeant.
Stationed at: Helston 17.4.1859. Truro 5.11.1877. Liskeard 27.9.1878. Bodmin 10.11.1883.
Removal: 5.1.1891 Pension £48.13.4.

P.C. 12 Zacharia Williams
A miner from Crowan, married aged 22.
Appointed: 8.3.1859.
Stationed at: Truro 6.5.1859
18.7.1859 Ordered to H.Q. At his own expense for drill for being absent from his conference point
11.2.1860 Resigned.

P.C. 151 George Timmons
A miner from Penryn, aged 21 years single.
Appointed: 29.3.1859.
Stationed at: Helston 5.6.1859.
27.10.1866 Resigned – going to keep a public house.

P.C. 131 William Brock
A single labourer from Stratton, Aged 20 years.
Appointed: 18.4.1859.
Promotion: 3.9.1863 to 1st class Constable.
Stationed at: Bodmin 22.6.1859 Liskeard 11.10.1863.
Removal: 14.10.1888. Pension on medical certificate £40.8.10. For one year and at the end of this time to come up for examination. Pension confirmed 13.10.1890.

P.C. 52 Thomas Clift
A carpenter from Marmchurch, single aged 20 years.
Appointed: 19.4.1859.
Stationed at: Bodmin 4.6.1859.
31.8.1859 Resigned.

P.C. 17 Samuel Symons
A 27 year old single miner from Gwinear.
Appointed: 24.4.1859.
Stationed at: Truro 5.6.1859.
30.11.1859 Dismissed the force for disgraceful conduct as a Police Officer.

P.C. 92 William Henry Carkeek
A 23 year old single carpenter from Ruanlanihorne.
Appointed: 27.4.1859.
Stationed at: Bodmin 3.7.1859.
20.9.1863 Resigned.

P.C. 29 David Brown
A single porter aged 29 years from Scotland.
Appointed: 4.5.1859.
Stationed at: Launceston 3.6.1859,
12.12.1859. Dismissed for drunkenness.

P.C. 36 Samuel Doidge
A 30 year old married labourer from Jacobstow.
Appointed: 4.7.1859.
Stationed at: Bodmin 17.8.1859.
Removal: 11.5.1889 Pension £40.8.10.

P.C. 14 Richard Cory
A married miner from Linkinhorne, aged 26 years.
Appointed: 11.7.1859.
Promotion: 9.10.1864 to 1st class Constable.
Stationed at: Launceston 24.10.1859. Bodmin 16.1.1872.
4.8.1872 Fined £1.0.0. For being absent from his conference point and making a false entry in his journal. 22.12.1872   Resigned with a gratuity of £60.13.4.

P.C. 68 John Perkin
A single shoe maker from South Petherwin aged 20 years.
Appointed: 20.7.1859.
Stationed at: Truro 27.9.1859. Bodmin 21.7.1861.
29.4.1860 Fined 10/- for neglect of duty. 9.12.1860 Fined 5/- for being absent from his conference point.
29.10.1861 Dismissed the force for being repeatedly absent from his conference points.

P.C. 112 John Hawkin
A married shoe maker from Stoke Climsland aged 23 years.
Appointed: 9.8.1859.
Stationed at: Penzance 27.9.1859.
9.11.1865 Resigned.

P.C. 52 William Coad
A 24 year old single farmer from St Ive.
Appointed: 5.9.1859.
Stationed at: Liskeard 24.10.1859.
22.7.1860 Fined 2/6 for taking refreshment in a public house at 2 am when he should have been on duty, and 2/6 for allowing a prisoner to be at large after he had taken him into custody.
12.4.1861 Resigned by order of the Chief Constable for inefficiency.

P.C. 86 Joseph Giles
A 33 year old married porter from Gwinear.
Appointed: 8.9.1859.
Promotion: 7.12.1862 to 1st class Constable.
Stationed at: Helston 24.10.1859. Penzance 10.11.1861.
13.12.1864 Resigned.

P.C. 86 Samuel Philp
A 30 year old married labourer from Veryan.
Appointed: 20.9.1859.
Stationed at: Penzance 24.10.1859.
21.2.1860 Resigned.

P.C. 34 Seth Dunn
A married miner from Crowan aged 27 years.
Appointed: 28.9.1859.
Stationed at: Bodmin 30.11.1859.
19.3.1860 Called upon to resign – inefficient.

P.C. 94 Edward Guy
A married fisherman from Mevagissey, aged 27 years.
Appointed: 28.9.1859.
Promotion: 27.4.1862 to 1st class Constable.
Stationed at: Truro 30.11.1859. Helston

18.5.1881.
Retired 5.1.1885. Pension £37.11.9.
Died 25.4.1888.

Inspector Elijah Middle

A former labourer from Bath. Transferred from Hampshire Police with 4 years service. Married aged 28 years.
Appointed: 7.10.1859.
Promotion: 15.1.1883 to Superintendent.
Stationed at: Bodmin Oct 1859. Launceston 31.12.1865. Helston 26.9.1870. Truro 18.5.1876. Bodmin 1.2.1883.
31.10.1889 Called upon to resign.

P.C. 149 Horatio Pollard

A 24 year old single fisherman from Paul, Penzance.
Appointed: 10.10.1859.
Stationed at: Liskeard 31.11.1859.
29.1.1861. Resigned by order of the Chief Constable.

P.C. 10 Robert Harris

A farmer from Paul, single aged 21.
Appointed: 14.10. 1859.
Stationed at: Bodmin 30.11.1859.
25.1.1860 Resigned.

P.C. 153 Samuel Prophet

A 20 year old single farmer from Gorran.
Appointed: 17.10.1859.
Stationed at: Bodmin 30.11.1859.
17.7.1860 Resigned.

P.C. 137 James Squire

A woolcomber from Crediton single aged 20.
Appointed: 27,10.1859.
Stationed at: Launceston 28,12.1859.
9.7.1860 Resigned.
March 1861 Rejoined as P.C. 6.
Stationed at: Helston 17.4.1861. Penzance 5.1.1862.
5.1.1862 Fined 10/- for being drunk and removed at his own expense to Redruth.
9.8/.1862. Dismissed for liberating a prisoner without going before a Magistrate.

P.C. 77 John Williams

A 20 year old married miner from Tywardreath.
Appointed: 31.10.1859.
Stationed at: Liskeard 27.12.1859.
28.4.1860. Called upon to resign for immorality of conduct.

P.C. 123 George Burnard

A stone cutter from Blisland single aged 34.
Appointed: 9.11.1859.
Stationed at: Launceston 27.12.1859.
7.2.1861. Resigned.

P.C. 30 Richard Michell

A 20 year old tin steamer from Bodmin, single.
Appointed: 24.10.1859.
Stationed at: Penzance 30.11.1859.
2.5.1860 Called upon to resign, Mr. Michell reported that he would never make an efficient Constable.

P.C. 147 James Walker

A 30 year old married slater from Aberdeen.
Appointed: 28.11.1859.
Stationed at: Truro 27.12.1859.
14.7.1861. Dismissed the force for drunkenness.

P.C. 28 Charles Truscott

A single shoe maker from St stephens-in-Brannel, aged 25.
Appointed: 22.12.1859.
Stationed at: Penzance 20.7.1860.
11.1.1861. Resigned. 23.11.1861
Reappointed: Launceston 9.1.1862.
6.1.1863 Fined 5/- for permitting a prisoner to get drunk when marching his to gaol.
Drowned whilst bathing at South Petherwin.

P.C. 96 James Harris Philp

A 20 year old single labourer from Veryan.
Promotion: 6.12.1863 to 1st class Constable. 16.12.1872 to Sergeant. 3.4.1881 to Inspector. 1.11.1889. To Superintendent. 27.11.1892 to Superintendent 1st Class.
Stationed at: Bodmin 20.6.1860. Helston 19.12.1872. Liskeard 6.4.1881. Bodmin 1.11.1884. Truro 13.1.1890. Liskeard 8.6.1894.
Retired 28.2.1899. Pension £106.9.2.

P.C. 41 James Thomas Byers

A single miner from Bodmin aged 20.
Appointed: 9.1.1860.
Promotion: 9.11.1862. to 1st class Constable.
Stationed at: Bodmin 20.2.1860. Penzance 14.10.1860. Helston 8.4.1861. Penzance 28.2.1864. Helston 4.12.1864.
24.6.1860 Fined 2/6 for being absent from his conference point.
14.10.1860 Fined 5/- and removed to St Just at his own expense fro being absent from his conference point.
3.5.1869 Died.

P.C. 104 Thomas Mutton

A labourer from Fowey married aged 27.
Appointed: 13.2.1860.
Stationed at: Liskeard 18.3.1860.
18.6.1861 Resigned.

P.C. 91 John Stephens

A labourer from Boscastle, single aged 20.
Appointed: 13.2.1860.
Promotion: 9.11.1862 to 1st class Constable. 9.10.1864 to Sergeant.
Stationed at: Truro 17.3.1860. Bodmin 9.10.1864.
6.5.1865 Dismissed the force for gross neglect of duty.

P.C. 10 John Talbot

A butcher from Bridgewater, single 20.
Appointed: 18.2.1860.
Stationed at: Launceston 17.3.1860. Penzance 17.5.1860.
8.5.1861 Dismissed for drinking in a public house and for general inefficiency.

P.C. 27 George Edward Hunt

An iron monger from Bristol, married aged 26.

Appointed: 23.2.1860.

Stationed at: Truro 20.3.1860. Bodmin 19.8.1860. Truro 21.7.1861.
22.1.1862 Called upon to resign for conspiring with Dr Dean to charge 2/6 to the County.

P.C. 1 Daniel Vosper

A 20 year old single labourer from Swansea.
Appointed: 23.2.1860.
Stationed at: Penzance 3.5.1860.
29.6.1860. Dismissed the force for conduct unbecoming a Police Officer.

P.C. 17 John Curtis J. Gynnirsley

A carpenter from Bristol, married aged 26.
Appointed: 25.2.1860.
Stationed at: Bodmin 10.3.1860.
27.8.1860 Resigned

P.C. 53 James Drewett

A single sawyer from Bristol, aged 22 years.
Appointed: 1.3.1860.
Promotion: 8.7.1872 to 2nd class Constable. 9.5.1875 to 1st class Constable.
Stationed at: Truro 17.3.1860. Helston 22.5.1864. Penzance 1.8.1878.
16.6.1867 Fined £1.0.0. For allowing a prisoner to escape. 16.2.1868 Fined 5/- for being absent from his conference point. 25.5.1885. Fined 5/- for not bringing his truncheon to parade for the Government Inspection.
Retired 3.11.1891. Pension £41.9.1.

P.C. 45 William Luxon

A 21 year old married miner from St Blazey.
Appointed: 5.3.1860.
Stationed at: Penzance 2,5.1860. Truro 10.11.1861. Truro 2.2.1862. Helston 27.4.1862.
23.5.1866 Resigned.

P.C. 89 Joseph Pascoe

A single stonemason from Luxulyan, aged 21.
Appointed: 5.3.1860.
Promotion: 9.10.1864 to 1st class Constable.
Stationed at: Penzance 2.6.1860.
3.10.1867 Resigned, alleged he was going to Australia.

P.C. 24 John Varcoe

A single stonemason from Luxulyan, aged 21.
Appointed: 5.3.1860.
Stationed at: Penzance 2.5.1860.
10.6.1860 Resigned.

P.C. 106 Frederick Evans

A 25 year old butcher from Axbridge, married.
Appointed: 8.3.1860.
Stationed at: Liskeard 3.5.1860.
1.7.1861. Dismissed the force for immorality of conduct.

P.C. 124 William Bath

A labourer from St Stephens by Launceston, single aged 24 years.
Appointed: 9.3.1860.
Stationed at: Truro 2.5.1860.
20.8.1860 Resigned.

P.C. 12 **Richard Coulan**
A 20 year old single labourer from St Austell.
Appointed: 17.3.1860
Stationed at: Launceston 2.5.1860.
16.7.1860. Dismissed the force with forfeiture of a weeks pay for neglect of duty and telling falsehoods.

P.C. 16 **John Werren**
A single labourer from Marhamchurch, aged 20 years.
Appointed: 17.3.1860.
Stationed at: Penzance 2,5,1860. Helston 14.10.1860.
11.4.1861 Resigned by order of the Chief Constable for inefficiency.

P.C. 84 **John LeWarne**
A 19 year old single miner from St Blazey.
Appointed: 19.3.1860.
Stationed at: Bodmin 11.6.1860. Truro 16.9.1860.
9.12.1860. Dismissed with forfeiture of a weeks pay for associating with prostitutes.

P.C. 85 **John Baker**
A married butcher from Cullumpton aged 31.
Appointed: 19.3.1860.
Stationed at: Liskeard 5.7.1860.
9.12.1860 Fined 5/- and to be moved at his own expense for being absent from his conference point and making a false entry in his journal.
29.12.1860 Dismissed the force for drunkenness.

P.C. 29 **Samuel Yeo**
A single labourer from Barnstable aged 24.
Public Service: 21 months with the Bristol Police.
Appointed: 19.3.1860.
Stationed at: Launceston 2.5.1860.
25.5.1861 Resigned.

P.C. 120 **John Riddler**
A single labourer from Bristol aged 22.
Public service: 17 months with Bristol Police.
Appointed: 19.3.1860.
Stationed at: Helston 2.5.1860.
7.7.1861 Resigned.

P.C. 82 **Frederick John Julian**
A single farmers son from Withiel, aged 22.
Appointed: 20.3.1860.
Stationed at: Penzance 2.5.1860 Liskeard 5.1.1862. Truro 22.6.1862.
22.6.1862 Fined 5/- and moved at his own expense for being absent from his conference point.
22.7.1862 Dismissed for drinking in a public house and dancing with prostitutes.

P.C. 34 **Thomas Hayden**
A 21 year old single labourer from Farnborough.
Appointed: 20.3.1860.
Stationed at: Liskeard 2.5.1860. Truro 21.7.1861.
1.4.1863 Resigned.

P.C. 32 **Edward Harper**
A single labourer from Plymouth aged 23

years. Public Service: 23 months with Devonport Police.
Appointed: 20.3.1860.
Stationed at: Penzance 3.5.1860. Helston 20.3.1863.
17.8.1865. Called upon to resign as his wife and him were continually quarrelling.

P.C. 86 **Henry Nicholls**
A labourer from Falmouth, single aged 20.
Appointed: 20.3.1860.
Stationed at: Launceston 2.5.1860.
30.8.1860. Called upon to resign.

P.C. 119 **Thomas Carlyon**
A 24 year old single seaman from Tywardreath.
Appointed: 2.4.1860.
Promotion: 21.5.1865 to 1st class Constable.
Stationed at: Penzance 11.6.1860. Bodmin 22.6.1862. Helston 14.9.1862. Liskeard 16.8.1863. Truro 6.7.1865.
16.8.1865 Resigned.

P.C. 72 **Thomas Butler**
A woolcomber from Bodmin single aged 20.
Appointed: 10.4.1860.
Promotion: 25.9.1870 to 1st class Constable. 13.9.1875 to Sergeant.
Stationed at: Bodmin 11.6.1860. Liskeard 16.8.1860. Bodmin 11.11.1860. Liskeard 13.9.1863. Truro 27.9.1870. Launceston 18.4.1881.
Retired 22.8.1891. Pension £57.11.4.

P.C. 15 **William Jenkin**
A 22 year old single miner from St Agnes.
Appointed: 7.5.1860.
3.3.1861 Fined 10/- for gross neglect of duty and for making a false entry in his occurrence book
17.8.1861 Dismissed for neglect of duty and making a false entry in his journal.

P.C. 118 **John Hicks**
A married malster from Jacobstow, aged 29.
Appointed: 7.5.1860.
3.10.1860 Resigned.

P.C. 135 **George Colinso**
A single shoe maker from Truro aged 23 years.
Appointed: 21.5.1860.
Promotion: 5.7.1861 to 1st class Constable.
Stationed at: Bodmin 11.6.1860. Helston 25.5.1862.
4.6.1862 Resigned, January 1865
Reappointed: as P.C. 68.
Promotion: 20.5.1866 to 1st class Constable. 7.11.1868 to Sergeant. 16.12.1872 to Inspector.
Stationed at: Liskeard 14.10.1880.
27.3.1881. Resigned.

P.C. 2 **William Hide**
A married butcher from Herts, aged 27 years. Public service. Six years in the Metropolitan Police.
Appointed: 19.5.1860.
Stationed at: Liskeard 28.4.1861.
2.1.1862 Dismissed for contracting debts.

P.C. 28 **Robert Bickle**
A labourer from South Petherwin, single aged 28.
Appointed: 19.5.1860.
Stationed at: Launceston 19.7.1860. Bodmin 3.3.1861. Launceston 21.6.1863.
26.7.1869 Resigned.

P.C. **Francis Gill**
A 24 year old single miner from St Agnes.
Appointed: 4.6.1860.
16.7.1860 Dismissed with forfeiture of a weeks pay for neglect of duty and telling the Chief Constable a falsehood.

P.C. 30 **William Chappel**
A wheel wright from Helston. Single aged 23.
Appointed: 16.6.1860.
Promotion: 9.10.1864 to 1st Class Constable.
Stationed at: St Austell 18.8.1860.
10.9.1865 Resigned.

Sergeant **John Newcombe**
A former labourer from Chumleigh, Devon, single aged 26. Transferred from Hampshire Police with a service of 5 years and 55 days.
Appointed: 3.7.1860.
Promotion: 1.11.1869 to Inspector.
10.10.1880. To Superintendent.
26.10.1886. To 1st class Superintendent.
Stationed at: Bodmin 16.7.1860. Launceston 18.8.1861. Bodmin 19.6.1864. Truro 5.11.1869. Bodmin 16.7.1871. Liskeard 19 .12.1872. Bodmin 14.10.1880. Penzance 29.10.,1888. Bodmin 11.10.1892. Launceston 8.6.1894.
9.2.1899 Died suddenly in his carriage at Canworthy Water whilst on duty.
Widow received a gratuity of £572.4.3.

P.C. 12 **Eli Winter**
A 24 year old single basket maker from Taunton.
Appointed: 21.7.1860.
Stationed at: Bodmin 29.8.1860. Helston 11.11.1862. Penzance 12.10.1862.
10.11.1864 Resigned.

P.C. 65 **William Pearce**
A miner from Tywardreath, single aged 21.
Appointed: 30.7.1860.
Promotion: 21.1.1867 to 1st class Constable.
Stationed at: Penzance 26.9.1860. Truro 6.12.1863.
1.12.1868 Resigned.

P.C. 137 **Luke Lukes**
A 20 year old single miner from St Blazey.
Apppointed: 30.7.1860.
Stationed at: Liskeard 25.10.1860.. ..28.11.1862. Resigned.

P.C. 153 **William Nicholls**
A miner from Perranzubaloe, aged 32 a widower.
Appointed: 13.8.1860.
Stationed at: Bodmin 26.9.1860.
20.4.1862 Resigned.

P.C. 60 **William Teague**
A single mason from St Teath aged 23 years.

Appointed: 13.8.1860.
Stationed at: Penzance 26.9.1860.
23.11.1860 Resigned.

P.C. 139 William Trevelyan Beckerlegg
Aged 24 years, a single sailor from Paul.
Appointed: 10.9.1860.
Promotion: 6.12.1863 to 1st class Constable.
Stationed at: Bodmin 27.10.1860.
Liskeard 25.3.1866. Launceston 8.6.1871.
26.12.1890 Retired Pension of £49.9.1.

P.C. 1 John Moushead
A 20 year old single miner from Pelynt.
Appointed: 18.9.1860.
Promotion: 1.3.1863 to 1st class Constable.
Stationed at: Truro 4.11.1860. Penzance
5.1.1862 Helston 30.3.1862.
7.10.1863 Died.

P.C. 17 Charles Nicholas
A miner from St Erth, single aged 21.
Appointed: 17.9.1860,
Stationed at: Truro 4.11.1860.
27.11.1861 Resigned.

P.C. 71 Henry Lean
A 19 year old single labourer from St Kew.
Appointed: 8.10.1860
Stationed at: Truro 9.12.1860. Helston
14.8.1864.
17.9.1864 Dismissed for marrying without
the Chief Constable's permission

P.C. 69 Nicholas Harring
A 20 year old single farmers son from St
Dominic.
Appointed: 15.10.1860.
Stationed at: Bodmin 9.12.1860.
13.6.1861 Dismissed with forfeiture of a
weeks pay for leaving his station to go to
Truro when he had been refused leave by his
Inspector.

P.C. 95 Thomas Allen
A single groom from Veryan, aged 23.
Appointed: 15.10.1860.
Promotion: 8.7.1872 to 2nd class Constable.
16.2.1873 to 1st class Constable.
Stationed at: Liskeard 19.12.1860.
Launceston 21.7.1861.
24.9.1867 Reported for getting refreshments
at a beer house after the hour for closing and
was moved at his own expense for so doing.
21.9.1891 Retired Pension £41.9.1.

P.C. 118 Christopher Rush
A labourer from St Breward, aged 22 single.
Appointed: 15.10.1860.
18.1.1861. Resigned.

P.C. 4 William Tolchard
A former labourer from Totnes, married aged
30. Transferred from the Hampshire
Constabulary after 4 years and 28 days.
Appointed: 22.10.1860.
Stationed at: Penzance 3.11.1860.
2.3.1862 Resigned.

P.C. 113 Nicholas Thomas Reed
A 24 years old married miner from St Blazey.
Appointed: 29.10.1860.

Stationed at: Liskeard 9.12.1860.
9.5.1861 Resigned.

P.C. 99 William Smale
From Stoke Climsland, a 30 year old married
miner
Appointed: 6.11.1860.
Promotion: 22.6.1863. To 1st class
Constable. 1.7.1872 to Sergeant.
Stationed at: Bodmin 21.1.1861.
Truro 1.5.1884.
4.8.1891 Retired Pension £51.11.4.

P.C. 60 Richard Oliver
A 22 year old single labourer from
Boconnoc.
Appointed: 3.12.1860.
Stationed at: Penzance 21.1.1861.
23.4.1862 Dismissed the force for being
frequently absent from his conference point.

P.C. 86 John Kite
A single miner from Stoke Climsland aged
24.
Appointed: 4.12.1860.
Promotion: 9.10.1864 to 1st class Constable,
Stationed at: Penzance 21.1.1861. Truro
27.4.1862.
5.9.1869 Resigned.

P.C. 124 Charles Riggs
A former labourer from Exeter, married aged
31. Public service. Four years in
Carmarthenshire Constabulary.
Appointed: 4.12.1860.
Stationed at: Liskeard 15.1.1861. Bodmin
28.5.1861. Helston 12.10.1862.
6.10.1863 Resigned.

P.C. 84 William Hunt
A married sailor from Bristol aged 31 years.
Appointed: 29.12.1860.
Stationed at: Truro 18.2.1861. Bodmin
30.6.1861.
10.7.1864 Dismissed for letting lodgings in
the house rented by the County.

P.C. 13 John Coombe
A single labourer from South Petherwin, aged
28. 29.4.1878 Married Elizabeth Campbell.
(Cook to W.H.P. Carew Esq., of St Anthony.)
Appointed: 10.1.1861.
Promotion: 14.9.1862 to 1st Class
Constable. 30.5.1871 to Sergeant.
11.10.1888 to Inspector. 1.12.1890 to
Superintendent.
Stationed at: Bodmin 18.2.1861. Liskeard
15.9.1868. Bodmin 8.6.1871. Liskeard
13.7.1872. Penzance 14.1.1886 Bodmin
29.10.1888. Penzance 9.12.1890.
16.10.1896 Retired Pension £106.9.2.

P.C. 85 James Dey
A former labourer from Aberdeen, aged 26
years and married. Public Service: Glasgow,
Somerset and Swansea Police for two years.
Appointed: 3.1.1861.
Stationed at: Truro 21.1.1861.
13.10.1861 Fined 2/6 for being absent from
his conference point and 2/6 for not filling in
his journal himself.
18.10.1861 Dismissed with forfeiture of all

pay due to him for being absent from his
station without leave.

P.C. 28 Thomas Simmons
A 21 year old single farmer from Pool.
Appointed: 18.1.1861.
Stationed at: Truro 18.2.1861.
6.3.1861 Dismissed for tendering his resignation within two months of his appointment.

P.C. 150 Charles Hamley
A single mason from St Mabyn, aged 20.
Appointed: 8.1.1861.
Stationed at: Launceston 18.2.1861. Truro
22.6.1862.
30.1.1863 Resigned.

P.C. 78 Thomas Congdon
From Launceston a 31 year old married
carpenter. Public service: In 'N' Division of
the Metropolitan Police for 19 months.
Appointed: 8.1.1861.
Stationed at: Liskeard 18.2.1861. Truro
28.4.1861.
28.4.1861 Fined 10/- for being the worse
for liquor and moved at his own expense.
2.9.1861 Dismissed for telling a falsehood.

P.C. 121 John Hutchings
A 26 year old married labourer from St
Buryan.
Appointed: 15.1.1861.
Stationed at: Penzance 20.4.1861. Helston
21.7.1861.
29.10.1861 Dismissed the force for being
absent from his conference point and letting
a prisoner go at large after having received
him.

P.C. 118 William Williams
A labourer from St Stephens-in-Brannel, aged
27, married.
Appointed: 21.1.1861.
Promotion: 20.5.1866 to 1st class
Constable.
Stationed at: Helston 20.5.1861. Truro
2.2.1862. Helston 3.2.1871.
22.8.1880. Resigned through ill-health
having injured his wrist in falling down in
frosty weather. Pension £23.2.4. For one
year. Pension then confirmed at the Quarter
Sessions of 1881 for life.

P.C. 3 William Pascoe
A single labourer from Bodmin aged 23.
Appointed: 18.2.1861.
Stationed at: Liskeard 13.4.1861.
2.9.1861. Dismissed the force with forfeiture
of a weeks pay for entering an orchard and
stealing apples.

P.C. 123 William Williams
A 20 year old single labourer from St
Columb. Public service: South Devon
Railway as porter and Policeman for nine
months.
Appointed: 22.2.1861.
Stationed at: Penzance 12.4.1861. Truro
21.5.1865.
25.10.1871. Dismissed for immoral and
highly improper conduct.

P.C. 152 George Harver
A labourer from Bedminster, married aged 24. Public service: Bristol Police for four years and two months.
Appointed: 5.3.1861.
Stationed at: Penzance 10.4.1861.
17.12.1861 Called upon to resign. Mr. Miller having reported that he was too intimate with a woman living near Harvers house.

P.C. 28 Anthony Furze
From South Petherwin aged 20, a single labourer.
Appointed: 4.3.1861.
Stationed at: Truro 21.6.1861.
11.2.1863 Resigned.

P.C. William Hambly
A 30 year old married blacksmith from Liskeard. Public service. Devon Constabulary for nine months.
Appointed: 15.2.1861.
11.3.1861. Dismissed having discovered that he had been previously dismissed from the Devon Constabulary in March 1859.

P.C. 23 Stephen Sluggett
A married labourer from Holsworthy aged 25.
Appointed: 14.3.1861.
Stationed at: Liskeard 21.5.1861.
14.3.1863. Dismissed with forfeiture of a weeks pay having been dismissed from other Police Force.

P.C. 149 Thomas Bray
A single shoe maker from St Agnes, aged 23.
Appointed: 25.3.1861.
Stationed at: Liskeard 21.5.1861. Helston 21.7.1861. Bodmin 9.11.1868.
26.4.1863 Fined 10/- for neglecting to serve some summons when he had them in his possession for a week. 25.5.1863. Fined 10/- for being absent from his conference point and making a false entry in his journal.
4.4.1859 Resigned, was going to America.

P.C. 128 Thomas Hedden
A single labourer from Hartland, aged 20.
Appointed: 8.4.1861.
Stationed at: Liskeard 21.5.1861.
24.4.1862 Dismissed for making false accusations against his Inspector.

P.C. 55 James Williams
A 22 year old single miner from St Leven.
Appointed: 9.4.1861.
Stationed at: Bodmin 21.5.1861.
10.6.1861 Dismissed the force with forfeiture of a weeks pay for tendering his resignation immediately after being sent from H.Q. And after being drilled at the expense of the County.

P.C. 16 William Williams
A 20 year old single carpenter from Veryan.
Appointed: 18.4.1861.
Stationed at: Liskeard 5.7.1861.
19.7.1862 Resigned.

P.C. 52 William Hocken Rundle
A labourer from Michaelstowe, aged 18 single.
Appointed: 16.4.1861.
Promotion: 9.10.1864 to 1st Class Constable.
Stationed at: Bodmin 5.7.1861
23.5.1862 Resigned.

P.C. 37 Richard Metherall
A farmers son from Holsworthy, aged 23 married.
Appointed: 22.4.1861.
Stationed at: Truro 5.7.1861.
22.6.1862 Fined 5/- for being absent from his conference point and 5/- for making a false entry in his journal.
28.4.1863 Resigned.

P.C. 113 Thomas Ackland
A 29 year old former labourer from Wellington. Married. Public service: 21 months in the Bristol Police.
Appointed: 9.5.1861.
Stationed at: Liskeard 5.7.1861. Liskeard 2.1.1865.
2.1.1887 Retired. Pension £21.1.0.

P.C. 10 George Allen
A 23 year old carpenter from Brixton, London. August 1873 married Elizabeth Williams of Feock.
Appointed: 13.5.1861.
Promotion: 29.11.1868 to 1st class Constable.
Stationed at: Penzance 5.7.1861. Helston 22.5.1866. Truro 8.9.1871 Liskeard 31.8.1887.
10.2.1878. Fined 5/- for having his accoutrements dirty and not filling in his journal for four days.
23.9.1878 Dismissed for drunkenness.

P.C. 29 Samuel Goodyear
A married miller from Kingsbridge, aged 32.
Appointed: 20.5.1861.
Stationed at: Penzance 5.7.1861.
9.8.1862. Dismissed for liberating a prisoner without taking him before a Magistrate.

P.C. Robert Buller
A 29 year old married labourer from Torrington.
Appointed: 24.6.1861.
2.8.1861. Dismissed for being in a hotel tap room the worse for liquor.

P.C. 55 Edwin Coleman
A blacksmith from St Allen, aged 24 single.
Appointed: 26.6.1861.
Stationed at: Bodmin 20.7.1861. Helston 12.10.1862.
28.12.1863 Dismissed with forfeiture of a weeks pay for fighting in a public house.

P.C. 9 Williams Bates
A single farm worker from Egloskerry, aged 20.
Appointed: 3.7.1861.
Stationed at: Truro 30.8.1861.
5.11.1861. Dismissed the force for disgraceful conduct.

P.C. 149 Thomas Nancarrow
A 22 year old single shoe maker from Grampound Road.
Appointed: 15.7.1861.
Stationed at: Launceston 30.8.1861. Penzance 2.2.1862.
6.10.1862. Dismissed with the forfeiture of a weeks pay for being the worse for liquor and speaking disrespectfully to his Sergeant.

P.C. 104 Richard Snell
A Groom from St Kew, aged 18 single.
Appointed: 29.7.1861.
Stationed at: Truro 28.10.1861. Helston 1.2.1863.
25.8.1862 Fined 5/- for leaving his journal exposed for anyone to read when he was out on duty.
14.3.1863 Resigned.

P.C. 129 Edward Jane
From St Austell, a single miner aged 21.
Appointed: 29.7.1861.
Stationed at: Liskeard 28.10.1861.
14.3.1864 Resigned.

P.C. 18 Daniel Henry Lord
A 20 year old single post boy from St Columb.
Appointed: 6.8.1861.
Stationed at: Bodmin 28.10.1861.
6.5.1863 Dismissed for telling the Chief Constable a falsehood.

P.C. 98 James Thomas
A married miner from Germoe aged 25.
Appointed: 27.8.1861.
Stationed at: Helston 25.10.1861.
5.1.1862 Fined 6/- for neglecting to report a robbery to his superior officer.
2.3.1862 Resigned.

P.C. 106 Jebez Darby
A single labourer from North Hill, aged 20.
Appointed: 29.8.1861.
Stationed at: Launceston 28.10.1861. Helston 16.8.1863. 25.8.1862 Fined 5/- for being absent from his conference point. 1.3.1863. Fined 10/- for being absent from his conference point.
22.5.1864 Resigned.

P.C. 3 Thomas Blackwell
From Ludgvan, Penzance, a 23 year old widower.
Appointed: 30.8.1861.
Stationed at: Bodmin 31.10.1861.
2.3.1862 Fined 10/- for falsely stating he had attended his conference point and making an entry to the same effect in his journal.
26.3.1862. Called upon to resign for inefficiency.

P.C. 133 George Arthur
A 22 year old single labourer from St Stephens by St Austell.
Appointed: 6.9.1861.
Stationed at: Penzance 23.11.1861.
6.8.1865 Resigned.

P.C. 76 John White
A single miner from Lelant aged 20 years.
Appointed: 21 9.1861.
Stationed at: Bodmin 23.11.1861.
17.12.1861 Dismissed for gross neglect of duty.

P.C. 78 Samuel Truscott
A married tailor from St Austell aged 22.
Appointed: 23.9.1861.
Promotion: 8.7.1872 to 2nd class Constable.
26.10.1873 to 1st Class Constable.
29.11.1880 reduced to 2nd class Constable.
28.12.1890 promoted to 1st Class Constable.
Stationed at: Launceston 2.12.1861.
Bodmin 23.4.1870. Truro 2.12.1880.
Liskeard 21.11.1884.
6.11.1864 Fined 2/6 for booking himself in
P.C. Tallerns journal. 29.11.1880 Reduced to
2nd class Constable for gross neglect of duty
in reference to a felony.
21.10.1894 Retired Pension £41.9.1.

P.C. 50 Walter Carlyon
A single seaman from Tywardreath aged 22.
Appointed: 30.9.1861.
Stationed at: Penzance 23.11.1861.
25.8.1862 Dismissed for using disgusting
language to a female.

P.C. 69 Edward Endacott
A married labourer from Bovey Tracey aged
29. Public service: Somerset Constabulary
and the South West Railway for 4 years and
6 months.
Appointed: 5.10.1861.
Promotion: 17.8.1862 to 1st class Constable.
Stationed at: Liskeard 4.11.1861. Bodmin
27.3.1863.
22.4.1864 Dismissed for appropriating to his
own use two pence given to him to pay for
the subsistence of a prisoner whilst marching
him to gaol.

P.C. 120 Samuel Pomeroy
A blacksmith from North Hill, aged 20.
Appointed: 3.10.1861.
Stationed at: Truro 23.11.1861. Penzance
27.4.1862.
27.4.1862 Fined 10/- for being drunk on
duty.
8.3.1863 Resigned.

P.C. 85 James Hicks
From Lanlivery a farmers son aged 23 single.
Appointed: 28.10.1861.
Stationed at: Truro 20.12.1861.
11.6.1862 Dismissed for neglect of duty.

P.C. 9 William Heard
A married labourer from South Petherwin
aged 23.
Appointed: 29.10.1861.
9.1.1862 Dismissed for being drunk on
duty.

P.C. 68 William Tabb
A groom from St Mewan, St Austell, aged 22
single.
Appointed: 4.11.1861.
Stationed at: Launceston 20.12.1861.
23.9.1864 Resigned.

P.C. 121 John Badcock
A 22 year old single labourer from St Veep.
Appointed: 4.11.1861.
Stationed at: Bodmin 17.12.1861.
18.1.1863 Dismissed with forfeiture of a
weeks pay for being indoors when he should
have been out on duty.

P.C. 7 William Bartlett
A single labourer from Morvah, Penzance
aged 25 single.
Appointed: 8.11.1861.
Stationed at: Bodmin 20.12.1861.
1.5.1862 Resigned.

P.C. 198 John Puckey
A 20 year old single labourer from St Ewe.
Appointed: 4,11,1861.
Promotion: 8.7.1872 to 2nd class
Constable. 13.10.1873 to 1st class
Constable. 7.11.1886 reduced to 2nd class
Constable for gross neglect of duty.
28.12.1890 to 1st Class Constable.
Stationed at: Truro 17.12.1861. Bodmin
14.1.1886.
14.8.1864 Fined 5/- for being absent from
his conference point.
15.2.1892 Retired Pension £41.9.1.

P.C. 46 Robert Rowlands
A former miller from Aberavon, single aged
29. Public service In the Borough of
Kidwelly Police.
Appointed: 15.11.1861.
Stationed at: Penzance 17,12.1861.
24.12.1862. Dismissed having previously
been dismissed from the Devonport Police.

P.C. 110 William May
A gardener from Ladock, aged 24 single.
Appointed: 19.11.1861.
Stationed at: Liskeard 20.12.1861. Bodmin
11.9.1864.
18.12.1864 Called upon to resign for having
his station dirty and for allowing his wife to
call all officers rogues.

P.C. 9 Nicholas Chapman
A single miner from Duloe aged 26.
Appointed: 21.12.1861.
Stationed at: Helston 7.2.1862. Penzance
4.12.1864. Launceston 13.8.1865.
10.10.1865 Resigned.

P.C. 2 William Davies
A 24 year old single labourer from Gorran.
Appointed: 2.1.1862.
Stationed at: Truro 7.2.1862. Liskeard
4.1.1863 .Fined 10/- and removed at his
own expense for being drunk.
18.6.1863 Dismissed for having his uniform
in a dirty state, and being found in a public
house in another officer's beat.

P.C. 76 Richard Faull
A farmers son from Crowan single aged 21.
Appointed: 8.1.1862.
Stationed at: Helston 21.3.1862. Liskeard
9.11.1862.
9.11.1862 Fined 5/- for being absent from
his conference point.
13.11.1862 Dismissed for having his

uniform in a disgraceful state when inspected
by his Superintendent.

P.C. 4 Thomas Harris Hunkin
A 28 year old single mason from St Hilary.
Appointed: 13.1.1862.
Stationed at: Helston 20.3.1862
23.8.1862 Resigned.

P.C. 46 William H. Udy
A 24 year old married miner from Luxulyan.
Appointed: 12.2.1862.
Stationed at: Truro 30.4.1862.
16.6.1862. Dismissed with forfeiture of a
weeks pay for neglect of duty.

P.C. 39 Samuel Martin
A shoe maker from Holsworthy, single aged
20.
Appointed: 26.2.1862.
Stationed at: Liskeard 30.4.1862. Bodmin
12.10.1862 Penzance 20.4.1864.
20.7.1862 Fined 5/- for disobedience to
orders and 10/- for being asleep whilst out
on duty.
16.9.1865 Dismissed for being in a public
house when he should have been on duty. And
also being absent from two conference points.

P.C. 98 William Henry Davey
From Tregoney a married labourer aged 22.
Appointed: 3.3.1862.
15.3.1862 Dismissed the force having
discovered that he had previously been
dismissed from the Cornwall Railway.

P.C. 98 Thomas Kneebone
A miner from Creed, married aged 26.
Appointed: 3.3.1862.
Stationed at: Liskeard 30.3.1862.
13.8.1862 Resigned.

P.C. 153 Robert Burnard
A carpenter from Altarnun, single aged 25.
Appointed: 26.3.1862.
Stationed at: Penzance 3.6.1862. Truro
26.4.1863.
25.5.1863 Resigned.

P.C. 81 Julias Thomas Bone
A farmers son from Jacobstow, single aged
19.
Appointed: 31.3.1862.
Stationed at: Bodmin 3.6.1862.
11.8.1863 Resigned.

P.C. 62 Robert Strike
A married miner from Callington, aged 24.
Appointed: 21.4.1862.
Stationed at: Launceston 3.6.1862.
Liskeard 1.3.1863
4.1.1866 Resigned.
Reappointed: 26.10.1866
16.11.1866 Resigned.

P.C. 128 Richard Pappin
A 24 year old carpenter from St Austell.
Married his third wife Mary A. Bolt of
Calstock on the 30.6.1875.
Appointed: 21.4.1862
Promotion: 20.5.1866 to 1st class
Constable.

Stationed at: Launceston 10.6.1862.
Liskeard 9.11.1883.
10.8.1891 Retired Pension £41.9.1.

P.C. 7 **Thomas Coleman Prout**
A 21 year old farmers son from Blisland,
single.
Appointed: 21.4.1862.
Stationed at: Penzance 3.6.1862
18.9.1864 Resigned.

P.C. 27 **George Williams**
From Tywardreath, a single miner aged 20.
Appointed: 16.4.1862.
Stationed at: Liskeard 3.6.1862 Launceston
19.7.1863. Bodmin 24.4.1864. Liskeard
21.5.1865.
19.7.1863 Fined 5/- for being absent from
parade and leaving H.Q. Without leave at
the Quarter Sessions. 24.4.1864. Fined 5/-
for neglecting to report to his superior officer
an occurrence which took place eight days
previously.
8.11.1865 Resigned.

P.C. 24 **Henry Mitchell**
A single miner from Tywardreath, aged 20.
Appointed: 8.5.1862.
Promotion: 3.12.1865 to 1st class Constable.
Stationed at: Bodmin 7.7.1862.
30.4.1887 Resigned.

P.C. 3 **Joseph Jay**
A 24 year old married miner from St
Pinnock.
Appointed: 8.5.1862.
Stationed at: Liskeard 7.7.1862.
8.11.1863 Fined 2/6 for being in his house
when he should have been on duty and 2/6
for making a false entry in his journal.
13.10.1864, Dismissed for being absent
from his conference point and making a false
entry in his journal.

P.C. 21 **John Rawling**
A labourer from St Columb Major aged 19
single.
Appointed: 11.6.1862.
Promotion: 3.12.1865 to 1st class Constable.
Stationed at: Penzance 11.8.1862.
Launceston 24.4.1864.
6.12.1866 Called upon to resign having had
an order in bastardy of 1/6 per week made
on him by the Justices in the Launceston
Division.

P.C. 46 **Thomas Pedlar**
A 29 year old married miner from St Blazey.
Appointed: 16.6.1862.
Stationed at: Truro 11.8.1862.
27.10.1862 Dismissed for having grossly
exceeded his duty and having received
money for his private use.

P.C. 122 **William Gartrell**
A 28 year old single miner from St Hilary.
Appointed: 23.6.1862.
Stationed at: Helston 11.8.1862.
6.9.1863 Resigned.

P.C. 85 **Thomas Finnemore**
A single miner from Tywardreath aged 20.

Appointed: 24.6.1862.
Stationed at: Helston 11.8.1862. Liskeard
12.10.1862. Penzance 7.12.1862.
7.12.1862 Fined 5/- for being absent from
his conference point
15.8.1863 Dismissed for allowing boys to
stone him out of Redruth and for buying fish
and selling them in the streets of Redruth.

P.C. 79 **Thomas Wenmouth**
A 26 year old single labourer from Quethioc.
Appointed: 30.6.1862.
Promotion: 20.5.1866 to 1st class Constable.
Stationed at: Penzance 11.8.1862. Helston
29.2.1864. Penzance 22.4.1870. Truro
7.8.1879.
Retired 3.8.1891. Pension £41.9.1.

P.C. 83 **Frederick Pascoe**
A 20 year old single stone mason from
Wendron.
Appointed: 2.7.1862.
Stationed at: Liskeard 11.8.1862.
21.9.1862. Dismissed for insubordination.

P.C. 135 **John Burn Sobye**
A single labourer from Bodmin aged 21.
Appointed: 14.7.1862.
Stationed at: Helston 22.9.1862. Truro
2.2.1863.
29.2.1864 Fined 10/- for being absent from
his conference point and making a false entry
in his journal.
22.9.1864 Resigned.

P.C. 5 **John Christopher**
A 27 year old single labourer from Paul,
Penzance.
Appointed: 16.7.1862.
Stationed at: Penzance 22.9.1862.
25.5.1863 Dismissed with forfeiture of a
weeks pay for being the worse for liquor and
behaving in a disgraceful manner in a
Railway carriage.

P.C. 16 **John James Pearce**
A single labourer from St Columb aged 19.
Appointed: 22.7.1862.
Stationed at: Bodmin 22.9.1862.
Launceston 21.5.1865.
1.1.1865 Fined 2/6 for being absent from his
conference point and 5/- for making a false
entry n his journal.
15.7.1865 Resigned.

P.C. 4 **Martin Strongman Burton**
A 26 year old single labourer from St Breoc.
Appointed: 22.7.1862.
Promotion:
6.10.1867 to 1st class Constable.
Stationed at: Liskeard 22.9.1862. Penzance
15.9.1868.
21.10.1873 Called upon to resign .

P.C. 32 **James Powell**
A 24 year old married miner from St Austell.
Appointed: 28.7.1862.
Stationed at: Truro 22.9.1862. Penzance
4.1.1863.
10.1.1863 Dismissed with forfeiture of all
pay due to him, for disobeying orders and
gross irregularity of duty.

P.C. 29 **Peter Spry**
A farmer's son from Ashwater, Launceston,
aged 30 married.
Appointed: 30.7.1862.
Promotion: 8.7.1872 to 2nd class Constable.
Stationed at: Bodmin 30.9.1862. Truro.
22.4.1870.
8.10.1865 Fined 5/- for being absent from
his conference point. 20.5.1866 Fined 5/-
for not filling in his journal daily. 20.3.1867
Fined 5/- for being absent from his conference point.
28.10.1879 Called upon to resign for
alleged immorality.

P.C. 6 **William Cole**
A miner from St Austell, single aged 21.
Appointed: 4.8.1862.
Stationed at: Liskeard 22.9.1862.
4.11.1863 Resigned.

P.C. 58 **Sampson Tamblyn**
A miner from St Columb single aged 27.
Appointed: 11.8.1862.
Stationed at: Truro 24.9.1862.
29.11.1862 Resigned.

P.C. 98 **Daniel Dunn**
A 20 year old miner from St Austell, single.
Appointed: 14.8.1862.
Stationed at: Truro 21.10.1862.
6.5.1864 Resigned.

P.C. 50 **James Richards**
A 25 year old labourer from St Stephens, St
Austell, married with one child. Public
service: Royal Marines for 139 days.
Appointed: 25.8.1862.
Stationed at: Liskeard 22.7.1862. Bodmin
31.1.1864.
9.3.1865 Dismissed with the forfeiture of a
weeks pay for drinking and dancing in a
public house.

P.C. 132 **John Stocker**
A 29 year old miner from St Austell, married
with four children.
Appointed: 13.8.1862.
Stationed at: Truro 28.10.1862.
9.9 1863. Resigned.

P.C. 83 **William Simpson**
A labourer from Alton, Hampshire, single aged
30. Public service: Hampshire Constabulary
for four years and eleven months.
Appointed: 23.9.1862.
Stationed at: Helston 27.10.1862. Truro
4.1.1863.
22.10.1863 Resigned.

P.C. 146 **Isaac Hendy**
A 23 year old married carpenter from
Ashburton.
Appointed: 27.9.1862.
Stationed at: Liskeard 2.12.1862.
22.12.1862 Dismissed having been previ-
ously dismissed from the Devonport Police.

P.C. 147 **Richard Williams**
A 20 year old single labourer from St
Columb. Public service: Metropolitan Police
for one year nine months.

Appointed: 6.10.1862.
Stationed at: Liskeard 1.12.1862. Helston 8.11.1863.
21.11.1867 Died.

P.C. 105 Robert Pascoe
A 20 year old labourer from Tregony, Truro. Single.
Appointed: 5.12.1862.
Stationed at: Penzance 12 1 1863.
8.3.1863 Resigned.

P.C. 137 John Hill Buddle
A miner from Redruth, aged 24 married with two children.
Appointed: 21.11.1862.
Stationed at: Truro 17.1.1862.
29.6.1869 Resigned, said he was going to America - doubtful as he was considerably in debt

P.C. 74 William Lawrey
A 21 year old sailor from St Hilary, Marazion, single. Public service: Merchant service for seven years.
Appointed: 9.12.1862.
Stationed at: Liskeard 27.1.1863.
4.9.1863 Resigned.

P.C. 146 James Berryman
A former miner from Ludgvan, Penzance, single aged 21.
Public service: Penzance Borough Police for two years.
Appointed: 17.12.1862.
Promotion: 8.7.1872 to 2nd class Constable. 26.10.1873 to 1st class Constable.
Stationed at: Truro 28.1.1863.
17.3.1875 Died. £40.0.0. Granted from the superannuation fund to his widow on the 6.4.1875.

P.C. 109 Nicholas Trevail
A 24 year old farmers son from Luxulyn, Bodmin, single.
Appointed: 22.12.1862.
Stationed at: Helston 28.1.1863.
31.7.1864 Resigned.

P.C. 46 Samuel Bawden
A 23 year old married sail maker from Phillack.
Appointed: 3.1.1863.
Stationed at: Truro 13.4.1863. Penzance 6.12.1863. Helston 28.2.1864.
17.11.1870 Dismissed for being drunk on duty.

P.C. 58 Aaron Dingle
A 19 year old gardener and miner from St Austell, single.
Appointed: 19.1.1863.
Promotion: 25.9.1870 to 1st class Constable. 15.1.1883 to Sergeant.
Stationed at: Penzance 11.3.1863. Helston 21.12.1876. Penzance 1.2.1883.
Retired 30.9.1895   Pension £51.11.4.

P.C. 76 David Rowe
A 22 year old married miner from St Blazey.
Appointed: 19.1.1863.
Stationed at: Liskeard 23.3.1863.

21.6.1863 Fined 10/- for being absent from his conference point.
19.7.1863 Dismissed for being absent from his conference point and being home when he should have been out on duty.

P.C. 82 John Johns
A 20 year old single miner from St Hilary, Penzance. Public service: Volunteers Artillery Marazion for 18 months.
Appointed: 19.1.1863.
Stationed at: Truro 11.3.1863. Bodmin 28.7.1865.
25.2.1865 Moved from Devoran to Mevagissey at his own expense for accepting a glass of ale from a landlord without paying for it.
28.5.1865 Called upon to resign for neglect of duty.

P.C. 150 William Chapman
A miner from Linkinhorne single aged 25.
Appointed: 2.2.1863.
Stationed at: Penzance 8.4.1863. Helston 28.2.1864
23.8.1866 Dismissed with the forfeiture of a weeks pay for drunkenness and gross impropriety of conduct.

P.C. 28 David Edwards
A labourer from Stonehouse, Plymouth. Single aged 24.
Appointed: 11.2.1863.
Stationed at: Truro 13.4.1863.
21 10.1864 Resigned.

P.C. 120 John May
A 23 year old married carpenter from Launceston.
Appointed: 9.3.1863.
Stationed at: Liskeard 8.5.1863
23.1.1864 Resigned through ill-health.

P.C. 105 Henry Thomas
A 21 year old labourer from Manaccon, married Emily Tregillis of Fowey on 10.3.1867.
Appointed: 17.3.1863.
Promotion: 8.7.1872 to 2nd class Constable. 1.5.1883 to 1st class Constable.
Stationed at: Penzance 9.5.1863. Launceston 22.4.1866. Bodmin 6.6.1871. Retired 11.1.1892. Pension £41.9.1.

P.C. 11 Samuel Marshall
A blacksmith from St Day, Redruth, single aged 22.
Appointed: 19.3.1863
11.10.1863 Resigned.

P.C. 127 William Henry Harry
A labourer from Camelford, aged 20. Married Elizabeth A. Westcot. Of Ruan Minor 11.12.1873.
Appointed: 19.3.1863.
Promotion: 18.2.1871 to 1st class Constable. 3.9.1893 to merit class Constable 1.8.1901 to special class Constable.
Stationed at: Bodmin 9.5.1863. Penzance 17.6.1866. Helston 28.11.1869. Truro 29.10.1881
Retired 31.10.1901 Pension £50.5.4.

P.C. 121 Michael Brown
A 23 year old miner from Newlyn East, Truro, single.
Appointed: 24.3.1863.
Stationed at: Bodmin 10.7.1863.
13.5.1864 Resigned.

P.C. 23 Stephen Thomas James
A 21 year old miner from Marazion, married with one child.
Appointed: 24.3.1863.
Stationed at: Helston 9.5.1863. Truro 22.5.1864.
29.6.1864 Resigned.

P.C. 104 Edwin Jewell
A 21 year labourer from St Teath, Camelford, single.
Appointed: 26.3.1863.
Stationed at: Penzance 9.5.1863 Bodmin 11.10.1863.
12.11.1863 Resigned.

P.C. 34 William Bunney
A 25 year old shoe maker from Penryn, married with one child. Public service: Coastguard volunteers for five years.
Appointed: 6.4.1863.
Stationed at: Liskeard 9.5.1863.
12.8.1863 Resigned.

P.C. 37 William Henry Johns
From Stithians, a married miner aged 21.
Appointed: 6.4.1863.
Stationed at: Penzance 3.6.1863. Truro 19.7.1863.
12.8.1863. Dismissed with the forfeiture of a weeks pay for riding in a millers cart when he should have been out on duty.

P.C. 90 John Bethy
A 23 year old single miner from Ludgvan, Marazion.
Appointed: 1.6.1863.
Stationed at: Truro 16.11.1863.
1.3.1864 Resigned.

P.C. 153 James Wyatt Ede
A labourer from Lostwithiel, single aged 20. Public Service: Cornwall Railway company for 3 months.
Appointed: 4.6.1863.
Promotion: 20.8.1863 to 2nd class Constable. 16.7.1873 to 1st class Constable.
16.6.1867 Fined 10/- for neglect of duty Resigned.

P.C. 5 Henry Kingdom
A 27 year old labourer from Blisland, Bodmin, married with two children.
Appointed: 8.6.1863.
Stationed at: Launceston 20.8.1863 Bodmin 28.11.1881.
Retired 2.11.1891 Pension £41.9.1.

P.C. 2 John Batten
From Launceston, a 20 year old labourer, single.
Appointed: 22.6.1863.
Stationed at: Penzance 20.8.1863. Helston 13.8.1865. Bodmin 8.10.1865.

28.7.1867 Resigned, stated he was going abroad.

P.C. 93 David Briggs
A 24 year old silk weaver from Manchester, married, no children. Public Service: Royal Artillery in Malta, 5 years and 194 days.
Appointed: 3.8.1863.
Stationed at: Liskeard 20.8.1863.
11.10.1863 Resigned.

P.C. 116 William Llewellyn Vosper
A labourer from St Dominic, Callington, aged 20 single.
Appointed: 21.8.1863.
Stationed at: Liskeard 6.10.1863. Penzance 17.7.1864.
17.7.1864 Ordered to pay for a new truncheon and a new whistle and to move at his own expense to Camborne.
13.12.1864 Resigned.

P.C. 148 Joseph Holmes
A 24 year old gardener from Torquay, married with two children.
Appointed: 24.8.1863.
Stationed at: Liskeard 15.10.1863.
24.2.1864 Fined 10/- for being absent from his conference point and making a false entry in his journal. 16.7.1865. Fined 5/- for being absent from his conference point.
15.2.1867 Dismissed with forfeiture of a weeks pay for being drunk on duty and losing stolen property.

P.C. 81 William Bate
A labourer from St Germans, single aged 22.
Appointed: 27.8.1863.
Stationed at: Bodmin 16.10.1863.
24.3.1867 Fined £1.0.0 . For gross neglect of duty, a man named Arthur used to come down from Devonport by the last train to steal fowls and go up by the first train next morning. Bate was put to watch this man but neglected to do so.
10.7.1871 Resigned.

P.C. 34 William T. Eddyvean
A 20 year old miner from Roche, single.
Appointed: 27.8.1863.
Stationed at: Helston 6.10/.1863.
28.12.1863 Dismissed with a forfeiture of a weeks pay for fighting in a public house.

P.C. 92 James Rowse
A tailor from Stoke Climsland, Callington, aged 21. Public Service. Plymouth Police for 12 months.
Appointed: 24.9.1863.
Stationed at: Bodmin 5.11.1863. Penzance 13.8.1865. Bodmin 25.3.1866.
22.7.1871 Resigned.

P.C. 37 Richard Stacey
A labourer from Launceston, aged 21 single.
Appointed: 19.10.1863.
Stationed at: Penzance 9.12.1863.
19.3.1864 Resigned.

P.C. 83 Richard Lobb
A 22 year old single labourer from Wadebridge.

Appointed: 26.10.1863.
Promotion: 14.5.1871 to 1st class Constable.
Stationed at: Liskeard 9.12.1863 Bodmin 20.10.1866. Penzance 12.11.1866.
29.9.1872 Resigned.

P.C. John Heale
A 21 year old seaman from Portsmouth single. Public Service. Plymouth Police for 4 days.
Appointed: 6.11.1863.
7.12.1863. Dismissed with the forfeiture of a weeks pay for being late on parade

P.C. 73 Edward Hatch
A 21 year old gardener, previously employed in Carhayes Castle, single. From Veryan, Truro. Public Service: Cornwall Railway for five months.
Appointed: 16.11.1863.
Stationed at: Helston 1.12.1863
5.8.1864 Resigned.

P.C. 15 William Mundy
A labourer from Mullion, single aged 20.
Appointed: 19.11.1863.
Stationed at: Truro 1.1.1864.
28.7.1864 Dismissed for being drunk.

P.C. 93 William Harris
A gardener from Veryan, Truro, aged 19 single.
Appointed: 26.11.1863.
17.1.1864. Dismissed with the forfeiture of a weeks pay for neglect of duty.

P.C. 104 Samuel Harris
A 20 year old miner from Perranarworthal, single.
Appointed: 26.11.1863.
Stationed at: Truro 1.1.1864.
26.11.1867 Fined 10/- for being absent from his conference point and making a false entry in his journal.
5.5.1868 Resigned, did not state the reason why.

P.C. 122 William Baker
A seaman from Plymouth, single aged 26.
Appointed: 26.11.1863.
Stationed at: Bodmin 1.1.1864. Helston 8.10.1865. Penzance 25.2.1866.
8.10.1865 Fined 10/- for being absent from his conference point and making two false entries in his journal. 23.2.1868 Fined 10/- for not filling in his journal daily according to orders and 1/- for having his handcuffs in a filthy state.
14.3.1870. Died.

P.C. 11 Lewis Jewell
A 24 year old labourer from Stratton, married with one child.
Appointed: 7.12.1863.
Stationed at: Penzance 11.7.1864.
18.7.1867 Resigned.

P.C. 74 John Carlyon
A 22 year old tailor from Tywardreath, single.
Appointed: 14,12.1863.
Stationed at: Liskeard 11.2.1864.
11.9.1864. Resigned.

P.C. 55 Edward Duff
A blacksmith from Truro, aged 23 single.
Appointed: 5.1.1864.
Stationed at: Penzance 11.2.1864.
6.7.1864 Resigned.

P.C. 6 John Hacker
A 24 year old married labourer from Kilkhampton. His wife died and he remarried Miss M.J.Stacey of Kilkhampton, 21.12.1883.
Appointed: 11.1.1864.
Promotion: 16.6.1867 to 1st class Constable. 26.2.1877 to Sergeant. 20.10.1886 to Inspector.
Stationed at: Launceston 24.3.1864. Bodmin 26.2.1877. Liskeard Oct. 1889.
28.10.1895 Retired. Pension £70.19.5.

P.C. 124 John Stapleton
A labourer from Bideford, single aged 23.
Appointed: 12.1.1864.
Stationed at: Liskeard 11.7.1864.
17.7.1864 Fined 5/- for being absent from his conference point.
12.2.1866 Dismissed for neglect of duty.

P.C. 140 William John Barker
A blacksmith from Phillack, Hayle. Single aged 21.
Appointed: 21.1.1864.
Stationed at: Helston 8.4.1864.
2.12.1866 Fined 10/- for neglecting to fill in his journal daily.
15.3.1868 Resigned.

P.C. 93 Joseph Thomas Semmins Ede Searle
A 21 year old single shoe maker from Camborne.
Appointed: 22.1.1864.
Stationed at: Truro 2.4.1864.
28.7.1864 Dismissed with forfeiture of a weeks pay for being drunk.

P.C. Joseph Chapman
A 20 year old labourer from St Kew, Wadebridge, single.
Appointed: 25.1.1864.
Promotion: 6.6.1867 to 1st class Constable. 8.4.

P.C. 1 William Thomas
A 19 year old labourer from St Anthony Helston, single.
Appointed: 25.1.1864.
Stationed at: 8.4.1864.
20.4.1864 Died.

P.C. 154 Thomas Blatchford
Appointed: 25.1.1864.
A labourer from Luxulyan, single, aged 25.
Promotion: 8.7.1872 to 2nd class Constable
Stationed at: Helston 8.4.1864.
26.10.1891 Retired Pension £39.8.8.

P.C. 132 John Lukes
A 22 year old labourer from Luxulyan, Single.
Appointed: 2.2.1864.
Promotion: 8.7.1872 to 2nd class Constable 9.2.1879 to 1st class Constable. 2.11.1890 to Sergeant. 30.11.1891 Reduced to 1st class Constable for gross inefficiency of duty.

Stationed at: Liskeard 8.4.1864. Bodmin 23.10.1890. Truro 4.12.1891.
24.7.1893 Retired Pension £41.9.1.

P.C. 120 Samuel Warren
A 21 year old labourer from Bridgewater, Somerset, married for the second time to Susan Northcott of Torquay on 16.12.1885. Public Service: South Devon Railway Company for 4 years and 6 months.
Appointed: 12.2.1864.
Promotion: 7.7.1872 to 1st class Constable. 3.4.1881 to Sergeant.
1.12.1890 to Inspector.
Stationed at: Bodmin 2.5.1864. Penzance 23.10.1882. Bodmin 19.12.1890.
7.3.1891 Died. His widow received a gratuity of £89.14.7. On 6.4.1891.

P.C. 37 John Brown
A farmer from Holsworthy aged 27, married with three children. Public Service: The North Devon Yeoman Calvary for 6 years.
Appointed: 19.3.1864.
Promotion: 16.5.1871 to 1st Class Constable.
Stationed at: Truro 12.5.1864. Helston 22.5.1864.
28.7.1872 Resigned.

P.C. 129 James Trurian
A 28 year old miner from St Agnes. Married with one child.
Appointed: 24.3.1864.
Promotion: 1.10.1871 to 1st class Constable. 24.6.1883 reduced to 2nd class Constable. For working at watch and clock cleaning and repairing in the village in which he was stationed.
Stationed at: Bodmin 12.5.1864. Liskeard 6.10.1867. Bodmin 19.12.1872. Launceston 5.6.1885.
Retired 22.8.1891 Pension £39.8.8.

P.C. 70 Thomas Cruse
A labourer from Kilkhampton, aged 22 single. Public Service with the Royal Cornwall Rangers Militia fir two years.
Appointed: 25.4.1864.
Promotion: 8.7.1872 to 2nd class Constable. 11.1.1886 to 1st class Constable. 27.11.1892 to merit class Constable.
Stationed at: Truro 2.7.1864.
25.7.1880 Fined 10/- for being absent from his conference point and making false entries in his journal.
Retired 17.9.1893. Pension £43.9.6.

P.C. 98 George Soloman
A labourer from St Columb, single aged 21.
Appointed: 25.4.1864.
Promotion: 7.7.1872 to 1st class Constable.
Stationed at: Liskeard 2.7.1864.
31.3.1878 Resigned.

P.C. John Renals
A 20 year old labourer from Bodmin, single.
Appointed: 5.5.1864.
30.5.1864 Dismissed for inattention to his duties and swearing in the Guardroom

P.C. 69 Robert Nicolls
A 25 year old miller from South Petherwin, married with one child.
Appointed: 9.5.1864.
Promotion: 8.7.1872 to 2nd class Constable.
16.7.1873 to 1st class Constable.
8.10.1888. To Sergeant.
Stationed at: Liskeard District 2.7.1864. 6.5.1895 Retired Pension £51.11.4.
22.2.1902 Died at 11pm at Penpoint, Altarnun.

P.C. William Taylor
Aged 22 years a single man from Telland, Looe. Fisherman. He did public service in the Duchy of Cornwall Volunteers for eighteen months.
Appointed: 4.3.1864.
Removal: 16.6.1864. Dismissed forfeiting one weeks pay for gross neglect of duty.

P.C. 1 Henry Taylor
Aged 23yrs., a married man from Lelant. A labourer.
Appointed: 30.5.1864.
Removal: 20.1.1865. Dismissed for contracting debts.

P.C. 33 Pascoe Kestle Deacon
Aged 18 yr., a single man from Tintagel. A labourer.
Appointed: 30.5.1864.
Promotion: 8.7.1872 2nd., Class Constable. 16.11.1879. Promoted to 1st, Class Constable
Stationed at: Helston 5.11.1864. Truro 6.10.1867. Bodmin 28.9.1871.
Retired 3.7.1888. Pension £33.19.0.

P.C. 121 Richard White
Aged 22 yr., a labourer from St Keverne, married.
Appointed: 7.6.1864.
Stationed at: Truro 5.11.1860.
Removal: 10.2.1867. Dismissed for being absent from his conference point and being impertinent to his superior officers.

P.C. 55 John Thomas
Aged 26 yr., a labourer from St Germans, married.
Appointed: 4.7.1864.
Stationed at: Launceston 24.11.1864
On the 1.3.1878. Reduced to 3rd., class Constable for drinking with a drunken man in a public house.
Removal: 6.4.1879. Called upon to resign owing to ill-health and received a gratuity of £40.0.0.

P.C. 23 William Henry Blatchford
A 22 year old labourer from Luxulyan, single.
Appointed: 1.7.1864.
Promotion: 2nd., class Constable on 8.7.1872. 1st class Constable on 8.11.1877.
Removal: 11.7.1892. Pension £41.9.1.

P.C. 84 Thomas Cory
A 20year old labourer from Launceston, single.
Appointed: 13.7.1864.

Stationed at: Bodmin 24.8.1864. Penzance 20,5.1866.
Removal: 8.6.1866. Dismissed for associating with a prostitute.

P.C. 90 Thomas Rice
A 23 year old labourer from Launceston, single.
Appointed: 24.6.1864.
Promotion: 2nd., class Constable 8.7.1872.
Stationed at:
Bodmin 24.8.1864.
Penzance 2.10.1872
Truro 5.12.1884.
Removal: 3.8.1897.
Pension. £39.8.8.

P.C. 73 John Skewes
A 25 year old shoemaker from Cury, Helston. Married with two children.
Appointed: 6.8.1864.
Stationed at:
Penzance 30.9.1864.
Removal: 27.10.1865 Resigned.

P.C. Thomas Fice
A 22 year old labourer from Tintagel, single.
Appointed: 8.8.1864.
Removal: 27.9.1864. Called upon to resign, it having come to the knowledge of the Chief Constable that Fice was a drunkard.

P.C. 109 Francis Luke
A 20 year old Blacksmith from Lanivet, single.
Appointed: 22.8.1864.
Stationed at: Bodmin 30.9.1864.
Removal: 14.11.1864. Resigned.

P.C. 111 Henry Richards
A 19 year old single man from Lanlivery who was a labourer.
Appointed: 5.9.1864.
Stationed at: Truro 1.11.1864. Liskeard 25.3.1866. Bodmin 29.11.1868. Truro 31.5.1869.
Removal: 2.1.1872. Resigned.

P.C. 152 William Cock
A 26 year old labourer from Mevagissey who was married with two children.
Appointed: 6.9.1864.
Stationed at: Truro 1.11.1864. Penzance 5.11.1865.
Removal: 10.6.1866. Called upon to resign owing to his wife being fond of drink and frequenting low beer houses.

P.C. 66 William Worth
A 26 year old from Hatherleigh in Devon, who was a labourer and married with one child.
Appointed: 12.9.1864
Stationed at: Liskeard 1.11.1864
Removal: 17.8.1867. Resigned.

P.C. 93 Joseph White
A 19 year old single man from St Keverne, labourer.
Appointed: 14.9.1864.
Promotion: 2nd Class Constable 8.7.1872.

1st Class Constable 8.11.1877.
Stationed at: Launceston 10.11.1864.
Removal: 4.7.1896. Pension £41.9.1.

P.C. 15 James Peter
A 19year old single man from St Keverne, labourer.
Appointed: 14.9.1864.
Stationed at: Launceston 1.11.1864
Removal: 9.3.1865. Asked to resign due to inefficiency.

P.C. John Hooper
A 20 year old from Linkinhorne, single miner.
Appointed: 19.9.1864.
Removal: 23.10.1864. Resigned.

P.C. 17 William Voisey
A 20year old single man from Tavistock, a shoemaker.
Appointed: 26.9.1864.
Stationed at: Penzance 1.11.1864.
Removal: 30.4.1869. Asked to resign having been reported for having connections with a servant girl in the vestry.

P.C. 88 William Henry Beare
A 20 year old labourer from Holsworthy, single.
Appointed: 3.10.1864.
Promotion: 18.7.1872 To 1st class Constable. 4.12.1876. to Sergeant 15.1. 1883. To Inspector. 6.1.1891. To Superintendent. 1.12.1902. To Deputy Chief Constable.
Stationed at: Bodmin 9.12.1864. Helston 16.6.1871. Penzance 15.12.1876. Truro 1.7.1883. Bodmin 14.1.1886. Bodmin 13.1.1891. Helston 11.10.1892. Falmouth 3.8.1897. Bodmin 27.11.1902.
Removal: 3.9.1910
Pension £140.0.0.
Kings Police Medal. The Chief Constable has much pleasure that among the list of recipients of the Kings Birthday Honours 1909 His Majesty was pleased to award the Kings Police Medal to William Henry Beare, Deputy Chief Constable. The Chief Constable was glad to take the opportunity on behalf of the Force in congratulating Deputy Chief Constable Beare on the well deserved award bestowed on him which is an honour not only to the Deputy Chief Constable but also to the whole Force.

P.C. Richard Colwell
Aged 21 years. A Labourer from St Germans, single.
Appointed: 5.10.1864.
Stationed at: Penzance 9.12.1864.
Removal: 31.12.1864. Dismissed from the Force for associating with a prostitute and convicted thief.

P.C. 125 Thomas Doidge
Aged 20 years a single man from Camelford, quarryman.
Appointed: 10.10.1864.
Stationed at: Penzance 2.8.1865.
Removal: 21.12.1865. Resigned.

P.C. 91 Richard Bant
Aged 21 years a single man from Lanteglos a quarryman.
Appointed: 10.10.1864.
Stationed at: 14.2.1864 Truro. 9.9.1869 Helston
Removal: 24.6.1869. Resigned

P.C. 135 Joseph Williams
Aged 20 years a labourer from St Keverne, single.
Appointed: 13.10.1864.
Stationed at: 14.12.1865 Penzance
Removal: 7.8.1866. Called upon to resign owing to his wife being dishonest.

P.C. 7 John Hitchens
Aged 25 years a Miner from Penzance, married with three children
Appointed: 17.10.1864.
Stationed at: 9.12.1864 Helston
Removal: 29.3.1866. Called upon to resign due to inefficiency.

P.C. 28 Jonus Ambrose Abrahams
A 20 year old gardener from Devonport, single.
Appointed: 31.10.1864.
Promotion:
11.7.1869 1st, class Constable.
Stationed at: 9.12.1864. Helston.
Removal: 27.4.1870. Resigned

P.C. 71 James Johns
A 20 year old labourer from Whitstone, single.
Appointed: 2.11.1864.
Stationed at: 9.12.1864. Bodmin.
Removal: 27.6.1865. Called upon to resign for inefficiency.

P.C. 109 Joseph Bassett
Aged 20 years a labourer from Mevagissey, single.
Appointed: 15.11.1864
Promotion: 8.7.1872. 2nd class Constable. 13.11.1882 1st class Constable. 5.11.1883 To Sergeant. 3.11.1889 To Inspector. 22.5.1894 To Superintendent. 13.2.1899 To 1st class Superintendent
Stationed at: 9.5.1865 Bodmin. 3.11.1867 Liskeard. 8.6.1894 Truro.
7.9.1866 Fined 5/- for neglecting to fill in his journal daily according to orders. 12.5.1881 Reduced to 2nd class Constable for allowing a prisoner to escape.
Favourable Record: For zeal and intelligence displayed in working up a case of Rex v Bullen convicted of Manslaughter in the summer Assizes of 1904.
Removal: 30.9.1905 Pension £113.6.8.

P.C. 3 William Harvey
A miner from Marazion aged 24 years married with two children.
Appointed: 28.11.1864.
Stationed at: 6.6.1865 Helston
Removal: 28.11.1865. Resigned.
P.C. 110 John Rowe
A miner from Ludgvan, Penzance. A 22 year old single man.
Appointed: 28.11.1864.

Stationed at: Liskeard 2.2.1865.
Removal: 10.4.1865. Resigned. Had the itch when he left the Force.

P.C. 97 Edwin Butler
A woolcomber from Bodmin. Aged 18 years, single.
Appointed: 8.12.1864.
Stationed at: Bodmin 2.2.1865.
Removal: 30.4.1865. Dismissed for making improper use of language to a brother Constable's wife.

P.C. 116 Francis Eva
A 23 year old single miner from Stithians.
Appointed: 9.1.1865.
Stationed at: Launceston 11.3.1865.
Removal: 26.6.1865.
On the 22.1.1865 was reprimanded for being absent from his lodgings after 10pm., and also for being drunk. Dismissed with forfeiture of a weeks pay for being absent from the station without leave and disobeying the order of his superior officer.

P.C. 12 Edmund Julian
A 23 year old farm labourer from Withiel, Bodmin. Single man.
Appointed: 30.1.1865.
Stationed at: Bodmin 11.3.1865. Penzance 14.7.1871.
Removal: 14.8.71.Resigned

P.C. 26 Henry Thomas
A 20 year old farm labourer from Bradstone. Single man.
Appointed: 13.3.1865.
Stationed at: Penzance 9.5.1865. Liskeard 8.10.1865. Bodmin 6.1.1868. Launceston 20.7.1868.
Removal: 20.5.1869. Resigned.

P.C. 50 Simon Warne
A 25 year old farm labourer from Wadebridge. Single man.
Appointed: 20.3.1865.
Promotion: 8.7.1872. To 2nd class Constable. 28.12.1890 To 1st Class Constable
Stationed at: Bodmin 7.7.1865. Helston 3.12.1865. Helston 2.12.1866.
Removal: 2.7.1892. Pension £41.9.1.

P.C. 1 Alexander Ellis Strick
A 20 year old miner from St Just. Married with one child
Appointed: 20.3.1865
Stationed at: Penzance 30.5.1865. Helston 25.3.1866
Removal: 17.6.1866. Called upon to resign for being absent from his conference point and for general inefficiency.

P.C. 18 Edward Mutton
A 21 year old farm labourer from Camelford.
Appointed: 29.3.1865.
Stationed at: Liskeard 9.5.1865. Penzance 8.10.1865.
Removal: 22.8.1866. Dismissed for general bad conduct.

P.C. 74 Silus Prophet
A married man from St Austell who was a farm labourer
Appointed: 3.4.1865.
Stationed at: Liskeard 9.5.1865
Removal: 31 .7.1865. Resigned

P.C. 110 Thomas Gummoe
An 18 year old farm labourer from Tregony, Truro.
Appointed: 17.4.1865.
Stationed at: Bodmin 5.7.1865. Helston 12.8.1866. Penzance 19.11.1870.
Removal: 21.12.1870. Dismissed for being drunk in a public house when he should have been out on duty. 2.12.1866. Fined 5/- for being absent from his conference point. 17.7.1870. Fined 5/- for making a false entry in his journal.

P.C. 101 Thomas Pengelly
A mason from Crediton, a married man aged 26 years.
Appointed: 6.5.1865.
Stationed at: Truro
Removal: 27.9.1866. Resigned.

P.C. 97 Charles Bellew
A labourer from Portsmouth aged 20 years and unmarried.
Appointed: 2.11.1865.
Stationed at: Truro 15.6.1865.
Removal: 17.9.1866. Resigned

P.C. 82 Thomas Hall
A 22 year old labourer and fisherman from Madron, single.
Appointed: 17.5.1865.
Promotion: 8.7.1872 2nd class Constable 16.11.1879. 1st class Constable. 29.11.1891 Sergeant
Stationed at: Bodmin 30.10.1865. Penzance 20.6.1866. Helston 19.11.1870. Truro 14.1.1886. Bodmin 4.12.1891
Removal: 6.5.1895 with a pension of £48.10.8.

P.C. 26 John Richard Williams
A miner from Liskeard. 18 years old and single.
Appointed: 28.7.1865
Stationed at: Penzance 14.9.1865
Removal: 9.7.1866. Resigned

P.C. 74 Samuel Goins
A 21 year old miner from Lostwithiel. Married.
Appointed: 31.7.1865.
Stationed at: Launceston 11.12.1865.
Removal: 10.10.1866. Resigned

P.C. 133 Frederick Snell
A miner from St Austell. 19 years old and single.
Appointment 20.3.1865.
Removal: 31.10.1866. Resigned stated he was going to California.

P.C. 7 John Lyle
A 25 year old single man, a labourer from Stratton.
Appointed: 2.10.1865.

Promotion: 7.7.1872 to 1st Class Constable.
Stationed at: Bodmin 1.12.1865. Penzance 25.3.1866.
Removal: 2.1.1893. Pension £41.9.1.

P.C. 87 Samson Sandercock
A 29 year old gardener from Launceston, Married.
Appointed: 4.10.1865.
Stationed at: Liskeard 1.12.1865.
Removal: 21 6.1868. Resigned. His wife could not agree with other women at the Police Station.

P.C. John Oliver
A 29 year old labourer from Holsworthy. Married with two children
Appointed: 21.10.1865.
Removal: 20.11.1865. Called upon to resign - a dissatisfied man.

P.C. 30 Charles Hill
A 20 year old labourer from St Tudy, Bodmin. Married.
Appointed: 8.11.1865.
Promotion: 8.7.1872. 2nd Class Constable 29.7.1877. 1st class Constable. 6.1.1891. Sergeant.
Stationed at: Bodmin 21.1.1866. Liskeard 12.7.1868. Bodmin 24.11.1869. Truro 8.7.1871. Helston 13.10.1873. Penzance 18.5.1882. Helston 13.1.1891. Penzance 16.8.1892.
Died 23.5.1894. Gratuity to widow £149.13.8.

P.C. 32 Thomas Bolitho
A 20 year old labourer from Helston, single.
Appointed: 13.11.1865.
Stationed at: Liskeard 21.1.1866.
Removal: 10.10.1867. Resigned. Said he was going abroad.

P.C. 9 Matthew Hugo
30 year old labourer from St Dennis, widower in Oct 1873 and subsequently remarried.
Appointed: 13.11.1865.
Promotion: 8.7.1872. 2nd class Constable. 9.5.1875 1st class Constable
Stationed at: Liskeard 21.1.1866.
Removal: 21.3.1892. Pension £41.9.1.

P.C. 112 John Rowe
28 year old miner and farm labourer from Lostwihiel. Married.
Appointed: 11.12.1865
Promotion: 8.7.1872. 2nd class Constable
Stationed at: Liskeard 5.2.1866
18.11.1877. Reduced to 3rd class Constable for taking a prisoner into a public house at Liskeard instead of the Police station for refreshments.
Removal: 23.4.1879. Resigned. Received a gratuity of £53.1.8.

P.C. 38 William Palmer
A 20 year old single man from Shrewsbury who was a game keeper.
Appointed: 3.1.1866.
Stationed at: Liskeard 1.3.1866.

11.8.1867 Ordered from H.Q. For a weeks drill for not standing to attention when addressed by the Chief Constable and having apparently forgotten his facings.
2.10.1868 Died of fever.

P.C. 116 Willam Tredinnick
A 20 year old miner from St Agnes, single.
Appointed: 1.3.1866.
Stationed at: Liskeard
Removal: 26.2.1867. Resigned to go to work in a mine in Scotland. Had a parchment certificate given to him which said conduct good, abilities never tested.

P.C. 62 William Henry Retallack
A 20 year old labourer from Luxulyn, single.
Appointed: 9.1.1866.
Stationed at: Penzance 22.3.1866.
Removal: 7.11.1869. Resigned - going abroad.

P.C. 125 John Wood
A single man from Holsworthy. A labourer.
Appointed: 10.1.1866.
Stationed at: Truro 22.3.1866.
Removal: 11.1.1867. Resigned.

P.C. 73 Achibald Arthur Keast
A 20 year old miner from St Neot, single.
Appointed: 10.1.1866.
Stationed at: Helston 1.3.1866.
Sept. 1866. Fined 10/- for being absent from his station without leave.
Removal: 28.9.1866. Dismissed for insubordination.

P.C. 39 Henry Lonn Moyle
A 21 year old labourer from London. Married with one child. Public service with Royal Volunteers for four years.
Appointed: 22.1.1866.
Stationed at: Penzance 22.3.1866. Truro 17.11.1869
Removal: 16.5.1872. Resigned.
On the 30.12.1866 fined 5/- for allowing prisoners to have beer in the street when near the gaol.
29.10.1871. Fined £1.0.0. For appropriating for his own use without leave from the Chief Constable a reward of 10/- given by the Excise.

P.C. 119 John Mutton
A 24 year old single man from Camelford, labourer.
Appointed: 1.2.1866.
Stationed at: Bodmin 26.4.1866. Truro 19 5 1867
Fined 10/- for neglecting to take a man out of a train who was in possession of tools which he was told were stolen.
Removal: 15.7.1868. Dismissed with a forfeiture of a weeks pay for playing cards at a public house.

P.C. 16 Tom Elias Truscott
A single man from St Austell, aged 18 years a labourer.
Public Service; With the Royal Volunteers 9th Comp, for five years.
Appointed: 4.2.1866.
Stationed at: Penzance 20.6.1866

Removal: 30.6.1966. Resigned due to ill-health.

P.C. 124 John Treleaven
A 21 year old china clay worker from Lostwithiel. Single.
Appointed: 20.2.1866.
Stationed at: Penzance 6.7.1866
Removal: 19.11.1868. Called upon to retire through ill-health.

P.C. Thomas Lean
Called upon to resign 8.3.1866 – A thick headed man – No other details recorded

P.C. 27 Josephus Nicholas
A 22 year old single miner from St Erth.
Appointed: 19.2.1866.
Stationed at: Liskeard 2.6.1866.
Removal: 12.10.1866. Resigned.

P.C. 35 Richard Tregise
A 23 year old shoemaker and fisherman from Helston, single.
Appointed: 21.2.1866.
Stationed at: Penzance 26.9.1866.
Removal: 14.7.1869. Resigned said he was going to New Zealand.

P.C. 115 George Pope
A labourer from Blandford Dorset, a 23 year old single man.
Appointed: 26.2.1866.
Stationed at: Bodmin 25.6.1866. Penzance 31.12.1868.
Removal: 12.3.1869. Dismissed having been found asleep in a cab.

P.C. 26 Thomas Tresize
A 20 year old farm labourer from Helston, single.
Appointed: 21.2.1866.
Stationed at: Truro 30.8.1866.
Removal: 17.10.1866. Resigned stating that his health had failed since he had joined the Force.

P.C. 130 Charles Lewis Colenso
A 24 year old mason from Truro, married with two children.
Appointed: 6.3.1866.
Stationed at: Bodmin 28,5.1866.
Removal: 17.3.1868. Dismissed for sleeping with a woman, not his wife, at the Lent Assize 1868.

P.C. 3 William Gay
A 21 year old labourer from Truro, single.
Appointed: 12.3.1866.
Stationed at: Bodmin 11.6.1866. Launceston 27.1.1867.
Removal: 22.2.1867. Resigned.

P.C. 7 John Hookyn
A 20 year old farm labourer from Truro, single.
Appointed: 31 .3.1866.
Stationed at: Helston 6.8.1866. Penzance 24.7.1867

Removal: 6.6.1867. Resigned to go home to live with his father.

P.C. 45 William Henry Harris
A 21 year old labourer a single man from Liskeard.
Appointed: 7.5.1866.
Promotion: 8.7.1872 2nd class Constable. 3.8.1877 1st class Constable. 20.11.1884 Sergeant. 7.12.1891 Inspector.
Stationed at: Bodmin 8.12.1866. Liskeard 18.5.1883. Penzance 29.10.1888. Helston 17.12.1891
Removal: 2.8.1897. Pension £70.9.5.

P.C. 145 John Willcocks
A 21 year old labourer from Launceston, single.
Appointed: 5.6.1866
Stationed at: Penzance 20.8.1866. Helston 2.12.1866. Bodmin 12.7.1868. Liskeard 29.11.1868.
Removal: 5.9.1869.
4.2.1869 fined 10/- for being absent from his conference point. 5.9.1869 fined 5/- and ordered to pay for a new cape and strap for having through gross neglect lost his old one. Called upon to resign for being a stupid man.

P.C. 84 William Biqrig McLean
A labourer from Lostwithiel, single aged 20 years.
Appointed: 26.6.1866.
Stationed at: Bodmin 26.9.1866. Helston 24.4.1867
Removal: 18.11.1869. Dismissed for being impertinent to the Chief Constable.

P.C. 152 John Tremain George
A 21 year old miller from Camelford, single.
Appointed: 21.6.1866.
Stationed at: Helston 13.9.1866.
Removal: 13.11.1868 Resigned to go and follow his trade as a miller.

P.C. 1 William Bryant
A 25 year old miner from St Austell. Married with one child.
Appointed: 22.6.1866.
Stationed at: Launceston 30.8.1866
Removal: 8.2.1867. Dismissed for being at a public house for several hours when he should have been on duty.

P.C. 16 Nicholas Doidge
A 18 year old quarryman, single, from Camelford. Public Service. Royal Cornwall Rangers for 3 years.
Appointed: 23.7.1866.
Stationed at: Liskeard 18.10.1866. Launceston 21.4.1869.
Removal: 30.10.1869.
21.4.1867. Fined 10/- and moved at his own expense for being absent from his conference point.
30.10.1867. Resigned when he was accused by P.C.Hacker of taking some flour.

P.C. 135 Charles Harper
Single, aged 20 years a miner from Lostwithiel.
Appointed: 13.8.1866
Stationed at: Truro 23.10.1866
Removal: 5.3.1867. Asked to resign due to inefficiency.

P.C. 76 James Rickard
A miner from Callington, single, aged 21. Public service : 5th Duke of Cornwall Volunteers for 3 months.
Appointed: 27.8.1866.
Stationed at: Bodmin 1.11.1866. Penzance 21.7.1867. Liskeard 12.7.1868.
Removal: 11.1.1870. Resigned said he was going to open a grocers shop at Callington.

P.C. 18 Alfred Tregonning
A 21 year old Miner from Perranzubaloe, single.
Appointed: 3.9.1866.
Stationed at: Penzance 23.10.1866
Removal: 12.12.1866. Resigned and told Mr.Vincent that the service did not agree with his health.

P.C. 150 John Cocking
A 20 year old farm labourer from Truro.
Appointed: 10.9.1866
Stationed at: Launceston 23.10.1866
Removal: 12.10.1868 Resigned
24.9.1867 Reported for getting refreshments from a beer house after closing hours and was moved at his own expense for doing so. 13.1.1868. Fined 5/- for being absent from his conference point and 5/- for making a false entry in his journal. Resigned and said he was going to serve in a drapers shop at Redruth
The Chief Constable said he could not give him a Character reference that would benefit him.

P.C. 73 Bennet John Tallack
A 20 year old farm labourer from Mylor, single.
Appointed: 20.9.1866.
Stationed at: Penzance 22.11.1866. Helston 19.11.1869.
Removal: 4.7.1870. Resigned.
18.6.1868. Fined 5/- for not filling in his journal daily

P.C. 74 James Pooley Carlyon
A 28 year old miner from Sithney. Married with three children.
Appointed: 28.9.1866.
Promotion: 8.7.1872. 2nd class Constable. 1.12.1890. 1st class Constable
Stationed at: Penzance 27.11.1866.
Removal: 31.3.1893. Pension £41.9.1.

P.C. 101 Francis Cornelius
A 22 year old farm labourer from Camelford, married with one child.
Appointed: 1.10.1866.
Stationed at: Truro 18.12.1866
Removal: 1.11.1867 Dismissed from the force for neglect of duty, drinking in a beer house with a man of bad character and when riding home at night in a wagon taking liberties with a married woman

P.C. 26 Richard Richards
A 21 year old single miner from St Ives.
Appointed: 16.10.1866
Stationed at: Bodmin 11.1.1867
Removal: 28.12.1868. Dismissed for being absent from his station without leave and bringing a false charge against his Sergeant.

P.C. 27 Elians Hockaday
A farm labourer from Holsworthy, single aged 18 years.
Appointed: 18.10.1866
Stationed at: St Columb, .31.1.1867
Removal: 28.6.1867. Called to resign for inefficiency

P.C. 156 Richard Landry
A 24 year old farm labourer from St Ive. Married.
Appointed: 22.10.1866.
Stationed at: Launceston 31.1.1867
Removal: 24.3.1867. Resigned

P.C. 157 William Henry Meagor
A 21 year old farm labourer from Lanhydrock. Single.
Appointed: 29.10.1866.
Stationed at: Truro 24.7.1867.
Removal: 11.12.1869. Resignation required Health delicate.

P.C. 117 Richard Brown
A 21 year old farm labourer from Launceston, single.
Appointed: 5.11.1866.
Promotion: 8.7.1862 to 2nd class Constable. 9.5.1875 to 1st class Constable
Stationed at: Bodmin 25.1.1867. Penzance 17.9.1867. Bodmin 31.12.1868.
Removal: 1.6.1881. Died.

P.C. 21 John Armstrong
A 22 year old single man from Stratton, farm labourer.
Appointed: 30.11.1866
Stationed at: 28.1.1867 Launceston. 21.4.1867 Liskeard
Removal: 14.5.1867. Reprimanded severely for that while on duty at the new police station on the evening of the 2.1.1867 was found by Sgt Major Piddock lying down fast asleep in that building. Resigned with a forfeiture of a weeks pay for being drunk on duty.

P.C. 18 John Minear
A 21 year old miner from St Austell, married.
Appointed: 17.12.1866.
Promotion: 8.7.1872. To 2nd Class Constable
Stationed at: 28.7.1867. Liskeard
Removal: 13.4.1873. Resigned.

P.C. 100 Thomas Tilley
A labourer from Camelford. A 24 year old married man. Public Service: Royal Cornwall Rangers for 3 years.
Appointed: 20.12.1866.
Stationed at: Bodmin 28.7.1867.
Removal: 1.10.1868. Dismissed for falsely accusing his superior officer of having been drunk on duty.

P.C. 148 Abraham Opie
A 24 year old miner from Stithians. Married with two children.
Appointed: 7.1.1867
Promotion: 8.7.1872. 2nd class Constable.
Stationed at: Bodmin 7.5.1867. Penzance 28.3.1870. Helston 1.8.1978.

Removal: 17.4.1881.
25.8.1878. Fined £1.0.0. For being in a public house when he should have been out on duty.

P.C. 99 Thomas Carter
A 24 year old miner from Germoe, single.
Appointed: 21.2.1867. Resigned 25.8.1868
Reappointed: 14.8.1872..
Promotion: 3.8.1873 to 2nd class Constable. 7.12.1884 to 1st class Constable. 1.12.1890. Sergeant
Stationed at: Bodmin 9.7.1867. Liskeard 22.9.1872. Bodmin 18.5.1883. Liskeard 9.12.1890.
Removal: 24.10.1898 Pension £51.11.4.

P.C. 125 John Pinch
A shoe maker from St Minver aged 22 years single. Public Service. South Devon Railway for about one month.
Appointed: 11.2.1867.
Stationed at: Liskeard 18.6.1867
Removal: 23.6.1868. Resigned. Going to Dartmoor as a Prison Warder.

P.C. 133 William Bluett
A 21 year old shoe maker from North Petherwin, single.
Appointed: 26.2.1867.
Stationed at: Truro 26.4.1867
Removal: 26.3.1869. Resigned going abroad.

P.C. 15 Robert Ebbett
A 19 year old groom from Gwithian, single.
Promotion: 18.7.1872 2nd class Constable. 27.7.1881 1st Class Constable. 14.7.1879 to Sergeant. 24.9.1894 to Inspector.
Stationed at: Bodmin 9.7.1867. Helston 12.7.1868. Liskeard 21.1.1869. Helston 6.8.1889. Truro 5.10.1894. Liskeard 26.10.1896.
Removal: 24.10.1898 £70.19.5.

P.C. Thomas Dyer
A single 21 year old miner from Roche.
Appointed: 5,3,1867
Removal: 29.3.1867. Dismissed for being found drunk in the guardroom

P.C. 1 William F.Harris
A 31 year old miller from Liskeard.
Appointed: 11.3.1867.
Stationed at: Liskeard 9.5.1867
Removal: 6.10.1867. Resigned alleging that Police duty did not agree with his health which was believed to be untrue.

P.C. John Dawe
A 22 year old gardener from Launceston, single.
Appointed: 11.3.1867
Removal: 27.3.1867. Resigned said he had a pain in his side ever since he had been in the Force and wished to go home.

P.C. 3 Richard Benny
A 21 year old single man from St Wenn, labourer.
Appointed: 2,4,1867
Stationed at: Penzance 9.7.1867.
Removal: 11,10.1870. Resigned due to ill-health.

P.C. 19 John Worth
A 28 year old farm labourer from Poundstock, single. Public Service: South Devon Railway for 7 months.
Appointed: 3.4.1867.
Stationed at: Truro 9.7.1867.
Removal: 20.7.1867. Called upon to resign - Dr.Leverton of Truro certified that he was suffering from "affection of the heart"

P.C. 156 William Gilbert
A 20 year old clay labourer from St Austell. Single.
Appointed: 8.4.1867.
Promotion: 8.7.1872 2nd class Constable
Stationed at: Launceston 23.8.1867. Helston 21.5.1873
Removal: 13.8.1873. Resigned.

P.C. 21 Joseph Retallick
A labourer from St Austell, Aged 20 single.
Appointed: 30.4.1867
Stationed at: Liskeard 23.8.1867. Bodmin 6.1.1868. Helston 4.2.1868. Truro 19.10.1869. Helston 8.9.1871
Removal: 23.1.1872. Dismissed for gross immoralities.

P.C. 136 Francis Bartlett
A 27 year old farm labour and miner from Camelford, single.
Appointed: 22.5.1867.
Promotion: 8.7.1872 2nd class Constable. 1.12.1890 1st class Constable
Stationed at: Truro 29.8.1867. Penzance 6.10.1867. Truro 17.9.1869. Penzance 7.3.1870. Truro 13.10.1873
Removal: 30.9.1895 Pension £41.9.1.

P.C. 135 John Morcomb Dowrick
A 22 year old water man from Ruan Highlanes. Married with one child.
Appointed: 25.5.1867.
Stationed at: Penzance 22.7.1867.
Removal: 8.6.1868. Dismissed for associating with prostitutes and general inattention to duty.

P.C. 7 William Thomas Treverton
A 20 year old miner from Gwennap Single.
Appointed: 26.9.1867.
Removal: 8.1.1868. Called on to resign for general inefficiency.

P.C. 27 William Henry Vercoe
A 20 year old clay labourer from St Austell. Single.
Appointed: 3.7.1867.
Promotion: 8.7.1872 2nd class Constable. 8.11.1877 1st Class Constable. 10.11.1884 to Sergeant. 23.3.1891 to Inspector. 22.5.1894 to Superintendent. 1.3.1899 to Chief Superintendent.
Stationed at: Bodmin 28.9.1867. Penzance 26.10.1896
Removal: 18.11.1904. Pension £113.6.8. 14.5.1871. Fined 5/- for approximating a fee to his own device.

P.C. 19 Charles Bone
A 25 year old labourer from St Stephens, St Austell. Married with two children.
Appointed: 22.7.1867.

Stationed at: Truro 27.9.1867
Removal: 16.12.1868 Dismissed for being the worse for liquor and using abusive language to his Sergeant.

P.C. 11 Hart Green
A 22 year old clay labourer from St Austell, single.
Appointed: 24.7.1867.
Promotion: 8.7.1872 2nd class Constable. 23.3.1891 1st class Constable.
Stationed at: Liskeard 8.10.1867. 29.10.1871 Fined 5/- for not filling in his journal daily.
Removal: 1.1.1895 Pension £41.9.1.

P.C. 2 Joseph Williams
A 22 year old miner from Breage
Appointed: 29.7.1867.
Stationed at: Penzance 8.10.1867. Helston 15.9.1868.
Removal: 11.7.1869. Called upon to resign owing to ill-health.

P.C. Albert Shepperd
A 31 year old labourer from Bristol. Married.
Appointed: 11.8.1867
Removal: 8.9.1867. Called upon to resign his wife addicted to drink.

P.C. 85 Alfred Julian
A farm labourer from Withiel. Single aged 23. Public service: Cornwall Railway for 10 months.
Appointed: 29.8.1867.
Stationed at: Bodmin 28.11.1867
Removal: 14.7.1872. Resigned

P.C. 20 John Yole
A 30 year old farm labourer from Tavistock, single. Public service: South Devon Railway for 16 months.
Appointed: 29.8.1867.
Stationed at: Bodmin 4.11.1867
Removal: 14.9.1870 Resigned

P.C. William Tink
Appointed: 16.9.1867.
Removal: 24.9.1867. Resigned stating he could not comply with the rules.

P.C. 66 Joseph Manhire
A 17 year old clay labourer from Roche. Single.
Appointed: 25.9.1867.
Stationed at: Launceston 20.12.1867. Penzance 20.7.1868. Liskeard 8.6.1869. Truro 14.3.1870. Penzance 28,4.1870
Removal: 24.6.1870. Called upon to resign for neglect of duty to be about with women.

P.C. 32 Joseph Lewis Jones
A 22 year old labourer from Holsworthy. Married.
Appointed: 8.2.1867.
Promotion: 8.7.1872 to 2nd class Constable. 17.12.1876 to 1st class Constable 14.7.1889 to Sergeant.
Stationed at: Liskeard 10.12.1868. Bodmin 18.4.1872. Penzance 23.7.1889. Bodmin 25.10.1898
Removal: 30.4.1907. Pension £55.9.4.

P.C. 32 Walter Quarem Mannell
A 28 year old labourer from Grampound. Married with three children.
Appointed: 10.10.1867
Promotion: 8.7.1872 to 2nd class Constable. 27.7.1881 to 1st class Constable
Stationed at: Liskeard 8.1.1868. Helston 30.9.1870
Removal: 6.1.1891 Pension £31.10.6. Died 26 Penlee Street, Penzance. On 1.3.1902.

P.C. 89 Thomas Sara Wills
A 21 year old shoemaker from Marazion, single. Public service : G.P.O. For 6 months.
Appointed: 14.10.1867
Stationed at: Bodmin 1.7.1868.
Removal: 23.7.1869. Dismissed with the forfeiture of a weeks pay for being absent from his station with out leave and making false entries in his journal.

P.C. 16 James Gibbons
A 19 year old waiter and cab driver from Gibraltar, single.
Appointed: 8.11.1867.
Promotion: 8.7.1872 to 2nd class Constable. 13.9.1875 to 1st class Constable
Stationed at: Truro 21.5.1868. Bodmin 3.6.1872. Liskeard 2.6.1873.
Removal: 4.4.1880. Resigned.

P.C. 101 John Budge
A 20 year old blacksmith from North Hill Launceston, married with one child.
Appointed: 6.11.1967.
Promotion: 8.7.1872 to 2nd Class Constable
Stationed at: Liskeard 20.3.1868. Bodmin 26.7.1878.
Removal: 11.11.1881.
25.8.1878 Fined 5/- for being absent from his station without leave and moved at his own expense for telling a falsehood. Called on to resign for not complying with an order from his Superintendent and telling the Chief Constable a false hood.
25.11.1981. A certificate of service was given him showing the punishment inflicted with this addition - that Budge had never been reported for drunkenness of any other improper conduct.

P.C. 147 Henry Thomas Julian
A 21 year old farmers son from Withiel, single.
Appointed: 28.11.1867.
Stationed at: Bodmin 2.5.1868. Truro 29.11.1868. Penzance 17.9.1869.
Removal: 23.12.1869. Dismissed for disobedience and for being absent without leave.

P.C. 7 Richard Jewells
A single 20 year old miner from Lostwithiel.
Appointed: 29.1.1868
Promotion: 8.7.1872 to 2nd class Constable. 1.12.1890 to 1st class Constable. 10.1.1895 to Merit Class Constable.
Stationed at: Bodmin 6.7.1868. Liskeard 24.8.1869.
Removal: 31.1.1898. Pension £43.9.6.

P.C. 133 Thomas Spry
A 29 year old labourer from Plymouth, Married with one child. Public service: Plymouth Police for 6 months.
Appointed: 3.2.1868
Stationed at: Penzance 6.6.1868
Removal: 17.11.1871. Resigned due to ill-health

P.C. 140 William Penrose
A miner from St Blazey a single man aged 22years. Public service: Artillery Volunteers in Cornwall for 9 months.
Appointed: 18.1.1868.
Promotion: 8.7.1872. 2nd class Constable. 28.12.1890 1st class Constable. 3.9.1892 Merit Class Constable.
Stationed at: Bodmin 27.10.1868. Liskeard 1.8.1870. Truro 21.11.1884.
Removal: 25.12.1898. Pension £43.9.6.

PC. 130 Henry Peters
A 19 year single labourer from St Germans.
Appointed: 27.3.1868.
Stationed at: Penzance 9.7.1868. Bodmin 12.11.1869.
Removal: 10.4.1871. Resigned.

P.C. 24 Thomas May
A 20 year old farmers son from Lanhydrock. Single.
Appointed: 13,5.1868.
Removal: 26.5.1868. Resigned did not like the work.
Reappointed: 11.5.1871
Removal: 12.9.1871.
3.6.1871. Fined 5/- for being in charge of a lunatic, locking him in a cell, and going to bed. 9.6.1871 Fined 10/- for using bad language in the Guardroom

P.C. 104 James Bennetts
A 21 year old single miner from Helston.
Appointed: 29.5.1868.
Stationed at: Bodmin 27.8.1868. Helston 19.7.1869.
Removal: 17.3.1872. Resigned.

P.C. 54 Janus Tilley
A 22 year old labourer from Treneglos, Launceston, single.
Appointed: 1.6.1868
Removal: 28.8.1868. Resigned.

P.C. 135 William Warring
A single man from South Petherwin, a farm labourer aged 20 years.
Appointed: 16.6.1868.
Promotion: 8.7.1872 2nd class Constable.
Stationed at: Bodmin 18.9.1868. Liskeard 3.4.1872. Bodmin 5.4.1873.
Removal: 29.11.1875. Gone to New Zealand.

P.C. John Meagor
A 20 year old labourer from Lanhydrock, single.
Appointed: 29,6.1868.
Removal: 24.7.1868. Resigned no complaint to make against the Force but thought he could do better.

P.C. Richard Pearce
A single 22 year old labourer from Stratton.
Appointed: 30.6.1868.
Removal: 17.7.1868. Resigned - a lazy recruit.

P.C. 87 John King
A 32 year old miner from St Hilary, single.
Public service: Metropolitan Police for about 10 weeks.
Appointed: 23.7.1868.
Promotion: 8.7.1872 2nd class Constable.
6.1.1881 1st class Constable. 24.8.1874 Sergeant
Stationed at: Liskeard 26.10.1868. Bodmin 13.12.1868. Launceston 20.7.1870. Bodmin 1.5.1884. Liskeard 21,11.1884.
Removal: 10.1.1895. Pension £51.11.4.
Died 16.5.1900.

P.C. Elias Birch
A 21 year old labourer from Launceston, married. Public service: Cornwall Railways for about 10 months.
Appointed: 27,7.1868.
Removal: 25.8.1868. Resigned a wretched scholar and too dull of comprehension for a Policeman.

P.C. 42 William Jenkin
A 23 year old mason from Lewannick.
Married with one child.
Appointed: 29.8.1868
Stationed at: Bodmin 29.10.1868
Removal: 21.3.1869. Resigned night air disagreed with him.

P.C. 54 Joseph Sartin
A 25 year old miner from Ludgvan. Married with three children
Appointed: 31.8.1868.
Stationed at: Helston 9.11.1868.
Removal: 9.12.1869. **Removal:** for disobedience of orders.

P.C. 125 Richard Prowse
A 25 year old farm Labourer from St Just, married with two children.
Appointed: 31.11.1868
Promotion: 8.7.1872 2nd class Constable
Stationed at: Truro 28.11.1868
Removal: 2.1.1893. Pension £33.2.1.
Pensioned on medical grounds as not fit for Police Force. Died at Perranporth 26.9.1900.

P.C. 121 Robert Pill
A 27 year old farm labourer from Probus .
Married with two children.
Appointed: 7.9.1868.
Promotion: 8.7.1872 to 2nd class Constable
6.2.1881 to 1st class Constable. 11.10.1886 to Sergeant.
Stationed at: Liskeard 9.11.1868.
Removal: 13.2.1893. Died and widow received gratuity of £134.8.0.

P.C. 151 John Snell
A 20 year old farm labourer from St Kew, single.
Appointed: 8.10.1868
Stationed at: Bodmin 27.1.1869. Penzance

3.4.1871.
Removal: 31.8.1871. Resigned.

P.C. 150 John Landers
A 20 year old carpenter from Egloshayle.
Single.
Appointed: 13.10.1868.
Promotion: 8.7.1872 to 2nd class Constable
Stationed at: 2.12.1868 Truro. 25.4.1870 Helston.
Removal: 4.3.1873 Resigned.

P.C. 100 Thomas Scantlebury
A 22 year old farm labourer from St Germans, single. Public service: Cornwall railway for 6 weeks,
Appointed: 13.10.1868.
Stationed at: Penzance 14.12.1868
Removal: 10.3.1872. Resigned.

P.C. 119 John Pearce
A 30 year old farm labourer from Mevagissey.
Married Hannah Emmett of St Anthony May 1874.
Appointed: 10.11.1868.
Promotion: 8.7.1872 to 2nd class Constable.
18.6.1888 to 1st class Constable. 3.9.1892 to Merit class Constable.
Stationed at: Helston 28.1.1869
Removal: 6.5.1895 Pension £43.9.6.

P.C. 68 William Prout
A 29 year old miner from Tavistock, single.
Public service South Devon Railway.
Appointed: 12.11.1868.
Promotion: 8.7.1872 to 2nd class Constable.
Stationed at: Launceston 6.2.1869.
Removal: 6.4.1879. Called upon to resign owing to ill-health and received a gratuity of £44.6.8.

P.C. 152 John Spry
A 23 year old farm labourer from North Tamerton, single.
Appointed: 19.11.1868
Promotion: 8.7.1872 to 2nd class Constable
Stationed at: Liskeard 25.5.1869
Removal: 14.5.1875. Died.
31.12.1873 Fined 5/- for being drunk on duty.

P.C. 38 John Henry Hambly
A 20 year old mason from St Mabyn, single.
Appointed: 20.11.1868.
Removal: 6.3.1871 Resigned
Reappointed: 31.10.1871 as P.C. 47.
Promotion: 6.7.1872 to 2nd class Constable.
3.2.1881 to 1st class Constable. 4.8.1891 to Sergeant. 25.5.1894 to Inspector.
Stationed at: Liskeard 28.1.1869. Truro 2.11.1871..Liskeard 8.6.1894. Launceston 11.7.1895.
Removal: 23.10.1899. Pension £70.19.5.
22.6.1884. Fined 5/- for being absent from his conference point and 5/- for making a false entry in his journal.

P.C. 124 James Wood
22 year old miller from Holsworthy, single.
Appointed: 2.12.1868
Stationed at: Penzance 12.2.1869.
Removal: 12.2.1870. Resigned, said he should join the convict service.

P.C. 65 William Hall
A 24 year old farm labourer from Madron.
Appointed: 7.12.1868.
Stationed at: Truro 28.1.1869.
Removal: 3.9.1869. Resigned.

P.C. 26 Thomas Harry
A Miner from Morvah, Penzance. Aged 20 single. Public Service: Artillery volunteers for 8 months
Appointed: 28.12.1868
Stationed at: Penzance 29.5.1869
Removal: 22.9.1869. Told the Chief Constable he thought he should go abroad in the spring when the Chief Constable told him to bring his clothing to H.Q. At once.

P.C. 115 William Nicholls
A 21 year old farmers son from Germoe, single.
Appointed: 4.1.1869.
Stationed at: Bodmin 29.5.1869
Removal: 23.9.1869. Resigned said he was going abroad.

P.C. 42 James Tucker
An 18 year old miner from Lewannick, single.
Appointed: 17 3.1869.
Stationed at: Bodmin 28.5.1869
Removal: 3.5.1871. Resigned

P.C. 19 Richard Harris Betts
A 20 year old single gardener from St Minver.
Public Service : Wadebridge Royal Volunteers for about 9 months.
Appointed: 19.3.1869.
Promotion: 8.7.1872 to 2nd class Constable
Stationed at: Bodmin 23.8.1869. Penzance 22.10.1870.
Removal: 21.11.1872. Resigned

P.C. 149 Edward Matthews
A 21 year old single miner from Saltash.
Appointed: 25.3.1869.
Removal: 12.9.1873.
Reppointed: 6.2.1974. P.C. 52
Promotion: 8.7.1872 to 2nd class Constable.
9.5.1875 to 1st class Constable. 25.7.1881 to 1st class Constable. 11.1.1886 to Sergeant.
11.10.1892 to Inspector. 26.10.1896 to Superintendent. 1.7.1901 to 1st class Superintendent.
Stationed at: Helston 11.8.1869. Bodmin 2.3.1874. Liskeard 14.1.1886. Bodmin 1.10.1889. Penzance 17.12.1891. Bodmin 11.10.1896. Liskeard 1.3.1899.
Removal: 11.11.1908. Superannuating £113.6.8..

P.C. 116 Richard Kerslake
A 20 year old farm labourer from Launceston, single.
Appointed: 31.3.1869.
Stationed at: Helston 24.6.1869. Penzance 2.4.1871
Removal: 28.5.1871. Resigned.

P.C. 17 Richard Oliver
A 23 year old farm labourer from Holsworthy. Married with one child.
Appointed: 11.5.1869
Promotion: 8.7.1872 to 2nd class Constable

Stationed at: Truro 23.7.1869
Removal: 22.7.1879. Died.

P.C. 41 Richard Lobb
A single 23 year old from Cardinham. Farm Labourer.
Appointed: 14.5.1869.
Stationed at: Penzance 28.9.1869.
Removal: 26.10.1869. Called upon to resigned for neglect of duty.

P.C. 97 Augustus Richard Hooper
A 22 year old labourer from Henley, Oxford.
Public Service: Callington Rife Volunteers for about 4 months.
Appointed: 18.5.1869.
Stationed at: Bodmin 21.7.1869
Removal: 16.6.1871. Resigned.

P.C. 106 Joseph Thomas Sleep Hocking
A 19 year old farm labourer from Callington, single.
Appointed: 9.6.1869.
Stationed at: Helston 15.10.1869.
Removal: 20.7.1870. Resigned.

P.C. 91 Richard Mellow
An 18 year old labourer from St Stephens, St Austell, single.
Appointed: 1.7.1869.
Stationed at: Penzance 27.9.1869.
Removal: 26.7.1870. Resigned

P.C. 137 John Barnicoat Harris
A 21 year old shipwright from Sussex.
Appointed: 12.7.1869.
Stationed at: Liskeard 27.9.1869
Removal: 16.11.1869. Called upon to resign for neglect of duty. A very stupid man.

P.C. 35 Edward Pope
A married man with two children, aged 29, a labourer from Egloshayle.
Appointed: 14.7.1869.
Promotion: 8.7.1872 to 2nd class Constable.
Launceston 27.7.1869
Removal: 8.12.1875. Died.

P.C. 89 Anthony Buckingham
A farm labourer from St Columb Major. 23 years and married with two children.
Public Service: Miners Artillery for 5 years.
Appointed: 24.7.1869.
Stationed at: Truro 27.9.1869.
Removal: 9.11.1870. Called upon to resign for inefficiency. 7.8.1869 Fined 10/- for taking money without permission of the Chief Constable.

P.C. 47 Edward Roberts
Farm labourer from Looe, single aged 24 years.
Appointed: 31.7.1869
Stationed at: Penzance 16.11.1869
Removal: 8.10.1871. Resigned.

P.C. 2 Ronald Renals
A miner from Linkinhorn, aged 19 single.
Appointed: 23.8.1869.
Stationed at: Bodmin 16.11.1869.
Removal: 14.1.1870. Resigned, said he was going as a bandsman in the Royal Navy.

P.C. 86 Symon Menhinnett
A miner from Callington, aged 22 a married man. Public Service: Plymouth Police for about 5 months.
Appointed: 16.9.1869.
Removal: 14.10.1869. Resigned, thought he could do better.

P.C. 145 William Wicks Doney
A shoe maker from Lewannick, aged 22, Married Martha Ann Reed from Gunnislake, 16.10.1869.
Appointed: 22.9.1869.
Removal: 24.9.1873. Resigned.
Reappointed: 24.3.1874.
Promotion: 8.7.1872 to 2nd class Constable.
9.11.1875 to 1st class Constable
Stationed at:
Penzance 16.11.1869. Helston 2.8.1872.
Helston 27.5.1874
Removal: 12.11.1882. Resigned.

P.C. 86 Joseph Stephens
A labourer from St Tudy, aged 28 married with three children.
Appointed: 13.10.1869.
Promotion: 8.7.1872 to 2nd class Constable.
18.6.1888 to 1st class Constable
Stationed at:
Liskeard 8.7.1870. Bodmin 10.10.1870.
Liskeard 18.5.1872. Bodmin 9.10.1874.
Penzance 1.1.1892
Removal: 18.5.1896. Pension £39.8.8.
17.7.1891. Reduced to 2nd class Constable for being drunk on duty.

P.C. 142 Francis Richardson
A labourer from Ladock, aged 21 married Rosina Sleeman of Newton Abbott on 6.9.1877.
Appointed: 16.10.1869
Promotion: 8.7.1872 to 2nd class Constable
Stationed at: Penzance 29.1.1870. Bodmin 8.10.1872. Truro 12 5.1877
Removal: 11.11.1877 Resigned.

P.C. 65 William Smith
Farm Labourer from Lifton, aged 19 single.
Public Service: Royal Cornwall Rangers Militia for 3 years.
Appointed: 18.10.1869
Stationed at: 18.12.1869 Helston
Removal: 25.11.1870. Dismissed for neglect of duty and when spoken to about it immediately sending his resignation.

P.C. 26 Thomas Jones
A farmers son from Holsworthy, aged 25 single. Public Service; North Devon Yeomanary for 2 years.
Appointed: 23.10.1869.
Stationed at: Truro 18.12.1869. Liskeard 14.3.1870.
Removal: 8.2.1872. Dismissed for gross neglect of duty making false entries in his journal and telling his Superintendent falsehoods.

P.C. Joseph S. Pearce
Appointed: 25.10.1869.
Removal: 25.10.1869. This man was passed by Dr.Couch, in the evening it was found

that his eyesight was weak, he was taken before Dr.Couch again the next day and he rejected him.

P.C. 41 Samuel Doney
A shoemaker from Lewannick, aged 24 years, married.
Appointed: 29.10.1869.
Promotion: 8.7.1872. To 2nd class Constable
Stationed at: Launceston 12.3.1870.
Truro 4.7.1873.
Removal: 5.5.1878. Resigned
On 6.6.1875 fined 5/- for making a false record in his journal.

P.C. 115 Robert Downing
A miner and labourer from St Keverne, aged 27 years, married with two children.
Appointed: 15.11.1869.
Promotion: 8.7.1872 to 2nd class Constable
Stationed at: Bodmin 12.3.1870.
Removal: 15.12.1872. Resigned.

P.C. 84 Thomas Symons
A labourer from Stratton, married with one child.
Appointed: 21 12 1869.
Stationed at: Bodmin 28.3.1870.
Removal: 28.11.1871. Resigned

P.C. 49 Richard Weeks
A farm labourer and blacksmith from Lostwithiel, a 21 year old single man.
Appointed: 8.1.1870.
Stationed at: Penzance 28.3.1870.
Removal: 25.9.1870. Resigned.

P.C. 157 John Winn
Stonecutter and labourer from Constantine, aged 21 and single.
Appointed: 11.2.1870.
Stationed at: Penzance 15.4.1870.
Removal: 10.10.1870. Resigned

P.C. 147 Richard Hall
A 19 year old labourer from Camborne, single.
Appointed: 18.1.1870.
Stationed at: Truro 27.4.1870.
Removal: 25.7.1870.
On 26.4.1870 was fined four days pay for not returning on the expiration of his leave.
On 25.7.1870 Dismissed for overstaying his leave a second time and for being in debt.

P.C. 76 George Neal
A farm labourer from Bideford, single aged 19 years.
Appointed: 31.1.1870.
Stationed at: Helston 5.5.1870. Penzance 14.11.1870
Removal: 18.12.1871 Resigned.

P.C. 2 William Tucker
A 23 year old mason from Lewannick, single.
Appointed: 28.1.1870
Stationed at: Penzance 2.7.1870.
Removal: 10.5.1871. Resigned.

P.C. 122 John Pardon
A stonemason from Budock, aged 22 single.
Appointed: 14.3.1870.

Stationed at: Truro 2.7.1870
Removal: 16.7.1872 resigned.

P.C. 54 Thomas Dawe
A 21 year old farm labourer from Stratton, single.
Appointed: 23.3.1870.
Stationed at: Bodmin 23.7.1870.
Removal: 29.10.1871. Resigned.

P.C. 134 James Richard Ould
A farm labourer from Helston, aged 20 single.
Appointed: 10.4.1870.
Stationed at: Helston 27.7.1870.
Removal: 28.6.1872. Called on to resign. 10.7.1870 Fined 10/- for being asleep in the Guardroom when he should have been out on duty.

P.C. 124 Edwin Baker
A Quarryman from Winckley, Devon. Single aged 20.
Appointed: 5.5.1870.
Stationed at: Truro 15.8.1870.
Removal: 17.5.1872.   Resigned.

P.C. William Henry Stribley
A miner and labourer from St Enodor, St Columb, aged 19 single.
Appointed: 10.5.1870.
Removal: 8.9.1870 Resigned.

P.C. 28 James Bryant Williams
A farm labourer from St Keverne, 20 year old single. **Public service:** The Rifle Volunteers for 2 years.
Appointed: 10.5.1870.
Stationed at: Bodmin 29.9.1870.
Removal: 2.4.1873. Dismissed for being drunk.

P.C. 66 James Richards
A 24 year old miner from St Keyne, married with four children. **Public service:** Navy for 3 months.
Appointed: 4.7.1870.
Promotion: 8.7.1872 to 2nd class Constable.
Stationed at: Bodmin 25.10.1870. Truro 15.8.1876.
Removal: 31.12.1889. Pension £21.17.0.

P.C. 106 William Jones
A farm labourer from Holsworthy aged 21 years.
Appointed: 25.7.1870.
Stationed at: Penzance 23.10.1870.
Removal: 31.8.1871. Resigned.

P.C. 73 William Henry Allen
A quarryman from St Kew, 22 single.
Appointed: 15.8.1870
Stationed at: Penzance 23.10.1870. Helston 14.11.1870.
Removal: 20.2.1871. Called upon to resign and to forfeit a weeks pay for disobedience of orders after having been previously forgiven for being drunk.

P.C. 147 John Cock
A 22 year old farm labourer from Gwithian. Single.
Appointed: 19.8.1870

Promotion: 8.7.1872 2nd class Constable. 28.12.1890 1st class Constable
Stationed at: Bodmin 23.10.1870. Helston 3.4.1872. Penzance 17.10.1873. Helston 9.5.1878. Truro 28.7.1893.
Removal: 11.3.1900. Pension £41 .11.4.

P.C. 20 Thomas Daveis
A farm labourer from Fowey, aged 27 married with one child.
Appointed: 15.9.1870.
Promotion: 26.10.1873 to 2nd class Constable. 11.1.1886 to 1st class Constable. 14.11.1881 to Sergeant
Stationed at: Bodmin 4.7.1871. Bodmin 1.8.1871. Liskeard 29.7.1878. Truro 18.11.1891.
Removal: 30.6.1900. Pension £51.14.2. On 4.8.1872 fined 10/- for being the worse for liquor.

P.C. 158 William Davis
A shoe maker from St Mellion, single aged 24 **Public Service:** The Rifle Volunteers for 6 years.
Appointed: 21.9.1870.
Stationed at: Penzance 30.11.1870.
Removal: 5.12.1874. Dismissed for drunkenness. On 9.7.1871 fined £1.0.0. For being drunk on duty and for being absent from his conference point.

P.C. 91 William Rowe
A 28 year old farm labourer from Callington, Married Sarah Friend of Beere ,Devon 22.4.1871.
Appointed: 29.9.1870.
Promotion: 23.11.1873 to 2nd class Constable. 4.10.1891 to 1st class Constable
Stationed at: Launceston 30.11.1870
Removal: 9.1.1896. Pension £14.9.1.

P.C. 157 James Richards
A 21 year old miner from Camborne, single.
Appointed: 20.9.1870.
Stationed at: Helston 30.11.1870
Removal: 10.3.1872. Resigned.

P.C. Thomas Hore
A 19 year old engine man from Roche, single.
Appointed: 17.10.1870.
Removal: 6.12.1870. Resigned.

P.C. 49 William Broad
A 22 year old shoe maker from Looe, single.
Appointed: 18.10.1870.
Stationed at: Helston 6.7.1871. Bodmin 23.8.1871. Penzance 8.10.1872.
Removal: 20.6.1873.
11.5.1873. Fined 5/- for not filling in his journal daily and 5/- making a false entry in his journal. 9.6.1873. Fined 10/- for being absent from his conference point, and 10/- for making a false entry in his journal. 20.6.1873. Dismissed for associating with prostitutes.

P.C. 144 Richard Benny
Farm labourer from St Enador, 21 year old single man. **Public service:** The Rifle Volunteers for 6 months.

Appointed: 29.10.1870.
Promotion: 16.7.1873 to 2nd class Constable
Stationed at: Helston 10.3.1871.
Removal: 9.8.1875. Resigned 10.7.1871 reprimanded for being found asleep (at H.Q. Station) when on duty.

P.C. 89 Richard Hawke
A 23 year old farm labourer from St Tudy, single. **Public service:** Army 65th Regiment. for 7 months.
Appointed: 15.11.1870.
Stationed at: Liskeard 10.3.1871
Removal: 29.9.1871. Resigned.

P.C. 3 Alfred Minear
Farm Labourer from St Austell. Aged 23 single.
Appointed: 24.11.1870
Stationed at: Truro 24.3.1871.
Removal: 28.2.1872 Resigned.

P.C. 44 George Milford
A 23 year old groom from St Austell, married.
Appointed: 28.11.1870.
Removal: 25.1.1871. Resigned.

P.C. 46 Lewis Thomas Watts
23 year old shoemaker from Poundstock, single.
Appointed: 28.11.1870
Stationed at: Penzance 17.4.1871. Helston 16.6.1871
Removal: 23.6.1872. Resigned. 21.1.1872. Fined 10/- for being absent from his conference point.

P.C. 65 George Evely
A farm labourer from Hatherleigh, aged 28 years, married with one child. **Public service:** Plymouth Police for 3 years and 2 months.
Appointed: 8.12.1870.
Stationed at: Liskeard 19.7.1871.
Removal: 31.5.1871. Dismissed with forfeiture of a weeks pay for being drunk and riotous.

P.C. 75 Thomas Penhall
A china clay worker from St Austell, aged 21 single.
Appointed: 9.12.1870.
Stationed at: Launceston 21.4.1871.
Removal: 15.5.1872. Resigned

P.C. 144 Richard Borlase
A clay worker from St Austell aged 19 single.
Appointed: 29.12.1870.
Stationed at: Penzance 20.4.1871.
Removal: 4.5.1873. Resigned.

P.C. 110 William Prout
A farm labourer from St Teath. Single.
Appointed: 30.1.1871
Stationed at: Bodmin 10.4.1871. Helston 23.8.1871. Launceston 13.4.1872.
Removal: 18.4.1880. Resigned.

P.C. 73 Thomas Philp
Farm labourer from St Teath, 21 years single.
Appointed: 20.2.1871.
Stationed at: Bodmin 16.6.1871.

Removal: 2.7.1871. Dismissed for being drunk on duty.

P.C. 61 John Wellington
20 year old labourer from Luxulyan, married.
Appointed: 1.3.1871
Removal: 6.10.1871. Dismissed for stealing Sergeant Trenerry's food. 6.10.1871 Fined 10/- for neglect of duty.

P.C. 38 Simon Teague
A mason from Camelford, aged 19 single.
Appointed: 27.3.1871.
Stationed at: Bodmin 16.6.1871
Removal: 28.1.1872 Resigned.

P.C. 62 Samuel John May
A miner from St Teath, aged 19 single. Public service: Duke of Cornwall Rifle Volunteers for one month.
Appointed: 24.4.1871
Stationed at: Truro 15.7.1871. Helston 16.7.1872 **Removal:** 12.1.1873. Resigned 11.6.1871 Fined 5/- for being quarrelsome and using bad language in the Guardroom.

P.C. 130 Henry Nicholls
A farm labourer from St Martins, Helston. Aged 20 single.
Appointed: 14.4.1871.
Removal: 13.6.1871 Resigned.

P.C. 42 John Davey Kendall
20 year old quarryman miner from Camelford, married 13.1.1872 to Elizabeth Hobbs of Mawgan East. Public service: Rifle Volunteers for 8 months
Appointed: 23.5.1871
Stationed at: Truro 17.7.1871.
Removal: 13.7.1873. Resigned.

PC. 97 Joseph Noy
29 year old miner from St Just. Married with one child. Public service: Marines for two years and eight months.
Appointed: 19.6.1871.
Promotion: 19.11.1873 to 2nd class Constable. 5.11.1883 to 1st class Constable. 6.9.1891 to Sergeant
Stationed at: Bodmin 2.8.1871. Launceston July 1881. Helston 4.10.1891
Removal: 7.10.1897. Pension £51.11.4.

P.C. 116 William Treglown Blight
Miner from St Mewan aged 18 years, single.
Appointed: 26.6.1871.

Stationed at: Liskeard 17.11.1871.
Removal: 18.5.1873. Resigned.

P.C. 2 James Hill
A 29 year old quarryman from Camelford, married Susan Baker of Camelford 29.10.1879.
Appointed: 28.6.1871.
Promotion: 26.10.1873 to 2nd class Constable. 1.12.1890 to 1st class Constable
Stationed at: Liskeard 12.9.1871. Bodmin 4.4.1872. Truro 19.1.1873. Launceston 18.11.1873. Helston 6.7.1878. Bodmin 5.11.1879.
Removal: 8.7.1897. Pension £41.9.1.

P.C. Francis Hawke
Appointed: 28.6.1871
Removal: 9.7.1871. Called upon to resign, Sergeant Major reported him as unfit for the Force - very illiterate and had no aptitude for learning.

P.C. 65 Thomas Brown
A 29 year old quarryman from Boscastle, married with one child. Public service: Duke of Cornwall Rife Volunteers
Appointed: 28.6.1871
Removal: 10.8.1871. Resigned
Reappointed: 31.10.1871
Promotion: 8.3.1873 to 2nd class Constable
Stationed at:
Liskeard 15.11.1871. Launceston 17.1.1887
Removal: 13.5.1888. Dismissed for making a false charge against his Sergeant.

P.C. 56 John Manhire
A farm labourer from St Enodor, aged 27 married Mary May of Ladock on 13.3.1872.
Appointed: 26.6.1871
Promotion: 3.8.1873 to 2nd class Constable. 28.12.1890 to 1st class Constable. 26.10.1896 to Merit Class Constable
Stationed at: Penzance 12.9.1871
Removal: 17.1.1898. Pension £43 .9.6.

P.C. 81 John Mitchell
Gardener from St Austell, 19 year old. September 1875 married Emma Pearce of Lelant. Later remarried Elizabeth Couch.
Appointed: 6.7.1871
Promotion: 3.8.1873 to 2nd class Constable. 28.7.1878 to 1st class Constable. 10.1.1895 to Sergeant
Stationed at: Penzance 18.12.1871. Helston 18.5.1882. Bodmin 10.1.1995
Removal: 14.10.1898. Pension £48.10.8. Retired on a medical certificate at 46 years old.

P.C. 102 Charles Harris
A miner from Tavistock, aged 19 single.
Appointed: 10.7.1871
Removal: 9.8.1871. Resigned.

P.C. 63 William Henry Thomas
A farm labourer from Helston, aged 23 single.
Appointed: 10.7.1871
Promotion: 16.2.1873 to 2nd class Constable
Stationed at: Penzance 14.9.1871. Helston 21.3.1872. Penzance 2.8.1872
Removal: 7.11.1875. Resigned.

P.C. 73 John Rowe Quick
21 year old miner from Sithney, married Louisia Gabriel of Gunwallow, August 1875.
Appointed: 10. 7 1871.
Promotion: 16.7.1873 to 2nd class Constable. 7.12.1884 to 1st class Constable. 3.11.1889 to Sergeant
Stationed at: Bodmin 2.11.1871. Truro 5.11.1879. Liskeard 7.11.1889. Helston 18.8.1991 Bodmin 4,1.1894. Launceston 24.4.1894
Removal: 30.11.1900. Pension of £54.17.2.

P.C. 13 James Reynolds
21 year old wood cutter from Lostwithiel, married with one child. Public service: Cornish Railway for about 3 weeks.
Appointed: 12.7.1871
Removal: 6.3.1872. Called upon to resign for beating his wife.

P.C. 106 Thomas Evans
Farm labourer from Bideford, aged 20 married.
Appointed: 11.9. 1871.
Stationed at: Bodmin 18.12.1871
Removal: 18.8.1872. Resigned.

P.C. 102 Joseph Johns
19 year old farm labourer from St Austell, single.
Appointed: 13.9.1871.
Stationed at: Penzance 18.12.1871
Removal: 8.7.1872. Dismissed for having connections with a prisoner in the Camborne Police cell.

P.C. 21 Silas Ward
20 year old farm labourer from Honiton, single.
Appointed: 17.10.1871.
Stationed at: Truro 29.1.1872
Removal: 24.6.1873. Resigned

P.C. 130 William Richard Matthews
Farm Labourer from Landolph, 19 single.
Appointed: 10.10.1871
Stationed at: Bodmin 29.1.1872. Truro 3.6.1872
Removal: 1.3.1876. Died.

P.C. 89 John Henry Box
A carpenter from Falmouth aged 22 years. Married Elizabeth Harris May 1873. Public service: Royal Cornwall Miners Artillery Munitions for four years seven months.
Appointed: 31.10.1871.
Promotion: 26.10.1873 to 2nd class Constable. 5.11.1883 to 1st class Constable.20.10.1889 to Sergeant 7.11.1891 reduced to 2nd class Constable for drunkenness. 3.8.1896 to 1st class Constable. 20.12.1897 to merit class Constable
Stationed at: Penzance 29.1.1872. Liskeard 24.11.1872. Truro 31.8.1877. Helston 5.2.1885. Liskeard 18.11.1891.
Removal: 10.4.1899. Pension £43.9.6. Favourable Record: for intelligence and energy when employed on special detective duty in prosecuting successfully a person selling liquor without a licence on 18.12.1897. Died at 55 Church Street, St Blazey, 22.7.1935.

P.C. 61 James Osborne
A farm labourer from Wadebridge, single aged 20 years.
Appointed: 31.10.1871.
Stationed at: Helston 2.2.1872. Penzance 21.3.1872. Liskeard 13.10.1873.
Removal: 17.12.1873. Called upon to resign for irregularities of conduct.

P.C. 92 James Hicks
A labourer from Barnstable, aged 22 single.
Appointed: 13.11.1871
Stationed at: Redruth 16.3.1872
Removal: 16.7.1872. Resigned

P.C. 151 James Lobb Kessell
A 25 year old farm labourer from St Breock.
Married Harriet Hambly from Summercourt
December 1872. Public service: Rifle
Volunteers for about four years.
Appointed: 20.11.1871
Promotion: 3.8.1873 to 2nd class Constable.
6.2.1881 to 1st class Constable.
Stationed at: Helston 11.3.1872. Truro
4.9.1873.
Removal: 2.5.1892.   Pension £24.17.1. For
one year at the end of the year to be
medically examined, if still unfit for duty.
Pension made permanent. 3.4.1893.

P.C. 133 William Hocking
A labourer from Truro, single aged 20.
Appointed: 14.12.1871.
Stationed at: Truro 4.3.1872.
Removal: 20.10.1873.   Resigned

P.C. 12 Edward Paine
A 30 year old farm Labourer from Kenwyn
Truro, single. Public service: 32nd Regiment
of Foot for 10 years.
Appointed: 8.12.1871.
Removal: 13.7.1872. Dismissed for being
drunk on duty.

P.C. 76 Samuel Lawrence
A blacksmith from Mullion, 18 years, single.
Appointed: 1.1.1872
Stationed at: Truro 20.3.1872.
Resigned. Date unknown.

P.C. 84 John Lambrick Lawrence
A 19 year old farm labourer from Mullion,
married with one child.
Appointed: 9.1.1872
Promotion: 17.12.1876 to 2nd class
Constable. 23.3.1891 to 1st class Constable
Stationed at: Helston 26.3.1872. Truro
14.10.1874. Bodmin 7.5.1893. Launceston
12.8.1896. Liskeard 3.9.1897. Truro
13.4.1898. Bodmin 26.9.1898.
Removal: 24.10.1898. Pension £41 .9.1.
Called upon to resign under medical certifi-
cate 45 years of age.

P.C. 123 Richard Warne
A shoemaker from St Germans, aged 20 single.
Appointed: 18.1.1872.
Stationed at: Bodmin 4.4.1872.
Removal: 4.7.1872. Resigned.

P.C. 54 Joseph Thomas Davey
A 22 year old farm labourer from Veryan,
Truro, Married Mary Ann Honey of St
Stephens, St Austell. May 1872.
Appointed: 22.1.1872
Stationed at: Penzance 20.3.1872
Removal: 30.3.1873. Resigned.

P.C. 38 John Hill Chadwick
A 20 year old shoemaker from Windsor,
Berks, single.
Appointed: 29.1.1872.

Promotion: 3.8.1873 to 2nd class
Constable.
Stationed at: Penzance 23.4.1872. Bodmin
8.10.1872
Removal: 3.12.1875. Resigned.

P.C. 12 John Pearce
A miner from St Mewan, St Austell, 19 years
single.
Appointed: 5.3.1872.
Promotion: 8.11.1877 to 2nd class
Constable. 28.12.1890 to 1st class Constable
Stationed at: Bodmin 20.8.1872. Helston
28.3.1873. Penzance 18.5.1881.
Removal: 13.4.1896. Pension £34.15.11.

P.C. 100 William Spry
A 27 year old farm labourer from
Launceston, single.
Appointed: 23.6.1872.
Promotion: 6.2.1876. To 2nd class
Constable
Stationed at: Bodmin 23.7.1872. Liskeard
2.7.1875.
Removal: 31.8.1882. Called on to resign.
Received character same time to this effect.
Conduct good up until the time he sent in
his resignation after which he told the Chief
Constable a deliberate falsehood and was
fined £1.0.0. And called upon to resign at
once.

P.C. William Pill Webb
A 30 year old coachman from St Austell,
married. Public service: Cornwall County
Asylum. For two and half years.
Appointed: 13.5.1872.
Removal: 16.5.1872. Called upon to resign
owing to his being in debt.

P.C. 26 William James Bawden
A farm labourer from Probus, 23 single.
Appointed: 23.11.1872
Removal: 11.6.1872. Called on to resign.

P.C. 124 William Giles
A labourer from St Columb, single aged 20.
Appointed: 21.5.1872.
Stationed at: Penzance 2.9.1872.
Removal: 19.1.1873. Resigned.

P.C. 37 William Endean
A 19 year old mason from Tregony, married
Emma Heard of Lawhitton 6.5.1874.
Public service: Cornwall Rangers Militia for 2
months.
Appointed: 10.6.1872.
Promotion: 18.11.1877 to 2nd class
Constable. 5.11.1883 to 1st class Constable.
12.1.1887 to Sergeant. 1.1.1894. To
Inspector. 13.1.1899 to Superintendent.
13.2.1904 to 1st class Superintendent.
Stationed at: Launceston 23.8.1872.
Penzance 11.2.1892. Bodmin 4.1.1894.
Lostwithiel 31.10.1895. Bodmin 1.3.1899.
Falmouth 28.11.1902.
Removal: 13.11.1907. Pension £113.6.8.

P.C. 52 Thomas Colwell
A farm labourer from Whitstone ,Stratton,
single aged 20.
Appointed: 24.6.1872.

Stationed at: Penzance 12.9.1872. Helston
11.7.1873.
Removal: 29.10.1873.   Resigned.

P.C. 157 Robert James Woodley
A mason from Stratton, aged 20 single.
Appointed: 7.8.1872.
Stationed at: Bodmin 11.11.1872.
Removal: 29.11.1872. Dismissed for being
drunk on duty.

P.C. 135 Edward Badcock
A 28 year old farm Labourer from Looe
married with two children.
Appointed: 13.8.1872.
Promotion: 13.9.1875 to 2nd class
Constable. 30.3.1885 reduced to 3rd class
Constable, for gross neglect in the discharge
of his duty. 28.12.1890 to 2nd class
Constable. 8.8.1892 to 1st Class Constable.
Stationed at: 5.11.1872 Bodmin.
Removal: 13.4.1896 to a yearly pension of
£32.6.2.

P.C. 92 John Osborne
A 23 year old farm labourer from Bideford,
married with one child. Public service:
Devon Constabulary for 1 year and 7
months.
Appointed: 19.8.1872.
Stationed at: Liskeard 3.10.1872.
Removal: 21.4.1873. Called upon to resign
for immorality.

P.C. 122 Thomas Shears
A 29 year old farm labourer from
Holsworthy, married Jane Thomas of
Whitstone 28.5.1873.
Appointed: 9.9.1872.
Stationed at: Truro 11.12.1872. Helston
27.5.1873. Penzance 21,7,1873.
Removal: 16.4.1875. Resigned

P.C. 26 George Parker
A farm labourer from St Ive, Liskeard. Aged
21, single. Public service: Preston Police for
6 months.
Appointed: 30.9.1872.
Stationed at: Bodmin 11.12.1872.
Removal: 29.10.1873. Resigned.

P.C. 34 Samuel Wills
A shoemaker from Wadebridge, aged 20
single.
Appointed: 2.10.1872
Stationed at: Penzance 30.12.1872.
Removal: 8.7.1873. Resigned.

P.C. 106 Henry Burley
A farm labourer from Tregony, aged 22 and
married with one child.
Appointed: 21.10.1872.
Stationed at: St Cleer 8.1.1873.
Removal: 21.12.1873. Resigned

P.C. 123 William Gill
A 22 year old farm labourer and game
keeper from St Erme. Married Jessie Harris
of St Erth 18.3.1876.
Appointed: 11.11.1872.
Promotion: 9.11.1875 to 2nd class
Constable. 18.6.1888 to 1st class Constable.
23.3.1891 to Sergeant. 26.2.1894 to

Inspector.
Stationed at:
Bodmin 5.1.1873. Helston 30.5.1873.
Helston 18.5.1881 Bodmin 24.3.1891.
Launceston 27.2.1894. Penzance 21.4.1897.
Falmouth 12.4.1899
Removal: 13.12.1901. Pension of £71.13.4.

P.C. 85 **William Rundle**
A miner from Liskeard aged 31 married with
two children.
Appointed: 4.11.1872
Removal: 27.11.1872. Resigned.

P.C. 21 **John Charles Nicholls**
A 21 year old fisherman from Paul,
Penzance, married Louisa Prin of Polwhele.
2.3.1880.
Appointed: 13.11.1872
Promotion: 13.9.1875 to 2nd class
Constable
Stationed at: Penzance 30.12.1872. Truro
18.11.1872.
Removal: 19.8.1881. Resigned.

P.C. 111 **Henry Clarke**
Farm labourer from Yeovil, single aged 23.
Appointed: 14.11.1872.
Stationed at: Helston 8.1.1873.
Removal: 10.7.1873. Resigned.

P.C. 75 **Nicholas Dunstan**
A blacksmith from Lelant, aged 22 married.
Appointed: 14.11.1872
Promotion: 16.12.1877 to 2nd class
Constable
Stationed at:
Bodmin 1.1.1873. Liskeard 9.10.1874.
Launceston 2.12.1875.
Removal: 9.10.1878. Resigned.

P.C. **Thomas Hawken**
A farm labourer from Quethiok, Liskeard.
Aged 20 single.
Appointed: 18.11.1872.
Removal: 27.11.1872. Resigned.

P.C. 102 **Charles Roger Grigg**
A 22 year old smelter from St Blazey. Married
with one child. Public service: Royal
Artillery, Cornwall, for 18 months.
Appointed: 25.11.1872.
Stationed at: Liskeard 30.12.1872.
Removal: 2.10.1873. Resigned.

P.C. 133 **John Evans**
A shoe maker from Jacobstow, Stratton.
Single aged 21.
Appointed: 25.12.1872.
Promotion: 9.5.1875 to 2nd class Constable
Stationed at: Liskeard 1.5.1873. Penzance
13.10.1873.
Removal: 16.9.1875. Resigned.

P.C. 19 **Peter Basher**
A 20 year farm labourer and fisherman from
Cury, Helston. Single.
Appointed: 26.11.1872.
Stationed at: Truro 26.2.1873. Bodmin
11.4.1873
Removal: 22.7.1873. Resigned.

P.C. 83 **Henry Kelly Stephens**
A farm labourer from Callington, single aged
24.
Appointed: 9.12.1872.
Promotion: 13.9.1875 to 2nd class
Constable.
Stationed at: Bodmin 26.7.1873.
Removal: 13.4.1879. Resigned.

P.C. 39 **Richard Hugo**
A farm labourer from Probus, aged 18 single.
Appointed: 9.12.1872
Stationed at: Bodmin March 1873. Helston
5.1.1875.
Removal: 9.4.1875. Dismissed for keeping
money belonging to a prisoner and denying
that he did so.

P.C. 157 **Thomas William Skewes**
A shoemaker from Cury, aged 21 married
Eliza Bray of Stithians 15.9.1874.
Appointed: 9.12.1872.
Promotion: 29.7.1877 to 2nd class
Constable. 28.12.1890 to 1st class Constable.
16.5.1895 to Sergeant.
Stationed at: Penzance 1.5.1873. Truro
26.1.1884. Bodmin 8.5.1895. Launceston
31.10.1899.
Removal: 30.9.1900. Pension £51.14.2.
Resigned under medical certificate. Died
23.12.1943.

P.C. 46 **Joseph Hodge**
Farm labourer from Cury, aged 20 single.
Appointed: 9.12.1872.
Promotion: 12.9.1877 to 2nd class
Constable. 3.11.1889 to 1st class Constable.
6.9.1891 to Sergeant.
Stationed at: Truro 1.5.1873. Penzance
13.10.1873.
Removal: 29.5.1905. Pension £55.9.4.

P.C. 85 **David Turner**
A 22 year old farm labourer from
Launceston, married Martha Luke of North
Tamerton on 6.11.1873. Public service:
Royal Cornwall Rangers Militia for 5 years.
Appointed: 27,1,1873.
Stationed at: Helston 11.7.1873. Liskeard
10.11.1873.
Removal: 12.2.1875. Called upon to resign
for inefficiency.

P.C. 96 **Henry Parnell**
A 24 year old farm labourer from Boynton,
single. Public service: South Devon Railway
for one month.
Appointed: 5.2.1873.
Removal: 18.5.1873. Resigned.
Reappointed: 19.1.1874.
Stationed at: Liskeard 19.7.1874.
Removal: 19 .4.1874 Called upon to resign.

P.C. 62 **William Brawn**
A farm labourer from Werrington,
Launceston, aged 22 ,married with one child.
Appointed: 7.1.1873.
Promotion: 9.2.1879 to 2nd class Constable
Stationed at: 10.7.1873 Launceston
Removal: 29.4.1888. Died.

P.C. 104 **Sampson Strike**
A 21 year old farm labourer from South Hill
Callington, single.
Appointment: 3.3.1873.
Removal: 14.7.1873.
7.7.1873 Fined 10/- for being found in the
porch of the H.Q. Station with a cell rug to
rest on instead of being out patrolling in the
front of the station. Resigned.

P.C. 156 **William Scantlebury**
A Farm labourer from St Germans, aged 19
single.
Appointed: 17.3.1873.
Stationed at: Bodmin 2.6.1873.
Removal: 8.7.1873. Dismissed the force
with a forfeiture of all pay due to him for
being the worse for liquor and insolent to his
superior officer.

P.C. 24 **William Dawe**
A farm labourer from Holsworthy, aged 24
married with two children.
Appointed: 24.3.1873
Promotion: 9.7.1879 to 2nd class Constable.
7.12.1884 to 1st class Constable. 17.3.1892
reduced to 2nd class Constable and to be
moved at his own expense for drinking in a
public house. 10.1.1895. To 1st class
Constable
Stationed at: Truro 27.6.1873. Bodmin
18.12.1874. Launceston 29.3.1892
Removal: 7.5.1899. Pension £41.9.1.

P.C. 54 **Thomas Barber**
A 19 year old farm labourer from
Launceston, married Annie Dymond of
Bodmin 26.4.1878.
Appointed: 24.3.1873.
Promotion: 9.7.1879 to 2nd class Constable.
28.12.1890 to 1st class Constable. 1.12.1896
to merit class Constable. 1.8.1901 to special
class constable.
Stationed at: Bodmin 20.8.1873. Penzance
24.4.1875. Truro 25.11.1886.
Removal: 30.9.1903. Pension £50.5.4.

P.C. **Walter Mutton**
A farm Labourer from Duloe, aged 24
married with two children.
Appointed: 22.4.1873.
Removal: 11.5.1873. Resigned.

P.C. 18 **William Henry Ellery**
A 20 year old miner from Lanlivet, married
Ellen Blee of Trenance Bridge, St Austell.
Public service: Manchester Police for about
3 months.
Appointed: 29.4.1873.
Promotion: 9.7.1879 to 2nd class Constable.
Stationed at: Bodmin 2.6.1873. Helston
11.12.1876.
Removal: 21.3.1883. Resigned.

P.C. 44 **Daniel Martin**
A 21 year old blacksmith from Bovey Tracey,
single. Public service: Cornwall Railway for
about one year.
Appointed: 12.5.1873.
Stationed at: Helston 31.10.1873.
Removal: 21.11.1875. Resigned.

P.C. 115 Samuel Bushcumbe
A 26 year old mariner from Egloshayle, married. Public service: Royal Naval Reserve for 5 years.
Appointed: 13.5.1873.
Promotion: 8.11.1877 to 2nd class Constable. 11.10.1876 to 1st class Constable.
Stationed at: Bodmin 3.11.1873. Liskeard 6.4.1879.
Removal: 14.6.1886. Deserted.

P.C. 28 Edward Thomas Williams
A 20 year old farm labourer from Helston, single.
Appointed: 1.7.1873.
Removal: 7.8.1873. Resigned.

P.C. 96 John Heard
A 21 year old quarryman from Tintagel, single.
Appointed: 11.7.1878.
Removal: 7.8.1873. Resigned.

P.C. 42 Alfred Nunn
An 18 year old game keeper from Newmarket, Cambs. Single.
Appointed: 25.7.1873.
Stationed at: Bodmin 31.10.1873. Liskeard 28.7.1875.
Removal: 7.6.1778. Dismissed for disgraceful conduct.

P.C. 19 William Took
A blacksmith from Milton Abbot, Devon. Aged 21 single.
Appointed: 11.8.1873.
Stationed at: Penzance 11.3.1873.
Removal: 25.12.1873. Dismissed with forfeiture of pay and taken before two magistrates and fined £1.0.0. And costs for neglect of duty.

P.C. 150 Richard Henry Bastard
At 29 year old sailor from St Germans, single. Public service: Exeter City Police and Devon County Police for 9 weeks.
Appointed: 18.7.1873.
Stationed at: Helston 18.11.1873.
Removal: 23.1.1877. Called upon to resign.

P.C. 24 William Blewett
A labourer from St Mabyn, Bodmin. Aged 24 married with one child. Public service: Cornwall Railway for two months.
Appointed: 16.9.1873.
Stationed at: Liskeard 13.1.1874
Removal: 22.8.1880. Dismissed for gross misconduct.

P.C. 104 Nicholas Sobye
A 20 year old farm labourer from Withiel.
Appointed: 16.9.1873
Stationed at: Penzance 8.1.1874
Removal: 19.9.1875. Resigned.

P.C. 111 William Frederick Sleeman
A farm labourer from St Columb. Aged 28 single.
Appointed: 29.9.1873.
Promotion: 29.7.1877 to 2nd class Constable. 3.11.1889 to 1st class Constable. 1.12.1896 to merit class Constable.
Stationed at: Truro 16.7.1874. Helston

10.1.1895.
Removal: 23.10.1899. Pension £43.9.6. Died. 1.1.1900 aged 54 years.

P.C. 12 Thomas Henry Hobb
A blacksmith and miner from St Columb. Aged 20 single.
Appointed: 6.10.1873.
Stationed at: Penzance 1.7.1874
Removal: 12.4.1878. Resigned.

P.C. 156 William Brown
A 24 year old farm labourer from Trewen, Launceston. Married with one child.
Appointed: 6.11.1873.
Promotion: 29.7.1877 to 2nd class Constable. 28.12. 1890 to 1st class Constable. 6.5.1895 to merit class Constable
Stationed at: Liskeard 26.7.1874
Removal: 11.3.1900. Pension £43.11.11.

P.C. 102 Amos Coomb Lane
A farm labourer from Linkinhorne, Callington. Aged 18 single.
Appointed: 15.12.1873
Stationed at: Penzance 2.3.1874. Truro 18.1.1875.
Removal: 12.5.1875. Dismissed with forfeiture of all pay due to him for making a false report against his superior officer.

P.C. 106 Charles Pomery
A 20 year old farm labourer from Menheniott. Married Elizabeth Ann Spear of Bodmin 27.11.1875.
Appointed: 29.12.1873
Promotion: 1.11.1879 to 2nd class Constable. 18.6.1888 to 1st class Constable. 3.9.1893 to merit class Constable 1.8.1901 to special class Constable
Stationed at: Penzance 4.1.1875. Helston 13.7.1878
Removal: 30.4.1903. Pension £50.5.4.

P.C. 19 Abraham Vanderwolf
A 20 year old farm labourer from Bodmin. Married Phillipa Bishop of Gwithian 20.3.1877.
Appointed: 19.1.1874.
Stationed at: Penzance 7.12.1874
Removal: 11.5.1877. Called upon to resign for general inefficiency.

P.C. 26 William Vartha Lukies
A 20 year old labourer from Sithney, single.
Appointed: 19.1.1874.
Stationed at: Bodmin 7.12.1874. Liskeard 29.5.1875.
Removal: 21.6.1875. Resigned.
22.11.1874 Fined 5/- for neglect of duty.

P.C. 34 Harry Chowins
A carpenter from Egloshayle. Aged 19 single,
Appointed: 20.1.1874.
Stationed at: Truro 2.3.1874. Penzance 1.3.1878
Removal: 1.4.1878   Resigned.

P.C 134 Robert Kitt
A 22 year old carpenter from Landrake, single.
Appointed: 26.1.1874

Stationed at: Truro 2.3.1874.
Removal: 3.4.1875. Called upon to resign through ill-health.

P.C. 28 John Hocking
A 21 year old labourer from Stithians,
Appointed: 26.1.1874.
Stationed at: Truro 26.3.1874. Penzance 18.1.1875.
Removal: 5.11.1876. Resigned.

P.C. 13 William Henry Thomas
Farm labourer from Endellion, Liskeard, 24 single.
Appointed: 26.1.1874.
Removal: 28.2.1874. Discovered that he had been convicted of a felony and he was sent away at once.

P.C. 61 William Asa Williams
A 21 year old miner from St Enodor, St Columb. Married 23.2.1875 to Miss M.E.Sleeman of Ladock.
Appointed: 26.1.1874
Promotion: 16.11.1879 to 2nd class Constable
Stationed at: Liskeard 29.3.1874.
Removal: 30.11.1884. Died suddenly.

P.C. 116 Christopher Yelland
A clerk from St Stephens, St Austell, 25 years single.
Appointed: 26.1.1874
Stationed at: Penzance 2.3.1874. Truro 19.4.1875. Helston 2.12.1875
Removal: 6.8.1876. Resigned.

P.C. 153 John Worden
A farm labourer from South Petherwin, aged 23 married with two children.
Appointed: 2.2.1874.
Stationed at: Liskeard 25.4.1874
Removal: 7.11.1877. Called upon to resign for inefficiency.

P.C. 92 William Hamlyn
A 19 year old farm labourer from Asburton, single.
Appointed: 5.2.1874.
Stationed at: Liskeard 22.4.1874
Removal: 14.8.1874. Resigned

P.C. 4 John Henry Mumford
A 30 year old engine driver from Canada. Single. Public service: Devon Constabulary and Rife Volunteers South Devon for 6 years.
Appointed: 6,2. 1874.

Stationed at: Bodmin 26.7.1874
Removal: 27.9.1874.

P.C. 49 John Tregwitha Bone
A fisherman from Paul, Penzance, aged 28 single. Public service: Naval Reserve for 3 weeks.
Appointed: 9.2.1874
Removal: 18.5.1874. Resigned - inefficiency.

P.C. 150 William Hawke
A 19 year old farm labourer from Lewannick, single.

Appointed: 9.2.1874
Stationed at: Helston 22.4.1874.
Removal: 31.10.1877. Resigned.

P.C. 145 John Henry Terrill
A 20 year old miner from Camborne, Single.
Appointed: 13.2.1874.
Stationed at: Helston 20.5.1874.
Removal: 30.6.1875. Resigned.

P.C. 52 James Alexander Fraser
A fisherman and gardener from Scotland, aged 32 single. Public service: 6th Comp., Inverness Volunteers for about one year.
Appointed: 16.2.1874.
Stationed at: Helston 27.4.1874.
Removal: 18.4.1874. Dismissed with a forfeiture of one weeks pay for being drunk.

P.C. 13 Thomas Woodcock
A farm labourer from St Martins , Isles of Scilly. Married aged 26.
Appointed: 25.3.1874.
Stationed at: Helston 10.11.1874. Truro 25.4.1876.
Removal: 5.10.1876. Called upon to resign for general inefficiency.

P.C. 99 Edwin Robins
A 22 year old stonecutter from St Blazey, single.
Appointed: 27.4.1874.
Removal: 3.8.1874. Resigned.

P.C. 49 Thomas Hocking
A gardener and miner from Wadebridge, aged 19 single.
Appointed: 27.5.1874.
Stationed at: Truro 20.5.1875. Penzance 21.4.1877.
Removal: 24.6.1877. Called upon the resign for general inefficiency.

P.C. 52 John Hick
A 28 year old miner from Kea, Truro. Married Rebecca Spear of Bodmin. 14.3.1876. Public service: Cornwall Railway for about 8 months.
Appointed: 10.8.1874
Stationed at: Bodmin 24.4.1875. Truro 25.8.1875
Removal: 21.9.1879. Resigned

P.C. 96 Frank Tamblyn
A warehouse man from St Columb. Aged 28 married with one child.
Appointed: 12.8.1874.
Stationed at: Truro 18.12.1874.
Removal: 1.12.1878.
8.4.1878 Fined 10/- for drinking in a public house with bad characters and without the permission of his superior officer to go into the public house to drink - called upon to resign after getting into debt.

P.C. 92 Thomas Henry Bevan
A mason from Okehampton, single aged 22. Public service: The Devon Constabulary.
Appointed: 31.8.1874.
Stationed at: Bodmin 27.7.1875.
Removal: 3.6.1877. Resigned.

P.C. 31 Edwin Peam
A 22 year old farmers son from Duloe, married with one child.
Appointed: 28.9.1874
Removal: 21.2.1875. Resigned.

P.C. 4 Thomas Hawke
A 21 year old farm labourer from Egloskerry. Married with one child.
Appointed: 26.10.1874
Stationed at: Penzance 19.4.1875.
Removal: 9.3.1879. Resigned.

P.C. 158 Martin Axworthy
A 21 year old gardener from Blisland. Married Annie Hobbs-Duke of Launceston. 10.6.1880.
Appointed: 8.12.1874.
Promotion: 6.2.1881 to 2nd class Constable
Stationed at: Bodmin 29.5.1875. Launceston 14.5.1877.
Removal: 28.9.1884. Resigned.

P.C. 85 Edward Burrows
A farm labourer from Pillaton, Callington. A 24 year old single man.
Appointed: 18.2.1875.
Promotion: 29.7.1877 to 2nd class Constable.
Stationed at: Helston 16.7.1875. Bodmin 2.5.1876
Removal: 14.12.1877. Resigned.

P.C. 31 Philip Kent
A 27 year old farm labourer from St Columb Minor, married with two children. Public service: Cornwall Railway for 7 weeks.
Appointed: 26.2.1875.
Stationed at: Bodmin 12.7.1875.
Removal: 8.7.1877. Resigned.

P.C. 134 Peter Doney
A 21 year old farm labourer from Lewannick. Married Mary Green of St Mawes 6.6.1877. Public service: Plymouth Police for 11 weeks.
Promotion: 16.11.1879 to 2nd class Constable. 3.11.1889 to 1st class Constable. 23.3.1899. To merit class Constable. 1.8.1901 to special class Constable
Stationed at: Bodmin 30.8.1875. Helston 15.8.1876. Bodmin 13.12.1881.
Removal: 31.1.1905. Pension £50.5.4. Favourable record for zeal and intelligence for tracing and prosecuting to conviction three offenders in a case of fowl stealing. 7.2.1898.

P.C. 146 George Bennett
A 22 year old farm labourer from Bodmin, married Elizabeth Chapple of St Columb. 6.11.1877.
Appointed: 6.4.1875.
Removal: 13.9.1885.
Reappointed: 1.4.1889 as P.C. 172.
Promotion: 27.7.1877 to 2nd class Constable. 28.12.1890 to 2nd class Constable. 24.1.1892 to 1st class Constable. 12.3.1900 to Merit class Constable. 1.11.1904 to special class Constable.
Removal: 13.6.1906. Pension £50.5.4. George Bennett, P.C. 146 joined the Cornwall Constabulary, 6.4.1875 and served

until 13.9.1885, being 10 years and 5 months. He then joined the Penryn Borough Police Force and served from 13.9.1885 to 1.4.1889 being 3 years six months and 12 days. On April 1st, 1889 he rejoined the Cornwall Constabulary his number then changed to P.C. 172.

P.C. 39 John Liddicoat
A 20 year old gardener from St Austell married Mary Bunney of Polmassick Sept 1875. Married Jane Lanyon of Lelant.
Appointed: 12.4.1875.
Promotion: 15.11.1879 to 2nd class Constable. 23.3.1891 to 1st class Constable. 1.8.1901 to special class constable.
Removal: 31.3.1905. Pension £50.5.4. 1.11.1895 Fined 10/- for being absent from his conference point and making a false entry in his journal.

P.C. 122 Richard Retallick
A 25 year old farm labourer from St Columb, married with one child.
Appointed: 26.4.1875
Promotion: 25.7.1881 to 2nd class Constable
Stationed at: Truro 25.11.1875.
Removal: 11.9.1890. Resigned

P.C. 102 William Henry Nicholls
A 21 year old farm labourer from Looe, married Elizabeth Mary Hugo, of Liskeard. 7.5.1881. Public service East Cornwall Railway for 7 months.
Appointed: 10.5.1875.
Promotion: 8.11.1877 to 2nd class Constable. 27.7.1881. To 1st class Constable. 1.12.1890 to Sergeant Major. 22.5.1894 to Inspector. 1.3.1899 to Superintendent. 1.3.1904 to 1st class Superintendent.
Stationed at: Bodmin H.Q. 1.12.1875. Bodmin/St Austell 8.6.1894. Launceston 1.3.1899.
Removal: 31.10.1905. Pension £106.13.4. Favourable record: 19.10.1899 For zeal and promptitude in detecting and prosecuting successfully in a case of robbery from the dwelling house.

P.C. 59 Henry Burnard
A 28 year old farm labourer from Bridgerule, Holsworthy, married Mary Yelland of Bridgewater 27.4.1876. Since dead then married Louisa Ham of Exminster Asylum.
Appointed: 17.5.1875
Promotion: 2.4.1883 to 2nd class constable. 24.1.1892 to 1st class Constable. 26.11.1898 to merit class Constable. 1.8.1900 to special class Constable
Stationed at: 21.9.1875 Penzance
Removal: 25.12.1901 Pension £50.5.4.

P.C. 152 Joseph Tippett
A 24 year old shoemaker from Padstow, married Mary Joliff of Jacobstow, 26.10.1875. Married Mary Rule of Redruth, 26.3.1886.
Appointed: 17.5.1875.
Promotion: 27.7.1881 to 2nd class Constable. 28.10.1895 to 1st class Constable. 1.8.1901 to special class Constable.
Stationed at: Helston 24.4.1876. Penzance

13.7.1878.
Removal: 30.9.1902. Pension £50.5.4.

P.C. 26 Thomas Kingdom
A 27 year old miner from Linkinhorne, married Eliza Hicks of Linkinhorne, 30.12.1875.
Appointed: 28.6.1875
Promotion: 16.11.1879 to 2nd class Constable
Stationed at: Launceston 22.1.1876.
Removal: 13 .2.1881.   Resigned.

P.C. 145 Thomas Freethy
A 21 year old miner from St Hilary, married Elizabeth Ann Coad of Rinsey, Breage. 27.12.1875.
Appointed: 19.7.1875.
Stationed at: Helston 4.1.1876.
Removal: 25.10.1876. Dismissed with a forfeiture of pay for drinking in a public house with bad characters.

P.C. 144 John Woodridge
A 25 year old minesmith from Calstock, single.
Appointed: 12.8.1875.
Stationed at: Bodmin 4.1.1876.
Removal: 30.9.1877. Resigned.

P.C. 133 William Wivill
A 24 year old farm labourer from Devon, married Elizabeth Langdon of Bodmin 8.7.1876. Public service: Devon Constabulary for about 12 months.
Appointed: 20.9.1875
Promotion: 13.11.1882 to 2nd class Constable. 28.12.1890 to 1st class Constable. 14.2.1898 to merit class Constable. 29.9.1901 to special class Constable.
Stationed at: Penzance 3.1.1876.
Removal: 21.12.1902. Pension £51.5.4.

P.C. 104 Luke Boundy
A miner from Launceston, married with two children.
Appointed: 20.9.1875.
Promotion: 13.11.1882 to 2nd class Constable. 1.12.1890 to 1st class Constable. 1.1.1900 to merit class Constable. 29.9 1901 to special class Constable.
Stationed at: Launceston 24.4.1876.
Removal: 13.8.1904. Pension £50.5.4.

P.C. 63 James Kingdom
A 23 year old farm labourer from Linkinhorne, widower. Married Ann Hancock. 30.9.1897.
Appointed: 18.11.1875
Promotion: 9.7.1879 to 2nd class Constable. 28.12.1890 1st class Constable. 23.11.1896 merit class Constable. 9.11.1901 special class Constable.
Stationed at: Liskeard 14.10.1876
Removal: 29.9.1904. Pension £50.5.4.

P.C. 77 Richard Vickel Kittow
A farm labourer from Alternun, married Annie Slanderwick of Axminster, Somerset 23.9.1885.
Appointed: 27.9.1875.
Promotion: 6.11.1879 to 2nd class

Constable. 4.11.1888 to 1st class Constable. 6.11.1891 to Sergeant. 20.4.1894 to Inspector.
Stationed at: Bodmin 29.1.1876. Launceston 1.5.1883. Bodmin 13.1.1891
Removal: 31 3 1909. Pension £71.13.4.
Favourable record: 7.2.1898 Zeal and intelligence in tracing and prosecuting to conviction of three offenders in a case of fowl stealing. 14.6.1898 Zeal and intelligence in tracing and prosecuting successfully a burglar.

P.C. 44 Thomas Bryant
A 21 year old farm labourer from Wadebridge, married Mary Wyatt of St Kew Highway on 10.2.1880. Married Mary Jane Tonkin of Tregony, 10.11.1890.
Appointed: 22.11.1875.
Promotion: 1.11.1879 to 2nd class Constable. 28.12.1890 to 1st class Constable. 26.10.1896 to merit class Constable. 1.7.1903 to special class Constable.
Stationed at: Truro 3.7.1877. Launceston 6.7.1878. Liskeard 4.9.1880.
Removal: 31.10.1903. Pension   £50.5.4.

P.C. 135 Thomas Kendall
A 31 year old farmer from St Columb, married with four children. Public service: Duke of Cornwall Rifle Volunteers for 5 years.
Appointed: 13.12.1875.
Promotion: 6.7.1881 to 2nd class Constable. 28.12.1890 to 1st class Constable.
Stationed at: Bodmin 19.8.1876. Launceston 1.7.1889.
Removal: 7.2.1901 Pension £41.11.4

P.C. 38 Benjamin Phillips
A 24 year old hedger from Gwithian, married Caroline LeCorrse of Jacobstow 20.6.1880. Public service: West Cornwall Railway for 4 months.
Appointed: 13.12.1875.
Promotion: 17.7.1881 to 2nd class Constable
Stationed at: Bodmin 15.8.1876. Launceston 19.6.1879.
Removal: 13.9.1885. Resigned.

P.C. 130 William Hewitt
A 20 year old blacksmith from St Tudy, Bodmin. Married Harriet Chegwiddon of Helston 6.6.1878.
Appointed: 31.1.1876.
Stationed at: Helston 13.1.1877. Penzance 19.10.1877
Removal: 3.5.1883. Resigned.
P.C. 35 John Pearn
A 20 year old railway porter from Duloe, Liskeard, single. Public service: East Cornwall Railway for one year seven months.
Appointed: 29.2.1876.
Removal: 11.7.1876. Called upon to resign.

P.C. 76 Frank Richards Smallcombe
A 22 year old farm labourer from Liskeard, married Tryphena Spear of Bodmin 26.9.1881.
Appointed: 11.7.1876.
Promotion: 6.2.1881 to 2nd class Constable. 4.11.1888 to 1st class Constable. 19.4.1891 to Sergeant. 22.5.1894 to Sergeant Major.

2.8.1897 to Inspector.
Stationed at: Bodmin 4.1.1877. Launceston 5.5.1891. Bodmin 24.4.1894. Launceston 3.8.1897. Camborne 3.12.1901. Launceston 13.5.1904.
Removal: 11.6.1914.   Pension £76.13.4.
Favourable Record. 24.3.1900 intelligence and promptitude in detecting and arresting three fowl stealers.

P.C. 35 Alfred Sturtridge
A 21 year old clay labourer from St Blazey, single.
Appointed: 25.7.1876
Stationed at: Penzance 6.7.1877.
Removal: 6.1.1879. Resigned.

P.C. 116 John Richards
A miner from Calstock, aged 19 single. Public service: Duke of Cornwall Rifle Volunteers 5th Corps. For three years.
Appointed: 21.8.1876.
Stationed at: Truro 16.4.1877.
Removal: 25.11.1877. Resigned.

P.C. 13 Richard Mitchell
A miner from Cubert, aged 21 married.
Appointed: 16.10.1876
Stationed at: Bodmin 15.3.1877.
Removal: 24.7.1881. Resigned.

P.C. 88 John Henry Ball
A 22 year old gardener from St Allen, Truro. Married Mary Jenkin of St Austell 25.3.1878. Public service: London and South Western Railway for one month.
Appointed: 15.11.1876.
Promotion: 27.7.1881. To 2nd class Constable. 28.12.1890 to 1st class Constable. 26.10.1896 to merit class Constable.
Stationed at: Bodmin 16.5.1877. Liskeard 26.11.1877.
Removal: 31.1.1905. Pension £46.16.0.

P.C. 28 Ammos Williams
A farm labourer from St Stephens, St Austell, 19 single. Public service; East Cornwall Railway for seven months.
Appointed: 18.12.1876.
Stationed at: Penzance 25.7.1877. Liskeard 9.7.1879.
Removal: 2.5.1880. Resigned.

P.C. 145 Jeremiah Bond
A gentleman's servant from St Columb, aged 20 single.
Appointed: 30.10.1876.
Stationed at: Liskeard 16.4.1877.
Removal: 2.9.1877 . Dismissed the force for being drunk.

P.C. 159 John Henry Boulden
Aged 20 a farm servant from Mylor.
Appointed: 8.1.1877.
Resigned 14.1.1878.
Reappointed: 24.9.1879.
Stationed at: Penzance 25.7.1877. Bodmin 15.1.1880.
Removal: 14.3.1880. Dismissed with the forfeiture of a weeks pay for being in a public house for three hours when he should have been on duty.

P.C. 149 **George Harris**
A farm labourer from St Agnes, aged 23 married with one child.
Appointed: 30.1.1877.
Stationed at: Liskeard 29.10.1877.
Removal: 1.5.1881. Resigned.

P.C. 6 **John Barber**
A 22 year old labourer and butcher from Linkinhorne, Married Catheryn Matthews of Porthallow, 10.9.1885.
Appointed: 26.2.1877.
Stationed at: Helston 19.10.1877.
Removal: 2.6.1878. Resigned.
Reappointed: as P.C. 96. 2.12.1878.
Promotion: 2.4.1883 to 2nd class Constable. 24.1.1892 to 1st class Constable. 24.10.1898 to 1st class Constable.
Stationed at: Truro 9.1.1879. Launceston 28.10.1881. Helston 7.11.1882.
Removal: 24.6.1905. Pension £45.1.4. 9.11.1895. P.C. 96 John Barber was reduced to 2nd class Constable for being absent from his conference point, making a false entry in his journal and telling his Superintendent falsehoods. 11.12.1900. P.C. John Barber was fined £1.0.0. For being drunk on duty on the 6th inst at Helston and also warned as to his future conduct in the Force.

P.C. 19 **Richard Benny**
A blacksmith from St Clements, Truro, aged 19 single.
Appointed: 17.5.1877.
Stationed at: Helston 7.11.1877. Bodmin 16.4.1881.
Removal: 25.9.1881. Resigned.

P.C. 92 **George William Williams**
A 25 year old farm labourer from Mawgan, Helston. Married Elizabeth A .Irwin of Callington, 16.7.1878.
Appointed: 11.6.1877.
Stationed at: Liskeard 7.11.1877.
Removal: 2.2.1885. Resigned

P.C. 49 **Albert Jewells**
An 18 year old miner from Lostwithiel Married Annie Kessell of Lostwithiel. 6.12.1872.
Appointed: 30.6.1877
Promotion: 18.6.1888 to 2nd class Constable. 4.10.1891 to 1st class Constable. 1.8.1901 to merit class Constable.
Stationed at: Helston 19.10.1877. Bodmin 13.4.1882. Penzance 23.10.1882.
Removal: 23.12 1910. Pension £46.16.0. 29.6.1882. Fined 10/- for being absent from his conference point and the worse for liquor.

P.C. 31 **Walter Couch**
A 27 year old butcher from Launceston, married with two children.
Appointed: 10.7.1877.
Promotion: 11.10.1886 to 2nd class Constable. 9.8.1891 to 1st class Constable. 24.10.1898 to merit class Constable. 1.8.1903 to special class Constable.
Stationed at: Liskeard 7.11.1877.
Removal: 15.10.1906. Pension £50.5.4.

P.C. 160 **William Henry Pollard**
A 21 year old farm labourer from Liskeard. Married Eva Hamley of Bodmin 23.3.1882.
Appointed: 16.7.1877.
Stationed at: Bodmin 6.7.1888
Removal: 28.3.1885. Resigned.
Reappointed: 9.11.1885
Promotion: 23.3.1891 to 2nd class Constable. 23.11.1896. To 1st class Constable. 1.2.1905 to merit class Constable
Stationed at: Bodmin 1.11.1885. Truro 26.9.1898.
Removal: 31.3.1908. Pension £46.16.0.

P.C. 161 **John Henry Strike**
A 26 year old miner from Stoke Climsland, married with one child.
Appointed: 23.7.1877.
Stationed at: Bodmin 26.11.1877.
Removal: 17.2.1880. Resigned.

P.C. 162 **Benjamin Coad**
A 27 year old carpenter from Bodmin married with one child. Public Service. Volunteers at Jarrow for one year.
Appointed: 6.9.1877
Promotion: 13.11.1882 to 2nd class Constable
Removal: 5.5.1886. Died.

P.C. 145 **William Henry Bunney**
A farm labourer from St Ewe, married Mary May of Gulval 21.3.1882.
Appointed: 14.9.1877.
Stationed at: Penzance 5.4.1878. Bodmin 1.7.1880.
Removal: 10.8.1883. Resigned.

P.C. 144 **John Thomas Penrose**
A 26 year old miner from St Just. Single.
Appointed: 1.10.1877.
Stationed at: Bodmin 13.4.1878. Penzance 1.7.1880.
Removal: 28.11.1880. Resigned.

P.C. 156 **Charles Spark**
A 25 year old farm labourer from Alternun, married Margretta Steer of Padstow. 16.11.1881.
Appointed: 6.11.1877.
Promotion: 27.7.1881 to 2nd class Constable. 4.11.1888 to 1st class Constable. 4.10.1891 to Sergeant. 24.10.1898 to Inspector. 19.11.1904 to Superintendent. 19.11.1909 to 1st class Superintendent.
Stationed at: Bodmin 12.4.1878. Launceston 4.10.1891. Bodmin 11.3. 1894. Liskeard 8.5.1895. Falmouth 25.10.,1898. Camborne 12.4.1899. Bodmin 18.11.1904. Truro 29.09.1905.
Removal: 30.9.1920. Pension £306.13.4.

P.C. 150 **John Knight**
A miner from Warleggan, aged 21 married with one child.
Appointed: 5.11.1877.
Stationed at: Launceston 15.4.1878.
Removal: 20.3.1882. Resigned.

P.C. **William Box**
A labourer from Launceston aged 19 single.
Appointed: 12.11.1877.

Removal: 19.11.1878. Called on to resign- not suitable for a Police Constable.

P.C. 142 **Richard Meagor**
A 19 year old miner from St Austell, single. Public Service Artillery Volunteers at Charlestown for 12 months.
Appointed: 12.11.1877.
Stationed at: Penzance 10.4.1878.
Removal: 3.11.1878. Resigned.

P.C. 57 **Edward John Thomas**
A 20 year old labourer from Budock. Public Service. Cornwall Railway for a short time.
Appointed: 12.11.1877.
Stationed at: Liskeard 16.5.1878.
Removal: 1.5.1881. Resigned..
Reappointed: 1.5.1889. On his return from America
Removal 11.8.1889. Resigned.

P.C. 14 **John Thomas Rowe**
A 21 year old farm labourer from Ruan Highlanes, Married Maria Rowse of Penvergate, Govian, 12.2.1879.
Appointed: 26.11.1877.
Promotion: 7.12.1884 to 2nd class Constable. 28.12.1890 to 1st class Constable. 13.10.1894. To Sergeant. 1.3.1899 to Inspector.
Stationed at: Penzance 14.5.1878. Bodmin 13.7.1879. Liskeard 23.11.1894. Bodmin 2.3.1899. Liskeard 1.7.1903. **Removal:** 30.6.1909
Pension £71.13.4.

P.C. 67 **William Henry Cobb**
A 22 year old cooper of St Pinnock.
Appointed: 4.1.1878.
Stationed at: Penzance 16.9.1879.
Removal: 22.11.1980 Resigned.
Reappointed: 16.5.1881. As P.C. 149.
Stationed at: Liskeard 20.6.1881.
Removal: 3.7.1886. Killed on the railway at Wivilscomb viaduct at St Stephens by Saltash.

P.C. 34 **John Mitchell**
A farm labourer from Cubert, aged 20 single.
Appointed: 3.4.1878.
Stationed at: Penzance 13.7.1879.
Removal: 28.12.1879. Resigned.

P.C. 98 **Symon Thomas Kent**
A 22 year old miner from Linkinhorne. Married with one child.
Appointed: 15.4.1878.
Removal: 6.3.1879. Dismissed for being drunk on duty.

P.C. 159 **William Robert Dennis**
A carpenter from Launceston. Married Bathsheba Blight of Blackwater, Scorrier. 5.10.1880.
Appointed: 15.4.1878.
Stationed at: Penzance 15.3.1879.
Removal: 1.12.1880. Called upon to resign, his eyesight was so bad he could not see his way about.

P.C. **William John Lenderyon**
Appointed: 15.4.1878.
Removal: 2.5.1878. Resigned.

P.C. 12 John David Menheer
A 20 year old farm labourer from Egloshayle, married Georgina Clemens of Hayle 6.10.1880.
Appointed: 6.5.1878.
Promotion: 18.6.1888 to 2nd class Constable. 21.1.1892 to 1st class Constable. 1.10.1900 to merit class Constable.
Stationed at: Penzance 5.11.1878.
Removal: 31.10.1907. Pension £46.16.0. 29.6.1879 Fined 10/- and moved at his own expense for neglect of duty and making a false entry in his journal. 4.11.1888 Fined £1.0.0. For gross neglect of duty.

P.C. 41 Harry Endean
A valet from Tregony aged 20 year single.
Appointed: 13,5,1878.
Stationed at: Liskeard 13.2.1879.
Removal: 6.7.1879. Resigned.

P.C. 42 William Smallcombe
A 28 year old farm labourer of Liskeard, married Elizabeth Stephens of Camborne, 9.10.1880.
Appointed: 4.6.1878.
Promotion: 2.4.1883 to 2nd class Constable.
Stationed at: Penzance 15.3.1879. Helston 30.8.1880.
Removal: 17.9.1890. Died. His widow received a gratuity of £28.16.4. On the 13.10.1890.

P.C. 6 William Grose
A 28 year old farm labourer from Roche. Married with one child.
Appointed: 10.6.1878.
Promotion: 5.11.1883 to 2nd class Constable. 9.8.1891 to 1st class Constable. 1.8.1907 to merit class Constable.
Stationed at: Bodmin 28.10.1878. Launceston 28.3.1881
Removal: 31.10.1904. Pension £46.16.0.

P.C. 10 Richard Sparks
A 19 year old farm labourer from Alternun. Married Sarah Varker of Copperhouse, Hayle, 14.11.1882.
Appointed: 25 9.1878.
Promotion: 18.6.1888 to 2nd class Constable. 9.8.1891 to 1st class Constable. 1.1.1901 to merit class Constable.
Stationed at: Penzance 15.3.1879. Liskeard 23.10.1882.
Removal: 4.3.1907. Died.

P.C. 75 Thomas Bennetts
A 22 year old miner from Sancreed, Penzance, Single. Public .Service. Rifle and Artillery Volunteers for about eight years.
Appointed: 8.10.1878.
Stationed at: Helston 4.6.1879. Bodmin 19.6.1879
Removal: 15.9.1880. Resigned.
Reappointed: 14.10.1880 as P.C. 67.
Stationed at: Helston 27.10.1880.
Removal: 9.3.1883. Resigned.

P.C. 142 Richard Glanville
A 19 year old farm labourer from Ruan, Truro, single.

Appointed: 4.5.1878.
Stationed at: Bodmin 17,4,1879.
Removal: 14.12.1879. Resigned.

P.C. 163 Daniel Olford
A 21 year old farm labourer from Fowey.
Appointed: 18.11.1878.
Stationed at: Helston 4.6.1879. Liskeard 19.6.1879.
Removal: 6.3.1882 Resigned.

P.C. 98 Samuel Tonkin
A 21 year old farm labourer from Menheniot, married Emma Jane Matthews of St Cleer. 7.8.1880. Public.Service. South Devon Railway for 12 months.
Appointed: 10.3.1879.
Promotion: 18.6.1888 to 2nd class Constable. 27.11.1892 to 1st class Constable. 1.10.1901 to merit class Constable
Stationed at: Penzance 31.7.1879. Helston 1.2.1883. Liskeard 18.5.1897. Launceston 6.9.1899.
Removal: 31.8.1907. Pension £46.16.0.

P.C. 83 John Barrett
A 24 year old clay labourer from St Austell. Single.
Appointed: 17.3.1879.
Stationed at: Launceston 31.7.1879.
Removal: 16.11.1879. Resigned.

P.C. 35 Abraham Spear
A coachsmith from Bodmin, aged 24 single.
Appointed: 7.1.1879.
Stationed at: Liskeard 13.6.1880.
Removal: 4.3.1883. Resigned

P.C. 112 Digory Ayers.
A 20 year old farm labourer from Bude, married Mary L.May of Penryn, late of Camborne. 5.8.1881. Was married at Illogan Church to Mary Burgan of Pool. 25.2.1904.
Appointed: 31.3.1879.
Promotion: 11.10.1886 to 2nd class Constable. 9.8.1891 to 1st class Constable. 1.10.1901. To merit class Constable.
Removal: 31.1.1909 Pension £46.16.0.
Re-engaged 18.10.1915
Resigned 30.4.1919.

P.C. 68 Henry Cowling
A 26 year old powder mill worker from St Austell, widower. Remarried G.Carlyon of Camborne 4.2.1885.
Appointed: 7.4.1879.
Promotion: 7.12.1884. To 2nd class Constable. 28.12.1890 to 1st class Constable. 1.8.1901 to merit class Constable. 1.5.1905 placed in special class.
Stationed at: Penzance 7.8.1879. Helston 11.10.1892
Removal: 30.9.1906 Pension £50.5.4.

P.C. 55 and 116 William Rowe
A 22 year old farm labourer from St Breok. Married Mary M.Kemp Berryman of Madron, 15.11.1884.
Appointed: 7.4.1879
Promotion: 5.11.1883 to 2nd class Constable. 23.3.1891 to 1st class Constable. 20.4.1894 to Sergeant. 13.10.1894 reduced

to 1st class Constable for gross irregularity. 26.10.1896 to Sergeant.
Stationed at: Penzance 15.1.1880. Bodmin 24,4,1894. Launceston 11.10.1894. Liskeard 23.10.1894
Removal: 18.12.1905 Died. Gratuity to widow of £180.0.0 Testimonials returned to widow,

P.C. 4 Alfred Dobb
A 20 year old miner from Duloe, single.
Appointed: 21.4.1879.
Stationed at: Helston 5.11.1879. Penzance 26.1.1882
Removal: 13.8.1882. Resigned.
February 1882 fined 10/- for associating with prostitutes.

P.C. 41 John Wroath
A 25 year old quarryman from Stonehouse, married with two children.
Appointed: 21.7.1879.
Stationed at: Launceston 24.11.1879
Removal: 3.9.1884. Called upon to resign by the Chief Constable for being in debt and never likely to make an efficient Constable.

P.C. 17 William Henry Stephens
A 24 year old miller from Stithians married with two children.
Appointed: 24.7.1879.
Promotion: 11.1.1886. To 2nd class Constable.
Stationed at: Truro 24.11.1879
Bodmin 2.12.1880
Removal: 13.10.1886. Dismissed for being drunk on duty.

P.C. 114 Thomas Prout
A 21 year old miner from St Agnes. Single.
Appointed: 28.7.1879.
Stationed at: Bodmin 15.1.1880.
Removal: 5.10.1880. Dismissed the force for gross immorality.

P.C. 40 John Leggo
A 22 year old miner from St Just, single. Public Service. Rife Volunteers of St Just for five years.
Appointed: 13.10.1879.
Stationed at: Bodmin 6.5.1880.
Removal: 29.4.1883 Resigned

P.C. 29 Daniel Miller
A 20 year old gardener from Sidmouth, widower. Married on 20.8.1895 to B.M.Brush a native of Tintagel. Lived 10 months at Liskeard.
Appointed: 31.10.1879
Promotion: 2.4.1883 to 2nd class Constable. 28.12.1890 to 1st class Constable. 8.8.1892 to Sergeant. 8.7.1895 to Inspector.
Stationed at: Liskeard 6.5.1880. Helston 1.8.1882. Penzance 26.10.1890. Truro 21.4.1897. Liskeard 10.1.1902. Bodmin 1.7.1903.
Removal: 13.7.1910. Pension £71.13.4. On 18.12.1908 Inspector Daniel Miller was severely censored by the Chief Constable and warned for dismissal for communicating with a fire insurance company with a view to obtaining money.

P.C. 83 Thomas Henry Roberts
A 20 year old miner from St Agnes, single.
Appointed: 17.11.1879.
Stationed at: Liskeard 13.4.1880
Removal: 24.4.1881. Resigned.
Reappointed: 25.7.1881
Stationed at: Bodmin 7.1.1881.
Removal: 29.9.1885. Resigned.

P.C. 85 William Ellery Meagor
A 22 year old porter (Queens Hotel,
Penzance) from St Breock. On 5.5.1884
married A. Holman of Camborne who died
in 1889. Remarried M.Wellington of Truro
12.8.1890.
Promotion: 7.12.1884. To 2nd class
Constable. 4.10.1891 to 1st class Constable.
1.10.1901 to merit class Constable.
Stationed at: Penzance 11.6.1880.
Removal: 31.5.1907. Pension £46.16.0.
Copy of G.O.31.10.1902. P.C. 85 William
E.Meagor was on the 16 inst, fined 10/- for
breach of confidence relative to a matter
which came to his knowledge only as a
Constable and 10/- for making a false statement in connection therewith.

P.C. 34 Joseph Pearce
A labourer from St Stephens by Launceston,
aged 22 years , married with one child
Appointed: 24.12.1879
Stationed at: Liskeard 11.6.1880.
Removal: 30.3.1882. Dismissed for being
drunk on duty.

P.C. 142 Thomas Folley Sheer
A 23 year old miller from Jacobstow, single.
Appointed: 29.12.1879.
Stationed at: Liskeard 6.5.1880.
Removal: 20.6.1886. Resigned.

P.C. 161 Richard Gearrons
A 25 year old mason from Stoke Climsland,
married with two children. Public.Service.
Volunteers 5th Comp., Callington, for two
years.
Appointed: 25.2.1880.
Stationed at: Bodmin 9.9.1880.
Removal: 13.10.1886. Dismissed for being
the worse for liquor.

P.C. 52 Samuel Dawe
A blacksmith from Boscastle, single aged 20.
Public Service. Volunteers 19th Comp.,
Camelford for about three months.
Appointed: 22.3.1880.
Removal: 20.8.1880   Dismissed with a
forfeiture of a weeks pay for gross misconduct.

P.C. 16 Alfred Webber
A 20 year old farm labourer from Liskeard,
married Rosina James of Camborne
13.8.1884.
Appointed: 14.4.1880.
Promotion: 17.12.1884 to 2nd class
Constable. 28.12.1890 to 1st Class
Constable. 17.12.1891 to Sergeant.
23.10.1899 to Inspector. 1.11.1905 to
Superintendent.
Stationed at: Penzance 4.9.1880. Bodmin
19.12.1891. Penzance 4.1.1894. Launceston
23.12.1894. Bodmin 1.12.1903. Launceston
1.11.1905. Record incomplete.

P.C. John M.Thomas
A 23 year old farm labourer from St Austell,
single.
Appointed: 9.4.1880.
Removal: 6.5.1880. Resigned.

P.C. 28 George Wallis
A 21 year old farm labourer from St Ive,
single. Public Service. Dorset Constabulary
for about one month.
Appointed: 3.5.1880.
Stationed at: Penzance 30.8.1880.
Removal: 21 8 1881. Resigned.

P.C. 110 John Pearce
A 27 year old shoe maker from St Ive. Single.
Public Service. 83rd., Regt., of Foot for 6
years 6 months.
Appointed: 8.5.1880.
Stationed at: Bodmin 27,10.1880.
Removal: 10.4.1881   Resigned.

P.C. 51 John Haley
A 20 year old farm Labourer from
Grampound, Married on 17.3.1888. To
Catheryn Maynard of Stratton who died
20.5.1894. Married 1.2.1899 Mary Venning
of Five Lanes.
Appointed: 24.8.1880.
Promotion: 11.1.1886 to 2nd class
Constable. 9.8.1891 to 1st class Constable.
10.8.1901 to merit class Constable.
Stationed at: Launceston 17.11.1880
Removal: 3.8.1910 Pension £46.16.0.
Favourable record 21.12.1899 Intelligence
and promptitude on pursuing and arresting a
notorious swindler who was prosecuted to
conviction.
Died 12.1.1911.

P.C. 52 Charles Hill
A 20 year old wheelwright from St Austell,
single. Public.Service. 4th Duke of Cornwall
Volunteers.
Appointed: 26.8.1880.
Removal: 10.9.1880. Resigned.

P.C. 118 Moses Evans
A 20 year old carpenter from Jacobstow,
single.
Appointed: 20.8.1880.
Stationed at: Helston 16.4.1881.
Removal: 7.1.1883. Resigned.

P.C. 24 Henry Osborne
A whip maker from Launceston, aged 24
years & married with one child.
Appointed: 21.8.1880
Stationed at: Bodmin 24.3.1881. Liskeard
16.3.1882.
Removal: 12.11.1882. Dismissed for
encouraging a boy to steal his masters
mangos, also for gross immoralities.

P.C. 67 Edmund Richards
A 20 year old granite labourer from St
Austell, single. Public.Service. 9th Duke of
Cornwall Volunteers for 18 months.
Appointed: 31.8.1880.
Removal: 1.10.1880. Resigned.

P.C. 52 Richard Carne
A 19 year old farm labourer from Newlyn
East, St Columb, single.
Appointed: 13.9.1880.
Stationed at: Bodmin 29.11.1880. Liskeard
7.1.1881.
Removal: 27.6.1881. Resigned.

P.C. 75 Thomas Buscombe
Aged 21 a labourer from St Issey.
Public Service. Duke of Cornwall's for 6
months.
Appointed: 20.9.1880.
Stationed at: Penzance 29.11.1880. Helston
3.11.1881. Bodmin 20.11.1883.
Removal: 22.8.1884   Called upon to resign.

P.C. 114 John Harris
A 21 year old farm labourer from
Menheniott, single.
Appointed: 4.10.1880
Stationed at: Bodmin 13.5.1881. Launceston
16.5.1888.
Removal: 13.11.1888. Dismissed for drunkenness on duty. 9.11.1884 Fined 5/- for
being absent from his conference point.
1.3.1885. Fined 10/- for being absent from
his beat.

P.C. 144 William Gard
A 21 year old labourer from St Minver married.
Appointed: 6.12.1880.
Promotion: 4.11.1888 to 2nd., class
Constable. 9.8.1891 to 1st class Constable.
2.8.1897 to Sergeant. 1.11.1905 to
Inspector. 1.12.1907 to Superintendent.
Stationed at:
Liskeard 4.6.1881. Bodmin 19.6.1896.
Truro 23.12.1897. Liskeard 2.3.1899.
Bodmin 9.5.1899. Falmouth 1.10.1902.
Liskeard 1.10.1903. Bodmin 1.11.1905.
Liskeard 11.11.1908.
Removal: 31.12.1920. Pension £306.13.4.
Favourable Record. For intelligence and
energy in detecting and prosecution success-
fully in a case of aggravated assault on a
female. 4.12.1898. Died 23.2.1941.

P.C. 159 Henry Walkey
A 24 year old cooper from St Austell,
married with one child. Public.Service.
Charlestown Artillery Volunteers for 4 years.
Appointed: 13.12.1880.
Removal: 23.3.1881. Dismissed with the
forfeiture of a weeks pay for bringing an
unfounded charge against Sergeant Major
Piddock.

P.C. 26 John Gill
A 23 year old farm labourer from Padstow,
married 29.11.1881 to Sarah Ellen Bidrick of
St Issey, who died. Remarried 21.4.1884
M.Wonnacott of Bude. Public Service. No1
Batt., Cornwall Artillery Volunteers for two
years.
Appointed: 28.3.1881.
Promotion: 4.11.1888 to 2nd class
Constable. 1.12.1890 to 1st, class Constable.
!.8.1901 to merit class Constable.
Stationed at: Liskeard 5.7.1881. Helston
30.1.1884.
Removal: 25.3.1908 Pension £46.16.0.

P.C. 120 John Marks
A 21 year old farm labourer from
Menheniott, single.
Appointed: 21.3.1881
Stationed at: Bodmin 11.7.1881. Liskeard
24.11.1881 Penzance 6.5.1882
Removal: 9.3.1883. Resigned.

P.C. 159 Joseph Cock
An 18 year old miner from St Agnes, Married
4.11.1888 to Mary Chenoweth of Bolster, St
Agnes.
Appointed: 4.4.1881.
Promotion: 3.11.1889 to 2nd class
Constable. 1.10.1893. To 1st class Constable.
1.10.1901 to merit class Constable.
Stationed at: Liskeard 9.8.1881.
Removal: 7.4.1907.   Pension £45.1.4.
20.9.1897 Reduced to 2nd class Constable
and transferred at his own expense from
Cargreen to St Neot on the 24.9.1897. Died
21.2.1941.

P.C. 110 John Edward Parkyn
A 22 year old shoe maker from Liskeard,
Married Jane Dawe of Liskeard. On
19.12.1885.
Appointed: 11.4.1881.
Promotion: 11.1.1886 to 2nd class
Constable. 4.11.1888 to 1st class Constable.
10.10.1892 to Sergeant.
Stationed at: Penzance 9.8.1881. Helston
25.1.1882. Launceston 11.10.1892.
Removal: 28.2.1909. Pension £55.9.4.
Died. 25.8.1952.

P.C. 57 Francis Edwards
A 19 year old miner from Linkinhorne,
single.
Appointed: 2.5.1881.
Stationed at: Truro 9.7.1881. Penzance
6.5.1882
Removal: 2.4.1884. Resigned.

P.C. 83 Davis Banfield
A 21 year old game keeper from St Austell,
married.
Appointed: 25.4.1881.
Promotion: 18.6.1888 to 2nd Class
Constable. 3.8.1892 to 1st class Constable.
Stationed at: Penzance 31.10.1881
Removal: 27.2.1902   Pension £29.14.10,
Pensioned on a medical certificate.

P.C. 148 Charles Richards
A 23 year old labourer from St Neot. Married
Maria Brinton Worden of Egloshayle.
Appointed: 24.4.1881.
Promotion: 7.12.1884 to 2nd class
Constable. 3.11.1889 to 1st class Constable.
8.7.1895 to Sergeant.
Stationed at: Penzance 21.8.1882.
Launceston 23.10.1882. Liskeard 11.7.1895.
Removal: 13.9.1908. Pension £55.9.4.

P.C. 117 John Charles Yeo
A blacksmith and farm labourer from
Lanreath, Liskeard. Aged 22 years single.
Appointed: 22.6.1881.
Stationed at: Bodmin 27.10.1881
Removal: 6.3.1882. Resigned.

P.C. 52 James Edward Bice
A miner from Tywardreath, aged 20.
Married Eliza Jane Hill of Helston 10.4.1885.
Appointed: 4.7.1881.
Promotion: 3.11.1889 to 2nd class
Constable. 9.8.1891. To 1st class Constable.
22.5.1894 to Sergeant.
Stationed at: Truro 27.10.1881. Penzance
6.5.1882. Helston 10.11.1882. Truro
8.6.1894.
Removal: 2.8.1895.   Reduced to 2nd class
Constable for drunkenness. Resigned.

P.C. 138 John Yeo
A 22 year old farm labourer and railway
porter, from Holsworthy, married with one
child. Public Service. London and South
West Railway for 16 months.
Appointed: 7.7.1881.
Promotion: 18.6.1888 to 2nd class
Constable. 9.8.1991 to 1st class Constable.
1.1.1894 to Sergeant.
Stationed at: Bodmin 22.11.1881. Helston
4.1.1894. Truro 20.10.1895.
Removal: 21.2.1897   Pension £21.16.3.
Resigned through ill-health.

P.C. 21 John Edward McCoy
A 19 year old hawker from Exeter, single.
Appointed: 25.8.1881.
Removal: 12.4.1882. Resigned.

P.C. 101 Philip Hill
A 19 year old labourer from Mevagissey,
single.
Appointed: 19.9.1881.
Stationed at: Launceston 10.5.1882. Bodmin
23.10.1882.
Removal: 11.11.1883. Resigned. Called
for by the Chief Constable for telling falsehood and irregularity of conduct.

P.C. 28 Thomas Warring
A 20 year old farm Labourer from South
Petherwin, Launceston. Married Bessie
Hockin of Camborne 2.5.1889.
Appointed: 3.10.1881.
Promotion: 4.11.1888 to 2nd class
Constable. 9.8.1891 to 1st class Constable.
24.9.1894 to Sergeant. 1.1.1902 to
Inspector.
Stationed at: Bodmin 16.5.1882. Penzance
9.4.1883. Helston 5.10.1894. Penzance
18.11.1904.
Removal: 30.11.1919 Pension £233.6.8.
Specially commended by the Sec of State in
connection with enquiries and reports relat-
ing to aliens and suspected persons, as the
result of appreciation expressed by Col. Kell
C.B. M.I.5 War Office. Since the outbreak of
was since Aug 1914. H.Q. Circular
28.2.1918.
Died at Newquay during the night of 5/6th
January, 1937, information received by Supt
W.J. Matthews, D.C.C. By phone from the
son-in-law Mr. Daniel. County Accountant
informed by letter.

P.C. 19 Thomas Nicholls
Aged 19 years a waggoner from Camelford,
Married Elizabeth A.Rowe of Camborne.
27.9.1885.

Appointed: 14.11.1881.
Promotion: 3.11.1889 to 2nd class
Constable. 4.10.1891 to 1st class Constable.
19.2.1893 to Sergeant. 26.10.1896 to
Inspector. 1.10.1905 to Superintendent.
Stationed at: Bodmin 23.3.1882. Penzance
9.4.1883. Launceston 16.9.1885. Liskeard
10.3.1893. Penzance 23.10.1894. Truro
30.10.1896. Launceston 21.4.1897. Helston
3.8.1897. Liskeard 25.10.1898 Truro
10.1.1902. Bodmin 29.9.1905. Falmouth
30.11.1908.
Favourable Record
6.4.1899   Zeal and intelligence in detecting
and successfully prosecuting a case of
larceny.
Retired 31.3.1930.

P.C. 163 Samuel Ware
A blacksmith from Calstock, Callington, aged
20 single.
Appointed: 6.3.1882.
Stationed at: Penzance 24.8.1882.
Removal: 17.5.1883. Resigned.

P.C. 34 John Bishop Cole
A 25 year old farm labourer from Dartmouth,
Married Ann Chubb of North Hill.
17.2.1884.
Appointed: 10.3.1882.
Promotion: 4.11.1888 to 2nd class
Constable. 9.8.1891 to 1st class Constable.
1.2.1902 to merit class Constable.
Stationed at: Penzance 24.10.1882.
Removal: Pension £46.16.0.

P.C. 150 Robert Davey Collett
A 21 year old farm labourer from Illogan,
Redruth. Married Elizabeth Ann Hancock of
St Issey. 18.8.1888. Married Jermima Bishop
of Wadebridge 14.2.1905.
Appointed: 23.3.1882.
Promotion: 28.12.1890 to 2nd class
Constable. 6.5.1895 to 1st class Constable.
Stationed at: Bodmin 20.12.1882.
Launceston 23.2.1884. Truro 30.12.1886
Bodmin 9.7.1888. Truro 28.3.1899.
Bodmin 10. 5.1900.
Removal: 28.2.1911. Pension £45.1.4.
1.7.1898. Was ordered to be transferred at
his own expense for unnecessary delay in
returning off duty and drinking in a public
house. 5.1.1900 . Fined £.1.0.0. For being
drunk and warned for dismissal. 27,5.1910.
Fined £1.0.0. For tippling in a public house
whilst on duty on 10.5.1910. And warned for
dismissal.

P.C. 117 John Hill
A farm labourer from Quethiock, Liskeard,
aged 20, married Mary F.Lake of Stithians,
1.5.1890.
Appointed: 4.4.1882.
Promotion: 9.8.1891. To 2nd class
Constable. 27.11.1892 to 1st class
Constable. 1.1.1902 to merit class Constable.
Stationed at: Truro 25.10.1882. Launceston
8.9.1884. Helston 9.2.1885. Launceston
21.12.1886.
Removal: 27.1.1913. Pension £52.0.0.
15.6.1890.   Fined 10/- for being the worse
for liquor.

P.C. 21 Samuel Smith
A farm labourer from Fowey, aged 20,
married Emily I. Cuff, of Falmouth on
30.12.1886.
Appointed: 17.4.1882
Promotion: 1.12.1890. To 2nd class
Constable. 27.11.1892 to 1st class Constable.
30.9.1895 to Sergeant.
Stationed at: Liskeard 20.12. 1882. Liskeard
13.1.1883. Penzance 8.10.1895. Launceston
3.12.1901.
Removal: 30.11.1911. Pension £55.9.4.
Died at 29 Penmore Road, Falmouth on
2.2.1939.

P.C. 13 Edwin Osborne Lane
A 22 year old gardener from Norfolk, single.
Appointed: 24.4.1882.
Stationed at: Penzance 20.12.1882. Helston
28.12.1883.
Removal: 15.10.1884. Dismissed the force
for being absent from his station without
leave.

P.C. 100 Thomas Paul
A miner from Calstock, aged 21 single.
Appointed: 14.8.1882.
Stationed at: Liskeard 5.2.1883.
Removal: 21.9.1884. Resigned

P.C. 4 Thomas Wallis
A labourer from Linkinhorne, aged 20 single.
Appointed: 30.9.1882.
Stationed at: Launceston 5.2.1883.
Removal: 29.4.1883. Resigned.

P.C. 14 Thomas Willcock
A farm labourer from St Issey, Wadebridge.
Aged 20 single.
Public Service. Artillery Volunteers for 4
years.
Appointed: 16.10.1882.
Stationed at: Truro 5.2.1883. Liskeard
3.8.1883.
Removal: 10.12.1890. Died.

P.C. 26 Richard James Roberts
A 20 year old groom from St Erth, single.
Appointed: 13.11.1882.
Stationed at: Bodmin 9.4.1883.
Removal: 28.10.1884. Resigned.

P.C. 143 Harry Crabb
A 21 year old farmer from Liskeard, single.
Public Service. Plymouth Police for about
five months.
Appointed: 21.12.1882.
Stationed at: Chyandour, Penzance.
9.4.1883.
Removal: 13.1.1884. Died.

P.C. 164 William Henry Glidden
A miner from Jacobstow, aged 19 single.
Appointed: 22.1.1883.
Stationed at: Liskeard 9.4.1883
Removal: 7.1.1885. Resigned
12.10.1884. Fined 10/- for being absent
from his conference point and making a false
entry in his journal.

P.C. 166 George Kendall
A 20 year old labourer from St Kew. Married

Mary Jane Ede of Dobwalls. 31.7.1884.
Married Mary Ann G.Sweet. A retired nurse,
from County Asylum, at Bodmin Bible
Christian Church 1.6.1911.
Appointed: 22.1.1883.
Promotion: 28.12.1890 to 2nd class
Constable. 1.10.1893 to 1st class Constable.
1.7.1900 to Sergeant.
Stationed at: Truro 9.4.1883. Bodmin
2.8.1884 Helston 7.8.1886. Truro 20.6.1900.
Removal: 13.1.1914. Pension £60.13.4.
Commendation: On 23.9.1897 for spirited
conduct in arresting a notorious poacher
when armed with a loaded gun and subse-
quently prosecuting him to conviction.
Summer Assizes in 1904. Zeal and intelli-
gence displayed in working up the case of
Rex v Bullen convicted of manslaughter.
Died 19.10.1946.

P.C. 58 James Dunstan
A miner from Calstock, aged 25 married with
one child.
Appointed: 23.1.1883.
Stationed at: Liskeard 13.6.1883. Bodmin
26.9.1883.
Removal: 8.2.1885. Resigned.

P.C. 92 Harry Johns
An 18 year old farm labourer from St
Germans, single.
Appointed: 21.1.1883.
Stationed at: Launceston 1.5.1883. Bodmin
7.8.1886.
Removal: 18.8.1887. Called upon to resign.

P.C. 165 Frederick Osborne
A 21 year old miner from St Agnes. Single.
Appointed: 29.1.1883.
Stationed at: Liskeard 19.9.1883.
Removal: 31.1.1886. Resigned.
3.9.1883. Fined 5/- for being in his station
when he should have been out on duty.

P.C. 188 John Baker
A 24 year old farm labourer from Tetcott,
Devon, Married Alice Bradford of Exeter,
21.10.1891.
Appointed: 29.1.1883.
Promotion: 28.12.1890 to 2nd class
Constable. 3.8.1892 to 1st class Constable.
30.8.1894 reduced to 3rd., class for being
drunk on duty. 28.10.1895 to 2nd class
Constable. 14.2.1898 to 1st class Constable.
1.7.1903 to merit class Constable.
Stationed at: Bodmin 9.4.1883. Truro
10.8.1890
Removal: 30.4.1909. Pension £46.16.0.
Favourable Record: For zeal and intelligence
displayed in the working up of a case of R v
Bullen convicted of manslaughter in the
summer Assizes in 1904.

P.C. 167 Harry Roberts
A 21 year old farm labourer of St Martins,
Liskeard. Married Ellen Harvey of Mawnan,
3.6.1885.
Appointed: 5.2.1883
Promotion: 28.12.1890 to 2nd class
Constable. 6.5.1895 to 1st class Constable.
1.8.1901 to merit class Constable.
Stationed at: Penzance 2.7.1883. Bodmin

22.12.1884.
Removal: 2.3.1885. Resigned.

P.C. 169 George Thomas Hooper
An 18 year old Railway porter from
Plympton, married Mary Pesteridge, of Mary
Tavy, on 18.9.1886.
Public Service. G.W.R. For about 3 years.
Appointed: 5.2.1883.
Promotion: 16.1.1886 to 2nd class
Constable. 4.10.1891 to 1st class Constable.
Stationed at: Penzance 9.4.1883. Helston
Oct 1889.
Removal: 14.11.1892 Dismissed for drunk-
enness.

P.C. 170 William Phillips Back
A 19 year old colt trainer from Ivybridge.
Appointed: 5.2.1883.
Stationed at: Truro 2.7.1883.
Removal: 7.6.1885. Resigned.
Reappointed: 1.4.1889. As P.C. 171.
Taken over from the Borough of Falmouth as
1st class Constable.
Promotion: 1.12.1902 to merit class.
Stationed at: Helston 1.4.1889. Camborne
7.10.1897.
Removal: 6.4.1907. Pension £52.0.0.
Favourable Record: Copy G.O.20.11.1902.
William Back is hereby granted a favourable
record and promotion to the merit class for
promptitude and courage in effecting the
arrest of three persons charged with forgery,
who were known to be armed.

P.C. 171 Frederick Duke
A 25 year old farm labourer from North
Petherwin, Launceston. Married with two
children.
Appointed: 5.2.1883.
Stationed at: Liskeard 3.5.1883.
Removal: 15.8.1886. Called on to resign
owing to ill-health.

P.C. 67 Benjamin Jose Rowe
A 22 year old farm labourer from Falmouth,
single.
Appointed: 5.3.1883.
Stationed at: Truro 2.7.1883.
Removal: 26.4.1885. Resigned.

P.C. 35 Richard Banfield
A 19 year old farm labourer from
Grampound. Married Bessie Currah of St
Germans. 2.8.1888
Appointed: 26.3.1883.
Promotion: 11.1.1886 to 2nd class
Constable. 3.11.1889 to 1st class Constable.
4.8.1891. To Sergeant. 28.10.1895 to
Inspector. 1.12.1902. To Superintendent.
1.10.1910 to Superintendent A.C.C.
Stationed at: Liskeard 19.1.1883. Bodmin
31.10.1895. Camborne 18.11.1904. Bodmin
23.11.1910.
Record not complete.

P.C. 120 Ernest Garibaldi Hugo
A stonemason from St Dennis, St Austell,
aged 20 years. Marriages: Kate A.Bassett of
Tavistock. 21.12.1884. Elizabeth Williams of
Duloe 31.1.1906.
Appointed: 20.3.1883.

Promotion: 1.12.1890 to 2nd class Constable. 21.4.1892 to 1st class Constable. 6.5.1895 to Sergeant. 1.12.1907 to Inspector.
Stationed at: Penzance 2.7.1883. Launceston 28.9.1884. Bodmin 6.5.1895. Liskeard 25.10.1898. Bodmin 13.11.1907.
Removal: 15.10.1920. Pension £233.6.8.

P.C. 130 John Lugger
A 20 year old blacksmith from Lifton, Devon.
Appointed: 18.4.1883.
Stationed at: Bodmin 21 11.1883. Helston 22.12.1884.
Removal: 5.2.1885. Resigned.
9.12.1883. Fined 10/- for telling falsehoods.

P.C. 140 Richard Johns
A 20 year old farm labourer from Veryan, Truro. Married Elizabeth Davies 2.8.1886.
Appointed: 30.4.1883.
Resigned 22.6.1884.
Reappointed: as P.C. 41 15.9.1884.
Promotion: 23.3.1891 to 2nd class Constable. 1.10.1893 to 1st class Constable.
Stationed at: Penzance 29.12.1883. Bodmin 29.10.1884. Liskeard 7.8.1896. Launceston 6.12.1896.
Removal: 17.12.1899. **Removal:** to the County Asylum Bodmin through mental infirmity. Pension £18.12.9.

P.C. James Jewell
Appointed: 22,5,1883.
Removal: 26.5.1883.
On the morning of the 27th May this man said he felt unwell and wished to return home and the Chief Constable permitted him to do so at once.

P.C. 163 John Uren
A 20 year old gardener from Lelant, single.
Appointed: 4.6.1883.
Removal: 11.11.1883. Called upon to resign by the Chief Constable for telling falsehoods and other irregularity of conduct.

P.C. 4 William Smeeth
A carpenter from Boscastle aged 19. Married Elizabeth Honey of Newquay on 20.9.1886.
Appointed: 23.7.1883.
Stationed at: Penzance 27.2.1884. Bodmin 10.5.1886.
Removal: 13.2.1887. Called on to resign for being drunk on duty and getting into debt.

P.C. 18 George Holwill
A 19 year old gardener from Tavistock. Married Jane Smith of St Austell 4.12.1894.
Appointed: 27.3.1883.
Promotion: 1.12.1890 to 2nd class Constable. 8.8.1892 to 1st class Constable. 7.6.1897 to merit class Constable.
Stationed at: Liskeard 10.3.1884. Bodmin 30.10.1884. Liskeard 7.8.1886. Penzance 12.6.1896. Bodmin 2.11.1899.
Removal: 15.10.1913. Pension £52.0.0.

P.C. 145 John Blythe
A 21 year old carpenter from St Neot, single.
Appointed: 22.8.1883.

Stationed at: Bodmin 10.3.1884.
Removal: 25.8.1884. Resigned.

P.C. 64 John Kent
A miner from Callington, aged 20 years. Married Elizabeth Smallcombe a widow of the late William Smallcombe. Later married Grace Gillas of Ludgvan 1.3.1911.
Appointed: 27.8.1883.
Promotion: 28.12.1890 to 2nd class Constable. 16.2.1894 to 1st class Constable. 14.10.1900 to Sergeant.
Stationed at: Bodmin 1.1.1884. Penzance 10.3.1884. Helston 29.9.1885. Launceston 15.11.1890. Truro 1.10.1895. Falmouth 9.10.1900. Camborne 25.5.1905.
Removal: 30.6.1912. Pension £55.9.4. 1.10.1895. P.C. 64 John Kent was moved at his own expense for refusing to obey an order of his superior officer.
Died. At 8 Wellington Place, Falmouth on 16.7.1944.

P.C. 109 Harry Roberts
A 22 year old china clay labourer from St Columb Major. Married Mary Elizabeth Clift. of Falmouth September 1887.
Appointed: 5.5.1883.
Promotion: 3.11.1889 to 2nd class Constable.
4.10.1891 to 1st class Constable. 22.5.1894 to Sergeant. 2.8.1897 to Sergeant Major. 1.3.1899 to Inspector.
Stationed at: Truro 8.9.1884. Helston 25.10.1884. Bodmin 30.8.1887 Truro 9.7.1888. Bodmin 8.6.1894. Truro 23.7.1897. Bodmin 27.7.1897. Liskeard 9.5.1899.
Removal: 14.8.1911. Pension £71.13.4.

P.C. John Warminton
A 19 year old labourer from Penryn, single.
Appointed: 3.12.1883.
Removal: 18.1.1884. Resigned.

P.C. 163 James Ackland
A farm labourer from Pelynt, Looe, single aged 20 years.
Appointed: 10.3.1884.
Stationed at: Bodmin 28.4.1884. Liskeard 20.4.1885.
Removal: 27.3.1887. Called on to resign for inefficiency.

P.C. 61 & 31 James Fuller
A farm labourer from Boyton Launceston. Married Ellen Hill a Nurse at the Lunatic asylum 20.10.1887.
Appointed: 4.1.1884.
Promotion: 28.12.1890 to 2nd class Constable. 17.11.1892 to 1st class Constable. 1.10.1900. To Sergeant. 1.9.1908 reduced to 1st class Constable.
Stationed at: Truro 8.9.1884. Helston 18.12.1886. Bodmin 13.11.1889. Liskeard 18.8.1891. Launceston 5.10.1900. Truro 29.3.1906. Liskeard 18.9.1908.
Removal: 25.3.1912. Pension £45.1.4. 7.4.1908. Sergeant Fuller was fined £1.0.0. For drunk on duty on 1.3.1908. 7.4.1908 Sergeant James Fuller was severely reprimanded for negligence in carrying out the

orders of his superior officer, he is further seriously cautioned as to his future conduct. 1.9.1908 Sergeant James Fuller was reduced to the rank of 1st class Constable for tippling and contracting debts and ordered to be transferred at his own expense. He is again severely cautioned as to his future conduct. The reduction in rank to take effect on and from 1.9.1908.
Died 31.1.1939 In formation by letter to the County Accountant.

P.C. 101 Samuel Henry Parkyn
A 25 year old farm labourer from Budock, Falmouth, single
Appointed: 11.2.1884.
Removal: 8.7.1884. Resigned Called for by the Chief Constable.

P.C. 143 Samuel Warren Jenkings
A farm labourer from South Petherwin aged 19, single.
Appointed: 18.2.1884.
Stationed at: Penzance 30.9.1884.
Removal: 15.1.1886. Dismissed for being drunk on duty.

P.C. 57 Robert Laskey
A 23 year old farm labourer from Kea, Truro. Married Edith Hopewell. From Gunnislake on 10.9.1895.
Appointed: 28.4.1884.
Promotion: 28.12.1890 to 2nd class Constable. 24.1.1892 to 1st class Constable. 24.10.1899 to Sergeant.
Stationed at: Liskeard 28.9.1884. Launceston 11.7.1895. Camborne 25.10.1895. Falmouth 1.10.1903.
Removal: 31.10.1912. Pension £60.13.4. Favourable record for zeal and intelligence displayed in detecting an offender, and bringing to justice, in a case of plate glass smashing.

P.C. 87 Walter Frederick Endean
A labourer from St Gluvias, Penryn, aged 20. Married E.M.Carlyon of St Gluvias on 23.10.1884.
Appointed: 5.6.1884.
Stationed at: Bodmin 21.11.1884
Removal: 9.11.1885. Called on to resign for misconduct.

P.C. 40 Edmund John Carpenter
A 22 year old farm labourer from Gunnislake, single.
Appointed: 23 6.1884.
Stationed at: Penzance 29.11.1884.
Removal: 8.11.1887. Resigned.

P.C. 145 Edward Wonnacott
A 21 year old packer from Newton Abbott, married Emily Way of Lympstone 14 9 1887.
Appointed: 18.8.1884.
Promotion: 28.12.1890 to 2nd class Constable. 1.1.1894 to 1st class Constable. 1.8.1901 to merit class Constable.
Stationed at: Launceston 29.11.1884. Bodmin 29.3.1892. Liskeard 26.10.1896. Bodmin 18.11.1904.
Removal: 15.10.1913. Pension £52.0.0. Died at Coomberry Place, Bodmin on 27.3.1935.

P.C. 75 **Philip Santo**
An 18 year old china clay labourer. Married Betty Nicholas from St Agnes, 26.9.1887. Public Service. D.C.L.I . 'D' Comp for two years.
Appointed: 25.8.1884.
Stationed at: Truro 9.2.1885.
Removal: 28.4.1889. Resigned.

P.C. 158 **Charles Penwill**
A 21 year old farm labourer from Ermington, Plymouth.
Appointed: 22.9.1884.
Stationed at: Launceston 9.2.1885.
Removal: 17.5.1885. Called on to resign - reported unfit for a Constable.

P.C. 101 **Philip Jenkin**
A 21 year old groom from Illogan, Redruth. Married Ellen Harris of Illogan 3.4.1885.
Appointed: 23,9.1884.
Promotion: 28.12.1890. To 2nd class Constable. 19.2.1893 to 1st class Constable. 2.9.1895 to Sergeant.
Stationed at: Penzance 9.2.1885. Truro 2.6.1894. Helston 9.10.1895. Camborne 19.12.1899. Falmouth 25.5.1905. Camborne 30.11.1907
Removal: 3.12.1911. Pension £55.9.4. Retired on medical certificate.

P.C. 100 **William James Hicks**
A 20 year old farm labourer from St Just-in-Roseland.
Appointed: 29.9.1884.
Stationed at: Bodmin 4.3.1885.
Removal: 14.2.1888. Reported for leaving the polling both at a school board election without permission and was fined 10/- and called upon to resign.

P.C. 24 **James Roach Grose**
A china clay labourer from St Austell, aged 19, single.
Appointed: 27.10.1884.
Stationed at: Bodmin 24.4.1885. Truro

2.7.1885.
Removal: 10.9.1886. Resigned.

P.C. 13 **Edmund John Retallick**
A china clay labourer from Luxulyan aged 19 years. Married Jane Pearce of Downderry on 13.11.1888.
Appointed: 12.11.1884.
Stationed at: Liskeard 20.4.1885.
Resigned 27.3.1890.

P.C. 45 **Robert Cole**
A 21 year old labourer from Lifton Devon, single.
Appointed: 24.11.1884.
Stationed at: Bodmin 24.4.1885. Truro 8.6.1885. Bodmin 4.2.1887.
Removal: 24.3.1887. Resigned.

P.C. 164 **Samuel Vanson**
A 19 year old china clay labourer from Tywardreath. Married Sarah Luke Oatey 21.11.1887. Public Service: Volunteer Artillery for about 4 years.
Appointed: 12.1.1885.

Promotion: 28.12.1890 to 2nd class Constable. 24.1.1892 to 1st class Constable. 26.3.1894 to Sergeant.
Stationed at: Penzance 22.9.1885. Bodmin 1.11.1886. Liskeard 10.1.1895. Penzance 26.10.1896. Liskeard 25.10.1898.
Removal: 31.10.1919. Pension £195.13.4. Died 21.1.1926. Widow Mrs Sarah Vanson granted a pension of £30.0.0. P.A. To date and from 1.4.1926.

P.C. 94 **Frank Hobb Vickery**
A 19 year old farm labourer from St Endellion Married Miss Ethel Rank of Bodmin 5.2.1918.
Appointed: 12.1.1885.
Promotion: 1.12.1890 to 2nd class Constable. 19.2.1893 to 1st class Constable. 24.10.1898 to Sergeant.
Stationed at: Bodmin 5.6.1885.
Removal: 29.2.1920. Pension £195.13.4.

P.C. 130 **John James Hill**
A farm labourer from Lifton, Devon. Single.
Appointed: 9.2.1885
Stationed at: Penzance 29.9.1885.
Removal: 18.7.1886. Resigned.

P.C. 58 **John Netherton**
A 20 year old farm labourer from Lanivet, Bodmin. Married Annie Verran of Bodmin 18.10.1888.
Appointed: 16 .2.1885.
Promotion: 28.12.1890 to 2nd class Constable. 1.10.1893 to 1st class Constable. 1.8.1901. To merit class Constable.
Stationed at: Bodmin 5.6.1885. Launceston 22.10.1888. Bodmin July 1889.
Removal: 30.4.1913. Pension £52 .0.0. Medical Certificate.

P.C. 170 **Walter Sleep**
A 20 year old farm labourer from Laneast, Launceston. Single.
Appointed: 20.3.1885.
Stationed at: Penzance 10.5.1886. Helston 16.9.1886. Launceston 6.12.1888.
Removal: 30.12.1889. Dismissed for drunkenness.

P.C. 67 **Charles Bray**
A 22 year old china clay labourer from St Austell. On 15.8.1886 married Mary A.Julian of St Austell.
Appointed: 27.4.1885.
Promotion: 1.12.1890 to 2nd class Constable. 19.2.1893 to 1st Class Constable.
Stationed at: Penzance 4.2.1886.
Removal: 13.2.1899. Resigned. 31.1.1886 fined 5/- for being absent from his conference point.

P.C. 168 **Edward Vincent**
A 24 year old block maker from Fowey, Married with two children. Public Service Artillery Volunteers, Cornwall.
Appointed: 2.3.1885.
Promotion: 3.11.1889 to 2nd class Constable. 24.1.1892 to 1st class Constable. 26.10.1896 to Sergeant
Stationed at: Bodmin 5.6.1885. Liskeard 30.10.1896. Liskeard 30.11.1907.

Removal: 30.6.1911. Pension £55.9.4. Died 25.12.1943.

P.C. 158 **Stephen George Hawke**
A miner from Grampound, single aged 18 years.
Appointed: 25.5.1885.
Stationed at: Liskeard 3.2.1886.
Removal: 23.3.1890. Dismissed for drunkenness.

P.C. 38 **Thomas Holman**
A 21 year old miner from St Agnes, single.
Appointed: 14.6.1885.
Stationed at: Penzance 14.9.1886.
Removal: 22.7.1890. Resigned.

P.C. 160 **William Henry Williams**
A blacksmith from Bodmin, 21 years, single.
Appointed: 15.6.1885.
Stationed at: Truro 4.2.1886.
Removal: 22.5.1887. Resigned.

P.C. 146 **Henry Pearn**
A 20 year old mine labourer from Stoke Climsland. 27.9.1890 Married Mary A.Tresidder of Camborne.
Appointed: 14.9.1885.
Promotion: 28.12.1890. To 2nd class Constable. 1.10.1893. To 1st Class Constable. 20.10.1895. To sergeant.
Stationed at: Bodmin 7.8.1886. Penzance 1.11.1886. Truro 31.10.1895. Liskeard June 1897. Launceston 13.9.1906.
Discipline: Sergeant Henry Pearn has been reprimanded and cautioned by the Chief Constable for being presented with a testimonial on licensed premises contrary to the G.O. Thereon. Died 31.12.32.

P.C. 102 **John Methven**
A 21 year old stone mason from Portsmouth, married. Public service: 5th Battery Duke of Cornwall Artillery Volunteers for 6 months.
Appointed: 11.1.1886.
Promotion: 28.12.1890 to 2nd class Constable. 1.1.1894 to 1st class constable.
Stationed at: Liskeard 17.9.1886.
Removal: 10.10.1898 Resigned.

P.C. 143 **Henry Rowe**
A 25 year old farm labourer from Egloshayle, Single.
Appointed: 18.1.1886.
Removal: 4.8.1886. Called on to resign for misconduct.

P.C. 165 **Abel Worth**
A 22 year old farm labourer from Egloskerry, Launceston. Single. Public service: Metropolitan Police for one month.
Appointed: 1.2.1886.
Stationed at: Launceston 7.8.1886.
Removal: 12.8.1888. Resigned.

P.C. 162 **Frederick George Rice**
A miner from Roche, aged 18 single.
Appointed: 10.5.1886.
Stationed at: Liskeard 4.11.1886.
Removal: 11.3.1888. Called on to resign for improper conduct with females in the street.

P.C. 142 John Tabb
A 19 year old farm labourer from Lostwithiel.
Appointed: 21.6.1886.
Stationed at: Penzance 4.11.1886.
Removal: 21.12.1887. Called on to resign for ill-health.

P.C. 149 John Ough
A 23 year old farm labourer from St Germans, married Thursa Eva of Linkinhorne 27.10.1891.
Appointed: 12.7.1886.
Promotion: 28.12.1890 to 2nd class Constable. 8.8.1892 to 1st class Constable. 22,5,1894 to Sergeant.
Stationed at: Bodmin 20.12.1886. Falmouth 18.12.1899.
Removal: 16.6.1914. Pension £60.13.4. Increase of pay from 6.9.1899.

P.C. 130 William Robert Jeffrey
A farm labourer from Madron, aged 18 Married Alice Sergeant Hatch of Madron Penzance 30.4.1892. Public service: Rifle Volunteers Penzance for two years.
Appointed: 12.7.1886.
Stationed at: Penzance 20.12.1886. Liskeard 27.12.1887
Removal: 27.3.1890. Resigned.
Reappointed: 25.8.1890. As P.C. 38.
Promotion: 9.8.1891 to 2nd class Constable. 13.10.1894 to 1st class Constable. 1.3.1899 to Sergeant.
Stationed at: Bodmin Aug 1890. Truro 2.3.1899. Camborne 27.3.1902. Truro 21.6.1902. Launceston 29.3.1906.
Removal: 10.4.1919. Pension £98.16.0. Granted 7.4.1919. Pension reassessed after Desborough Report and granted £195.13.4. From 1.5.1919. 1.1.1888 Fined 10/- and moved at his own expense for being drunk on duty.

P.C. 27 George Lea's
A 19 year old Porter on Railway from St Blazey. Public Service. Great Western Railway for two years and nine months.
Appointed: 30.8.1886.
Stationed at: Launceston 7.3.1887.
Removal: 12.5.1887. Resigned.

P.C. 133 William Henry Pethick
A farm labourer from Bodmin aged 23 years. Married Rosina L.Jolliffe from the Isle of Wight. 29.10.1896.
Appointed: 13.9.1886.
Stationed at: Truro 5.3.1887. Bodmin 6.12.1888.
Removal: 3.4.1890 Resigned.
Reappointed: 2,6.,1890
Promotion: 28.12.1890 to 2nd class constable. 22.5.1894 to 1st class Constable. 1.3.1899 to Sergeant.
Stationed at: Bodmin 16.6.1890. Truro 21.5.1892. Helston 9.9.1892.
Removal: 12.9.1900 Died Widow granted a gratuity of £60.16.8.

P.C. 24 Philip Harvey Pascoe
A miner from Scotland now living at St Neot, single.
Appointed: 20.9.1886

Stationed at: Bodmin 14.2.1887. Helston 13.8.1887
Removal: 15.1.1888. Resigned.

P.C. 121 John Penno
A 24 year old farm labourer from Lostwithiel, single.
Appointed: 25.10.1886.
Stationed at: Bodmin 8.8.1887. Truro 6.12.1888.
Removal: 20.8.1890. Resigned.

P.C. 17 Josiah Spear
A 21 year old labourer from Stoke Climsland. Married Emma England of St Ives 21.12.1891.
Appointed: 25.10.1886.
Promotion: 23.3.1891 to 2nd class Constable. 22.5.1894 to 1st Class Constable.
Stationed at: Truro 23 .5.1887. Penzance 10.4.1889. Liskeard 12.6.1896. Helston 10.5.1897.
Removal: 29.8.1898 Resigned.

P.C. 161 John James Jenkin
A 24 year old labourer from Madron. Married Annie Reynolds of Madron 17.4.1888. Public Service: West Cornwall Railway for 5 months.
Appointed: 11.11.1886.
Promotion: 8.8.1892 to 2nd class Constable. 30.8.1896. To 1st class Constable. 1.11.1904 to merit class Constable.
Stationed at: Liskeard 7.6.1887 Penzance 8.12.1897. Truro 10.8.1890.
Removal: 9.1.1915 Pension £52.0.0. Died at Heamoor, Quintrell Downs 10.2.1937.

P.C. 113 Daniel James Chapman
A 19 year old miller from St Issey, single.
Appointed: 18.1.1887.
Removal: 15.3.1887. Resigned.

P.C. 4 Alfred Butler
A 21 year old carpenter from Torpoint, Single.
Appointed: 25.2.1887.
Stationed at: Bodmin 23.9.1887.
Removal: 1.7.1888. Resigned 1.7.1888 Fined 10/- for being absent from his conference point.

P.C. 113 Woodman Cowling
A 20 year old farm labourer from Kenwyn, Truro, single.
Appointed: 23.3.1887.
Stationed at: Truro 23.9.1887. Penzance 6.4.1889.
Removal: 24.3.1891. Resigned.
11.9.1887 Fined 5/- for disobedience of orders in creating a noise at 11 p.m. at the H.Q. Station.

P.C. 163 William Trezise
A farm labourer from Helston. Aged 21 and single.
Appointed: 28.3.1887.
Stationed at: Bodmin 23.9.1887.
Removal: 9.2.1890. Resigned.
11.9.1887. Fined 10/- for being found sitting down and asleep when out on duty.

P.C. 45 William John Dyer
A labourer from Kenwyn, Truro, aged 18. Married Ada Louisa Skews. 31.3.1891.
Appointed: 4.4.1887.
Promotion: 23.3.1891 to 2nd class Constable. 1.12.1896 to 1st class Constable. 1.2.1908 to merit class Constable.
Stationed at: Helston 16.1.1888. Penzance 18.8.1891. Liskeard 15.2.1902. Truro 14.1.1915.
Removal: 30.6.1917. Pension £52.0.0. On medical certificate. 2.2.1915. Fined 15/- for failing to investigate a very serious case of selling government stores and for being guilty of conduct prejudicial to the interests of the force and for stating a falsehood to his superior officer.

P.C. 27 John Varcoe
A china clay labourer from St Stephens, St Austell, aged 22 single.
Appointed: 23.5.1887.
Promotion: 7.8.1891 to 2nd class Constable. 13.10.1894 to 1st class Constable. 21.10.1902 to merit class Constable.
Stationed at: Bodmin 9.4.1888. Launceston 31.8.1893.
Removal: 31 .7.1915. Pension £52.0.0. Died 1.3.1948.

P.C. 160 William Cornelius
A 20 year old farm labourer from Camelford. Married Jane Carhart of St Minver on 1.3.1890.
Appointed: 3.5.1887.
Promotion: 9.8.1891 to 2nd class Constable. 22.5.1894 to 1st class Constable. Oct 1897 to Sergeant. 24.7.1910 to Inspector.
Stationed at: Liskeard 9.4.1888. Helston 26.10.1897. Liskeard 2.3.1899. Camborne 1.10.1903.
Removal: 31.8.1920. Pension £233.6.8. Died 27.5.1935 at 36 Church View Road, Tuckingmill, Camborne.

P.C. 92 John Symons Brawn
A 20 year old farm labourer from Launceston, single.
Appointed: 22.8.1887.
Stationed at: Penzance 9.7.1888
Removal: 11.2.1889. Dismissed for drunkenness when on duty.

P.C. 40 James Pethick
A 22 year old farm labourer from St Mabyn. Single.
Appointed: 7.11.1887
Stationed at: Liskeard 4.7.1888.
Removal: 30.3.1890. Resigned.
Reappointed: 4.6.1890 as P.C. 13.
Stationed at: Liskeard 25.6.1890
Removal: 13.7.1891. Resigned.

P.C. 142 John Harry Rundle
A 22 year old farm labourer from Looe.
Appointed: 26.12.1887.
Stationed at: Truro 9.7.1888. Bodmin 24.5.1890.
Removal: 1.6.1890. Resigned.

P.C. 162 Ernest Richards
A 19 year old miner from St Neot, single.

Appointed: 20.2.1888.
Promotion: 25.3.1891 to 2nd class Constable. 8.7.1895 to 1st class Constable. 27.9.1904 reduced to 2nd class Constable. 1.11.1907 to 1st class Constable.
Stationed at: Bodmin 18.7.1888. Launceston 8.5.1895. Truro 30.9.1904. Bodmin 11.5.1910.
Removal: 31.1.1920 Pension £165 4.7. Copy of G.O. 30.9.1904. 1st Class P.C. Ernest Richards was on the 27th inst, reduced to 2nd class of his rank and ordered to be transferred at his own expense, for gross irregularities in the performance of his duties. The reduction to take place from the 1st approximately. Died 5.10.1940.

P.C. 100 Richard Harvey
A 19 year old farm labourer from St Columb Minor, single.
Appointed: 20.2.1888.
Stationed at: Launceston 18.8.1888. Helston 6.12.1888. Penzance District 2.5.1889.
Removal: 1.5.1890. Dismissed for being drunk.

P.C. 24 Fred Tabb
A farm labourer from St Columb, aged 20. Married Grace Ann Soloman from Colan, Truro, 12.11.1890.
Appointed: 19.3.1888.
Promotion: 9.8.1891 to 2nd class Constable. 20.10.1896 to 1st class Constable. 1.8.1901 to merit class Constable.
Stationed at: Liskeard 29.10.1888.
Removal: 31.7.1918. Pension £52.0.0. Resigned on medical certificate. Favourable record, 18.12.1897 for intelligence and energy when employed on special detective duty in prosecuting successfully a person selling liquor without a licence.

P.C. 62 William Henry Pethick
A 23 year old plumber from St Stephens, Launceston. Married Mary E. Quest. of Linkinhorne 31.9.1890. Public Service: Royal Volunteers for 4 years.
Appointed: 30.4.1888.
Promotion: 14.10.1891 to 2nd class Constable. 10.1.1895 to 1st class Constable. 24.10.1898 to Sergeant. 1.10.1905 to Inspector.
Stationed at: Liskeard 30.10.1888. Bodmin 26.10.1896. Camborne 28.10.1898. Truro 29.9.1905. Bodmin 15.7.1910.
Removal: 9.12.1914. Pension £76.13.4. Died 27.4.1935. At The Village, Pensilva.

P.C. 65 John Symons
A 23 year old farm labourer from Duloe, Liskeard. Married Ellen Maud Nicholas of St Martins, 13.11.1889.
Appointed: 21.5.1888
Promotion: 4.10.1891 to 2nd class Constable. 1.12.1896 to 1st class Constable. 1.5.1905 to merit class Constable.
Stationed at: Penzance 2.3.1889.
Removal: 24.8.1914. Pension £52.0.0. Died at Redruth 6.1.1939.

Sergeant Major David Roberts
A 37 year old clay labourer from St Columb,

married with two children.
Public Service: For 12 years and 47 days in the Royal Artillery.
Appointed: 28.3.1888
Removal: 10.9.1890. Called on to resign.

P.C. 4 Albert Ead
A 26 year old mason's labourer from Bodmin. Married Mary Lawndry Dean on May 18. Married Betty Courts
Appointed: 20.6.1888
Promotion:
23.3.1891 to 2nd class Constable. 6.5.1895 to 1st class Constable. 21.10.1902 to merit class Constable.
Stationed at: Bodmin 18.12.1898.
Removal: 30.9.1914. Pension £52 .0.0. Died 30.11.1944.

P.C. Joseph William Dingle
A carpenter from St Austell, 20 years single. Public Service: D Comp., Rifle Volunteers St Austell for two years.
Appointed: 16.7.1888.
Removal: 22.7.1888. Resigned.

P.C. 25 William Toms
A 20 year old farm labourer from St Mabyn, Bodmin. Married Mary Elizabeth Ann Scantlebury. Of Bodmin 17.8.1892.
Appointed: 20.7.1888.
Promotion: 4.10.1891 to 2nd class Constable. 1.12.1896 to 1st class Constable. 1.11.1904 to merit class Constable.
Stationed at: Bodmin 27.10.1888 Truro 6.4.1889. Launceston 4.1.1890.
Removal: 9.10.1913. Pension £48.7.2. On medical certificate.

P.C. 115 James Allen
A 19 year old carter from St Mewan, St Austell. Single.
Appointed: 21.7.1888.
Stationed at: Launceston 18.12.1888. Penzance 30.3.1889.
Removal: 24.11.1889. Resigned.

P.C. 33 Samuel Smale
A 20 year old carpenter of Bodmin Married Maud Voss of St Columb 14.9.1892.
Appointed: 23.7.1888.
Promotion: 23.3.1891. To 2nd class Constable. 27.11.1892 to 1st class Constable. 22.2.1897 to Sergeant. 17.4.1899 to Sergeant Major. 19.11.1904 to Inspector. 12.11.1908 to Superintendent
Stationed at: Bodmin 1.11.1888 Falmouth 18.11.1904. Bodmin 13.11.1908. Camborne 27.11.1910.

P.C. 165 Frederick Botterell
A 19 year old farm labourer from Sancreed. Married E.A.May of Camborne. 31.10.1896.
Appointed: 21.8.1888
Promotion: 9.8.1891 to 2nd class Constable. 23.11.1896 to 1st class Constable.
Stationed at: Penzance/Redruth 2.3.1889. Truro 22.11.1896. Liskeard 30.4.1898
Removal: 30.9.1919. Pension £165.4.7.

P.C. 22 Henry Knight
A 21 year old single labourer from St

Winnow.
Appointed: 10.9.1888
Promotion: 9.8.1891 to 2nd class Constable. 30.9.1895 to 1st class Constable. 1.10.1903 to merit class Constable.
Stationed at: Bodmin 20.9.1899. Liskeard 19.8.1892. Launceston 22.6.1898. Bodmin 8.10.1912.
16.6.1898 Fined 10/- for insubordination towards his Sergeant. 25.3.1917 Retired Pension £52.0.0.

P.C. 131 James Thomas Simmons
A single labourer from Madron aged 19.
Appointed: 25.10.1888.
Stationed at: Penzance 21 6.1889. 26.4.1890 Resigned.

P.C. 69 John Trethewey
From St Blazey, a 19 year old single grocer.
Appointed: 29.10.1888.
Stationed at: Truro 28.6.1889. 26.1.1890 Resigned.

P.C. 114 William Truscott
A 23 year old labourer from St Columb. Married Alma Lobb of St Columb in March 1890.
Appointed: 3.12.1888.
Stationed at: Launceston 20.9.1889. Liskeard 8.4.1890.
5.5.1891 Called upon to resign.

P.C. 92 William Clark
A 20 year old labourer from Kenwyn. 8.8.1891. Married Martha Jane Trevithick of Sithney. Public Service: 2 years 3 months with the Third Batt D.C.L.I.
Appointed: 25.2.1889.
Promotion: 9.8.1891 to 2nd class Constable. 26.10.1896 to 1st class Constable.
Stationed at: Penzance 20.9.1899. Bodmin 22.8.1901.
1.2.1905 P.C. 92 Walter Clark was ordered to be transferred at his own expense in consequence of unfavourable reports as to the performance of his duties. 16.9.1913 Retired on medical certificate Pension £43.13.7.

P.C. 174 James Jennings
A married Police Officer from Penryn, aged 56 years. Public Service: Penryn Borough Police for 14 years.
Appointed: 1.4.1889.
Promotion: 28.12.1890 to 2nd class Constable. 8.8.1892 to 1st class Constable. 1.12.1896 to merit class Constable.
Stationed at: Helston 1.4.1889.
31.12.1900 Retired. Pension £43.11.11. 30.12.1901 Died.

P.C. 75 Thomas Annear
A single blacksmith from Camborne, aged 22.
Appointed: 1.5.1889.
Promotion: 8.8.1892 to 2nd class Constable.
Stationed at: Liskeard 20.9.1889. 4.2.1895 Resigned.

P.C. 36 William John Holloway
A 20 year old shoe maker from Tavistock.
27.10.1891. Married Caroline Scantlebury
of Liskeard.
Appointed:. 20.5.1889.
Promotion: 9.8.1891 to 2nd class
Constable. 19.2.1893 to 1st class Constable.
19.11.1904 to Sergeant. 1.7.1909 to
Inspector.
Stationed at:
Liskeard 20.9.1889. Bodmin 18.11.1904.
Liskeard 5.1.1906. Truro 13.11.1907.
Liskeard 1.7.1909.
31.1.1924 Retired

P.C. 177 Wallace Dunstan
A 19 year old farmers son from St Columb.
On 22.10.1892 Married Emily Chappel of
Falmouth.
Appointed: 8.7.1899.
Promotion: 24.1.1892 to 2nd class
Constable. 9.7.1897 to 1st class Constable.
1.10.1909 to merit class Constable.
Stationed at: Helston 6.12.1889. Bodmin
30.5.1891. Penzance 27.6.1891. Turo
Bodmin 1.9.1915.
30.11.1921   Retired.

P.C. 118 William Hodge
A woodsman from Helston aged 23.
In February 1891 married Elizabeth James of
Mullion.
Appointed: 15.7.1889.
Promotion: 8.8.1892 to 2nd class Constable.
26.10.1896 to 1st Class Constable. 1.6.1907
to merit class Constable.
Stationed at: Liskeard 22.11.1889.
10.12.1908 Retired Pension £33.13.11.
10.1.1910.
Reappointed: as P.C. 118
Stationed at: Truro 1.3.1910.
31.10.1919 Pension £165.4.7.
5.7.1935 Died at St Michaels Hospital at
Hayle from injuries received in a road acci-
dent whilst riding a pedal cycle.

P.C. 178 George Holloway
A 21 year old labourer from Tavistock.
Married Jane Matthews from the Lizard on
the 23.3.1893.
Appointed: 15.7.1889
Promotion: 24.1.1892 to 2nd class
Constable. 20.8.1896 to 1st class Constable.
5.3.1907 to merit class Constable.
Stationed at: Launceston 21.12.1889. Truro
27.8.1890. Helston 18.8.1891.
Retired 30.9.1920 Pension £165.4.7.
Died 1.12.1826. Widow granted a pension
of £30.0.0. Per annum to date on and from
1.1.1927.

P.C. 179 William Bowden
A farmers son from Budock, aged 20 single.
Appointed: 15.7.1889.
18.10.1889 called upon to resign.

P.C. 180 James Downing Allen
A single labourer from St Teath, aged 19
years. Records show number 180 deleted
and 55 inserted.
Appointed: 29.7.1889.
Promotion: 8.8.1892 to 2nd class Constable.

Stationed at: Penzance 21.12.1889. Helston
28.7.1893.
1.4.1895 Fined 10/- for being under the
influence of liquor whist on duty. 6.2.1897
Fined £.1.0.0. And cautioned for dismissal.
21.10.1897 Dismissed for drunkenness on
duty.

P.C. 1 Samuel Ley
A 19 year old labourer from St Teath, single.
Appointed: 29.7.1889.
Promotion: 24.1.1892 to 2nd class
Constable. 2.8.1897 to 1st class Constable.
Stationed at: Truro 4.1.1890. Helston
7.4.1893. Camborne 2.6.1907.
21.12.1905 P.C. 1 Samuel Ley was fined
10/- for being absent from his conference
point on the 16.11.1905 at 4,30 am. And
also fined the sum of 10/- for making a false
entry in his journal.
Retired 31.3.1923   Died 1.6.1937.

P.C. 176 Thomas Henry Mitchell
A 23 year old single tanner from Penryn.
Public service: K Comp., Rifle Volunteers.
Appointed: 29.7.1889.
Stationed at: Truro 12.2.1890.
23.7.1890 Resigned.

P.C. 15 Albert Bunt
A 23 year old single saddler from St Teath.
Appointed: 5.8.1889.
Promotion: 24.11.1892 to 2nd class
Constable.
Stationed at: Liskeard 26.3.1890
30.5.1892 Resigned.

P.C. 173 Robert Miller Hill
A 21 year old single labourer from St Breock.
Appointed: 15.8.1889.
1.2.1890. Dismissed for being drunk.

P.C. 73 William John Bate
A groom from St Merryn aged 21 years.
3.3.1890 married Miss Watts of Padstow.
Appointed: 4.11.1889.
Promotion: 4.10.1891 to 2nd class
Constable. 10.1.1895 to 1st class Constable.
1.12.1900 to Sergeant.
Stationed at: Bodmin 25.4.1890. Launceston
4.12.1900. Liskeard 13.9.1906. Launceston
12.4.1918.
30.9.1822 Retired.

P.C. 89 Joseph Hocking
A 21 year old married mason from S.Ives.
Appointed: 11.11.1889.
Stationed at: Helston 20.10.1890.
22.3.1892 Called upon to resign.

P.C. 179 James Henry Harris
A 19 year old single labourer from Feock.
Public service. K Comp., Rifle Volunteers
D.C.L.I.
Appointed: 11.11.1889.
Stationed at: Liskeard 25.4.1890.
26.12.1890 dismissed for drunkenness.

P.C. 115 Joseph Chapman
A farm labourer from St Cleer , 19 single.
Appointed: 2.12.1889.
5.1.1890   Resigned.

P.C. 170 Richard I. Rowland
A 24 year old labourer from Bodmin.
9.11.1893. Married Isabella Bickford of
Week St Mary.
Appointed: 15.1.1890.
Promotion: 8.12.1892 to 2nd class
Constable. 22.2.1897 to 1st class Constable.
9.4.1907 to merit class Constable.
Stationed at: Launceston 25.4.1890. Truro
12.10.1893. Bodmin 12.8.1896. Truro
19.9.1917.
31.3.1919. Retired Pension £86.13.4.

P.C. 115 Sidney Lawrence
A 26 year old miller from Blanford.
Appointed: 16.1.1890.
14.1.1897 Married Maud Rogers of
Dorchester.
Promotion: 8.8.1892 to 2nd class
Constable. 27.9.1897 to 1st class Constable.
1.4.1908 to merit class Constable.
Stationed at: Bodmin 25.4.1890. Helston
2.2.1891.
31.1.1920 Retired. Pension £165.4.7.
Died at Fore Street, Flushing, near Falmouth
on 5.7.1938.

P.C. 173 Thomas Whell
A 20 year old woodsman from St Neot.
Appointed: 10.2.1890.
15.2.1894 Married Alice Bickford of
Launceston.
Promotion: 10.2.1893 to 2nd class
Constable. 20.12.1897 to 1st class Constable.
1.9.1907 to merit class Constable.
Stationed at: Launceston 28.8.1890. Truro
11.1.1892. Penzance Aug 1894.
29.2.1920 Retired. Pension £165.4.7.
Died 10.11.1952.

P.C. 69 William Wherry
A 20 year old single labourer from St Meryn.
Appointed: 10.2.1890.
Stationed at: Penzance 26.6.1890.
20.7.1890. Resigned.

P.C. 40 Harry Ough
A gardener from Morval, single aged 25.
Appointed: 24.3.1890.
Stationed at: Penzance 11.10.1890.
27.4.1891 Resigned.

P.C. 143 Alfred Cobblebdick
A 22 year old single labourer from Bere
Alston.
Appointed: 24.3.1890.
Stationed at: Bodmin 15.8.1890. Truro
3.10.1891.
30.11.1891 Resigned.

P.C. 130 John Northcott
A labourer from Boscastle aged 22 years.
Appointed: 7.4.1890.
6.7.1898 Married Mary Jane Daniel of
Redruth.
Promotion: 24.1.1892 to 2nd class
Constable. 28.10.1895 to 1st class Constable.
1.12.1902 to Sergeant. 14.7.1910 to
Inspector.
Stationed at: Penzance 11.10.1890. Helston
10.4.1891. Penzance 18.8.1891. Liskeard
1.12.1902. Bodmin 5.1.1906. Truro

19.7.1910.
Favourable Record: Zeal and intelligence displayed in detecting and bringing an offender to justice in a case of plate glass smashing
Favourable Record. 25 4.1902 at Camborne. Spirited and brave conduct in stopping a runaway horse at great personal risk and thereby preventing harm to life and property.
31.10.1919. Retired Pension £233.6.8.
29.10.1935 Died Robarts Road, Newquay.

P.C. 131 William Henry Cocking
A teacher from Linkinhorne, single aged 22 years.
Appointed: 10.5.1890.
Stationed at: St Ives 11.10.1890. Truro 27.8.1891. Helston 9.9.1892.
16.3.1893 Called on to resign for neglect of duty, having received a report of a death and not updating it. And for general inattention.

P.C. 158 John Henry Crowle
A 19 year old single man from St Blazey.
Appointed: 19.5.1890.
Promotion: 24.1.1892 to 2nd class Constable. 6.5.1895 to 1st class Constable. 1.11.1907 to merit class Constable. 1.7.1911. To Sergeant.
Stationed at: Penzance 11.10.1890. Truro 11.4.1896. Bodmin 15.7.1908. Liskeard 6.7.1911. Camborne 9.7.1912. Truro 5.11.1919.
Retired 30.9.1921. Died 5.11.1944.

P.C. 142 Richard Thomas Roberts
A 25 year old single labourer from Phillack, Hayle. 19.10.1891 Married Mary E. Hile of Hayle.
Appointed: 27.5.1890.
Promotion: 22.5.1894 to 2nd class Constable. 5.6.1899 to 1st class Constable. 1.2.1909 to merit class Constable.
Stationed at: Bodmin 22.12.1890. St Germans 14.4.1895.
31.10.1918 Retired. Pension £165.4.7.

P.C. 66 Walter Wright
A 23 year old porter from Essex. Public Service: Metropolitan Police for two years. July 1890 Married Mary Hobba Gardino of London.
Appointed: 9.6.1890.
Promotion: 24.1.1892 to 2nd class Constable. 10.1.1895 to 1st class Constable. 23.10.1899 to Sergeant. 1.12.1902 to Inspector.
Stationed at: Liskeard 2.7.1890. Launceston 1.12.1902. Camborne 13.5.1904.
Favourable Record. Inspector Walter Wright was on the 3rd, Inst granted a Favourable Record for exhibiting, on the 16th of August last, special zeal and intelligence and promptness in dealing with a swindler subsequently convicted.
23.7.1910 Died whilst walking on Praa Sands.

P.C. 121 James Henry Holman
A 28 year old miner from Stoke Climsland. March 1891 Married Emma Grylls.
Appointed: 25.8.1890.
Promotion: 30.8.1896 to 2nd class Constable. 29.8.1898 to 1st class Constable.

Stationed at: Launceston 17.1.1891. Liskeard 1.11.1903.
30.9.1919. Retired Pension £86.13.4. Reassessed in accordance with the Desborough Report and granted £165.4.7. On and from 1.10.1919.

P.C. 69 Reuben Fitze.
A 24 year old single miner from Calstock.
Appointed: 25.8.1890.
Stationed at: Penzance 15.1.1891.
18.5.1891 Resigned.

P.C. 176 George John Oliver
A blacksmith from Madron aged 21 years. 6.9.1904 Married at St Annes Church, Newlyn, to Edith Collins of Florence Place, Newlyn.
Appointed: 8.9.1890.
Promotion: 24.1.1892. To 2nd class Constable. 1.6.1902 to 1st class Constable.
Stationed at: Bodmin 3.2.1891. Liskeard 17.9.1895. Camborne 12.7.1899. Truro 11.6.1901. Camborne 12.3.1903. Launceston 17.6.1903.
Fined 10/- for being absent from his conference point and 10/- for making a false entry in his journal.
31.10.1919 Retired Pension £165.4.7.

P.C. 122 Edward Smith
A 22 year old farmers son, married, from Brisbane, Australia.
Appointed: 30.9.1890.
11.11.1890 Absconded.

P.C. 132 William Henry Slanton
A farmers son from St Germans aged 22 years. 1.4.1893 Married Elizabeth Hill of St Martins.
Appointed: 6.10.1890.
Promotion: 27.11.1892 to 2nd class Constable.
Stationed at: Helston 7.2.1891. Truro 28.7.1893.
15.2.1894 Resigned.

P.C. 102 Henry Taylor
A single porter from Menheniott aged 19 years.
Appointed: 20.11.1890.
Stationed at: Truro 17.2.1891
17.7.1891 Resigned.

P.C. 14 Henry Reynolds
A 19 year old single gardener from Mawnan Smith.
Appointed: 31.12.1890.
Promotion: 8.12.1892. To 2nd class Constable.
Stationed at: Penzance 30.4.1891.
7.1.1893 Resigned.
1.9.1893
Reappointed: as P.C. 8
Stationed at: Bodmin 15.9.1893.
8.4.1895 Resigned.

P.C. 179 Thomas Lillington
A 22 year old single labourer from Wareham. 24.5.1894 Married Bertha Hambly of Landrake.
Appointed: 5.1.1891.
Promotion: 22.11.1892 to 2nd class

Constable. 28.10.1895 to 1st class Constable.
Stationed at: Penzance 13.4.1891. Bodmin 20.5.1892. Truro 25.10.1898.
Discipline: P.C. 179 Lillington was on the 26.3.1898 fined for disrespect to his Superintendent.
Pension on Doctor's Certificate of £45.1.4. Retired 31.3.1907

P.C. 122 William John Crocker
A labourer from, Tywardreath aged 19 years. 10.4.1895 Married H.Bone of Cawsand.
Appointed: 5.1.1891.
Promotion: 27.11.1892 to 2nd class Constable. 1.3.1899 to 1st class Constable. 1.7.1911 to merit class Constable.
Stationed at: Liskeard 26.6.1891. Bodmin 8.5.1895.
31.12.1919 Retired Pension £165.4.7.

P.C. 32 William Robert Ellory
A 20 year single labourer from Tywardreath.
Appointed: 7.1.1891.
Promotion: 1.10.1893 to 2nd class Constable
Stationed at: Liskeard 26.5.1891. Bodmin 1.7.1897.
30.8.1897 Resigned under medical certificate. Granted a gratuity of £20.0.0.

P.C. 42 Thomas Curtis
A carpenter from Roche aged 21 years. 1.9.1891. Married Alma Ada Moyses of Roche
Appointed: 28.1.1891.
Stationed at: Liskeard 17.4.1891.
16.5.1892 Resigned.

P.C. 77 Robert Henry Benney
A 20 year old miner from Duloe. 21.11.1891 married Margaret Jane Johns of Illogan.
Appointed: 2.2.1891.
Promotion: 24.1.1892 to 2nd class Constable. 26.10.1896 to 1st class Constable. 1.7.1908 to merit class Constable.
Stationed at: Bodmin 5.8.1891. Truro 20.5.1892.
Favourable Record: For zeal and promptitude and intelligence displayed in the successful prosecution for a child murder (Rex v Ellen Phillips) on the 28.11.1901.
Favourable Record: For courageous conduct in a prolonged struggle with two poachers at the risk of his own life. Both poachers being armed with loaded guns.
30.4.1919 Retired Pension £165.4.7.

P.C. 99 Richard Henry Matthews
A labourer from Ludgvan aged 20 years married
Appointed: 2.3.1891
Promotion: 24.1.1892 to 2nd class Constable. 26.10.1896 to 1st class Constable. 1.5.1909 to merit class Constable. 14.7 1910 to Sergeant.
Stationed at: Bodmin 19.4.1891. Truro 15.7.1908. Bodmin 19.7.1910.
Favourable Record: P.C. 99 Richard H.Matthews was on the 14th of July last granted a favourable record for zeal and intelligence displayed in tracing and arresting

under difficulties five men charged with burglary, on the 25.2.1906.
30.9.1919 Retired Pension £195.13.4.

P.C. 30 Henry Edwin Pearce
A labourer from Stratton, aged 20 years.
20.10.1892 Married Elizabeth Tripp of Falmouth.
Appointed: 9.3.1891.
Promotion: 13.10.1894 to 2nd class Constable. 1.12.1900 to 1st class Constable.
Stationed at: Helston 7.7.1891. Truro 30.10.1892. Liskeard 12.8.1908.
31.5.1922 Retired. Pension £145.4.7.
Died 3.1.1926.

P.C. 113 Joseph Robert Burnett
A 21 year old married cab driver from Gerrans.
Appointed: 2.4.1891.
Promotion: 13.10.1894 to 2nd class Constable. 23.10.1899 to 1st class Constable.
Stationed at: Liskeard 28.8.1891.
Launceston 2.4.1893
16.8.1907 Resigned on medical grounds Pension £21.12.7.

P.C. 123 John Haley
A single groom from Menabilly aged 19 years.
Appointed: 20.4.1891.
Stationed at: Truro 18.8.1891. Launceston 14.1.1892. Bodmin 27.8.1892.
9.10.1893 Resigned.

P.C. 40 William James Balsdon
A labourer from Holsworthy aged 21 years.
28.10.1896 Married Miss M.J.Chynoweth of Nanstallon.
Appointed: 27.4.1891
Promotion: 21.11.1892 to 2nd class Constable. 1.7.1900 to 1st class Constable.
1.7.1911 to merit class Constable.
Stationed at: Penzance 7.7.1891. Bodmin 20.10.1891. Penzance 7.4.1893. Truro 11.5.1906. Bodmin 20.5.1914.
31.12.1919. Retired Pension £165.14.7.

P.C. 76 Frank Boundy
A 20 year old single labourer from St Columb Minor.
Appointed: 4.9.1891.
Stationed at: Liskeard 18.8.1891.
19.3.1892 Resigned.

P.C. 114 William John Keast
A 19 year old labourer from Fowey.
22.6.1899 married Emma Rundle,
Appointed: 11.5.1891.
Promotion: 27.11.1892 to 2nd class Constable. 7.6.1897 to 1st class Constable.
1.10.1905 to Sergeant. 13.11.1908 to Inspector.
Stationed at:
Helston 18.8.1891. Bodmin 7.4.1893.
Truro 5.10.1894. Penzance 11.4.1896.
Falmouth 31.10.1899. Camborne 29.9.1905. Falmouth 30.11.1907.
Launceston 26.1.1919.
No further record.

P.C. 69 Mark Bennetts
From Creed, a 24 year old coachman,
1.2.1893 Married Sarah Bennett of Par.

Appointed: 6.7.1891.
Promotion: 27.11.1892 to 2nd class Constable. 1.8.1901 to 1st class Constable.
Stationed at: Launceston 10.9.1891. Truro 12.1.1892.
13.5.1894 Fined 5/- for not filling in his journal according to orders.
27.4.1905 Retired on medical grounds with a gratuity of £73.4.8.

P.C. 13 George Bear
A single labourer from Ludgvan aged 19 years.
Appointed: 13.7.1891.
20.9.1891 Dismissed with forfeiture of a weeks pay for drunkenness and disorderly conduct.

P.C. 126 George Scown
A widower from Truro aged 21 years, a blacksmith.
Appointed: 20.7.1891.
20.9.1891 Dismissed with forfeiture of one weeks pay for drunkenness and disorderly conduct.

P.C. 102 William Lyndon
A 19 year old labourer from Probus.
14.11.1896 Married Sarah Holman of Bodmin.
Appointed: 20.7.1891.
Promotion: 19.2.1893 to 2nd class Constable. 24.10.1898 to 1st class Constable.
24.7.1910 to Sergeant.
Stationed at: Bodmin 1.10.1891. Penzance 5.7.1896. Bodmin 3.6.1903.
31/.12.1921 Retired.

P.C. 90 Wesley Juliff
A single labourer from Ladock aged 20 years.
Appointed: 4.8.1891.
9.9.1891 Resigned.

P.C. 47 William Courtis
A 21 year old single labourer from Stofford, Devon.
Appointed: 7.8.1891.
Stationed at: Helston 4.11.1891. Truro 9.9.1892. 7.1.1893 Removal to Newquay at his own expense. Penzance 20.8.1893.
Launceston 14.12.1893.
17.4.1894 Dismissed for insolence to his Inspector.

P.C. 79 Willie Taylor
A 20 year old single labourer from Tywardreath.
Appointed: 10.8.1891.
Stationed at: Truro 16.10.1891. Penzance 15.6.1892. Truro 28.4.1893.
15.7.1893 Dismissed for gross neglect of duty and telling falsehoods.

P.C. 128 Francis Cowling
A 25 year old married labourer from Lewannick.
Appointed: 19.8.1891.
Promotion: 30.9.1895 to 2nd class Constable. 1.3.1899 to 1st class Constable.
Stationed at: Launceston 7.10.1891.
24.7.1911 Reprimanded and cautioned as to future conduct on that he, on his rest day,

received information as to alleged fowl stealing and did not take the necessary steps to deal properly with the matter.
28.2.1912. Fined £1.0.0. And severely cautioned as to future conduct for neglect of duty and for drinking in a Public House on 8.1.1912.
1.2.1919 Fined 10/- for absence from a conference point and making a false entry in his journal and has also been called upon to resign.
28.2.1919. Resigned Pension £86.13.4.

P.C. 80 William Jeffery
A 24 year old single farmer from Paul, Penzance.
Appointed: 31.8.1891.
Stationed at: Bodmin 15.10.1891.
21.12.1891 Resigned.

P.C. 155 John Henry Hodge
A married groom from Helston aged 25 years. 13.8.1901 2nd marriage to Mary Bennetts of Ludgvan.
Appointed: 31.8.1891.
Promotion: 19.2.1893 to 2nd class Constable.
23.10.1899 to 1st class Constable.
Stationed at: Camborne 12.10.1891.
Penzance. Camborne
Retired 31.12.1921. Died 31.1.1952.

P.C. 129 Edward Henry Rogers
A 22 year old married miner from Sithney.
Appointed: 31.8.1891.
Promotion: 19.2.1893 to 2nd class Constable.
Stationed at: Penzance 31.12.1891.
23.5.1898 Resigned.

P.C. 60 John Wickett
A carpenter from Stratton, married aged 22 years.
Appointed: 7.9.1891.
Promotion: 1.10.1893 to 2nd class Constable.
Stationed at: Launceston 18.1.1892.
Liskeard 21.5.1902.
Copy of G.O. 31.10.1901. P.C. 60 John Wickett hereby fined 10/- for failing to carryout a Conference point and 10/- for making a false entry in his journal. Relative thereto, both offences being aggravated by denial in the first instant. The Constable is to be transferred at his own expense to another Station and is warned for dismissal if reported against within a considerable time.
Copy of G.O. 3.6.1902 P.C. John Wickett was on the 20th ult., fined 5/- for improper conduct as a Policeman on the 12th ult., and also fined 5/- for disobeying his Sergeants orders on the same date. Also again warned for dismissal.
7.5.1904 Called upon to resign by the Chief Constable.

P.C. 97 John Libby
A single labourer from Polperro, aged 21 years.
Appointed: 7.9.1891.
Stationed at: Bodmin 23.11.1891. Truro 20.2.1892.
25.3.1892 Resigned.

P.C. 13 Samuel Oatey
A 20 year old labourer from Crowan.
6.8.1894 Married Suzy Harvey of Germoe.
Appointed: 21.9.1891.
Promotion: 1.10.1893 to 2nd class
Constable. 30.8.1896 to 1st class Constable.
19.9.1908 to Sergeant.
Stationed at: Liskeard 3.12.1891. Truro
18.9.1908.
30.6.1919 Retired Pension £195.13.4.

P.C. 90 John Stephens
A single labourer from Breage, Helston, aged
19 years.
Appointed: 21.9.1891.
Promotion:. 1.10.1893 to 2nd class
Constable.
Stationed at: Penzance 3.12.1891. Truro
10.1.1895.
2.9.1895 Resigned.

P.C. 126 William Thomas Hall
A 20 year old labourer from Breage, Helston.
24.8.1898 Married Sarah Nicholls of
Ludgvan, Penzance.
Appointed: 24.9.1891.
Promotion: 26.10.1896 to 2nd class
Constable. 1.1.1901 to 1st class Constable.
1.4.1912. To Sergeant.
Stationed at: Launceston 9.1.1892. Bodmin
20.8.1895 . Falmouth 26.3.1912.
H.Q. Letter dated 28,2.1918. Specially
commended by the Secretary of State for
good work in connection with enquiries and
reports relating to aliens and suspected
persons as a result of appreciation expressed
by Col., Kell C.B. M.I.5 War Office, since
the outbreak of war Aug 1914.
Retired 30.9.1919. Pension £195.13.4.

P.C. 46 Edward John Pooley
A 20 year old single labourer from
Davidstow.
Appointed: 19.10.1891.
Stationed at: Bodmin 23.2.1892.
29.2.1892 Resigned.

P.C. 95 Ezia Menear
A single labourer from St Austell, aged 22.
Appointed: 16.10.1891
Stationed at: Launceston 6.2.1892.
4.4.1892 Called on to resign.

P.C. 153 John George Rogers
A 23 year old single labourer from Liskeard.
Appointed: 16.10.1891.
Promotion: 19.2.1893 to 2nd class
Constable. 28.12.1898 to 1st class
Constable. 1.9.1910 to merit class Constable.
Stationed at: Liskeard 13.12.1891.
Camborne 6.7.1903. Truro 27.4.1905.
30.4.1919 Retired Pension £165.4.7.

P.C. 107 John Warden
A labourer from Callington, single aged 22
years.
Appointed: 9.11.1891.
31.12.1891 Dismissed for drinking in public
houses and inattention to duty.

P.C. 154 Phillip Nicholls
A 23 year old single market gardener from

Liskeard.
Appointed: 9.11.1891.
Stationed at: Bodmin 22.2.1892.
29.8.1892 Resigned.

P.C. 5 George Francis
A single bakers assistant from Paul, aged 20
years.
Appointed: 16.11.1891.
9.12.1891. Resigned.

P.C. 80 Richard Henry Boundy
A 20 year old single labourer from St Clether.
Appointed: 18.1.1892.
Stationed at: Truro 28.3.1892.
13.5.1892 Dismissed for associating with a
female of immoral character and disobedience to orders.

P.C. 5 Cyrus Lampshire
A single labourer from Perran aged 21 years.
19.9.1892 Married Annie M.Dyer of Truro.
Appointed: 18.1.1892.
Stationed at: Liskeard 25.3.1892.
18.1.1893 Dismissed for telling falsehoods.

P.C. 143 William Thomas Giles
A married blacksmith from St Winnow, aged
23 years.
Appointed: 19.1.1892.
Promotion: 6.5.1895 to 2nd class Constable.
12.3.1900 to 1st class Constable.
Stationed at: Bodmin 17.2.1892. Liskeard
18.11.1904.
20.1.1905 Fined 10/- for displaying serious
indiscretion in making an arrest.
28.2.1921 Retired   Pension £165.4.7.
Died 11.2.1945.

P.C. 105 Thomas Chappele
A 21 year old single wheelwright from St
Columb.
Appointed: 27.1.1892.
Stationed at: Bodmin 9.4.1892.
10.3.1894 Fined 5/- for not filling in his
journal according to orders.
16.4.1894 Called upon to resign.

P.C. 35 Charles Deacon
A 20 year old labourer from North Hill.
20.8.1902 Married Bessie Termouth of
Millbrook.
Appointed: 1.2.1892.
Promotion: 1.1.1894 to 2nd class Constable.
1.10.1901 to 1st class Constable.
Stationed at: Penzance 9.4.1892. Bodmin
19.4.1894. Liskeard 29.12.1895. Truro
26.2.1903.
14.2.1897 Fined 10/- for being drunk on
duty and cautioned as to his future conduct.
Favourable Record: For intelligence and
promptitude in the detection and arrest of
three soldiers convicted of larceny
29.2.1920 Retired   Pension £165.4.7.
17.1.1956 Died.

P.C. 43 Samuel John Kellow
A 24 year old single labourer from Cubert.
Appointed: 2.2.1892.
Stationed at: Bodmin 11.4.1892. Launceston
27.8.1892.
1.7.1893. Resigned.

P.C. 107 Albert John Hooper
A single clay labourer from St Austell, aged
19 years.
Appointed: 8.2.1892.
12.2.1892 Resigned.

P.C. 107 Samuel Bice
A 20 year old porter from Tywardreath.
14.8.1895 Married Miss E.Treffry of
Calstock.
Appointed: 15.2.1892.
Promotion: 6.5.1895. To 2nd class
Constable.
Stationed at: Launceston 4.4.1892.
On January 4th was ordered to be trans-
ferred at his own expense for conduct unbe-
coming a Constable.
15.1.1900 Resigned.

P.C. 48 Joseph John Symons
A 22 year old single clay labourer from
Roche.
Appointed: 22.2.1892.
Stationed at: Liskeard 3.6.1892.
10.2.1894 Resigned.

P.C. 46 John Sweet
A single labourer from St Breock, aged 20
years.
Appointed: 3.3.1892.
Stationed at: Penzance 20.5.1892.
8.11.1892. Resigned.

P.C. 141 James Rickard
A 23 year old labourer from North Hill.
6.10.1897 Married Miss Pope of Bodmin.
10.9.1902 2nd marriage to Anna Leech of
Alcombe, Somerset.
Appointed: 9.3.1892.
Promotion: 10.1.1895. To 2nd class
Constable. 1.5.1905 to 1st class Constable,
Stationed at: Bodmin 20.5.1892. Truro
27.7.1896. Bodmin 1.8.1897. Liskeard
28.2.1900.
13.2.1900 Fined 10/- for unnecessary delay
in returning to his station, 5/- for drinking in
a public house, and 10/- for being drunk.
The last offence being aggravated by denial.
30.11.1921. Retired   Pension £165.4.7.

P.C. 16 John Vincent Burnett
A 24 year old coachman from Gerrans.
30.12.1894. Married Miss M.E.Vincent of
Truro.
Appointed: 7.3.1892.
Promotion: 25.5.1894 to 2nd class constable.
Stationed at: Truro 20.5.1892. Penzance
10.1.1895. Liskeard 1.2.1905.
31.12.1922 Retired Pension of £165.4.7.
Died 16.2.1949.

P.C. 53 William Tamlin Mitchell
A carpenter from Duloe, aged 23 years.
10.4.1897 married Sarah A.Hoskin of
Camelford.
Appointed: 7.3.1892.
Promotion: 1.10.1893 to 2nd class
Constable. 1.10.1900 to 1st class Constable.
1.1.1912 to Sergeant.
Stationed at: Helston 9.4.1891. Liskeard
10.1.1895. St Tudy 5.9.1895. Camborne
16.12.1903.
15.3.1922 Retired.

P.C. 108 John Charles Dyer
A married labourer from St Blazey aged 24 years.
Appointed: 7.3.1892.
Stationed at: Liskeard 4.4.1892. Launceston 17.2.1895.
Fined 10/- for sleeping whilst out on duty and being absent from his conference point. 11.11.1895 Resigned.

P.C. 37 Ernest George Carpenter
A single farm labourer from St German, aged 20 years.
Appointed: 21.3.1892.
Promotion: 10.1.1895 to 2nd class Constable. 16.1.1900 to 1st class Constable.
Stationed at: Bodmin 30.8.1892. Falmouth 2.3.1899. Camborne 2.2.1912.
31.10.1919 Retired Pension £165.4.7.

P.C. 97 George Broad
A 19 year old single labourer from Pelynt.
Appointed: 30.3.1892.
Promotion: 26.2.1894 to 2nd class Constable.
Stationed at: Penzance 25.5.1892.
27.7.1895 Dismissed for being drunk.

P.C 76 Thomas Henry Broad
A 21 year old labourer from Pelynt.
20.6.1895 married Lucy J.Rogers of St Austell.
Appointed: 30.3.1892.
Promotion: 26.2.1894 to 2nd class Constable. 13.2.1899 to 1st class Constable. 1.11.1905 to Sergeant. 18.8.1911 to Inspector.
Stationed at: Bodmin 25.5.1892. Liskeard 8.5.1895. Launceston 5.9.1897. Liskeard 1.11.1900.
Favourable Record: 26.1.1898 Promptitude in arresting and preventing the suicide of a man charged with forgery.
9.7.1903 Displaying zeal and promptitude in tracing under difficulties two motorists subsequently convicted of furious driving.
31.3.1923 Retired. 1.5.1943 Died.

P.C. 181 Thomas Beer
A 21 year old single farmer from Camelford.
Appointed: 4.4.1892.
21.7.1892 Resigned.

P.C. 89 William Thomas Hooper
A farm labourer from Pelynt aged 21 years.
21.2.1895. Married Hannah J.Clemo from Camelford.
Appointed: 4.4.1892
Promotion: 1.10.1893 to 2nd class Constable.
Stationed at: Truro 14.6.1892.
13.3.1899 Resigned.
30.7.1952 Died.

P.C. 9 William Martin
A 22 year old married farm labourer from Padstow.
Appointed: 5.4.1892.
21.7.1892 Resigned,

P.C. 95 Richard Marshall
A Farm labourer from Helland aged 21 years.

13.6.1898 Married Mary E.Rudlin of Flushing
Appointed: 18.4.1892.
Promotion: 10.1.1895. To 2nd class Constable. 1.9.1902 to 1st class Constable.
Stationed at: Truro 10.9.1892. Helston 25.7.1893. Camborne 7.12.1898. Bodmin 2.3.1909.
31.12.1920 Retired Pension £165.4.7.

P.C. 151 John Davey
A labourer from Key, Truro. Aged 21 years.
12.8.1899 Married Edith Harris.
Appointed: 5.5.1892.
Promotion: 8.7.1895 to 2nd class Constable. 24.10.1898 to 1st class Constable.
Stationed at: Liskeard 8.7.1892. Bodmin 28.2.1900.
30.6.1922 Retired

P.C. 42 William Quintrele
A 25 year old labourer from Truro.
4.11.1896 married Miss K.Rowe of St Just.
Appointed: 23.5.1892.
Promotion: 28.10.1895 to 2nd class Constable. 1.7.1903 to 1st class Constable.
Stationed at: Penzance 9.9.1892. Falmouth 2.7.1912.
31.5.1920 Retired. Pension £165.4.7.
Died at St Ives on 21.3.1935.

P.C. 80 James Henry Collett
A 21 year old labourer from Truro. 4.4.1900 married Miss E.J.Bull.
Appointed: 23.5.1892.
Promotion: 30.8.1896 to 2nd class Constable. 1.1.1902 to 1st class Constable.
Stationed at: Liskeard 22.10.1892. Truro 11.4.1894. Bodmin 10.8.1895. Launceston 6.6.1899.
31.12.1922 Retired.

P.C. 15 William Henry Rogers
A carpenter from Padstow aged 20 years.
21.4.1904 married Louisa Jane Hughes of Falmouth.
Appointed: 30.5.1892.
Promotion: 22.5.1994. To 2nd class Constable. 24.10.1898 to 1st class Constable. 1.4.1913 to sergeant. 1.9.1920 to Inspector.
Stationed at: Helston 21.10.1892. Penzance 11.4.1897. Helston 12.6.1897. Camborne.. 17.3.1901. Bodmin 10.6.1901 Camborne 10.3.1902. Bodmin 25.6.1902. Liskeard 31.10.1903. Camborne 7.4.1913.
1.10.1908 Reprimanded for failing to report a serious crime occurring on his beat and for omitting to make any references thereto in his occurrence book and cautioned against a repetition of such irregularity.
28.2.1925 Retired. Died 2.3.1947.

P.C. 23 Henry Hebbard
A farmer from Germoe aged 20 years.
19.10.1900 married Mary E.Coad of Bodmin.
Appointed: 11.7.1892.
Promotion: 6.5.1895 to 2nd class Constable. 24.10.1898 to 1st class Constable. 1.4.1909 to Sergeant.
Stationed at: Liskeard 27.7.1893. Bodmin 5.10.1994. Penzance 14.3.1997. Bodmin

12.6.1897. Camborne. 12.3.1898. Bodmin 7.6.1898. Camborne. 5.12.1899. Bodmin 4.12.1900. Launceston 2.3.1909 Liskeard 15.8.1911.
31.12.1921. Retried. Died 10.6.1923.

P.C. 29 William Rouse
A labourer from St Austell. Aged 20 years.
14.11.1900 Married Annie Powell from St Columb.
Appointed: 5.9.1892.
Promotion: 6.5.1895 to 2nd class Constable. 1.2.1901 to 1st class Constable.
Stationed at: Helston 16.3.1893. Penzance 28.7.1893. Truro 20.8.1893. Penzance 6.2.1896. Liskeard 15.5.1899. Camborne 8.11.1907
4.2.1896 Fined £1.0.0 for leaving his station twice in plain clothes and going out of his division with out leave, when he should have been on duty.
Favourable Record: 13.10.1900 Zeal and promptitude in detecting and arresting two fowl stealers.
12.1.1920 Retired. Pension £165.4.7.

P.C. 154 William Samuel Jenkin
A 24 year old labourer from Helston.
30.11.1904 married Mary Jane Andrew of St Just.
Appointed: 5.9.1892
Promotion: 20.10.1895 to 2nd class Constable. 1.8.1901 to 1st class Constable.
Stationed at: Liskeard 30.11.1892. Camborne 8.11.1898. Falmouth 3.7.1906.
1.6.1903 Copy of G.O. P.C. 154 William Jenkin was on the 12th ult., fined 5/- for carelessness in the discharge of his duty.
8.4.1909 Fined 5/- for neglect of duty in failing to be on a conference point on the 30th March last and 5/- for making a false entry in his journal relative thereto, and also 5/- for making a false statement to his Sergeant relative thereto.
26.8.1916 Died. Widow's gratuity of £149.10.0.

P.C. 125 Albert Moor
A shoe maker from Looe aged 23 years,
24.1.1898 Married Fanny C.Nicholls of Kenwyn.
Appointed: 12.9.1892.
Promotion: 20.10.1895 to 2nd class Constable. 1.10.1901 to 1st class Constable.
Stationed at: Liskeard 18.11.1892. Truro 28.12.1898.
13.6.1919 Retired. Pension £165.4.7.
Died 25.5.1952.

P.C. 50 Frederick Bunney
A 20 year old single labourer from St Blazey.
Appointed: 10.10.1892.
19.10.1892 Resigned.

P.C. 50 Edward H. Keat
A 25 year old married labourer from St Kew.
19.10.1907 2nd marriage to Eunice Ann Evans of Looe.
Appointed: 17.10.1892.
Promotion: 26.10.1896 to 2nd class Constable. 1.2.1901 to 1st class Constable.
Stationed at: Launceston 16.11.1892.

Liskeard 6.9.1899. Camborne 2.9.1914.
31.10.1919. Retired Pension £165.4.7.
2.1.1947 Died.

P.C. 46 Joseph Andrew
A labourer from St Columb Minor aged 23
years. 1.2.1899 married Mary Jane Chinn of
Phillack.
Appointed: 24.10.1892.
Promotion: 10.1.1895 to 2nd class
Constable. 1.10.1901 to 1st class Constable.
1.12.1911 to Sergeant.
Stationed at: Penzance 27.1.1893.
Launceston 10.5.1899. Liskeard 17.4.1918.
Favourable Record: For promptitude and
intelligence in effecting the arrest on
13.10.1905 of a man subsequently convicted
for arson, at the Autumn Assize 1905.
31.1.1923 Retired.

P.C. 110 James Truscott
A labourer from Creed, aged 20 years.
Married Mary Jane Balhatchet of
Marhamchurch.
Appointed: 14.11.1892.
Promotion: 30.8.1896 to 2nd class
Constable. 1.2.1902 to 1st class Constable.
Stationed at: Launceston 1.5.1893.
31.10.1922 Retired.

P.C. 72 Maurice Light
A porter from St Neot aged 22 years.
28.4.1895 married Bessie Congdon of
Dobwalls.
Appointed: 21.11.1892.
Promotion: 1.1.1894 2nd class Constable.
24.10.1898 to 1st class Constable. 13.7.1909
to Sergeant. 1.4.1923 to Inspector.
Stationed at: Truro 7.4.1893. Bodmin
5.10.1894. Truro 8.5.1895. Liskeard
13.7.1909. Falmouth 1.11.1912.
28.2.1918. Specially commended by the
Sec Of State for good work in connection
with enquiries and reports relating to aliens
and suspected persons. As the result of
appreciation expressed by Col.Kell C.B.
MI5 War Office since the outbreak of war
1918. 30.6.1930 Retired.

P.C. 169 Joseph B.Stephens
A 21 year old labourer from Looe. 6.9.1893
married Rose Evrill of Looe.
Appointed: 21.11.1892.
Promotion: 30.8.1896 to 2nd class
Constable. 1.12.1902 to 1st class Constable.
Stationed at: Helston 1.5.1893. Penzance
14.9.1893. Bodmin 25.10.1898. Camborne
24.6.1905.
31.12.1921 Retired 12.12.1945 Died.

P.C. 71 George Beynon
A 22 year old married Master Mariner of
Penbroke, South Wales.
Appointed: 9.1.1893.
Stationed at: Liskeard 7.4.1893.
26.2.1894 Resigned.

P.C. 139 Daniel Rundle
A 21 year old single labourer from Pleynt.
Appointed: 9.1.1893.
Stationed at: Launceston 4.7.1893.
13.10.1893 Dismissed for drunkenness.

P.C. 14 James Drew
A single sawyer from Mylor. 3.7.1895
married Esther Jane Spargo of Mylor Bridge.
Appointed: 9.1.1893.
Promotion: 30.8.1896 to 2nd class
Constable. 12.3.1900 to 1st class Constable.
1.10.1905 to Sergeant. 1.4.1909 to
Inspector. 1.1.1921 to Superintendent.
Stationed at: Bodmin 12.9.1893. Liskeard
6.10.1894. Camborne 29.9.1903. Bodmin
1.4.1909. Liskeard 30.12.1920.
Favourable Record. P.C. 14 James H. Drew
was on the 6.1.1902 granted a favourable
record for his ready knowledge and prompt
action in restoring to life a boy who was
apparently drowned. P.C. Drew was on the
16.1.1902 presented with the honorary
certificate from the Royal Humane Society
for his action on the same occasion.
Favourable Record. Sergeant H.Drew was on
the 1st 7. 1907. Granted a favourable
record for his zeal and energy displayed in
connection with the working up with a difficult case of child murder (Rex V Polmere)
31.12.1933 Retired.

P.C. 5 Willy Stoot
A 21 year old gardener from Truro. 4.9.1894
married Jessie Odgers of Truro.
Appointed: 26.1.1893.
Stationed at: Helston 28.7.1893. Bodmin
23.7.1894.
25.11.1895 Resigned.

P.C. 19 Charles Pollard
A 25 year old single labourer from Liskeard.
Public Service: 1st Batt. D.C.L.I. For 7 years
and 4 months.
Appointed: 20.3.1893.
16.7.1893 Dismissed for being the worse for
liquor while on duty.
P.C. 131 Richard I.May
A labourer from Tregoney, aged 20 years.
25.9.1897 married Sarah I.Johns of
Camborne.
Appointed: 23.2.1893.
Promotion: 26.10.1896 to 2nd class
Constable. 1.10.1903 to 1st class Constable.
31.7.1906 reduced to 2nd class Constable.
Stationed at: Penzance 15.9.1893. Truro
29.3.1906.
12.3.1906 warned by the Chief Constable
against repeating the offence of tippling with
which offence he had been charged.
31.7.1906, Reduced to the 2nd class of his
rank and again severely warned.
16.4.1909 Fined £1.0.0. For tippling at St
Columb on 19.3.1909 with the result that he
was drunk at his station on that day. The
Constable was also cautioned severely.
14.7.1909 Resigned on medical certificate.
Granted a pension of £19.19.4.

P.C. 74 Richard Marks
A single labourer from Launceston, aged 20
years.
Appointed: 17.4.1893.
Stationed at: Bodmin 14.12.1893.
Penzance 3.8.1894.
23.8.1895 Dismissed for associating with
bad characters and drinking in public houses.

P.C. 43 Albert Bunt
A 26 year old single saddler from Camelford.
Appointed: 3.7.1893.
24.7.1893 Called on to resign.

P.C. 79 Alfred Kean Honey
A labourer from Luxulyan, 28.3.1895
married Lilly Broadway of Falmouth.
Appointed: 17.7.1893
Stationed at: Helston 15.9.1893.
15.11.1895 Fined 10/- for being absent from
his conference point and making a false entry
in his journal.
10.3.1896 Dismissed with forfeiture of all
pay due to him for being absent from his
conference point, making a false entry in his
journal and telling a falsehood.

P.C. 19 Preston W. Jewels
A 19 year old single mine labourer from St
Germans.
Appointed: 25.7.1893.
Promotion: 23.11.1896 to 2nd class
Constable.
Stationed at:
Penzance 6.1.1894. Truro 9.8.1897.
Camborne 25.10.1898. Falmouth
20.6.1900. 9.5.1897 Fined 10/- for drunkenness and moved at his own expense.
19.6.1900 Fined 10/- for drunkenness on the
night of the 18th., also 5/- for absence from
his conference point on the same occasion and
ordered to be transferred at his own expense.
3.9.1900 Dismissed from the force with the
forfeiture of all pay due for repeated drunkenness.

P.C. 43 John T. Ruse
A labourer from South Petherwin aged 24
years. 15.4.1895 married E.Couch from
Coads Green.
Appointed: 28.7.1893.
Promotion: 1.12.1896 to 2nd class
Constable. 1.11.1904 to 1st class Constable.
Stationed at: Liskeard 27.2.1894.
Launceston 15.3.1907
31.5.1922 Retired.

P.C. 82 John Rogers
A 20 year old miner from Sithney. 31
10.1899 married R.H.Oates. Of Crowan.
Appointed: 28.7.1893.
Promotion: 22.7.1897. To 2nd class
Constable. 21.10.1902 to 1st class
Constable.
Stationed at: Bodmin 27.2.1894. Camborne
12.3.1898. Liskeard 31.10.1899.
31.12.1921 Retired.

P.C. 139 John Chapman
A 22 year old married labourer from
Manaccan. 22.11.1902. 2nd marriage to
Edith Cook of Frogpool.
Appointed: 16.10.1893.
Promotion: 1.12.1896 to 2nd class
Constable. 1.8.1906 to 1st class Constable.
Stationed at:
Bodmin 4.1.1894.
13.2.1900 Fined 5/- for unnecessary delay in
returning to his station and 5/- for drinking in
a public house. 10.11.1919 Reduced in pay
as Constable viz., from 90/- to 80/- per week

for conduct unbecoming a Constable and calculated to bring discredit on the force.
30.11.1919 Retired Pension £139.2.10.
1.3.1931 Died.

P.C. 70 Richard J.Jose
A single tin streamer from Perranzubaloe, aged 20 years.
Appointed: 23.10.1893.
Stationed at: Liskeard 26.4.1894.
12.8.1895 Dismissed with forfeiture of all pay due to him, for being in a public house drinking in plain clothes after closing time, when he should have been on duty.

P.C. 48 John Smitheram
From Camborne a labourer aged 24 years.
14.1.1902 Married Frances E.Waters.
Appointed: 12.2.1894
Promotion: 9.7.1897 to 2nd class Constable.
1.11.1905 to 1st class Constable.
Stationed at: Launceston 25.10.1894.
Penzance 11.4.1897. Bodmin 2.6.1897.
Truro 23.8.1897. Camborne 29.12.1900.
Liskeard 25.6.1902. Launceston 8.3.1911.
31.3.1920 Retired. Pension £165.4.7.

P.C. 132 James Reynolds
A 19 year old single gardener from Mawnan.
Appointed: 15.2.1894.
Stationed at: Penzance 26.4.1894,
21.12.1894 Resigned.

P.C. 138 William Odgers
A blacksmith from Ludgvan, single aged 19 years.
Appointed: 1.1.1894
Stationed at: Liskeard 9.8.1894.
8.6.1896 Resigned.

P.C. 71 Frederick Holloway
A shoe maker from Tavistock, aged 21 years.
1.6.1897 married Elizabeth A.Ellacott from Boyton.
Appointed: 26.2.1894.
Stationed at: Launceston 12.7.1894.
Camborne 25.11.1898. Launceston
2.8.1894. Camborne 25.11.1898.
19.9.1900 Resigned.
Gratuity of £29.13.1.

P.C. 164 Albert Johns
A 22 year old gardener from Veryan,
15.12.1896 Married lena Davey of Truro.
Appointed: 28.2.1894
Promotion: 27.10.1896 to 2nd class Constable. 1.8.1901 to 1st class Constable.
1.12.1907. To Sergeant.
Stationed at: Helston 24.1.1894. Liskeard
30.11.1907. Truro 1.7.1909. Falmouth
12.2.1913.
30.9.1920. Retired Pension £195.13.4.

P.C. 47 William John Matthews
A grocer from Bodmin aged 20 years
Appointed: 18.4.1894.
4.11.1899 Married D.F.Giles of Glamorgan.
Promotion: 1.12.1896. To 2nd class Constable. 1.10.1900 to 1st class Constable.
1.5.1907 to Sergeant. 12.6.1914 to Inspector. 1.9.1922 to Superintendent.
1.10.1935 to Deputy Chief Constable.
Stationed at: Bodmin 9.8.1894. Penzance

22.11.1896. Bodmin 13.6.1907. Camborne
5.8.1910. Launceston 12.6.1914. Falmouth
16.1.1919.
14.2.1939 Awarded the Kings Police Medal for Distinguished Service.
31.5.1939 Retired 24.8.1947 Died.

P.C. 102 Richard Werren Sandercock
A 24 year old butcher from North Petherwin.
Appointed: 19.4.1894.
15.10.1895 married Bessie Perry from Linkinhorne.
Promotion: 26.10.1896 to 2nd class Constable. 1.8.1907 to 1st class Constable.
Stationed at: Penzance 5.10.1894. Truro
8.10.1895.
30.4.1920 Retired Pension of 165.4.7.
21.8.1945 Died.

P.C. 109 Harry Jenkin
A labourer from Illogan, single aged 20 years.
Appointed: 28.5.1894.
Promotion: 30.8.1896 to 2nd class Constable.
Stationed at: Penzance 2.1.1895
4.7.1898 Resigned.

P.C. 149 Thomas Treleven
A labourer from Bodmin, single aged 21 years.
Appointed:. 12.6.1894.
Stationed at: Liskeard 17.2.1895
16.9.1895 Resigned.

P.C. 52 Henry Warren
A 20 year old labourer from St Erth.
Appointed: 23.7.1894.
27.9.1998 married Honor James
Promotion: 27.9.1897 to 2nd class Constable. 1.8.1907 to 1st class Constable.
Stationed at: Helston 10.1.1895. Launceston
25.10.1898.
12.6.1922 Retired.

P.C. 28 William Henry Dowrick
A single blacksmith from St Just in Roseland.
Appointed: 1.10.1994.
Stationed at: Truro 25.3.1895. Liskeard
4.7.1995. Bodmin 17.9.1995. Penzance
14.3.1897.
17.12.1897 Fined 10/- for being drunk when returning off duty on the 8.12.1897 at 7.pm. 4.7.1895 Moved at his own expense from Newquay to Liskeard for neglect of duty.
7.11.1898 Dismissed from the Force for drunkenness and disorderly conduct.

P.C. 18 John Stapleton
From St Germans a labourer aged 20 years.
Appointed: 22.10.1894.
12.7.1904 married Eleanor Webb from Somerset.
Promotion: 25.10.1897 to 2nd class Constable. 1.12.1907 to 1st class Constable.
Stationed at: Bodmin 3.5.1895. Liskeard
8.1.1896. Truro 15.4.1899. Bodmin
25.1.1900. Truro 7.5.1900. Camborne
9.5.1903. Falmouth 27.3.1918
31.3.1923 Retired 12.8.1944 Died.

P.C. 132 John Hicks
A miner from St Just, single aged 20 years.
Appointed: 27.12.1894.
Stationed at: Bodmin 8.5.1895.
10.2.1896. Resigned.

P.C. 11 Alfred Thomas Davey
A labourer from Tregoney aged 20 years.
Appointed: 7.1.1895.
25.1.1899 married Emma Rescorla
Promotion: 24.10.1898 to 2nd class Constable. 1.10.1905 to 1st class Constable.
Stationed at: Helston 8.5.1895. Camborne
13.2.1899. 21.5.1908 Resigned.

P.C. 81 Samuel John Clark
A labourer from St Germans aged 21 years.
Appointed: 16.1.1895.
13.12.1900. Married Mary Annie Merryfield
Promotion: 24.10.1898 to 2nd class Constable. 19.11.1904 to 1st class Constable.
Stationed at: Truro 11.7.1895. Camborne
29.4.1905. Bodmin 9.10.1907.
P.C. 81 Samuel J.Clark has been reprimanded and cautioned by the Chief Constable for serious indiscretions in the performance of his duty.
31.10.1912. Resigned on Medical Certificate. Pension £25.12.8.

P.C. 75 Henry Martin
A stone mason from Kea, Truro, aged 25 years.
Appointed: 4.2.1895.
14.4.1900 Married Sarah L.W.Chegwiddon of Probus.
Promotion: 20.12.1897 to 2nd class Constable. 1.1.1906 to 1st class Constable.
Stationed at: Liskeard 7.9.1995.
28.2. 1921 retired. Completed Service Pension not fixed. 11.12.1947 Died.

P.C. 8 James Kingdom
A labourer from Linkinhorne aged 21 years.
Appointed: 10.4.1895.
15.6.1898 married Lucy Heddon of South Petherwin.
Promotion: 14.2.1898 to 2nd class Constable. 1.5.1905 to 1st class Constable.
Stationed at: Truro 10.8.1895. Penzance
9.5.1897. Launceston 12.6.1897. Falmouth
10.6.1898. Camborne 1.2.1905.
31.12.1913 Pensioned on medical certificate of £27.2.10.

P.C. 120 Hubert John Pope
A 24 year old single tailor from Bodmin.
Appointed: 6.5.1895
Stationed at: Penzance 26.8.1895.
Launceston 25.5.1897.
19.8.1897 Called upon to resign , insufficient ability.

P.C. 157 William John Martin
A labourer from Calstock aged 21 years.
Appointed: 6.5.1895.
8.2.1900 Married Lilly Stephens of Redruth.
Promotion: 23.5.1898 to 2nd class Constable. 1.4.1907 to 1st class Constable.
Stationed at: Camborne 9.9.1895. Bodmin
10.6.1898. Camborne 15.4.1899. Truro
25.1.1900. Launceston 20.9.1904.
31.5.1921 Retired. Pension £165.4.7.

P.C. 119 Ernest Dunn
A wheelwright from Lewannick. Aged 21 years single.
Appointed: 6.5.1895.
Stationed at: Liskeard 15.8.1895.
7.12.1895 Resigned.

P.C. 148 Thomas Henry Coad
A 22 year old single farmer from Lanhydrock.
Appointed: 8.7.1895.
Stationed at: Liskeard 17.9.1895.
6.1.1896 Resigned.

P.C. 97 William Roberts
A farmers son from Crowan. Single aged 22 years.
Appointed: 30.7.1895.
5.8.1895 Resigned. Forfeited six days pay.

P.C. 70 Ernest Crabb
A labourer from Liskeard single aged 20 years.
Appointed: 5.8.1895.
Stationed at: Penzance 31.10.1895.
5.7.1897. Resigned.

P.C. 97 Thomas Moorshead Dingle
A labourer from St Austell aged 19 years.
Public Service: Five years with 2nd Batt D.C.L.I.
Appointed: 5.8.1895.
5.8.1903 married Maud J.Osborne of Bodmin.
Promotion: 16.2.1896 to 2nd class Constable. 1.11.1904 to 1st class Constable. 1.10.1919 to Sergeant. 1.10.1923 to Inspector.
Stationed at: Launceston 31.10.1895. Penzance 25.5.1897. Bodmin 7.5.1900. Camborne 13.12.1900. Truro 24.6.1905. Camborne 27.10.1915. Falmouth 14.10.1919. Also Trispen, Perranporth , Marazion, Mawgan and Newquay.
30.11.1930 Retired.
24.7.1959 Died.

P.C. 74 William Osborne
A gardener from St Ewe aged 19 years. (Residence at time of joining Heligan)
Appointed: 19.8.1895
15.12.1904 Married Ida Wilmot of Mylor Bridge.
Promotion: 29.8.1898 to 2nd class Constable. 1.10.1904 to 1st class Constable. 13.11.1908 to Sergeant. 1.1.1915 to Inspector. 1.10.1922 to Superintendent.
Stationed at: Helston 31.10.1895. Camborne 10.4.1900. Truro 25.8.1900. Camborne 11.4.1901. Truro 7.6.1901. Camborne 27.3.1902. Bodmin 21.6.1902. Falmouth 25.4.1903. Camborne. 27.4.1905. Falmouth 13.11.1908. Truro 12.2.1913. Bodmin 7.1.1915.
30.9.1937 Retired.

P.C. 101 Thomas Chapman
From St Breock, a labourer aged 21 years.
Appointed: 27.8.1895.
Public Service: 8 Months with 2nd Vol.Batt., D.C.L.I. 27.4.1899 Married Kate Webber.
Promotion:
29.8.1898 to 2nd class Constable.
Stationed at: Bodmin 8.1.1896. Liskeard

1.4.1903.
16.5.1907 Fined 10/- for frequenting public houses and for tippling habits. Ordered to be transferred at his own expense.
13. 1 .1909 Fined £1.0.0. For improperly entering a public house whilst on duty.
31.1.1909 Resigned.

P.C. 90 William Strike
A Miner from Linkinhorne, aged 21 years single.
Appointed: 3.9.1895.
Stationed at: Bodmin 29.12.1895. Penzance 14.3.1897. Bodmin 12.6.1897. Truro 23.11.1897. Liskeard 9.5.1898. 6.6.1898 Resigned.

P.C. 149 William George Bond
A 21 year old single labourer from St Blazey.
Public Service: Three Years with the 5th Batt, Volunteers, Royal Artillery, and four moths with the Marine Artillery.
Appointed: 23.9.1895.
26.9.1895 Called upon to resign.

P.C. 136 John Wherry
A labourer from Warleggen, aged 19 years.
Appointed: 30.9.1895.
24.4.1902 married Florence Jane White Whitell of Millbrook.
Promotion: 13.2.1899 to 2nd class Constable. 1.12.1907 to 1st class Constable.
Stationed at: Liskeard 6.2.1896. Camborne 5.9.1902.
Copy of G.O. 3 .6.1902. P.C. 136 John Wherry was on the 26th ult., fined 10/- for being drunk whilst on duty.
31.3.1924 Retired. 8.4.1944 Died.

P.C. 21 Enoch Mitchell
A labourer from Phillack, aged 26 married with three children.
Appointed: 30.9.1895.
Promotion: 7.6.1897 to 2nd class Constable.
Stationed at: Penzance 31.10.1895. Liskeard 25.11.1895.
Copy of G.O. 1.10.1902. P.C. 21 Enoch Mitchell, was on the 4th Ult. Fined £1.0.0. For absence from his conference point on the 21st ult., the offence being aggravated by a false statement in his explanation and a false entry in his journal.
P.C. Mitchell was also transferred at his own expense
31.3.1903 Resigned.

P.C. 149 William Collett
A labourer from Truro, married aged 20 years.
Appointed: 30.9.1895.
Promotion: 1.3.1899 to 2nd class Constable. 1.9.1907 to 1st class Constable.
Stationed at: Truro 9.3.1896. Liskeard 8.2.1907. Camborne 26 .11.1914.
31.10.1920 Pensioned in consequence of an injury received on duty, £182.12.6 p.a. Or £3.10.0. per week.

P.C. 146 William Berry
A miner from Illogan, married aged 25 years.
Appointed: 28.10.1895.
Promotion: 24.10.1895 to 2nd class

Constable. 1.8.1901 to 1st class Constable.
Stationed at: Bodmin 2.1.1896. Liskeard 7.9.1916.
31.10.1932 Retired.

P.C. 108 Erwin French
A 19 year old single coach smith from Kenwyn. **Public Service:** 1st Vol.Batt., D.C.L.I. For four and half years.
Appointed: 11.11.1895.
Promotion: 5.6.1899 to 2nd class Constable. 1.3.1909 to 1st class Constable.
Stationed at: Penzance 19.3.1896. Truro 25.10.1898. Bodmin 19.2.1901. Truro 20.5.1914.
17.12,1897 Was fined 10/- for being absent from his conference point, at Roskear Church at 4.30.am on 12.12.1897.
8.8.1905 Reprimanded for conduct on the 3rd July last unbecoming to a Constable and warned against again infringing the rule as to driving in conveyances (Para 10 Book of Rules).
7.7.1906 Fined £1.0.0. For improper conduct and seriously warned as to his future conduct.
30.6.1923 Retired.

P.C. 5 John Williams Matthews
A 22 year old farm labourer from St Leven.
Appointed: 26.11.1895.
22.8.1907 Married Fanny Meek of Falmouth.
Promotion: 24.10.1898 to 2nd class Constable. 1.8.1901 to 1st class Constable. 1.4.1909 to Sergeant. 1.12.1919. To Inspector.
Stationed at: Helston 11.4.1896. Camborne 17.3.1901. Falmouth 3.5.1901. Camborne 1.4.1909.
H.O. Letter 25 .2.1918. Specially commended by the Sec of State for good working connection with enquiries and reports relating to aliens and suspected persons as the result of appreciation expressed by Col.Kell Q.B. MI5 War Office. Since the outbreak of war since Aug 1914
31.3.1934 Retired.

P.C. 119 William Henry Pomery
From Bodmin a farm labourer aged 23 years.
Appointed: 17.12.1895.
11.3.1903 Married Mary Rodda Westcott of Dawlish.
Promotion: 24.10.1898 to 2nd class Constable. 1.7.1905 to 1st class Constable.
Stationed at: Penzance 27.4.1896. Bodmin 9.5.1903. Launceston 1.9.1910.
31.8.1919 Granted a Special Pension of £2.10.0. Per week in accordance with Sec 1 (2) of the Police Act 1890 reassessed and granted £3.10.0. Per week as from 1.4.1920.
23.5.1924 Died. Widow Mrs Rodda Pomery granted a pension of £30.0.0. p.a. To take effect on and from 1.7.1924.

P.C. 148 Charles Osborne
A 24 year old fisherman from Paul, Penzance.
Appointed: 13.1.1896.
3.8.1897 married Mary A.Nicholls of Paul.

Promotion: 25.4.1899 to 2nd class Constable. 1.10.1905 to 1st class Constable.
Stationed at: Liskeard 24.6.1896. Bodmin 23.7.1897.
30.9.1922 Retired.

P.C. 132 Richard John Banfield
A 21 year old single fisherman from Veryan.
Appointed: 10.2.1896.
Promotion: 12.3.1900 to 2nd class Constable.
Stationed at: Penzance 5.7.1896.
21.8.1901 Dismissed.

P.C. 79 Stephen Kendall
A labourer from St Germans single aged 26 years. Public Service: 1st and 2nd Batt DC.L.I. For seven years and 323 days.
Appointed: 11.3.1896.
Promotion: 28.12.1898 to 2nd class Constable.
Stationed at: Bodmin 5.7.1896. Launceston 10.6.1898, Camborne 3.11.1898.
24.4.1899 Resigned.

P.C. 3 John Charles Lewis Pearce
A 20 year old single carpenter from Gwennap.
Appointed: 13.4.1896.
Stationed at: Truro 28.9.1896.
8.2.1897 Resigned.

P.C. 137 Richard Henry Warren
A 22 year old labourer from St Erth.
Appointed: 7.5.1896.
14.5.1894 married Elizabeth Grey of Baldhu.
Promotion: 23.10.1899 to 2nd class Constable. 1.4.1908 to 1st class Constable.
Stationed at: Bodmin 21.10.1896. Camborne 22.8.1901. Truro 16.2.1907.
P.C. 137 Richard Warren before the bench of St Austell Petty Sessions for an assault on William James Crowle of Nanpean, St Stephens, on Aug 2nd 1901. Was fined 10/- and costs of £1.12.6.
26.5.1922 Retired
21.3.1937 Died.

P.C. 86 William Brown
A 21 year old labourer from Roche.
Public Service: 2nd Vol Batt, D.C.L.I. For 3 years.
Appointed: 10.5.1896.
10.9.1903 married Phillipa Chinn of Hayle at Phillack Church.
Promotion: 1.3.1899 to 2nd class Constable. 5.3.1907 to 1st class Constable.
Stationed at: Penzance 5.12.1896. Liskeard 5.9.1902. Camborne 19.11.1903. Bodmin 23.12.1903.
17.8.1919 Died of Typhoid Fever.
26.7.1953 Widow died at Phillack Hospital aged 81 years.

P.C. 138 William Cleave
A 21 year old single farm labourer from St Wenn.
Appointed: 8.6.1896.
8.5.1901 married Elizabeth Ann Ellis of St Just.
Promotion: 10.4.1899 to 2nd class

Constable. 9.4.1907 to 1st class Constable.
15.8.1911 to sergeant.
Stationed at: Penzance 2.11.1896. Launceston 15.8.1911.
30.6.1922 Retired.
18.4.1953 Died.

P.C. 93 Harry Gomm
A 24 year old carpenter from Aylesbury Bucks. Public Service: Devon port Police.
Appointed: 4.7.1896.
11.6.1895 married Amelia Furze. Of Devonport.
Promotion: 12.5.1900 to 2nd class Constable. 1.11.1910 to 1st class Constable.
Stationed at: Truro 12.8.1896. Bodmin 25.10.1898. Launceston 19.2.1901. Truro 1.9.1915.
4.7.1922 Retired.

P.C. 168 James Hocking
A labourer from St Keverne aged 26 years.
Appointed: 26.10.1896.
8.3.1900 married Mary E.Jenkin at Redruth.
Promotion: 24.10.1898 to 2nd class Constable.
Stationed at: Penzance 14.3.1897. Falmouth 30.6.1900. Camborne 29.11.1901.
19.11.1903 Resigned.

P.C. 91 Frederick Ernest Crossman
A butcher/labourer from Tavistock, aged 20 single,
Appointed: 9.11.1896
27.11.1896 Called upon to resign - violent temper.

P.C. 116 Samuel James Lean
A 24 year old married labourer from Stithians.
Appointed: 23.11.1896
Stationed at: Bodmin 11.4.1897.
1.8.1897 Resigned. Afraid to go on duty, wanting in courage.

P.C. 91 James Baker
A 26 year old single shoe maker from Lanteglos. Public Service: 1st Batt D.C.L.I. For 8 years and forty days.
Appointed: 4.12.1896.
Stationed at: Penzance 14.3.1897.
6.6.1897 Resigned.

P.C. 3 John Henry Harris
A 25 year old married labourer from St Teath. Public Service. 2nd Vol.Batt., D.C.L.I. For seven and half years.
Appointed: 11.2.1897.
Stationed at: Truro 29.6.1897
20.8.1897 P.C. 3 Harris is fined 10/- and warned that if again reported for drunkenness within a period of six months from this date he may expect dismissal.
22.10.1897 Resigned.

P.C. 33 George Barnet Kersey
A 22 year old single stonemason from Constantine Public Service: 1st Vol.Batt., D.C.L.I. For 6 years.
Appointed: 22.2.1897
Stationed at: Liskeard 9.7.1897.
16.9.1897 Resigned.

P.C. 91 Isaac Penberthy
A gardener from Ludgvan, married aged 27 years. Public Service: Penzance Borough Police for three years and ten months.
Appointed: 19.6.1897.
Promotion: 16.1.1900 to 2nd class Constable. Later to 1st class Constable.
Stationed at: Bodmin 12.7.1897. Launceston 8.10.1912.
22.10.1912. Was severely reprimanded and warned as to his future conduct for being in a public house after closing time.
30.11.1922 Retired.

P.C. 70 Arthur Truscott
From Kenwyn, and organ builder aged 21 years.
Appointed: 5.7.1897
22.5.1915 married Violet E. Gilbert at St Georges Parish Church, Truro.
Promotion: 16.1.1900 to 2nd class Constable. 9.4.1907 to 1st class Constable. 1.11.1910. To Sergeant Clerk. 1.10.1920 to Inspector Chief Clerk. 1.4.1930 to Superintendent.
Stationed at: Liskeard 9.11.1897. Bodmin 20.9.1902. Truro 13.7.1909. 6.8.1909 H.Q.
31.7.1930 Retired. 13.2.1952 Died.

P.C. 2 William Thomas Banfield
A 26 year old fisherman from Devoran.
Appointed: 9.7.1897
14.9.1917 married Miss Clara Jenkin of Torpoint at Torpoint Parish Church.
Promotion: 1.7.1902 to 2nd class Constable. 1.7.1908 to 1st class Constable.
Stationed at: Bodmin 9.11.1897. Truro 17.6.1900. Liskeard 2.5.1904. Camborne 1.1.1912.
1.10.1908 P.C. 2 William T.Banfield was cautioned against omitting to make any reference in his occurrence books as to enquiries relative to a serious crime.
30.6.1927 Retired.
5.10.1946 Died.

P.C. 144 William Warren
A 23 year old married labourer from St Erth.
Appointed: 2.8.1897.
28.1.1913 married for the 2nd time to Laura Tracey at St Columb Minor Parish Church.
Promotion: 16.1.1900 to 2nd class Constable. 1.3.1905 to 1st class Constable.
Stationed at: Launceston 9.11.1897. Truro 6.2.1912. Liskeard 6.11.1913.
29.10.1913 Fined 10/- for tippling whilst on duty.
31.12.1923 Retired 29.10.1943 Died.

P.C. 116 James Arthur Stephens
A 19 year old railway porter from Lostwithiel.
Appointed: 25.8.1897.
24.8.1899 married Louise Hocking.
Stationed at: Bodmin 9.11.1897. Liskeard 15.8.1898. Truro 8.2.1907.
30.9.1924 Retired. 31.3.1948 Died.

P.C. 120 Matthew Martin Blake
A 22 year old single carpenter from St Teath.
Appointed: 25.8.1897
20.9.1997 Resigned.

P.C. 32 Charles Thomas French

A 22 year old single linesman, G.W.R. From East Teignmouth, Devon.
Appointed: 6.9.1897.
Married Alice M.Carne at St Thomas in Exeter on 16.12.1894.
Promotion: 1.10.1900 to 2nd class Constable.
1.12.1908 to 1st class Constable.
Stationed at: Liskeard 9.11.1897. Bodmin 1.4.1898. Truro 10.5.1900. Launceston 6.2.1912. Liskeard 7.11.1916.
Favourable Record: Special promptitude and intelligence in arresting on 23.10.1899 a tramp subsequently convicted of stealing a large sum of money.
7.6.1914 P.C. 32 Charles French was granted a favourable record for rendering assistance in company with a coast guard by descending a rope ladder over a cliff and recovering the body of a lady who had fallen over.
16.6.1914 P.C.. 32 French was granted a favourable record for stopping a horse at Bude at great personal risk.
11.2.1916 In recognition to his tact and strict attention to duty on the night of 11.2.1916 when the S.S. *Mettleton* was wrecked on the coast at Morwenstow and rendering valuable assistance in rescuing the whole of the crew and two lady passengers.
11.4.1916 P.C. 32 Charles French of Bude. Was granted one year's acceleration in pay to take effect on and from the 6th Sept, next.
5.9.1919 Retired Pension £118.19.4.

P.C. 33 Albert Edward Sidney Annear

A 23 year old single wheelwright from St Clements. Public Service: Royal Engineers for seven years.
Appointed: 20.9.1897.
Stationed at: Falmouth 9.11.1897. Launceston 14.6.1899.
13.7.1899 Fined 5/- for being drunk when required for duty and ordered to be transferred at his own expense for disobedience of orders. Called out to rejoin the colours on the 8.10.1899 and did not rejoin in consequence of ill-health.

P.C. 120 William Patrick

A 24 year old married tinplate worker from Birmingham. Public Service: The 32nd., C.I.I. For five years and sixteen days.
Appointed: 29.9.1897.
9.10.1899 Called out to rejoin the colours. Rejoined the force 1.10.1902 as P.C. 152.
Promotion: 21.10.1902 to 2nd class Constable. 1.9.1907 to 1st class Constable. 1.10.1908 to Sergeant. 1.11.1919 to Inspector.
Stationed at: Truro 9.11.1897. Bodmin 2.3.1899. Bodmin 1.10.1902. Truro 4.2.1914.
30.9.1923 Retired.

P.C. 55 Albert John Davies

A 24 year old tailor from Tywardreath.
Appointed: 21 10.1897.
28.7.1902 married Ethel Wilkinson of Bodmin at the Congregational Church.
Promotion: 23.10.1899 to 2nd class

Constable. 21.10.1902 to 1st class Constable.
1.1.1906 to Sergeant. 1.11.1910 to Inspector and Chief Clerk. 1.10.1920 to Superintendent. 16.1.1927 to Deputy Chief Constable.
Stationed at: Bodmin 12.2.1898. Camborne 3.3.1899. Bodmin 16.3.1899. Truro 1.10.1920.
Specially commended by the Sec of State for good work in connection with enquiries and reports relating to aliens and suspected person as a result of appreciation expressed by Col.Kell C.B. MI 5., War Office since the outbreak of war in 1914. H.Q. Letter dated 28.2.1918.
3.6.1933 Awarded the M.B.E. By his Majesty King George V in the birthdays honours of 1933.
30.9.1935 Retired 8.9.1946 Died

P.C. 3 Henry Phillips

A 23 year old groom/gardener from Sherborne in Dorset. Public Service: D Comp Volunteers for six months.
Appointed: 26.10.1897.
Promotion: 1.10.1900 to 2nd class Constable. 1.11.1910 to 1st class Constable.
Stationed at: Liskeard 8.2.1898 Camborne 15.5.1899
21.7.1921 Retired.

P.C. 160 Arthur Toms

A 20 year old single railway porter from Hounslow.
Appointed: 4.11.1897.
Stationed at: Falmouth 22.1.1898. Camborne 12.3.1898. Falmouth 1.6.1898. Camborne 21.12.1898.
20.12.1898 P.C. 160 Arthur Toms was fined 10/- and moved at his own expense to Camborne.
3.2.1899 Dismissed for repeated neglect of duty.

P.C. 7 William John Trythall

A labourer from Ludgvan aged 19 years.
Appointed: 31.1.1898.
13.8.1902. Married Louisa Edwards of Ludgvan.
Promotion: 1.1.1901 to 2nd class constable. 1.5.1907 to 1st class constable. 1.2.1914 to Sergeant. 16.10.1920 to Inspector.
Stationed at: Bodmin 9.5.1898. Truro 18.10.1901. Bodmin 4.2.1914.
Specially commended by the Sec., of State for good work in connection with enquiries and reports relating to aliens and suspected persons as a result of appreciation expressed by Col. Kell C.B. MI5 War Office since outbreak of war 1914. H.Q. Letter dated 28.2.1918.
31.3.1938 Retired.

P.C. 56 Thomas Bryant

A 21 year old single railway porter from Marazion.
Appointed: 14.2.1898.
Stationed at: Camborne 29.8.1898. Bodmin 12.7.1899. Launceston 11.1.1900.
20.12.1900 P.C. Thomas Bryant was dismissed for grossly improper conduct. He having been previously warned for dismissal.

P.C. 129 Thomas James Harfoot

A labourer from Kenwyn, aged 23 years.
Appointed: 1.6.1898.
4.8.1904 married Annie Mitchell of Bodmin.
Promotion: 1.1.1901 to 2nd class Constable. 1.1.1911 to 1st class Constable.
Stationed at: Bodmin 31.10.1898. Falmouth 5.8.1903. Liskeard 29.9.1904. Truro 12.8.1908. Camborne 1.3.1910.
18.4.1908 P.C. 129 Thomas Harfoot was fined 10/- for drinking in a public house whilst on duty.
5.11.1909 P.C. Thomas Harfoot was fined 10/- for making a false entry in his journal and 5/- for failing to be at his conference point.
23.6.1914 P.C. 129 Thomas Harfoot was fined 15/- and deprived of one conduct badge for 12 months. For being found drinking in a public house in Camborne on 13.6.1914 whilst on duty and warned for dismissal should he again be reported for misconduct.
31.10.1924 Retired.
21.4.1952 Died.

P.C. 90 Edwin LeMin

A labourer from Roche aged 22 years.
Appointed: 13.6.1898.
23.5.1907 married Hannah Richens of Redruth.
Promotion: 1.1.1901 to 2nd class Constable. 1.11.1910 to 1st class Constable.
Stationed at: Falmouth 31.10.1898. Camborne 11.4.1901. Falmouth 13.5.1901 Camborne 1.1.1904. Bodmin 3.2.1905. Camborne 13.4.1905. Liskeard 26.11.1914. Camborne 2.9.1920.
20.12.1920 P.C. 90 Edwin LeMin was reprimanded for failing to work his beat in accordance with orders
30.6.1924 Retired.

P.C. 109 Claudius Bate

A 21 year old labourer from Lanlivet.
Appointed: 4.7.1898.
10.5.1902 married Ethel Weller of Bodmin.
Promotion: 1.3.1901 to 2nd class Constable. 1.5.1909 to 1st class Constable.
Stationed at: Bodmin 31.10.1898. Camborne 3.12.1902. Liskeard 7.4.1913. 31.7.1924. Retired.

P.C. 17 William John Osborne

A labourer from St Wenn aged 19 years.
Appointed: 29.8.1898.
7.1.1903 married Rosina Jane Pethick, widow of the late Sergeant Pethick.
Promotion: 1.2.1900 to 2nd class Constable. 1.6.1908 to 1st class Constable.
Stationed at: Launceston 18.11.1898. Falmouth 14.7.1899. Truro 4.10.1901. Bodmin 2.6.1903. Launceston 13.8.1904. Bodmin 5.8.1910.
Favourable Record 31 .10.1904 P.C. 17 William J.Osborne was awarded a favourable record for perseverance and skill in successfully trying a case of robbery of money, resulting in a conviction. The had been originally no clue as to the offender.
Favourable Record: 30.8.1907 P.C. 17 Williams J.Osborne was granted a favourable

record for stopping a runaway horse at great personal risk on the 22.8.1907. His conduct in applying first aid on the same occasion was commended by the Chief Constable.
3.9.1926 Retired 14.6.1952 Died.

P.C. 103 Francis Kelly Bartlett
From Veryan a 21 year old ironmonger.
Appointed: 24.10.1898.
5.2.1900 married Mary Polkinhorne of St Columb.
Promotion: 1.12.1901 to 2nd class Constable. 1.11.1910 to 1st class Constable. 10.7.1912 to Sergeant.
Stationed at: Liskeard 25.1.1899. Launceston 19.1.1900. Liskeard 15.3.1907. Falmouth 1.10.1920.
31.10.1930 Retired.

P.C. 94 Alfred Williams
A single labourer from St Stephens-in-Brannel, aged 17 years.
Appointed: 24.10.1898
14.11.1898 Permitted to resign.

P.C. 62 James Martin
A 19 year old single wheel wright from Trewen.
Appointed: 14.10.1898.
31.7.1900 Resigned.

P.C. 57 William John Ough
A 23 year old labourer from East Looe.
Appointed: 24.10.1898.
17.5.1902 married Alice Basher of St Martin.
Promotion: 1.2.1901 to 2nd class Constable. 1.11.1910 to 1st class Constable.
Stationed at: Launceston 26.6.1899. Falmouth 5.9.1899. Camborne 1.10.1902 Falmouth 31.3.1905.
31.10.1924 Retired.

P.C. 84 John Cadwell
A 19 year old single blacksmith from Camborne.
Appointed: 31.10.1898.
Promotion: 1.9.1902 to 2nd class Constable.
Stationed at: Falmouth 26.1.1899. Bodmin 8.12.1902.
24.11.1900 P.C. 84 John Cadwell was fined 2/6 for absenting himself from his conference point on the 19.11.1900. The Constable was also ordered to be transferred at his own expense for offering an improper and untrustworthy explanation.
31.12.1904. Resigned.

P.C. 94 Edward Brown
A 19 year old groom from Mevagissey.
Appointed: 16.11.1898
1.10.1903 married Edith F. Burt from St Minver.
Promotion: 1.1.1901 to 2nd class Constable. 1.4.1909 to 1st class Constable.
Stationed at: Truro 13.2.1899. Bodmin 21.8.1899. Truro 24.11.1899. St Minver 17.6.1900. Launceston 5.6.1907. Bodmin 8.3.1911. Launceston 13.2.1918.
31.1.1926 Retired.

P.C. 28 John Coumbe
A labourer from St Austell aged 19 years.
Appointed: 12.12.1898.
10.8.1904 married Annie Maud Harris of Constantine.
Promotion: 1.12.1900. To 2nd class Constable. 1.2.1909 to 1st class Constable.
Stationed at: Bodmin 2.3.1899. Falmouth 9.2.1901.
21.10.1917 Granted a favourable record for bravery displayed in stopping a powerful runaway horse at Falmouth. His action is further recognised by a grant of six months' seniority in respect of his next rise in pay.
1.7.1922 Granted a favourable record form brave conduct at Falmouth on the 18.5.1922 when he with great promptitude on seeing a runaway horse attached to a cab without a bridle galloping through the Moor. He warned the people in the vicinity and noticing a Mr. Medlyn aged 77 years in imminent danger raced to his assistance and moved him to safety, by this gallant action the Constable no doubt prevented a serious loss of life.
1.4.1927 Granted a favourable record for brave conduct when he at great personal risk stopped a runaway horse thereby preventing what might have been a serious accident.
31.10.1929 Retired 16.8.1938 Died.

P.C. 140 Edward John Burley
A 19 year old game keeper from Gorran.
Appointed: 2.1.1899.
2.12.1903 married Florence Burral Curtis of Camborne.
Promotion: 1.2.1902 to 2nd class Constable.
Stationed at: Truro 28.3.1899. Camborne 14.5.1901. Liskeard 11.5.1904.
13.1.1906 Fined 10/- for being absent from his conference point and also 10/- for making a false entry in his journal relative thereto. The Constable was at the same time ordered to send in his resignation.
23.1.1906 Called upon to resign.

P.C. 67 Herbert John Crocker
A 19 year old boiler-smith from Tywardreath.
Appointed: 24.2.1899.
6.4.1902 married Caroline I. James of St Ives.
Promotion: 1.12.1901. To 2nd class Constable. 1.10.1908 to 1st class Constable. 2.6.1914 to Sergeant. 1.10.1922 to Inspector.
Stationed at: Camborne 29.4.1899. Camborne 9.1.1903. Liskeard 30.5.1901. Falmouth 1.4.1909. Camborne 12.6.1914. Bodmin 14.2.1920.
28.2.1931 Retired. 14.2.1941 Died.

P.C. 38 John Henry Couch
A 19 year old single labourer from Davidstow.
Appointed: 4.3.1899.
Promotion: 1. 1.1901. To 2nd class Constable.
Stationed at: Camborne 12.7.1899. Truro 29.1.1901. Liskeard 11.9.1908.
1.10.1902 Copy of G.O. P.C. 38 John H.Couch was on the 13 ult., fined 10/- for

being drunk on duty on the 2nd inst, the Constable was also transferred at his own expense.
20.10.1903 Dismissed the force for being drunk on duty.

P.C. 89 Thomas Lee
A labourer from Bideford aged 22 years.
Born 22.9.1876
Appointed: 23.3.1899.
28.1.1901 married Elizabeth Ebely at Liskeard.
Promotion: 1.2.1907 to 2nd class Constable. 1.9.1910 to 1st class Constable. 27.6.1914 to Sergeant. 1.9.1922 to Inspector.
Stationed at: Liskeard 12.7.1899. Bodmin 24.8.1900. Camborne 25.6.1901. Falmouth 17.6.1914.
30.11.1928 Retired. 24.1.1947 Died.

P.C. 160 Matthew Buckingham
A 20 year old single plate layer from Truro.
Appointed: 27.3.1899.
Stationed at: Falmouth 10.6.1899.
26.8.1899 Resigned.

P.C. 100 Christopher Cock
A 23 year old married plate layer from St Neot.
Appointed: 1.4.1899.
30.10.1899 Resigned.

P.C. 79 Titus Hambly
A labourer from Kilkhampton aged 25 years.
Appointed: 9.5.1899
Public Service: Royal Artillery for eight years.
28.3.1901 married Maria Venner of Marhamchurch.
11.2.1900 Left the force to join the colour Re-joined 1.1.1901 as P.C. 73
Service during absence with colours to count towards pension. R.M.H.C.C. 12.1.1901.
Promotion: 1.12.1901 to 2nd class Constable. 1.11.1910 to 1st class Constable.
Stationed at: Bodmin 23.10.1899. Camborne 11.4.1901. Truro 27.10.1915. Retired 30.6.1925.

P.C. 20 Andrew Burrough
An 18 year old store porter from Bodmin.
Appointed: 10.5.1899.
Public Service: 2nd Vol Batt D.C.L.I. For four years.
11.11.1902 married Alice Miners of the Cornwall County Asylum, Bodmin, at Porthpean Bible Christian Chapel.
Promotion: 1.1.1901 to 2nd class Constable. 24.7.1910 to 1st class Constable. 1.11.1915. To Sergeant. 1.1.1921 to Inspector.
Stationed at: Camborne 2.11.1899. Truro 3.9.1903. Camborne 16.2.1906. Falmouth 9.7.1907. Liskeard 7.1.1915. Bodmin 30.12.1920.
31.10.1930 Retired.

P.C. 24 William Henry Bone
A 26 year old married quarryman from Cumberland. **Public Service:** Penzance Borough Police for one year and ten months.
Appointed: 12.6.1899.
Promotion: 1.10.1900 to 2nd class Constable. 13.7.1909 to 1st class Constable.

Stationed at: Liskeard 12.7.1899. Bodmin 7.9.1916.
30.6.1925 Retired.

P.C. 160 **Edward Osborne**
A 18 year old labourer from St Columb.
Appointed: 11.9.1899
10.3.1901 married Grace Mitchell of Camborne.
Promotion: 1.12.1902. To 2nd class Constable.
Stationed at: Camborne 25.1.1900. Truro 31.10.1901. Bodmin 24.6.1905. Camborne 9.10.1907.
9.11..1908 P.C. 160 Edward Osborne was fined 5/- for frequenting public houses when on duty and ordered to be transferred at his own expense.
4.12.1908 P.C. 160 Edward Osborne was fined 10/- for disobedience to orders and warned as to his future conduct.
31.3.1909 Resigned.

P.C. 33 **Alfred John Ching Hunt**
A 20 year old single butcher from Bideford.
Appointed: 25.10.1899.
Stationed at: Liskeard 25.1.1900.
8.5.1900 Resigned.

P.C. 66 **Thomas Tonkin**
A 26 year old stone cutter from Paul, Penzance.
Appointed: 26.10.1899.
14.7.1900 married Mary Jane Reynolds of Newlyn.
Promotion: 1.1.1902 to 2nd class Constable. 1.11.1910 to 1st class Constable.
Stationed at: Truro 28.1.1900.
31.5.1926 Retired. 20.1.1947 Died.

P.C. 100 **John Bunney**
A 20 year old labourer from Gorran.
Appointed: 13.11.1899.
Married at Penwerris Church, Falmouth to Mary Betty Kunckey of Stithians on 5.11.1903.
Promotion: 21.10.1902 to 2nd class Constable.
Stationed at: Falmouth 23.3.1900. Camborne 11.4.1901. Camborne 14.3.1902. Falmouth 5.8.1903. Truro 8.3.1904
31.12.1906 Resigned
Reappointed: 18.6.1907
Promotion: 1.4.1908 to 2nd class Constable. 1.11.1910 to 1st class Constable.
Stationed at: Falmouth 18.6.1907.
29.8.1912 Severely reprimanded and warned as to his future conduct for neglect of duty and for making false statements to his superior officer and in his journal and was also ordered to be reduced to a lower rate of pay to which he was entitled.
28.2.1913 Resigned. Granted £10.0.0. Portion of rateable deduction .S.J.C. Meeting on 7.4.1913.

P.C. 41 **Harry Williams**
A 22 year old single labourer from Calstock.
Appointed: 26.12.1899.
Stationed at: Camborne 7.5.1900.
Copy of G.O. 31.10.1902 P.C. 41 Harry

Williams was on the 6th inst, fined 10/- for absenting himself from his beat without permission, on the 21st, inst, at Redruth.
21.3.1904 Dismissed.

P.C. 120 **John Jacob**
A 18 year old single grocer from Portsmouth.
Appointed: 8.1.1900.
Stationed at: Liskeard 7.5.1900. Falmouth 15.5.1902.
21.9.1903 Resigned.

P.C. 107 **Robert Cowling**
A 25 year old married seaman from St Endellion.
Appointed: 15.1.1900.
Promotion: 1.5.1903 to 2nd class Constable. 1.11.1910 to 1st class Constable.
Stationed at: Falmouth 7.5.1900. Truro 10.5.1900. Camborne 25.9.1900.
31.1.1926 Retired. 31.5.1945 Died.

P.C. 123 **Francis Thomas Basher**
A single labourer from Constantine.
Appointed: 22.1.1900.
13.10.1906 married at St James Church, Torpoint, to Ethel Troon of Mawnan Smith.
Promotion: 1.6.1902 to 2nd class Constable. 1.11.1910 to 1st class Constable. 1.11.1912 to Sergeant. 1.11.1919. To Inspector. 16.1.1927 to Superintendent.
Stationed at: Liskeard 7.5.1900. Truro 7.1.1915. 5.11.1919 H.Q.
30.6.1933 Retired.

P.C. 111 **John Andrew**
A 24 year old labourer from Wadebridge.
Appointed: 25.1.1900.
28.9.1904 married Mary Judith Perry of Bodwyn, North Wales, at St Germans Church.
Promotion: 1.12.1902 to 2nd class Constable. 1.11.1910 to 1st class Constable.
Stationed at: Liskeard 7.5.1900. Falmouth 11.4.1901. Liskeard 10.1.1902. 31.1.1926 Retired.

P.C. 79 **William John Stidwell**
A 20 year old single farm Labourer from Boyton.
Appointed: 12.3.1900.
18.6.1900 Resigned.

P.C. 156 **Frederick Thomas**
A 21 year old farm labourer from Perranzubloe.
Appointed: 12.3.1900.
Stationed at: Falmouth 30.6.1900. Camborne 21.12.1900.
10.5.1901 Resigned through ill-health.

P.C. 147 **Harry Haley**
A baker from Tywardreath, aged 21 years.
Appointed: 19.3.1900.
12.6.1900 married Bessie Bassett of Lostwithiel.
Promotion: 1.10.1903 to 2nd class Constable. 1.11.1910 to 1st class Constable.
Stationed at: Camborne 30.6.1900. Liskeard 5.10.1900. Launceston 21.6.1902. Liskeard 14.1.1915.
21.4.1918 By direction of the Sec of State

released to join the army for hostilities. Re-joined on 3.2.1919.
31.3.1926 Retired.

P.C. 33 **John Trehane**
A single labourer from St Ives, aged 22 years.
Appointed: 14.5.1900.
5.5.1904 married Bessie B. Annear of Camborne, at St Martins Church, Camborne.
Promotion: 1.11.1904 to 2nd class Constable. 1.11.1910 to 1st class Constable.,
Stationed at: Camborne 25.8.1900. Falmouth 29.9.1905. Truro 8.5.1919.
15.5.1927 Retired.

P.C. 79 **Robert Ashford**
A 21 year gardener from St Marys Isles of Scilly.
Appointed: 19.6.1900.
3.11.1904 married Mary Ellen Rogers of Tregonissey at St Austell Parish Church.
Promotion: 31.10.1903 to 2nd class Constable. 1.11.1910. To 1st class Constable. 1.11.1919 to Sergeant.
Stationed at: Bodmin 25.8.1900. Truro 12.3.1903. Camborne. 27.10.1904 Truro 5.11.1919.
30.9.1931 Retired. 26.10.1945 Died.

P.C. 180 **Joseph Olliver**
A 17 year old single miner from St Neot.
Appointed: 9.7.1900.
Stationed at: Truro 5.10.1900. 8.12.1900 Resigned.

P.C. 181 **Thomas Chapman**
A 20 year old labourer from Lanlivet.
Appointed: 14.7.1900.
23.9.1905 At Truro Bible Christian Chapel married Leonora Pengelly of Newquay.
Promotion: 1.7.1903 to 2nd class Constable. 1.2.1908 to 1st class Constable. 1.7.1922 to Sergeant.
Stationed at: Bodmin 17.9.1900. Camborne 11.4.1901. Bodmin 13.6.1901. Camborne 27.3.1902. Bodmin 25.6.1902. Camborne 1.10.1903.
6.4.1926 Retired.

P.C. 166 **Edward James Thomas**
A labourer from Gulval aged 24 years.
Appointed: 14.7.1900.
19.10.1905 at Probus Weslyan Chapel married Mary Rowe Symons of Grampound Road.
Promotion: 1.12.1903 to 2nd class Constable. 1.11.1910 to 1st class Constable.
Stationed at: Camborne 11.10.1900. Bodmin 9.7.1901. Camborne 9.3.1902 Camborne 25.6.1902. Liskeard 26.2.1903. Truro 1.1.1907. Bodmin 3.12.1913.
30.9.1926 Retired. 17.12.1937 Died.

P.C. 62 **Fred Barrett**
A 24 year old married butcher from Lostwithiel.
Appointed: 16.7.1900.
Promotion: 19.11.1904 to 2nd class consta-ble. 1.11.1911 to 1st class Constable.
Stationed at: Falmouth 17.9.1900. Camborne, Truro 10.10.1917.
28.7.1909 P.C. 62 Fred Barrett was fined 5/- for failing to carry out a conference point on

13.7.1909. The same Constable was also fined 15/- for neglect of duty on the same occasion by absenting himself from his beat. When on duty the Constable neglected his duty in a manner calculated to bring discredit on the force and has aggravated his offence by falsehoods and prevarication.
31.7.1926 Retired.

P.C. 182 William Thomas Osborne
A 21 year old labourer from Egloshayle. Married with two children.
Appointed: 17.7.1900.
Stationed at: Camborne 1.10.1900.
27.12.1900 William Thomas Osborne was dismissed for drunkenness and violent conduct when on duty on the 25th inst.

P.C. 183 William Horace Ede
An 18 year old single corn trader from Holloway.
Appointed: 10.9.1900.
Stationed at: Falmouth 21.12.1900.
30.4.1902 Called on to resign.

P.C. 185 Alfred George Jago
A 20 year old gardener from Bodmin
Appointed: 10.9.1900.
22.5.1907 At Helston Church married Mary Ellen Pascoe of Helston
Promotion: 1.11.1904 to 2nd class Constable. 1.11.1919 to 1st class Constable. 1.10.1920 to Sergeant. 1.2.1924. To Inspector.
Stationed at: Launceston 21.12.1900. Camborne 7.3.1903. Liskeard 17.5.1904. Falmouth 24.6.1905. Truro 12.4.1907. Bodmin 7.10.1919.
29.2.1932 Retired 16.6.1956 Died.

P.C. 184 Samuel James Prime
A coach builder from Kea, Truro, single aged 19 years.
Appointed: 10.9.1900.
Stationed at: Launceston 21.12.1900. Camborne 11.4.1901.
14.11.1903.   Resigned.

P.C. 39 John Roberts
A 23 year old single labourer from Cubert.
Appointed: 10.9.1900.
Promotion: 1.1.1905 to 2nd class Constable. 1.11.1910 to 1st class Constable.
Stationed at: Camborne 21.12.1900. Launceston 11.6.1901. Camborne 10.12.1901. Liskeard 1.12.1903. Camborne 1.6.1907. Falmouth 10.6.1908. Bodmin 14.10.1913. Falmouth 26.11.1914.
31.1.1928 Retired.

P.C.19 Nicholas Deacon
A gardener from Pelynt aged 19 years, single.
Appointed: 17.9.1900.
3.10.1900 Resigned.

P.C. 163 George Strike
A 20 year old labourer from Linkinhorne.
Appointed: 17.9.1900
8.9.1908 At St Mewan Church married Lucy A.Kent of Bodmin Road.
Promotion: 1.3.1905. To 2nd class Constable. 1.11.1910. To 1st class

Constable. 1.5.1919 to Sergeant.
Stationed at: Falmouth 21.12.1900. Camborne 11.4.1901. Falmouth 13.6.1901. Falmouth 21.6.1902. Bodmin 5.8.1903 Launceston 3.6.1919.
13.12.1925 Retired. 1.8.1961. Died.

P.C. 71 Joseph Kent
A single quarryman from St Teath.
Public Service: 2nd., Vol Batt., D.C.L.I. For five years.
Appointed: 8.10.1900.
24.10.1900 Resigned.

P.C. 61 Samuel Henry Pomery
A 20 year old single labourer from Liskeard.
Appointed: 22.10.1900.
Stationed at: Bodmin 9.2.1901.
21.8.1901 Called upon to resign by the Chief Constable.

P.C. 71 George Henry Bingley
A farmer from Yorkshire aged 21 years single.
Public Service: Artillery Volunteers for seven months.
Appointed: 22.10.1900.
28.2.1903 Resigned.

P.C. 19 Henry Davey
A 22 year married Plumber from Liskeard.
Appointed: 1.11.1900.
Stationed at: Bodmin 18.3.1901. Liskeard 30.7.1901. Falmouth 10.1.1902.
21.1.1904 P.C. 19 Henry Davey was on 31.12.1903 fined 10/6 for being drunk when required on duty on 25.12.1903. Resigned.

P.C. 64 Ephriam Hancock
An 18 year old single railway porter from St Austell.
Appointed: 3.12.1900.
Stationed at: Falmouth 18.3.1901. Camborne 3.4.1901.
23.11.1901 fined 10/- for being drunk at St Austell on the 16th inst., and was ordered by the Chief Constable to resign on 30.11.1901.

P.C. 180 George Brooking
A 21 year old labourer from South Brent.
Appointed: 29.1.1901.
21.9.1904 married Mary Glasson at St Johns Church, Penzance.
Promotion: 1.1.1906 2nd class Constable. 1.1.1911 1st class Constable. 1.3.1920 to Sergeant.
Stationed at: Camborne 14.6.1901. Falmouth 1.1.1904. Truro 1.7.1904. Bodmin 8.10.1914.
30.4.1927 Retired.

P.C. 182 William Botheras
A 19 year old labourer from Paul, Penzance.
Appointed: 16.2.1901.
15.10.1910. Married Norah Heller at Fowey Parish Church,
Promotion: 1.6.1905 to 2nd class Constable. 1.11.1910 to 1st class Constable. 1.9.1920 to Sergeant.
Stationed at: St Columb 14.6.1901. Camborne 2.7.1901. Bodmin 1.7.1903.

Camborne 5.10.1910.
30.6.1931 Retired.

P.C. 56 Nigel Elford Prout
A 19 year old single stonemason from South Petherwin. Public Service: 2nd., Vol., Batt., D.C.L.I. For 18 months.
Appointed: 1.4.1901.
Promotion: 1.10.1905 to 2nd class Constable.
Stationed at: Bodmin 24.7.1901. Truro 9.5.1903. Falmouth 27.6.1904. Liskeard 23.1.1907.
Favourable Record: P.C. 56 Nigel Prout was on the 9.6.1906 granted a favourable record for brave and spirited action in stopping a runaway horse on 31.5.1906.
16.1.1907 P.C. 56 Nigel Prout was reprimanded for indiscipline and disrespect to his superior officer and ordered to be transferred at his own expense.
30.9.1907 Resigned.

P.C. 135 Ira Sloman
A 24 year old farmer's son from Warbstow.
Appointed: 1.5.1901.
21.4.1903 married Ethel Rose Boundy of Canworthy Water at Warbstow Church.
Promotion: 1.11.1905 to 2nd class Constable. 1.1.1911 to 1st class Constable.
Stationed at: Falmouth 2.7.1901. Camborne 25.3.1905. Liskeard 1.12.1911. 30.11.1915 To H.M. Forces
4.2.1919 Rejoined from the army
8.2.1919 Camborne.
30.4.1927 Retired 28.1.1949 Died.

P.C. 174 Henry Pearce Johns
From Tavistock a miller aged 20 years, single.
Appointed: 1.4.1901.
Stationed at: Bodmin 9.9.1901. Falmouth 8.10.1901.
10.5.1904   Resigned on ill-health.

P.C. 156 Ernest Alfred Ede
A 21 year old single labourer from St Pinnock.
Appointed: 20.5.1901.
Promotion: 1.5.1905 to 2nd class Constable. 1.11.1910 to 1st class Constable.
Stationed at: Truro 16.9.1901. Falmouth 4.10.1901. Camborne 3.3.1911. Liskeard 13.5.1911.
24.4.1911 Ordered to be transferred at his own expense from St Just to Liskeard for riding his bicycle when on duty contrary to regulations and for inefficiency patrolling his beat at Cury on 24.2.1911.
2.6.1913 Fined 10/- for making a false entry in his journal and 10/- for being absent from his station without permission.
31.7.1913 Resigned.

P.C. 61 Francis Robert James
A 26 year old blacksmith from St Germans.
Appointed: 9.9.1901
Stationed at: Falmouth 7.2.1902. 31.4.1902 Resigned.

P.C. 132 George Edward Wilkinson.
A carpenter from Bodmin aged 21 years single.

Appointed: 11.9.1901.
Stationed at: Launceston 7.2.1902. Bodmin 3.3.1902. Truro 26.6.1902. Bodmin 2.3.1903. Truro 6.5.1903. Camborne. 23.12.1903. Liskeard 18.11.1904.
25.10.1904 P.C. 132 George E.Wilkinson was fined 10/- for being drunk when required for duty. He was ordered to be transferred at his own expense and warned.
20.12.1905 P.C. 132 George E.Wilkinson was dismissed from the force for being drunk whilst on duty on the 15.12.1905.

P.C. 127 **Bedford Ernest Jewels**
A 20 year old railway shunter from St Germans.
Public Service: Artillery Vol., for three years.
Appointed: 1.12.1901.
30.3.1905 Married Lily Hughes of Falmouth at Pikes Hill Weslyan Chapel.
Promotion: 1.7.1905 to 2nd class Constable.
Stationed at: Falmouth 1.6.1902. Launceston 1.11.1905. Bodmin 5.6.1907.
21.6.1907 Resigned.

P.C. 64 **Sidney Thomas Bowden**
A 20 year old parcels booking porter from Lydford.
Appointed: 1.1.1902.
5.9.1903 married Mary Lydia Lousia Menhenick of Newton Abbot at Newton Abbot Bible Christian Chapel.
Promotion: 1.10.1905 to 2nd class Constable. 1.11.1910 to 1st class Constable.
Stationed at: Camborne 15.5.1902. Liskeard 3.6.1903. Falmouth 23.1.1904.
31.12.1931 Retired.

P.C. 183 **Owen Barrett**
A carpenter from St Veep, single aged 20 years.
Appointed: 1.5.1902.
Stationed at: Falmouth 20.9.1902.
31.5.1903 Resigned.

P.C. 61 **Richard George**
A single blacksmith from Polperro aged 20 years.
Appointed: 5.5.1902.
31.7.1902 Called on to resign.

P.C. 61 Ernest Clark A 20 year old carpenter from St Germans.
Appointed: 27.8.1902.
15.10.1907 married Annie Hubber at Weslyan Chapel, Newquay.
Promotion: 1.4.1907 to 2nd class Constable. 1.4.1912 to 1st class Constable.
Stationed at: Liskeard 15.1.1903. Truro 3.5.1904. Falmouth 3.10.1906. Bodmin 26.11.1914.
9.1.1929 Retired 23.7.1952 Died.

P.C. 83 **Henry John Randall**
A footman from Pulborough, Sussex, aged 22 years single.
Appointed: 1.9.1902.
Promotion: 1.2.1906 to 2nd class Constable.
Stationed at: Camborne 12.12.1902. Falmouth 22.5.1905. Truro 31.1.1908.
8.5.1908 Resigned.

P.C. 59 **Ernest Edwin Steer**
A 21 year old railway porter from Modbury, Devon.
Appointed: 8.9.1902.
16.10.1907 married Edith Mary Hancock. At St Austell Parish Church.
Promotion: 1.1.1907 to 2nd class Constable.
Stationed at: Bodmin 12.3.1903. Launceston 1.12.1903.
30.9.1911. Was fined 5/- and warned as to his future conduct for failing to report lost property, which had been found and brought to the Superintendent of his Division.
6.4.1912. Was fined 5/- and seriously warned as to his future conduct for failing to visit his 10.30.pm. Conference point on 1.4.1912.
30.9.1929 Retired.

P.C. 138 **Thomas Henry Grose**
A 23 year old Police Office from St Austell.
Public Service. Royal Irish Constabulary for three years and three months.
Appointed: 1.12.1902.
21.2.1907 married Elizabeth Jane Nicholls at St Martins Church Looe.
Promotion: 31.5.1904 to 2nd class Constable. 1.11.1910. To 1st class Constable. 1.7.1919 to Sergeant.
Stationed at: Launceston 1.12.1902. Falmouth 1.10.1903. Bodmin 13.5.1905. Falmouth 28.9.1906. Liskeard 12.5.1907. Truro 1.7.1919.
31.3.1927 Retired 22.6.1953 died.

P.C. 133 **William James Steed**
A 23 year old single gardener from Landrake.
Appointed: 1.1.1903.
Stationed at: Bodmin 9.5.1903. Camborne 1.10.1903. Bodmin 1.2.1905.
31.5.1905 Resigned

P.C. 71 **William John Harris**
A 19 year old single coachman from St Neot.
Appointed: 16.3.1903.
Stationed at: Bodmin 22.7.1903. Camborne 26.4.1906.
Copy of G.O. 29.9.1906 P.C. 71 William J. Harris was on the 21 inst., called on by the Chief Constable to resign his position in the force owing to misconduct.
26.9.1906 Resigned.

P.C. 21 **Fred Rockey**
A 24 year old naval seaman from Bere Ferris.
Public Service: His Majesty's Navy for eight years and five months.
Appointed: 9.4.1903.
28.3.1905 married Alice Doney from North Hill at North Hill Church.
Promotion: 9.4.1907. To 2nd class Constable. 9.4.1912. To 1st class Constable.
Stationed at: Truro 1.8.1903. Launceston 1.10.1903. Bodmin 26.5.1904. Liskeard 7.2.1908.
2.6.1914 P.C. 21 Rockey was fined 5/- for making a false entry in his journal
9.4.1929 Retired. 17.2.1957 died.

P.C. 106 **Ernest John Bennett**
A blacksmith from Newton Abbott, 19 years single.
Appointed: 11.5.1903.

Stationed at: Camborne 5.8.1903.
31.10.1906 Resigned.
P.C. 183 **Henry Thomas Mapston**
A 26 year old labourer from Nottingham.
Public Service: H.M. Army, Gloucestershire for nine years and 209 days. Reserve for two years and 155 days.
Appointed: 1.6.1903.
8.10.1904 married Elsie Louisa Burrows at the Wesleyan Chapel, Newquay.
Promotion: 9.4.1907 to 2nd class Constable. 1.6.1912. To 1st class Constable. 1.1.1921 to Sergeant.
Stationed at: Bodmin 11.7.1903. Liskeard 30.12.1920.
31.7.1915 Joined the army under the Police (emergency provisions) Act 1915.
20.7.1919 Rejoined as P.C. 44.
Favourable Record: 31.7.1912 granted a favourable record for praiseworthy conduct on the 17.7.1912 in that he dived repeatedly into the river Camel at Trevilling, Wadebridge, in the hope of rescuing a boy named Frederick J.H.Harris aged 12 years, accidentally drowned whilst bathing.
31.7.1929 Retired. 19.2.1939 Died.

P.C. 120 **Thomas Colwil Harris**
A 23 year old single carpenter from Tregoney.
Appointed: 5.10.1903.
13.12.1903 Resigned.

P.C. 168 **Ernest Sampson White**
A 19 year old labourer from St Erth.
Public Service: 1st Vol., Batt., D.C.L.I. For two years.
Appointed: 7.11.1903.
11.6.1907 At Phillack Parish Church married to Elizabeth Phillips of Phillack.
Promotion: 1.6.1907 to 2nd class Constable. 1.7.1912 to 1st class Constable.
Stationed at: Falmouth 5.3.1904. Bodmin 26.4.1906. Launceston 1.12.1911.
23.11.1907 P.C. 168 Ernest S.White is hereby granted a favourable record for exhibiting at Port Isaac conspicuous coolness under difficult circumstances and also firmness and bravery in facing a large hostile crowd whereby the rescue of a prisoner and injury to property was prevented.
28.2.1912 Reprimanded for neglect of duty and drinking in a public house on the 8.2.1912.
31.1.1918 Dismissed the force for serious improper conduct.

P.C. 44 **William Wilton**
A 22 year old labourer from St Cleer.
Appointed: 26.11.1903.
13.11.1905 At the United Methodist Free Church, Camborne, to Mary Elizabeth Laity of Camborne.
Stationed at: Camborne 5.3.1904. Liskeard 29.9.1905.
12.5.1906 Resigned.

P.C. 184 **William John Osborne**
A 22 year old single plumber from Torquay.
Public Service: 1st Devon and Somerset Vol., for four years and six months.
Appointed: 21.12.1903.
Stationed at: Liskeard 29.3.1904.

29.4.1904 William John Osborne was fined 5/- for improper conduct and 5/- for omitting to make the proper entries in his journal and transferred at his own expense and warned. 20.10.1904 Dismissed the force for improper conduct and inefficiency.

P.C. 38 Albert Edwin Perkin
A blacksmith from Landrake, aged 22 years single.
Appointed: 28.12.1903.
Stationed at: Camborne 2.4.1904. Bodmin 22.11.1906.
21.11.1906 P.C. 38 Albert E.Perkin was fined 15/- for failing to keep his conference points on the 15th., inst., and ordered to be transferred at his own expense. The offence was aggravated by falsehoods.
30.11.1906 Resigned.

P.C. 19 William Henry Morgan
A 19 year old single moulder from Phillack.
Public Service: No 6 Batt., D.C.L.I. For three years.
Appointed: 16.1.1904.
Stationed at: Bodmin 4.4.1904. Camborne 30.4.1904. Falmouth 13.4.1907
4.4.1907 P.C. 19 William H.Morgan was fined 2/6 and ordered to be transferred at his own expense for being drunk on duty.
14.6.1907 P.C. 19 William H.Morgan was fined 5/- for overstaying his leave and 10/- for making false statements relative thereto.

16.8.1907 Dismissed the force for drunkenness on duty.

P.C. 120 William Henry Edyvean
A 24 year old labourer from St Columb.
Appointed: 21.1.1904,
28.9.1907 At St Germans Parish Church married Kate Scantlebury of St Germans.
Promotion: 1.5.1907 to 2nd class Constable. 1.5.1912 to 1st class Constable.
Stationed at: Launceston 30.5.1904. Liskeard 23.12.1905.
30.4.1930 Retired.

P.C. 54 James Ball
An 18 year old single labourer from Mevagissey.
Appointed: 15.2.1904.
Stationed at: Camborne 11.5.1904.
2.7.1905 Resigned.

P.C. 41 Harry White Turner
A 20 year old labourer from Perranzabaloe.
Public Service: 1st., VOl., Batt., D.C.L.I. For five years.
Appointed: 24.3.1904.
15.9.1916 At St Marys Church Penzance married Hetty Case of S.Ives.
Promotion: 1.7.1907 to 2nd class Constable. 1.7.1912. To 1st class Constable. 1.11.1919 to Sergeant.
Stationed at: Camborne 14.6.1904. Truro 24.8.1908. Bodmin 8.10.1908. Camborne 1.12.1911. Truro 25.3.1914. Bodmin 3.6.1919. Camborne 5.11.1919.
Also Newlyn, Chyandour, Newquay, St Austell, Padstow, Boscastle, Gloweth, Port Isaac and Hayle.

24.7.1915 Joined the army under the Police (Emergency Provisions) Act 1913.
Rejoined from the Army on 26.5.1919.
Favourable Record: P.C. 41 Harry White Turner who on the 12th., November 1911, displayed bravery in volunteering and going out in the lifeboat to assist in saving life from a vessel in distress near Padstow.
5.1.1914 Was granted the King's Police Medal for Conspicuous Gallantry at Padstow.
Favourable Record: 1.3.1924 for brave conduct at Hayle on the 13.2.1924 when he at great personal risk stopped two runaway horses attached to a cart loaded with sand, the driver having been killed, thereby preventing what might have been a further loss of life.

P.C. 174 Thomas Richard Hyde
A 21 year old labourer from East Looe.
Appointed: 11.5.1904
11.3.1908 Married Emily Louisa Soady at St Martins Church, near Looe.
Promotion: 1.9.1907 to 2nd class Constable.
Stationed at: Falmouth 1.9.1904. Liskeard 22.5.1906. Falmouth 10.7.1906.
30.9.1930 Retired.

P.C. 60 William James Gilbert
A miner from Stoke Climsland, aged 24 single. Public Service. 2nd., Vol., Batt., D.C.L.I. For three years.
Stationed at: Liskeard 21.10.1904.
15.12.1905 Resigned.

P.C. 63 George Edwin Doney
A 24 year old single labourer from St Germans.
Appointed: 12.10.1904.
Promotion: 1.9.1907 to 2nd class Constable.
Stationed at: Falmouth 3.2.1905. Camborne 2.3.1909. Launceston 5.1.1911.
19.1.1910 Fined 10/- for tippling and neglect of duty and seriously warned as to his future conduct. 6.5.1910. Fined £1.0.0. For drinking and being under the influence of liquor whilst on duty. On the 5.5.1910 and seriously warned as to his future conduct. 13.7.1912 Called on to resign and died two days after leaving force.
£3.16.5. Portion of rateable deduction applied to funeral expenses July 1912.

P.C. 184 Charles Ernest Toy
A labourer from Mabe aged 22 years.
Public Service: 1st., Vol. Batt.., D.C.L.I. For three years.
Appointed: 31.10.1904.
21.7.1910. Married Ann Evans Opie at Mabe Parish Church.
Promotion: 1.11.1907 to 2nd Class Constable
Stationed at: Camborne 3.2.1905.
19.11.1910. Fined 10/- for tippling and neglect of duty and seriously warned as to his future conduct.
31.12.1933 Retired 7.4.1944 Died.

P.C. 6 Mark Prust
A carpenter from Hartland, Devon.
Appointed: 2.11.1904

19.5.1909 Married Maud Westcott at the Methodist Chapel, Tregonissey, St Austell.
Promotion: 1.3.1908 to 2nd class Constable. 1.2.1923 to Sergeant.
Stationed at: Bodmin 3.2.1903 Falmouth 13.4.1909. Truro 1.5.1909.
Favourable Record: 1.1.1919 Awarded the Merit Class in addition to the above for close attention to duty and bravery displayed in securing in the street at great personal risk a large rabid dog which savagely attacked him.
30.11.1934 Retired.

P.C. 36 Albert William Clifton
A carpenter from Broadwoodwidger in Devon.
Appointed: 28.12.1904.
16.8.1915 married Florence N.Smith of Saltash at the Baptist Church, Saltash.
Promotion: 1.12.1907 to 2nd class Constable. 16.3.1922 to Sergeant.
Stationed at: Bodmin 21.6.1905. Camborne 10.8.1907. Bodmin, Truro 20.7.1910. Liskeard 30.1.1913.
Favourable Record: 1.10.1927 for brave conduct at Chacewater on 4.7.1927 when he at great personal risk stopped a runaway horse thereby preventing what might have been a serious accident.
31.7.1933 Retired.

P.C. 104 Frederick Nankivell Thomas
A 21 year old single carpenter from Bodmin.
Appointed: 12.1.1905.
Stationed at: Camborne 22.5.1905.
14.3.1906 Resigned.

P.C. 134 William John Harper
A 19 year old plumber from Bodmin.
Public Service: 2nd., Vol., Batt., D.C.L.I. For 2 years and six months.
22.9.1909 married Emma Cowling at St Neot Church
Appointed: 13.2.1905
Promotion: 9.4.1908 to 2nd class Constable.
Stationed at: Falmouth 13.5.1905. Bodmin 13.9.1907. Truro 6.8.1909.
4.11.1912 Reprimanded and fined 10/- for making a false entry in his journal and stating a falsehood to his superior office.
20.11.1904 fined 10/- for making a false entry in his journal and false statements to his superior officer and seriously warned as to his future conduct.
31.12.1914 Resigned.

P.C. 84 Thomas Prout
A 21 year old foreman from Launceston.
Appointed: 17.2.1905.
Married Alice A.O. Basher of Newtown at St Stephens Church Treleigh.
Promotion: 1.2.1908 to 2nd class Constable. 1.1.1924 to Sergeant. 13.4. 1931 to Inspector.
Stationed at: Liskeard 13.5.1905. Truro 1.7.1905. Falmouth 1.11.1905. Liskeard 4.12.1907. Falmouth 19.12.1907. Camborne 20.3.1909.
3.6.1936 Retired 17.2.1947 Died.

P.C. 88 Samuel John Mitchell
A 30 year old labourer from Holsworthy.

Appointed: 17.4.1905.
25.9.1906 married Blanche Pooley at Tetcott Parish Church.
Promotion: 1.10.1907 to 2nd class Constable.
Stationed at: Bodmin 5.8.1905. Camborne 26.8.1905. Liskeard 15.3.1907.
1.10.1908 P.C. 88 Samuel Mitchell was cautioned against omitting to make any reference in his occurrence book as to his enquiries relative to a serious crime.
30.4.1912 Resigned.

P.C. 69 William Morley Pill

A farmer from St Austell aged 19 years.
Appointed: 15.5.1905.
25.9.1911 married Rosa Lilly Luke of St Stephens in Brannel.
Promotion: 1.7.1908 to 2nd class Constable. 1.12.1919 to Sergeant. 1.1.1924 to Inspector. 1.8.1930 to Superintendent.
Stationed at: Launceston 9.9.1905. Bodmin 6.7.1911. Camborne 4.12.1919.
16.4.1940 Died.

P.C. 133 William Prideaux

A 23 year old labourer from Ugborough, single.
Appointed: 14.6.1905
Promotion: 1.7.1908 to 2nd class Constable.
Stationed at: Camborne 30.9.1905.
7.11.1908 Resigned through ill-health.

P.C. 96 Frederick Hawkin

A 21 year old labourer from St Germans.
Appointed: 21.8.1905
18.2.1908 married Florence Annie Scantlebury of Morval.
Promotion: 1.10.1908 to 2nd class Constable. 1.11.1919 to Sergeant.
Stationed at: Falmouth 1.12.1905. Liskeard 5.11.1919. Porkellis, Helston Perranwell and St Germans.
22.12.1913 Favourable Record: For tracing and bringing to justice two fowl stealers.
No further record.

P.C. 54 George Ferrell

A 21 year old game keeper from Mylor Bridge, single.
Appointed: 6.9.1905.
Stationed at: Liskeard 1.12.1905. Camborne 22.11.1906. Launceston 20.4.1907.
15.4.1907 P.C. 54 George Ferrell was fined 10/- for conduct unbecoming a Constable and 5/- for absenting himself from his station without leave and ordered to be transferred at his own expense.
31.5.1907 Resigned.

P.C. 114 Frederick Charles Trebilcock

A 21 year old labourer from St Mellion, Callington.
Appointed: 2,10.1905.
26.4.1912 married Nora Ann Lee of Bodmin.
Promotion: 1.12.1908 to 2nd class Constable.
Stationed at: Falmouth 8.1.1906. Camborne 2.4.1912. Bodmin 4.12.1919. Falmouth, Carnel Green, St Dennis, Camelford and

Lewannick.
6.3.1911 A Favourable Record granted for courage displayed in stopping a runaway horse at great personal risk to himself, in Falmouth on 28.2.1911.
30.11.1931. Retired.

P.C. 14 Samuel William Norish

A 20 year old labourer from Stoke Climsland.
Appointed: 5.10.1905.
1.6.1909 married Alice May Pellows of Budock Water.
Promotion: 1.1.1909 to 2nd class Constable. 1.1.1922 to Sergeant. 1.8.1930 to Inspector. 1.10.1935 to Superintendent.
Stationed at: Bodmin 11.2.1906. Falmouth 10.3.1907. Camborne 1.4.1909. Falmouth 8.5.1919. Tywardreath, St Ives. Stratton, Wadebridge, Torpoint and Falmouth.
30.6.1941 Retired.

P.C. 76 James MacDonald Piper

A 26 year old moulder from Illogan, Redruth. Transferred from Norfolk Constabulary where he served for three years and seven months.
24.3.1913 married Ellen Pengelly of Burraton, Saltash.
Appointed: 1.11.1905.
Promotion: 5.3.1907 to 2nd class Constable. 6.3.1912 to 1st class Constable. 1.10.1920 to Sergeant.
Stationed at: Falmouth 7.11.1905. Liskeard 6.1.1906. Also Pensilva, Callington, Cargreen, St Ann's Chapel.
31.8.1926 Retired.

P.C. 60 William Henry Ead

A 18 year old labourer from Cardinham, Bodmin. 30.8.1911 married Annie Weller from Essex.
Appointed: 1.1.1906.
Promotion: 1.3.1909 to 2nd class Constable.
Stationed at: Camborne 10.4.1906. Also Zennor, Nancledra, Sennen, Pool, Goldsithney, Pendeen and Padstow.
1.12.1928 Granted a Favourable Record for brave conduct at Padstow on 23.10.1928 when he at great personal risk stopped a runaway pony thereby preventing what might have been a serious accident.
30.6.1932 Retired. 10.10.1945 died.

P.C. 132 Martin Stephens

A 19 year old labourer from Roche, St Austell. 9.1.1909 married Janie Clemow of Camborne.
Appointed: 1.1.1906.
Promotion: 1.2.1909 to 2nd class Constable.
Stationed at: Camborne 14.10.1906. Liskeard 1.2.1909. Also Anthony, St Cleer. 7.3.1910. Fined 10/- for failing to work a conference point and 5/- for making a false entry in his journal relative thereto.
3.9.1933 Retired.

P.C. 55 Edward John Cortis

A mason from Kea, Truro aged 18 years.
6.6.1911 married Beatrice Mary Vigus of Mutley, Plymouth.
Appointed: 16.1.1906.
Promotion: 1.4.1909 to 2nd class Constable.

Stationed at: Liskeard 12.5.1906. West Looe 1.7.1919. Also Liskeard, Calstock and West Looe.
3.4.1934 Retired

P.C. 140 John Burrough

From Bodmin, a 19 year old grocers assistant.
8.2.1913 married Amelia Coad of Truro.
Appointed: 5.2.1906.
Promotion: 1.10.1920 Sergeant Clerk. 1.4.1930 Inspector. 1.1.1935 Superintendent.
Stationed at: Liskeard 1.2.1907. Truro 16.4.1908. Bodmin H.Q. 14.6.1909. Also Helston, Launceston, Truro.
31.12.1943 Retired 24.10.1944 Died.

P.C. 104 Joseph Reginald Crocker

A porter on the G.W.R. Aged 21 years of Tywardreath.
Appointed: 2.4.1906.
23.1.1909 married Beatrice Molly Olver of Tywardreath.
Appointed: 2.4.1906.
Promotion: 10.8.1909 to 2nd class Constable.
Stationed at: Truro 16.7.1906. Liskeard 16.10.1907. Camborne 1.2.1909.
21.7.1910 Dismissed the force for gross irregularities and serious neglect of duty.

P.C. 44 Bertram Louis Rundle

A 21 year old horse trainer from Stoke Climsland, Callington. Public Service. Royal Field Artillery for three years, Army Reserve for nine years.
Appointed: 12.5.1906.
13.4.1909 married Eliza Ann Kneebone of Redruth.
Promotion: 1.4.1909 to 2nd class Constable,
Stationed at: Bodmin 1.10.1906. Launceston 17.11.1906. Camborne 8.4.1907.
31.3.1912 Resigned in consequence of incapacity on medical certificate.
8.4.1912 Granted a gratuity of £26.0.0.

P.C 172 John David McGlenon

A labourer from Hampshire aged 20 years.
Appointed: 5.7.1906.
21.1.1909 married Miss N.Hubbard of Newquay.
Appointed: 5.7.1906
Promotion: 1.1.1911 to 2nd class Constable.
Stationed at: Bodmin 9.10.1906. Camborne 1.11.1906. Bodmin 15.3.1910. Falmouth 15.9.1911. Launceston 21.7.1914.
11.3.1910 Fined 10/- for being drunk and neglecting his duty thereby bringing discredit to the force and ordered to be transferred at his own expense.
1.9.1915 joined the army under the Police(Emergency Provisions) Act .
1.9.1919 rejoined the force. As P.C. 167.
Stationed at: Camborne 17.9.1919. Bodmin 5.2.1920. Also Bodmin, Camborne, St Just, St Austell, Helston, Bude, Camborne and Roche.
31.10.1933 Retired. 2.11.1944 Died.

P.C. 68 Albert Lobb

A 21 year old labourer from Kenwyn, Truro.

30.3.1910 married Annie Lobb from Tywardreath.
Appointed: 1.10.1906
Promotion: 13.7.1909 to 2nd class Constable.
Stationed at: Camborne 19.12.1906. Truro Aug. 1909. Bodmin 26.3.1912. Also Camborne, Newquay, St Columb, Newquay, Luxulyan and St Austell.
31.3.1939 Retired.

P.C. 71 Bertee Jane
A 20 year old miner from Tavistock, single.
Public Service: Vol.2nd., Batt., D.C.L.I. For 12 months.
Appointed: 1.10.1906
Stationed at: Truro 19.12.1906.
30.11.1907 Resigned.

P.C. 106 Francis Bulford
A 20 year old seaman from Devonport.
23.4.1907 married Emily M.Coyne of Fowey.
Appointed: 1.11.1906.
Promotion: 19.7.1910 to 2nd class Constable.
Stationed at: Bodmin 26.1.1907. Camborne 17.5.1907. Falmouth 30.11.1907. Camborne 27.3.1918. Also Padstow, Chyandour, Porthleven, Nancledra and Blue Anchor .
31.1.1908 was fined 10/- for making a false statement to his Inspector.
19.2.1923 Granted a Favourable Record that he at Giew Mine, Towednack, on the 23.1.1923 at great personal risk descended a disused mine shaft and rescued a dog who had fallen in.
29.2.1936 Retired.

P.C. 31 Charles Cory
A 21 year old miner from Calstock, Callington. Married Rose Sarah Tom of Tavistock, 18.4.1906.
Appointed: 1.11.1906.
Promotion: 1.5.1909 to 2nd class Constable.
Stationed at: Falmouth 26.1.1907. Launceston 16.8.1907. Bodmin 30.12.1920.
Also Penryn, Stratton and Port Isaac.
31.10.1932 Retired.

P.C. 38 Arthur Henry Warne
A stone mason from St Tudy, Bodmin, aged 22 years. Married Annie Searle of St Tudy 26.8.1919.
Appointed: 10.1.1906.
Promotion: 24.7.1910 to 2nd class Constable.
Stationed at: Camborne 16.4.1907. Bodmin 5.11.1910. Launceston 1.7.1915.
18.9.1915 Joined the army under the Police (Emergency Provisions) Act 1915.
1.8.1919. Rejoined as P.C. 183.
Stationed at: Bodmin 1.9.1919. Launceston 6.4.1920. Also Camborne, Pool, Fowey, Bugle, Bude, St Austell, Bude and Kilkhampton.
30.9.1936 Retired.

P.C. 100 Samuel John Granger
A fireman from Redruth aged 19 years.
Appointed: 21.2.1907.

Promotion: 1.7.1910 to 2nd class Constable.
1.10.1922 to Sergeant.
Stationed at: Camborne 25.5.1907. Bodmin 1.3.1910. Launceston 16.9.1915. Liskeard 1.12.1915. Falmouth 1.3.1916. Camborne 7.11.1916.
5.2.1917 Joined the army under Police (Emergency Provisions) Act 1915.
1.10.1919 Rejoined the force.
Stationed at: 21.10.1919. Cury. Also Camelford, Rilla Mill, Gunnislake, Week St Mary, Mawgan-in-Meneage and Slades.
31.10.1934 Retired.

P.C. 10 Wilfred Webber
A 20 year old labourer from South Petherwin, single.
Appointed: 13.3.1907.
12.7.1907 Resigned.

P.C. 159 Charles Francis
A 22 year old labourer from Gibraltar, Single.
Public Service: Volunteers 1st Cornwall R.G.A. For three years.
Appointed: 22.4.1907.
8.5.1907 P.C. 159 Charles Francis was on the 8.5.1907 dismissed from the force with forfeiture of all pay for making false statements.

P.C. 179 Sidney Valentine Rose
An 18 year old postman from Bodmin. Married Mary Ann Berryman of Camborne 7.5.1907.
Appointed: 6.5.1907.
Promotion: 1.11.1910 to 2nd class Constable.
Stationed at: Camborne 13.8.1907. Bodmin 21.2.1912. 10.1.1920 H.Q. Also Camborne, Newlyn, Camborne, Bodmin, St Mabyn, St Kew Highway, and H.Q.
31.3.1939 Retired 8.1.1956 Died.

P.C. 47 Martyn John Hawken
A 21 year old labourer from St Minver. Married Winifred Douglas Rogers from Helston 13.9.1910.
Appointed: 20.5.1907.
Promotion: 1.11.1910. To 2nd class Constable.
Stationed at: Bodmin 13.8.1907. Helston 17.8.1907. Bodmin 1.9.1910. Also Helston, Newtown, Wadebridge, Sticker and Wadebridge.
31.5.1933 Retired. 11.6.1953 Died.

P.C. 171 Richard Alfred Weary
From Bodmin a store porter aged 19 years. Married Annie Sandercock in Clapham, Surrey.
Appointed: 20.5.1907
Promotion: 16.10.1911 to 1st class Constable. 1.10.1921 to Sergeant. 1.7.1930 to Inspector.
Stationed at: Bodmin 29.8.1907. Truro 14.6.1909.
18.6.1910 Resigned to join Devonport Borough Police.
16.10.1911
Reappointed: as P.C. 104
Joined the army under the Police (Emergency

Provisions) Act 1915. Awarded the Meritorious Service Medal for service in Selonika 6.8.1918 Rejoined the force on discharge from the army.
Stationed at: Bodmin. Truro 11.10.1918. Bodmin 28.10.1918. Launceston 7.11.1918. Also Mawgan, St Austell, Torpoint and Wadebridge.
Favourable Record. On 10.5.1912 for stopping at great personal risk a runaway horse at St Austell on 9.4.1912.
3.9.1939 Retired.

P.C. 159 William John Richards
A baker from St Winnow aged 21 years. Married Clara Matthews of Camborne 10.10.1913.
Public Service: 2nd., Batt., D.C.L.I. For four years.
Appointed: 27.5.1907.
Promotion: 1.1.1911 to 2nd class Constable.
Stationed at: Bodmin, Camborne.
7.10.1908 P.C. 159 William J.Richards was fined 5/- for absence from a conference pint.
15.5.1915 resigned.

P.C. 127 Christopher Charles Wadge
From Tremayne, Launceston, a 20 year old single carpenter.
Appointed: 5.6.1907.
Promotion: 1.11.1910 to 2nd class Constable.
Stationed at: Falmouth 6.9.1907.
31.3.1914 Resigned to join the New Zealand Police.
Reappointed: 1.6.1921
Stationed at: St Ives, Tregoney, Gunnislake, Veryan and Luxulyan.
Favourable Record. 16.6.1909 P.C. 127 Chistopher C.Wadge was granted a favourable record for stopping a runaway pony thereby displaying pluck and coolness in danger.
13.2.1936 Retired.

P.C. 85 Thomas Sambles
A labourer from St Keyne , aged 21 years. Married Blanch Ellen Searle 27.10.1908.
Appointed: 1.7.1907.
Promotion: 1.11.1910 to 2nd class Constable.
Stationed at: Falmouth 21.9.1907. Camborne 13.11.1908. Truro 13.7.1909. Mawgan-in-Pydar and St Issey.
3.6.1933 Retired.

P.C. 19 Courtney Doney
A 19 year old single labourer from North Hill.
Appointed: 9.9.1907.
Stationed at: Bodmin 13.12.1907.
28.2.1910. Resigned.

P.C. 98 Henry Peters
A 20 year old labourer from Wendron, Helston. Married Ethel Sleeman of Callington on 14.9.1911. Public Service: 1st., Vol., Batt., D.C.L.I. For three years.
Appointed: 9.9.1907.
Promotion: 1.11.1910 to 2nd class Constable. 1.11.1921 to Sergeant. 1.12.1928 to Inspector. 1.1.1934 to Superintendent.

Stationed at: Liskeard 27.11.1907. Bodmin 8.12.1917. Mevagissey. Also Tywardreath, Saltash, Helston, Mawgan and Launceston. 31.12.1934 Retired.

P.C.113 Francis Rogers
A 22 year old single butcher from Treveglos, Launceston. Public Service: 2nd Vol.,Batt., D.C.L.I. For two years.
Appointed: 9.9.1907.
Promotion: 1.11.1910. To 2nd class Constable.
Stationed at: Liskeard 27.1.1907. 22.5.1912. Resigned to join Devonport Borough Police.

P.C. 56 William Pearce
A 20 year old G.W.R. Porter from South Petherwin.
Married Alice Bray of Camborne on 22.7.1915.
Appointed: 15.10.1907.
Promotion: 1.11.1910 to 2nd class Constable.
Stationed at: Camborne 22.2.1908. Bodmin 4.11.1915. Also Newlyn, Camborne, Troon, Camborne, Blisland and Bodmin.
7.12.1921 Died.

P.C. 10 Henry George Balsdon
A 19 year old single labourer from Landulf.
Appointed: 25.11.1907.
Promotion: 1.12.1910 to 2nd class Constable.
Stationed at: Falmouth 22.2.1908. 13.9.1911 Resigned.

P.C. 164 Edward Henry Stevens
A 21 year old single coachman from St Keverne. 21.4.1912 married Sarah Jane Dorcus Tom of St Minver at St Minver Parish Church.
Appointed: 28.12.1907.
Promotion: 1.1.1911 to 2nd class Constable.
Stationed at: Liskeard 16.4.1908. Camborne 10.5.1911. Liskeard 8.5.1912. 31.3.1916 Resigned. Joined army for duration of war.
Reappointed: as P.C. 35 1.4.1920
Stationed at: Bodmin 27.4.1920. Launceston 9.2.1921. Also Liskeard, Torpoint, St Just, Kingsand, Lostwithiel, Five Lanes, Tintagel, and Lostwithiel.
30.9.1938 Retired.

P.C. 71 Joseph Lobb
A 19 year old single labourer from Kenwyn.
Appointed: 28.12.1907.
Stationed at: Redruth 1.4.1908. 5.1.1909 Fined 5/- for failing to attend his conference point and also a further sum of 5/- for making a false entry in his journal relative thereto. 15.1.1909 Dismissed the force for repeated irregularities.

P.C. 12 Wilfred Harold Rogers
A 21 year old single labourer from South Brent. 16.10.1913 married Beatrice Ellen Nicholls at All saints Church, Falmouth.
Appointed: 28.12.1907.

Promotion: 1.1.1911 to 2nd class Constable. 1.10.1922 to Sergeant. 1.3.1931 to Inspector.
Stationed at: Falmouth 1.4.1908. Bodmin 2.7.1911. Camborne 21.2.1912. Also Padstow, St Ives and Stratton. 2.4.1931 Retired.

P.C. 87 William John Garland
A 20 year old single postman from St Eval.
Appointed: 1.9.1908.
Promotion: 1.2.1911 to 2nd class Constable.
Stationed at: Launceston 18.4.1908. Camborne 1.2.1909. Launceston 5.8.1910. 22.2.1916 Joined Army under Police(Emergency Provisions) Act 1915.
Reappointed: 18.2.1919
Stationed at: Falmouth 22.2.1919. Also Newtown, Jacobstow, Stratton, Whitstone, and The Lizard.
28.2.1938 Retired.

P.C. 26 Ernest Hawking
A 19 year old single gardener from St Mellion.
Appointed: 6.4.1908.
Stationed at: Camborne 17.7.1908 31.3.1909 Resigned.

P.C. 88 Edward Charles Dustow
A 19 year old footman from St Austell. 8.1.1911 married Mary Jane Hollicoumbe Odgers of Helston.
Appointed: 16.4.1908.
Promotion: 17.4.1911 to 2nd class Constable
Stationed at: Launceston 13.7.1908. Falmouth 22.6.1909. 11.6.1917 joined the army.
Reappointed: 18.7.1919 as P.C. 186.
Stationed at: Camborne 1.8.1919. Also Bude, Launceston, Falmouth, Helston, Chyandour and Camborne.
31.3.1939 Retired.

P.C. 11 John Oliver Draydon Bligh
A 21 year old driver from St Neot, single.
Appointed: 22.6.1908.
Promotion: 22.6.1911 to 2nd class Constable.
Stationed at: Falmouth 1.10.1908. 13.10.1911 Resigned.

P.C. 34 William Ernest Boon
A labourer from Kilburn, London. 8.6.1914 married Mabel Wills of Falmouth.
Appointed: 1.7.1908.
Promotion: 1.7.1911 to 2nd class Constable. 1.9.1922 to Sergeant. 1.11.1930 to Inspector.
Stationed at: Bodmin 23.11.1908. Falmouth 3.5.1909. Truro 14.10.1920. Also Bodmin, Falmouth, The Lizard, Newquay, Falmouth and Fowey.
30.4.1936 Retired. 1.8.1958 Died.

P.C. 152 Ernest James Hosking
A labourer from St Stephens by Saltash. Public Service: 2nd., Lifeguards for three months. 16.11.1911 married Edith Wright of Redruth.
Appointed: 3.10.1908.

Promotion: 31.10.1911 to 2nd class Constable. 16.10.1920 to Sergeant. 1.3.1925 to Inspector. 1.7.1933 to Superintendent. 1.4.1939 to Deputy Chief Constable. 1.1.1943 to Assistant Chief Constable.
Stationed at: Camborne 15.1.1909. Truro 26.3.1912. Camborne 14.10.1920. Also Redruth, Newlyn, Chyandour, Newquay, Camborne, Redruth, H.Q. Falmouth, Camborne and Bodmin.
31.10.1948 Retired.

P.C. 133 William Henry Wilkins
A single miner from St Agnes. Aged 20.
Appointed: 16.11.1908.
Stationed at: Camborne 1.3.1909. 23.11.1910 Resigned,.

P.C. 74 George Mayne
A farmer from Illogan, aged 19 years. 17.7.1916 married Evelyn Bowden of Falmouth.
Appointed: 23.11.1908.
Promotion: 24.11.1911 to 2nd class Constable.
Stationed at: Falmouth 1.3.1909. 31.3.1916 joined the army.
Reappointed: 30.1.1919
Stationed at: Bodmin 3.3.1919. Also Falmouth, Helston, Falmouth, Foxhole and Millbrook.
29.2.1936 Retired.

P.C. 175 William Francis Pooley
A skilled labourer from H.M.Dockyard from St Germans aged 22 years. 30.3.1912 married Kate Pollard of Bodmin.
Appointed: 11.1.1909.
Promotion: 12.1.1912 to 2nd class Constable.
Stationed at: Liskeard 3.4.1909. Bodmin 2.10.1909. Liskeard 26.3.1912. Truro 6.11.1913. Also Liskeard, Bodmin, Padstow, St Germans, Cargreen, St Columb Minor, Portscatho and St Mawes.
10.1.1935 Retired.

P.C. 101 Archie Hillman
From Launceston a tailor aged 22 years. 9.8.1911 married Florence Scantlebury of Launceston. Public Service. C Comp., 5th., Batt., Cornwall's for four years.
Appointed: 1.3.1909.
Promotion: 1.3.1912 to 2nd class Constable. 1.4.1923 to Sergeant.
Stationed at: Liskeard 4.5.1909. Bodmin 1.12.1911. Camborne. 14.10.1919. Also Liskeard, St Germans, St Minver. Marazion, Truro and Penryn.
30.9.1936 Retired.

P.C. 23 William Henry Rowe
A labourer from Mawnan Smith aged 23 and single.
Appointed: 16.3.1909.
Stationed at: Bodmin 29.5.1909. Liskeard 2.10.1909. Truro 18.8.1910. Camborne 3.10.1910.
30.11.1911 Resigned.

P.C. 112 Samuel John Rowe
A single labourer from Mawgan in Meneage.

Appointed: 23.3.1909.
Promotion: 24.3.1912. To 2nd class Constable.
Stationed at: Camborne 5.6.1909.
28.2.1913 Resigned.

P.C. 71 Francis John Roseveor
A 23 year old labourer from Newlyn East. Public Service: 4th., Batt., D Comp., Cornwall's for two years and nine months.
30.7.1912. Married Polly Hore of Bugle.
Appointed: 23.3.1909.
Promotion: 24.3.1912 to 2nd class Constable.
Stationed at: Truro 5.6.1909. Bodmin 12.10.1909. Camborne 26.4.1910. Truro 1.6.1910. Liskeard 9.7.1912. Also Newquay, Lostwithiel, Newlyn, Truro, Dobwalls, and Burraton.
31.3.1935 Retired.

P.C. 26 Herbert John Luke
A 22 year old blacksmith from Egoshayle.
1.2.1916 married Gertrude K.Share of Tresmeer, Egloskerry.
Appointed: 17.4.1909.
Promotion: 17.4.1912 to 2nd class Constable.
Stationed at: Camborne 17.7.1909. Launceston 25.1l 1913
31.5.1915 joined the army
13.4.1918 died from wounds received in action.

P.C. 160 Charles Henry Smith
A labourer from St Clether aged 21 years, single.
Appointed: 17.4.1909.
Stationed at: Bodmin 17.7.1909. Camborne 15.3.1910.
18.2.1911 resigned.

P.C. 5 Thomas Peu Horwood
A 21 year old single footman from Egloskerry.
Appointed: 1.5.1909.
Stationed at: Truro 17.7.1909.
31.12.1911 Resigned in consequence of ill-health.

P.C. 118 Herbert L.Tresidder
A 24 year old single labourer Stithians.
Appointed: 29.5.1909.
Stationed at: Bodmin 6.8.1909. Camborne 1.10.1912.
17.1.1910 Called upon to resign for neglect of duty and other irregularities.

P.C. 186 John Henry Eddy
A 23 year old labourer from St Austell.
22.8.1912 married Edith Gill of Falmouth.
Appointed: 1.6.1909.
Promotion: 1.6.1912 to 2nd class Constable. 14.12.1925 to Sergeant. 1.3.1932 to Inspector.
Stationed at: Launceston 20.10.1909. Falmouth 5.1.1911. Liskeard 1.4.1914. Falmouth 7.1.1915. Also Launceston, Liskeard, Callington, Helston, and Falmouth.
31.7.1940 Retired.

P.C. 72 George Frederick Howe
A 26 year old single carpenter from Uxbridge, Middlesex. Public Service: 5th.,

Dragoon Guards for eight years.
Appointed: 5.8.1909
31.12.1909 Resigned.

P.C. 131 Ernest Hosking
A 21 year old single carpenter from Camelford.
Appointed: 8.9.1909.
Promotion: 1.7.1930 to Sergeant. 9.2.1936 to Inspector.
Stationed at: Bodmin 1.3.1910. Falmouth 19.10.1911.
30.11.1914 Resigned for war service.
Reappointed: 16.6.1919 as P.C. 15
Stationed at: Camborne 19.6.1919. Also St Austell, Falmouth, Penryn, Falmouth Newlyn, Lelant, Newquay St Austell, Falmouth, Redruth and Truro.
3.3.1914. P.C. 131 Ernest Hosking was granted a favourable record for stopping a runaway horse at Penryn at 25.2.1915.
31.1.1946 Retired.

P.C. 72 William George Davey
An 18 year old groom and gardener from Linkinhorn.
Appointed: 25.1.1910.
Stationed at: Camborne 22.7.1910.
30.6.1913 Resigned.

P.C. 19 Mark Percival Holman
A 19 year old single blacksmith from Linkinhorn.
Appointed: 1.3.1910
Stationed at: Bodmin 23.7.1910. Camborne 5.8.1910.
11.8.1912 Resigned.

P.C. 171 George Hedley Basher
An 18 year old single mason from Helston.
Appointed: 22.6.1910.
Stationed at: Liskeard 26.9.1910.
23.5.1913 Resigned.

P.C. 99 Phillip Cundy
A fisherman from Looe aged 20 years.
Married Annie Droyer of Tipperary, Ireland, at Sclerder House Polperro.
Appointed: 14,7,1910.
Stationed at: Bodmin 26.9.1910. Camborne 5.1.1911. Liskeard 1.11.1912.
8.11.1913 Resigned.

P.C. 104 Thomas Henry Jane
A 21 year old single labourer from Gwinear. Public Service: I Comp., 4th., Batt., D.C.L.I. For three years.
Appointed: 25.7.1910.
Stationed at: Bodmin 5.5.1911. Falmouth 3.8.1911
4.10.1911 Resigned.

P.C. 51 Nelson George Humphries
A 22 year old single labourer from Swindon.
Appointed: 28.7.1910.
Stationed at: Camborne 5.1.1911.
31.10.1912 Resigned.

P.C. 102 William Thomas Broad
A labourer from Phillack aged 20 years.
18.7.1917 married Mabel Toy of Camborne.
Appointed: 3.9.1910.

Promotion: 1.4.1921 to Sergeant.
Stationed at: Camborne 8.3.1911. Bodmin 1.10.1912. Camborne 25.3.1914.
13.3.1917 Joined the army under Police (Emergency Provisions) 1915.
Reappointed: 16.6.1919
Stationed at: Camborne 19.6.1919. Truro 1.7.1919. Also Bodmin, Redruth, Bodmin, Nanpean, Camborne, Sennen, Camborne, Devoran, Newlyn, St Just and Truro.
31.1.1937 Retired.

P.C. 70 Charles Clymow
A porter from Gwennap aged 21 years.
9.6.1917. Married Evelyn Johns from Bude.
Appointed: 10.10.1910.
Promotion: 1.2.1924 to Sergeant.
Stationed at: Bodmin 8.3.1911. Launceston 6.7.1911. Falmouth 21.7.1914.
13.3.1917 Joined army for war service.
Reappointed: 27.3.1919 as P.C. 86.
Stationed at: Falmouth 28.3.1919. Also Bodmin, Padstow, Bude, Helston, Falmouth, Veryan, Mawnan Smith, Mawgan in Meneage, St Columb and Padstow.
31.1.1937 Retired.

P.C. 133 Herbert John Knight
A 22 year old single quarryman from St Teath.
Appointed: 24.11.1910.
Stationed at: Bodmin 8.5.1911. Falmouth 24.7.1911.
31.1.1913 Resigned.

P.C. 49 Albert Ernest Jago
A 19 year old labourer from St Austell.
9.11.1918 married Ada Matthews Brush of Heamoor.
Appointed: 6.1.1911.
Stationed at: Bodmin 24.7.1911. Truro 1.8.1911. Liskeard 6.11.1913. Camborne 21.7.1914. 18.7.1916 Joined the army.
Reappointed: 11.10.1919
Stationed at: Camborne 5.11.1919. Bodmin, Newquay, Millbrook, Chyandour, Camborne, Praze, and Penryn.
1.10.1938 Retired.

P.C. 150 James Henry Tresidder
A 20 year old single farmer from Mabe.
Appointed: 25.2.1911.
Promotion: 1.5.1923 to Sergeant.
Stationed at: Camborne 15.8.1911. Also St Ives, Boscaswell, St Just, Sennen, Camborne, St Ives, North Hill, Tinagel, Week St Mary, Camelford and Penryn.
26.1.1920 P.C. 150 James H.Tresidder was fined £1.0.0. For visiting a public house at St Ives whilst on duty, contrary to the regs of the force. The breach of rules being aggravated by prevarication. The Constable is warned as to his future conduct.
31.8.1939 Retired.

P.C. 160 Herbert Edward Richards
An 18 year old fisherman from Looe.
17.6.1916 married Winifred Hendra from St Austell.
Appointed: 1.3.1911.
Promotion: 1.9.1928 to Sergeant.
Stationed at: Bodmin 15.9.1911. Truro 31.3.1913.
31.5.1915 joined army for duration of war.

Reappointed: 1.8.1919. as P.C. 9.
Truro 2.8.1919.
Stationed at: St Austell, Padstow, Newquay, Truro, Newquay, St Columb Minor, Newquay, St Anne's Chapel, Launceston, Tregoney and Truro.
7.4.1939 Retired.

P.C. 158 William James Tonkin
A 24 year old G.W.R. Porter from Gwennap.
5.4.1913 married Mary Annie Rank of Bodmin.
Appointed: 1.7.1911.
Stationed at: Bodmin 1.12.1911. Also Blisland, Lanivet, Polruan, Tywardreath and St Breward.
30.6.1937 Retired.

P.C. 138 Robert Matthews
A 19 year single gardener from Paul, Penzance.
Appointed: 15.8.1911.
Stationed at: Bodmin 1.12.1911. Camborne 16.12.1911. Truro 23.3.1914
6.9.1915 joined the army.
Reappointed: 20.3.1919 as P.C. 128.
Stationed at: Truro 1.4.1919. Also Bodmin, Redruth, Sennen, Newquay, Gloweth and Truro.
30.6.1939 Retired.

P.C. 11 John Henry Dann
A fisherman from East Looe aged 19 years.
3.6.1917 married Miss F.A.Emmett of Newquay at the Registry Office, St Coloumb.
Appointed: 15.9.1911.
Stationed at: Falmouth 7.2.1912. Truro 1.7.1912. Camborne 25.3.1913. Liskeard 21.7.1914.
31.5.1915 Joined the army.
Reappointed: 17.4.1919 as P.C. 170.
Stationed at: Liskeard 19.4.1919. Truro 7.5.1919. Also Falmouth, Newquay, Newlyn, Millbrook, Grampound Road, Blue Anchor, Mawgan in Pydar, Tywardreath and Polruan.
30.9.1938 Retired.

P.C. 10 James Philip Hawton
A single stone cutter from Greenwich, London. Public Service: Penzance Borough Police for 3 months.
Appointed: 25.9.1911.
Stationed at: Liskeard 7.2.1912.
12.8.1913 Dismissed for 1. Stating false-hoods 2. Conduct calculated to bring the force into disrepute.

P.C. 23 Leonard Warne
A porter, aged 19 years, G.W.R. From St Germans. 24.11.1917 married Miss Ruth Peterson at St Marylebone Church, London.
Appointed: 1.12.1911.
Promotion: 1.6.1926 to Sergeant.
1.1.1935 to Inspector.
Stationed at: Bodmin 26.3.1912.
31.5.1915 joined the army.
Reappointed: 20.8.1919
Stationed at: Bodmin 13.9.1919. St Austell. Also Padstow, St Austell, St Minver, Illogan, Week St Mary, Bodmin, Helston, and Callington.
30.9.1939 Retired.

P.C. 46 James Gerrey Valance
A 26 year old clay cutter from Newton Abbott. 12.3.1916 married Miss Kate Carsarthe of St Ives.
Appointed: 1.12.1911.
Stationed at: Camborne 18.3.1912.
30.11.1915 joined the army.
Reappointed: 23.9.1919
Stationed at: Liskeard 3.10.1919. Also St Ives, Anthony and Kingsand.
30.6.1927 Retired.

P.C. 53 Horace George Kinsman
A 21 year old single miner from Callington
Appointed: 15.1.1912.
Stationed at: Bodmin 1.4.1912.
30.6.1912 Resigned.

P.C. 5 William Samuel Matthews
A 23 year old gardener from Devonport.
5.8.1914 married Hilda K.Martin of Liskeard.
Appointed: 22.1.1912.
Stationed at: Bodmin 1.4.1912. Liskeard 1.10.1912. Bodmin 1.1.1914. Truro 4.9.1914.
11.6.1917 joined the army.
Reappointed: 10.2.1919.
Stationed at: Truro 10.2.1919. Camborne 16.1.1920. Also Bodmin, Liskeard, Wadebrige, Lostwithiel, St Wenn, Pool and Praze.
28.2.1938 Retired.

P.C. 190 Clarence Clifton
A 19 year old single carpenter from Holsworthy. Public Service: 6th Batt., Devon Regt., two years and nine months.
Appointed: 27.3.1912.
Stationed at: Falmouth 1.7.1912.
28.2.1915 Resigned.

P.C. 88 Samuel Charles Rowe
A butcher from St Blazey, aged 22 years single. Public Service: Royal Garrison Artillery, 47th., Comp.., for five years and 349 days.
Appointed: 1.4.1912.
Stationed at: Liskeard 1.7.1912.
4.8.1914 Reservist recalled to the colours. Killed in action.

P.C. 44 Cyril Dawe
A 20 year old single stonemason from Linkinhorne.
Appointed: 1.4.1912.
Stationed at: Falmouth 1.7.1912
31.12.1915 joined the army.
Reappointed: 1.7.1919 as P.C. 130.
Stationed at: Falmouth 20.7.1919. Also Penryn, Bodmin, and Falmouth.
31.12.1945 Retired.

P.C. 88 William Walter Hodge
A drapers assistant from St Germans, single aged 20 years. Public Service: 5th Batt/., D.C.L.I. For three years.
Promotion: 1.4.1930 to Sergeant. 1.7.1933 to Inspector, Chief Clerk. 1.4.1939 to Superintendent.
Stationed at: Bodmin 1.7.1912. H.Q. 2.8.1919. Bodmin. Also St Minver, Bodmin,

Chief Constable's Office, Bodmin and Camborne.
20.5.1940 Retired.

P.C. 189 Jonathan Greet
A 21 year old single labourer from St Enoder.
Appointed: 1.4.1912.
Stationed at: Truro 9.7.1912.
31.12.1915 joined the army.
Reappointed: 2.2.1919
Stationed at: Truro 7.2.1919. Also St Agnes, Truro, Newquay, Blackwater and Devoran.
30.4.1938 Retired.

P.C. 13 William Moyse
A labourer from Lewannick aged 20 years.
4.10.1913 married Maud N.Wilton from Launceston.
Appointed: 1.4.1912.
Stationed at: Launceston 1.7.1912. Liskeard 9.11.1913.
21.4.1918 joined the army.
Reappointed: 4.2.1919
Stationed at: Launceston 10.9.1919. Also St Germans, Cargreen, Saltash, Launceston, Camelford and Launceston.
1.2.1929 Favourable Record for brave conduct at Launceston on 8.1.1929 when he at great personal risk and with great courage and determination entered a burning house and endeavoured to hold the fire in check pending the arrival of the Brigade.
Retired through ill-heath in 31 .12.1938.

P.C. 191 William Charles Scott
A carpenter from Camelford aged 23 years.
8.9.1915 married Elizabeth Nicholls a widow.
Appointed: 8.4.1912.
Promotion: 1.11.1930 to Sergeant.
Stationed at: Falmouth 18.6.1912.
21.4.1918 joined the army
Reappointed: 22.1.1919
Stationed at: Falmouth 25.1.1919. Also Flushing, Falmouth, Mawnan Smith.
31.7.1938 Retired. 2.4.1965 Died.

P.C. 113 John Charles Gerrans
A 23 year old single blacksmith from Gwennap. Public Service: Lancashire County Constabulary for two years.
Appointed: 1.5.1912.
Stationed at: Bodmin 1.5.1912.
Liskeard 23.5.1912.
1.1.1913 Resigned.

P.C. 126 Charles Doney
A wool comber from Liskeard aged 21 years.
28.4.1915. Married Kate E.S.Williams of Gulval.
Appointed: 23.5.1912.
Stationed at: Camborne 1.10.1912.
11.6.1917 joined the army.
Reappointed: 16.4.1919
Stationed at: Camborne 17.4.1919. Also Redruth, Chyandour, Sennen, Camborne, Redruth Highway, St Ives, Pool, Foxhole and Mevagissey.
31.5.1938 Retired 19.8.1944 Died.

P.C. 193 Ernest Burrough
A 23 year old attendant from the Cornwall

County Asylum, Bodmin. 1.9.1918 married Edith Ruth Chasney of Thetford, Norfolk.
Appointed: 1.7.1912.
Stationed at: Camborne 1.10.1912.
Truro 3.6.1915.
9.8.1915 joined the army.
Reappointed: 29.8.1919
Stationed at: Truro 5.9.1919. Bodmin 5.11.1919. Also Camborne, St Just, Newquay, Truro, Egloshayle and St Austell.
3.6.1915 P.C. Ernest Burrough was ordered to transfer at his own expense for being under the influence of liquor on the 21.5.1915 and seriously waned as to his future conduct.
30.6.1938. Retired.

P.C. 103 Richard Edward Hopgood Badcock
A 21 year old groom from Morval, Liskeard. 28.5.1914 married Lillian Bennett of Menheniott. Public Service: 1st., Batt., Coldstream Guards for three years.
Appointed: 1.7.1912.
Stationed at: Camborne 1.10.1912.
4.8.1914 reservist called to the colours.
Reappointed: 1.2.1919. as P.C. 27.
Stationed at: Camborne 3.2.1919. Redruth, Illogan, Carnel Green and Marazion.
As 1st Police Reserve 312 Favourable Record for zeal and efficiency displayed in connection with a series of larcenies at Millpool in the Parishes of St Hilary and Germoe which resulted in the clearing up of a number of crimes and the conviction of ten people.
31.6.1938 Retired.

P.C. 53 Archibald Hendy
A labourer from Lanivet, single aged 21 years.
Appointed: 1.7.1912.
Stationed at: Launceston 1.10.1912.
19.11.1914. Resigned.

P.C. 192 Ernest Weary
A store porter from Bodmin aged 19 years. 25.9.1917 married Miss B.Penna of Redruth.
Appointed: 1.7.1912.
Stationed at: Falmouth 1.10.1912. Camborne 4.7.1913. Launceston 7.8.1914.
31.8.1915 joined the army.
Reappointed:29.8.1919
Stationed at: Falmouth 17.9.1919. Truro 5.11.1919. Also Falmouth, Redruth, Launceston, Helston, St Columb Major, Veryan and Highertown.
30.9.1938 retired 1.12.1944 Died.

P.C. 194 Frederick Hoskin
A labourer from St Germans aged 20 years. 8.2.1914. Married Maud Sowden of Bodmin.
Appointed: 1.7.1912.
Promotion: 1.,10.1923 to Sergeant. 1.1.1934 to Inspector. 1.7.1937 to Superintendent.
Stationed at: Camborne 1.10.1912. Falmouth 17.3.1913.
12.3.1917 joined the army.
Reappointed: 9.4.1919.
Stationed at: Launceston 4.4.1919. Also

Camborne, Penryn, Tintagel, St Columb Major, Truro, St Ives, Newquay and St Austell. 26.10.1922 Favourable Record in that he at Tintagel on 3.8.1921 at great personal risk to himself went down a cliff and assisted in searching for a man who had fallen and who was subsequently found drowned.
18.1.1934 At Newquay Police Court Inspector Frederick Hosken was complimented by the Chairman of the bench in the satisfactory and quick following of clues which resulted in John Henry Summers, aged 25 years being committed for trial at the Assizes on three charges of burglary and one charge of having in his possession a certain firearm other than that for a lawful purpose.
18.9.1948 Died.

P.C. 63 James Penrose
A 23 year old skilled labourer from St Blazey. 1.10.1919 Married Lilly Pascoe of Camborne
Appointed: 15.7.1912.
Stationed at: Camborne 1.10.1912.
13.4.1917 Joined the army for war service.
Reappointed: 1.5.1919 as P.C. 199.
Stationed at: Falmouth 6.5.1919. Camborne 3.3.1920. Also Falmouth, Cury, Mousehole, Hessenford, Liskeard, Halworthy.
31.12.1938 Retired.

P.C. 167 Samuel Thomas Bishop
A 23 year old miner from Crowan, Married.
Appointed: 1.9.1912.
Stationed at: Bodmin 1.1.1913.
14.11.1915. Joined the army for war service.
Reappointed: 3.3.1919 as P.C. 103.
Stationed at: Liskeard 10.3.1919. Bodmin 8.4.1920. Also Wadebridge, Port Isaac, Liskeard, Bodmin, Wadebridge, Bodmin, Mawgan.
1.4.1920. Awarded the Kings Police Medal for distinguished bravery for stopping a runaway horse at Liskeard on the 9.8.1919. (This man was given an ill-health pension for injuries received on duty)
31.1.1924 Retired through ill-heath.

P.C. 19 Harry Hoskin
A single farmer from Morval, Liskeard, aged 20 years.
Appointed: 1.10.1912.
Stationed at: Camborne 1.1.1913. Bodmin 16.5.1914.
31.5.1915. Joined the army for war service.
Reappointed: 26.8.1919
Stationed at: Truro 17.9.1919. Bodmin 1.1.1920. Also Camborne, Bodmin, St Austell. Tregoney, St Austell.
14.5.1914. P.C. 19 Hoskin was reprimanded for conduct while on duty calculated to bring the force into disrepute and transferred at his own expense.
7.1.1921 P.C. 19 Hoskin was suspended from duty and called upon to resign for neglect of duty and discreditable conduct.

P.C. 195 Ernest Doney
A 20 year old farm hand from Helland, Bodmin. 29.7.1916 Married Molly L.Winnon of Falmouth.
Appointed: 1.10.1912.

Promotion: 1.12.1928 to Sergeant. 1.4.1938 to Inspector.
Stationed at: Launceston 1.1.1913. Falmouth 5.8.1914.
22.4.1918 joined the army for war service.
Reappointed: 1.2.1919. as P.C. 202.
Stationed at: Camborne 3.2.1919. Also Launceston, Falmouth, Pool, Redruth, Goldsithney, Fowey, Pleynt, Chacewater, Truro, Fowey , Newquay , Launceston.
1.7.1916. P.C. 193 Ernest Doney was granted a Favourable Record for zeal and tact displayed in the execution of his duty particularly in regard to the successful prosecution which had resulted from his vigilance. Granted a months seniority in service whilst holding the rank of Constable.
31.10.1944 Retired.

P.C. 196 John Henry Pellow
A single baker from Falmouth, aged 21 years. Public Service: Army Service Corps., for three years.
Appointed: 1.10.1912.
Stationed at: Bodmin 1.1.1913.
8.4.1914 Reservist recalled to the colours. Letter attached to Record.
Rouen, France.
19.3.1919.

The Chief Constable.
C.C.C.
Sir,
Owing to the changed circumstances brought about by the war, I beg most respectfully to tender my resignation from the Cornwall County Police. Before being recalled to the colours my Police No. Was 196.
I remain Sir Your obedient servant,
Sergeant John H.Pellow
10th., Batt., Royal Fusiliers (Attached),
Intelligence Corps.,
C/o Intelligence Officer
Rouen,
B.E.F. France.

P.C. 197 Sidney Goad
A 20 year old wood man from Illogan, Redruth. 11.2.1915. Married Flossie Cliss.
Appointed: 17.10.1912.
Stationed at: Falmouth 1.1.1913. Bodmin 1.3.1916.
13.2.1917 joined the army for war service.
Reappointed: 14.1.1920
Stationed at: Liskeard 4.3.1920. Also Penryn, New Town, Cury, Bodmin, St Neot and Polruan.
14.10.1924 Resigned.

P.C. 123 George Pearce
A 23 year old grocers assistant from Bodmin. 20.9.1917 Married Miss M.Rowling of Moor Street, Camborne. At the United Methodist Church, Camborne.
Appointed: 1.11.1912.
Promotion: 1.3.1931 to Sergeant.
Stationed at: Camborne 1.1.1913.
31.12.1915. Joined the army for war service.
Reappointed: 21.9.1919.
Stationed at: St Ives, Camborne, Marazion, St Just, Falmouth, St Columb.
31.10.1938 Retired.

P.C. 81 John Edward Ough
A 24 year old from Morval Liskeard, labourer, single.
Appointed: 1.11.1912.
Stationed at: Camborne 1.3.1913.
13.10.1913 Resigned.

P.C. 51 William John Babbage
A 19 year old labourer from Menheniot.
10.8.1915. Married Elizabeth Gill of Falmouth.
Appointed: 1.11.1912.
Stationed at: Falmouth 1.2.1913.
11.9.1918 joined army for war service.
Reappointed: 1.2.1919
Stationed at: Falmouth, Constantine , Comford, St Day, Breage.
2.9.1914 P.C. 51 William J.Babbage was granted a Favourable Record for stopping a runaway pony at Falmouth at great personal risk.
31.3.1940 Retired.

P.C. 117 Richard Curgunven
A 20 year old mason from St Agnes.
7.2.1918 married Miss A.Critchley of St Keverne at the Parish Church, Busford, Oxfordshire.
Appointed: 1.1.1913.
Stationed at: Bodmin 1.4.1913.
31.5.1915 Joined army for war service.
Reappointed: 1.3.1919 as P.C. 159.
Stationed at: Falmouth 12.4.1919. Liskeard 1.7.1919. Also St Austell, Tywardreath, Cury, Calstock, Pensilva.
12.3.1914 Granted a Favourable Record for stopping a runaway horse at St Austell on 10.3.1914 at great personal risk.
31.3.1935 Retired through ill-health (Injuries received whilst on duty)

P.C. 113 Frederick Stanley Benney
A 20 year old labourer from Illogan, Redruth.
23.8.1914 Married Miss Osborne from Lanreath.
Appointed: 1.1.1913.
Stationed at: Liskeard 1.4.1913.
21.4.1918 joined the army for war service.
Reappointed: 13.1.1919 as P.C. 20.
Stationed at: Liskeard 14.1.1919. Duloe, West Looe, Dobwalls.
1.10.1923 Granted a favourable Record for that he at a recent fire in Dean Street, Liskeard, at great personal risk, gallantly made two attempts to rescue, from a burning building an aged woman who was subsequently found suffocated.
31.3.1939. Retired 10.9.1948 Died.

P.C. 133 Oscar Foulsham Woods
A 22 year old single cabinet maker from Leiston, Suffolk. Public Service: Royal Engineers fir three years.
Appointed: 11.1.1913.
Stationed at: Camborne. 1.4.1913.
9.11.1913 Resigned.

P.C. 198 Samuel Tom
A 20 year old single labourer from St Minver.
Appointed: 21.1.1913.
Stationed at: Bodmin 31.3.1913. Camborne 20.4.1915. Liskeard 1.7.1915 Bodmin 20.11.1915.

12.12.1915 joined the army for war service. Killed in Action.

P.C. 199 Oliver William Dickinson
A gardener aged 20 years from Ireland.
22.10.1919 married Miss L.M.Mitchell of St Austell.
Appointed: 1.2.1913.
Stationed at: Bodmin 1.6.1913.
31.5.1915. Joined the army for war service.
Reappointed: 13.8.1919 as P.C. 11.
Stationed at: Bodmin , Padstow, Bodmin, Torpoint, St Breward, Redruth Highway, St Blazey.
31.1.1940 Retired.

P.C. 200 John Tonkin James
A 20 year old single fisherman from Paul.
Appointed: 3.2.1913.
Stationed at: Camborne 1.5.1913. Liskeard 7.11.1916
31.12.1916 joined army for war service.
Reappointed: 1.1.1919
Stationed at: Bodmin 27.1.1919. Liskeard 1.10.1920. Also Camborne, Torpoint, Mevagissey, East Looe, Mullion, St Ives.
30.9.1939 Retired. 26.6.1950 Died.

P.C. 54 John Kessel Prynne
A 21 year old labourer from St Wenn.
17.12.1914 married Katherine Buckley of Newquay.
Appointed: 10.3.1913.
Stationed at: Truro 3.7.1913.
19.12.1915 Resigned.
Reappointed: 1.5.1920 as P.C. 105.
Stationed at: Launceston 27.5.1920. Also Newquay, Trispen, South Petherwin, Boscastle and Egloskerry.
30.4.1945 Retired.

P.C. 201 Frederick John Bray
A grocers assistant from Liskeard, single aged 18 years.
Appointed: 1.4.1913.
Stationed at: Falmouth 3.7.1913. Truro 14.11.1914.
9.1.1916 joined the army for war service
3.5.1917 Died of wounds received in action.

P.C. 112 William George Ralf Chellew
A blacksmith from St Minver, single aged 20 years.
Appointed: 7.4.1913.
8.5.1913 Resigned.

P.C. 15 George Thomas Tapley
A 24 year old clerk from Phillack, Hayle. Public Service. Royal Engineers for three years. Married Miss Taylor of Lanner without obtaining the necessary permission.
Appointed: 7.4.1913
Stationed at: Falmouth 4.7.1913.
4.8.1915 Reservist recalled to the colours.
Reappointed: 10.2.1919
Stationed at: Liskeard 18.2.1919.
5.3.1919 Resigned.

P.C. 202 William Reginald George Williams
A 24 year old single Royal Navy Seaman

from Gosport. Public Service. Royal Navy, H.M.S. Angus for five years.
Appointed: 21.4.1913.
Stationed at: Liskeard 3.7.1913.
4.8.1915 Naval Reservist recalled to the Navy.
Reappointed: 1.1.1919 as P.C. 58.
Stationed at: Liskeard 14.1.1919. Bodmin 3.3.1920. Also Liskeard, Lanreath, Liskeard, St Stephens, Lezant , North Hill, Halworthy, Menheniot, Polperro, St Germans , Duloe.
9.3.1946 Retired.

P.C. 112 Arthur John Kitt
A 21 year old married farm labourer from Landrake, Saltash.
Appointed: 1.6.1913.
Stationed at: Bodmin 30.7.1913. Truro 8.10.1914.
11.6.1917 joined the army for war service.
Reappointed: 7.4.1919.
Stationed at: Truro 8.4.1919. Also Wadebridge, St Agnes, Comford.
31.10.1939 Retired 23.9.1951 Died.

P.C. 71 John Hicks
An 18 year old single labourer from Crowan. Public Service. Household Cavalry for 10 months.
Appointed: 26.5.1913.
Promotion: 1.4.1933 to Sergeant.
Stationed at: Bodmin 11.8.1913.
23.2.1916 joined the army for war service.
Reappointed: 26.2.1919
Stationed at: Camborne 1.5.1919. Also Mevagissey, Tywardreath, St Ives, Portreath, Illogan, Heamoor, St Ann's Chapel.
3.6.1938 Retired. 29.6.1943 Died.

P.C. 202 Edgar Ead
A gardener from Egloshayle, single aged 22 years.
Appointed: 26.5.1913.
Stationed at: Bodmin 23.8.1913. Falmouth 1.4.1914.
31.12.1915. Joined the army for war service.
Reappointed: 8.10.1919 as P.C. 97.
Stationed at: Liskeard 14.10.1919. Falmouth 3.1.1921. Also Bodmin, Cury, Lanreath, Cury, Mullion, Flushing and Mylor Bridge.
30.11.1944 Retired..

P.C. 203 Samuel Reynolds Bennetts
A 19 year old mason from Paul, Penzance.
15.12.1917 married Agatha M.Wright of Penzance.
Appointed: 2.6.1913.
Stationed at: Liskeard 23.8.1913.
30.6.1915 joined the army for war service.
Reappointed: 1.2.1919 as P.C. 63.
Stationed at: Camborne 8.2.1919. Falmouth 5.11.1919. Bodmin 11.11.1919. Liskeard 2.9.1920. Also Callington, Saltash, Redruth, Perranwell, Fowey, Lerryn, Polperro, Duloe, St Erth.
31.10.1939 Retired.

P.C. 204 Gerald Rogers
From Looe a labourer aged 20 years.
4.12.1917. Married Beatrice M.Carpenter of Redruth.
Appointed: 3.12.19.

Promotion: 1.8.1929 to Sergeant.
Stationed at: Camborne 20.11.1913.
31.12.1915 joined the army for war Service.
Reappointed: 4.6.1919
Camborne 11.6.1919. Also Fowey, Redruth, Camborne, Carnel Green, Copperhouse, Launceston, Camborne.
7.7.1940. Retired. 4.6.1950. Died.

P.C. 72 Thomas Newery Stamp
A 23 year old labourer from Brixham.
14.1.1915. Married Annie Philp of Grampound.
Appointed: 3.7.1913.
Stationed at: Launceston 20.11.1913.
21.4.1918 joined the army for war service.
Reappointed: 10.2.1919 as P.C. 83.
Stationed at: Launceston 10.2.1919. Bodmin 9.2.1921. Also Launceston, Canworthy Water, Five Lanes, St Austell, Bodmin Road, Fowey.
2.7.1940. Retired through ill-health.

P.C. 205 William Henry Hocking
From St Cleer an 18 year old single gardener.
Appointed: 14.7.1913.
Stationed at: Camborne 20.11.1913.
31.7.1915 Joined the army for war service.
War Service 3.8.1915 to 1.8.1919.
Metropolitan Police, 5.10.1919 to 28.12.1919.
Reappointed: 1.2.1920 as P.C. 29.
Stationed at: Truro 16.2.1920. Camborne 5.5.1920.
12.4.1920 P.C. 29 William H.Hocking was fined £2.10.0. For absenting himself from his station without permission and stating false-hoods to his superior officer. The Constable has been seriously warned and ordered to be transferred at his own expense.
30.11.1920 Resigned.

P.C. 206 John Gifford England
A 21 year old single groom from Illminster.
Appointed: 27.7.1913.
8.8.1913 Resigned.

P.C. 156 Edwin George Cock
A 20 year old single G.W.R. Shunter from Kenwyn. 27.2.1916 married Miss J.A.Hyde at St Martins-by-Looe.
Appointed: 4.8.1913.
Stationed at: Falmouth 20.11.1913.
30.11.1915. Joined the army for war service.
Reappointed: 17.2.1919
Stationed at: Bodmin 24.2.1919. Also Falmouth, Penryn, St Kew Highway, Chyandour, Illogan, Porkellis, Blackwater.
31.8.1940 Retired.

P.C. 206 Thomas Henry Bastion
A 24 year old farmer from Breage, Helston.
10.11.1915 Married Emma S.Thomas of Crowlas.
Appointed: 12.8.1913
Stationed at: Camborne 25.11.1913.
21.4.1918 joined the army for war service.
Reappointed: 20.1.1919
Stationed at: Camborne 20.1.1919. Also St Ives, St Just, Boscaswell, Lelant, Newlyn East, Praze, Pool.
30.9.1939. Retired.

P.C. 207 Henry Charles Walters
A 21 year old single soldier from Guilford, Essex. **Public Service:** 3rd., Batt., Grenadier Guards for three years.
Appointed: 15.8.1913.
Stationed at: Bodmin 23.10.1913.
4.8.1914. Recalled to the colours.
Reappointed: 28.1.1919
5.5.1919 Resigned.

P.C. 10 Sydney Henry Hocking
A 21 year old married labourer fro m St Austell.
Appointed: 28.8.1913.
Stationed at: Truro 5.12.1913.
31.8.1914 Resigned.

P.C. 92 William Avery Bray
A 21 year old farm Labourer from Lanteglos by Fowey. 10.1.1916 Married Mary Glass of Anderton at the Parish Church of Millbrook.
Public Service: Royal Engineers for two years 74 days.
Appointed: 17.9.1913.
Stationed at: Liskeard 1.1.1914.
15.1.1916 Joined the army for war service.
Reappointed: 10.2.1919 as P.C. 70.
Stationed at: Liskeard 11.2.1919. Millbrook, East Looe, Cargreen.
16.10.1923 Resigned.

P.C. 18 William John Brooking
A G.W.R. Plate layer from Kingsbridge, aged 25 single. **Public Service:** D.C.L.I. For eight years and one month.
Appointed: 6.10.1913.
Stationed at: Truro 1.1.1914. Falmouth 1.4.1914.
4.8.1914 joined the army for war service.
Reappointed: 25.2.1919
Stationed at: Camborne 1.3.1919. Also Newquay, Falmouth, Newlyn, Redruth.
1.5.1924 Granted a Favourable Record for brave conduct at Redruth on 2.4.1924 when he at great personal risk stopped two runaway horses thereby preventing what might have been a serious accident.
2.5.1924 Awarded the Kings Police Medal for distinguished bravery in stopping two runaway horses at Redruth on 2.4.1924.
30.11.1939 Retired.

P.C. 133 William Toy
A 23 year old gardener from St Minver.
20.5.1916 Married Mabel A.Chapman of Moorswater, Liskeard.
Appointed: 1.12.1913.
Promotion: 7.4.1926 to Sergeant. 1.4.1934 to Inspector.
Stationed at: Liskeard 14.3.1914.
12.12.1915 Joined the army for war service.
Reappointed: 10.2.1919
Stationed at: Liskeard 14.2.1919. Bodmin 3.4.1919. Also Torpoint, Sticker, Camelford, Falmouth, Chyandour, Liskeard.
16.1.1950. Retired. 14.12.1955. Died.

P.C. 81 Charles Leonard Webb
From Menheniot, a 23 years old single mason.
Public Service: 1st Search Light Comp., Royal Engineers, Aldershot for three years.
Appointed: 1.12.1913.

Stationed at:. Camborne 1 4.3.1914
4.8.1915 Reservist recalled to the colours.
Died whilst prisoner of war in Germany.

P.C. 45 Gerald Hyde
A 22 year old single labourer from Looe.
Public Service: R.H. And R.F.A. Artillery, 11th., Batt., for three years.
Appointed: 1.12.1913.
Stationed at: Truro 25.3.1914.
4.8.1914 Reservist recalled to the colours.
Reappointed: 16.4.1918
Stationed at: Bodmin 8.2.1919. Truro 4.3.1921. Also Saltash, St Austell, Truro, Slades, St Austell, St Stephens.
29.1.1938. Retired. 6.11.1954. Died.

P.C. 99 Cecil Pedlar
A 19 year old single clay labourer from St Austell.
Appointed: 1.12.1913
Stationed at: Camborne 25.3.1914.
30.11.1915 joined the army for war service.
Reappointed: 1.7.1919 as P.C. 37.
Stationed at: Bodmin 2.8.1919. St Ives, Bodmin.
31.1.1942 Retired.

P.C. 25 Erwin Edgar Hodge
A miner from Lansallas, Polperro, single aged 20 years. **Public Service:** 5th Batt., D.C.L.I. G.Comp.
Appointed: 1.12.1913.
Promotion: 9.2.1936 to Sergeant.
Stationed at: Falmouth 14.3.1914.
4.8.1914 Recalled to the Territorials from which he had not been discharged.
Reappointed: 1.3.1919 as P.C. 22
Stationed at: Bodmin 1.4.1919. Liskeard 4.2.1920. Also Falmouth, Fowey, Tywardreath, Fowey, Torpoint, St Ives, St Buryan, St Stephens, Tywardreath, Bodmin, Wadebridge.
31.5.1941 Retired.

P.C. 8 Joseph Edward Trays
A 20 year old gardener from Torpoint.
20.4.1916 Married Miss E.Gardener of Newquay.
Appointed: 1.1.1914.
Promotion: 1.8.1930 to Sergeant.
Stationed at: Truro 10.4.1914.
Bodmin 16.9.1915.
17.10.1915 Joined the army for war service.
Reappointed: 20.8.1919
Stationed at: Liskeard 17.9.1919. Bodmin 4.3.1920. Also Newquay, Gloweth, St Austell, Liskeard, St Neot, St Austell, St Stephens, Padstow, St Columb, Falmouth, Tywardreath,
30.6.1941. Retired.

P.C. 209 Percy Mitchell
A butcher from Illogan aged 21 years.
Appointed: 1.1.1914.
Promotion: 1.10.1939 to Sergeant.
Stationed at: Liskeard 1.4.1914.
19.1.1916 Joined the army for war service.
Reappointed: 14.2.1919.
Stationed at: Bodmin 18.2.1919. Truro 1.3.1919. Also Saltash, Bodmin. Newquay, Fowey, St Blazey, St Columb Minor, Liskeard, Camborne.
14.10.1944 Retired. 28.8.1956 Died.

P.C. 208 Percy Job
A 22 year old labourer from Gerrans.
Appointed: 1.1.1914.
6.6.1915 Married Annie Keast (widow) of
Higher Enys Road, Camborne. At the United
Methodist Church, Camborne.
Appointed: 1.1.1914.
Stationed at: Bodmin 1.4.1914. Camborne
16.5.1914. Truro 21.12.1915.
11.6.1917 Joined the army for war service.
Reappointed: 1.2.1919 as P.C. 38.
Stationed at: Falmouth 3.2.1919. Also
Bodmin, Camborne, St Just, Trispen,
Perranwell, Helston, St Keverne, The Lizard,
South Downs, Camborne.
6.10.1945 Retired. 25.3.1953 Died.

P.C. 7 Richard Claude Colwill
A 20 year old single labourer from Stratton.
Appointed: 16.3.1914.
Stationed at: Bodmin 5.8.1914.
9.1.1916 Joined the army for War Service.
Reappointed: 9.11.1919 as P.C. 118.
Stationed at: Camborne 11.11.1919. Also
Wadebridge, Fowey, Bodmin, Redruth,
Camborne, Bodmin.
31.1.1945. Retired.

P.C. 127 James Edwin Botheras
A 21 year old single dairyman from St
Buryan, Penzance.
Appointed: 26.3.1914.
Stationed at: Bodmin 5.8.1914. Falmouth
18.3.1915. Liskeard 1.7.1915. Camborne
1.12.1915.
13.3.1917. Joined the army for War Service.
Camborne 18.2.1919.
31.8.1920 Resigned.

P.C. 211 Walter Gray
A Royal Marine from Wiltshire, aged 23
years, single. Public Service: Royal Marine
Light Infantry for 6 years and 182 days.
Appointed: 1.4.1914.
Stationed at: Launceston 9.7.1914.
4.8.1915 Reservist recalled to the colours.
3.8.1916 Killed in action.

P.C. 210 Thomas Cecil Grigg
A gardener from Mabe, Falmouth, aged 21
years.
Appointed: 1,4.1914.
16.2.1918 Married Louie Andrews of
Stithians.
Stationed at: Camborne 7.7.1914. Truro
20.4.1915.
31.5.1915 Joined the army for war service.
Reappointed: 7.8.1919
Stationed at: Liskeard 16.8.1919. Also
Redruth, Newquay, Liskeard, Landrake,
Torpoint, Callington, Stratton.
28.11.1936 Granted a Favourable Record as
the result of a commendation at Callington
Juvenile Court on 12.11.1936 for exception-
ally good work performed and zeal and intelligence shown in the detection of a number
of cases of housebreaking and larceny at
Callington.
29.5.1943 Granted a Favourable Record for
zeal and devotion to duty between the 17th
and 19th 4.1943 as the result of which
number 13026500 Private George Grubb

was arrested and committed for trial at the
Assize on charges of burglary, shop breaking
and housebreaking.
31.12.1945 Retired.

P.C. 212 Leonard Richards
A 20 year old mason from Bodmin.
11.6.1918 Married Miss R.L.Symons of
Falmouth.
Appointed: 1.4.1914.
Stationed at: Falmouth 11.7.1914.
Launceston 1.7.1915.
31.8.1915 Joined the army for war service.
Reappointed: 4.9.1919
Stationed at: Launceston 6.9.1919. Also
Falmouth, Launceston, South Petherwin,
Canworthy Water, Lezant, St Austell, South
Downs, Blue Anchor.
31.12.1945 Retired.

P.C. 213 George Henry Fradd
A 19 year old single carpenter from Bodmin.
Appointed: 27.4.1914.
Promotion: 1.11.1930 to Sergeant.
Stationed at: Falmouth 26.8.1914.
Camborne 1.6.1915.
30.11.1915. Joined the army for war service.
Reappointed: 24.2.1919
Stationed at: Liskeard 1.3.1919. Also
Falmouth, Helston, Callington, St Mellion,
Cargreen, Saltash, Week St Mary, Bodmin.
30.6.1943 Retired through ill-health.

P.C. 214 Richard Henry Palmer
An 18 year old labourer from Plymouth.
7.4.1919 Married Ruth Sandy at St Winnow
Parish Church.
Appointed: 27.4.1914.
Promotion: 1.12.1930 to Sergeant.
Stationed at: Falmouth 28.8.1914.
17.12.1915 Joined the army for war
Service.
Reappointed: 2.10.1918
Stationed at: Falmouth 8.10.1919. Truro
16.1.1920. Also Helston, Falmouth, St Wenn,
Truro, St Ann's Chapel, St Germans,
Launceston.
12.6.1937 Retired 31.3.1940 Drowned
in Werrington Park, Launceston.

P.C. 67 Albert Hoskin
A 22 year old single fireman from St
Winnow.
Appointed: 12.6.1914.
Stationed at: Liskeard 2.9.1914. Launceston
31.8.1915.
15.3.1917 joined the army for was service.
Reappointed: 1.10.1919
Stationed at: Launceston 2.10.1919. Also
Torpoint, Launceston, Pipers Pool, Sticker,
Charlestown, Boscastle.
11.6.1940 Retired.

P.C. 89 William Roger Tremethick
From Paul, Penzance, aged 20 years, a
labourer. 12.4.1919 Married Ida Morris of
Truro.
Appointed: 1.7.1914.
Stationed at: Truro 19.11.1914.
14.11.1915 joined the army for war service.
Reappointed: 6.2.1919 as P.C. 160.
Stationed at: Bodmin 15.2.1919. Falmouth

11.11.1919. Also Truro, Fowey, Perranwell,
South Downs, St Austell, Sticker.
31.12.1945 Retired.

P.C. 15 Nicholas Mayne
A 21 year old farmer from Illogan.
12.12.1918 Married Miss A.Taylor of
Hertfordshire.
Appointed: 20.8.1914.
Stationed at: Bodmin 19.11.1914. Falmouth
22.12.1914.
22.11.1915 joined the army for war service.
Reappointed: 16.9.1919 as P.C. 119.
20.9.1919 Was on the 22.11.1915 fined 5/-
for being the worse for liquor whilst on duty
at Falmouth on the 20 inst.,
26.1.1920 Fined 50/- for drinking in a
public house whilst on duty and seriously
warned as to his future conduct.
8.3.1921 Fined £1.0.0. For failing to work
his beat in accordance with orders and
leaving same without due permission of suffi-
cient cause.(G.O. No 6 1.4.1921).
Stationed at: Camborne, Bodmin, Falmouth,
St Ives, Chacewater, Grampound, Mawnan,
Sticker, Truro.
13.5.1947 Retired.

P.C. 211 William Henry Mallett
A 19 year old single labourer from Lanivet.
Appointed: 26.8.1914.
Promotion: 1.3.1931 to Sergeant. 1.5.1936
to Inspector. 1.6.1940 to Superintendent.
Stationed at: Camborne 19.11.1914.
31.10.1915 joined the army for war service.
Reappointed: 15.9.1919
Stationed at: Camborne 17.9.1919. Truro
4.3.1921. Also Chyandour, Truro, Delabole,
Hayle, Camborne, Fowey, St Austell,
Launceston.
31.5.1949 Retired.

P.C. 25 Arthur James Bray
A 17 year old single stoker from Crowan.
Appointed: 31.8.1914.
Stationed at: Liskeard 19.11.1914.
31.5.1915 Joined the army for war service.
Reappointed: 11.8.1919
Stationed at: Truro 16.8.1919. Bodmin
4.9.1920. Also Callington, Newquay, Fowey,
Troon, Pool, Camborne, Redruth.
31.12.1935 Resigned.

P.C. 145 William Henry Taylor
A skilled labourer from St Stephens by
Saltash, married aged 23 years.
Appointed: 31.8.1914.
Stationed at: Bodmin 19.11.1914.
11.6.1917 joined the army for war service.
Reappointed: 22.1.1919
Stationed at: Wadebridge, St Mabyn, St
Dennis,
28.2.1946 Retired. 7.1.1949 Died.

P.C. 81 Vincent Arnold Cecil Burrows
A 21 year old gardener from Langport,
Somerset.
Appointed: 1.9.1914.
Stationed at: Liskeard 19.11.1914.
17.1.1916 Joined the army for war service.
Reappointed: 10.3.1919
Stationed at: Truro 20.3.1919. Also

Liskeard, Torpoint, Liskeard, Newquay, Landrake, Liskeard.
31.8.1939 Retired. 7.2.1951 Died.

P.C. 58 Percy Berryman
A farm labourer from Budock, Falmouth, aged 23 years. Married Lezetta J.Drew of Penzance on 2.5.1915.
Appointed: 5.9.1914.
Stationed at: Bodmin 19.11.1914.
Launceston 1.9.1915.
11.6.1917 joined the army for war service.
Reappointed: 10.2.1919 as P.C. 172.
Stationed at: Liskeard 4.3.1921. Also St Austell, Pipers Pool, Liskeard, Landrake and St Mellion.
31.1.1945 Retired.

P.C. 10 William George Mooney
A 20 year old single labourer from Plymouth.
Appointed: 9.9.1914.
Stationed at: Bodmin 19.11.1914.
30.6.1915 joined the army for war service.
Reappointed: 18.11.1918
Stationed at: Launceston 8.2.1919. Also Bodmin, Padstow, St Austell, Launceston.
30.6.1921 Resigned.

P.C. 196 William John Soloman
A labourer from St Stephens-in-Brannel, aged 18 years single.
Appointed: 9.9.1914.
Stationed at: Camborne 19.11.1914.
30.4.1915 joined the army for war service.
Died of wounds received in action in France.

P.C. 65 Reginald Rowland
A 17 year old single plate layer from Tavistock.
Appointed: 14.9.1914.
Promotion: 16.1.1927 to Sergeant.
1.10.1935 to Inspector. 1.5.1940 to Superintendent. 1.11.1948 to Deputy Chief Constable. 1.3.1949 to Assistant Chief Constable.
Stationed at: Liskeard 22.12.1914. Truro 7.1.1915.
30.11.1915 joined the army for war service.
Reappointed: 14.10. 1919
Stationed at: Camborne 20.10.1919. Also Liskeard, Newquay, Camborne, St Ives, Chyandour, Saltash, Truro, Torpoint, Camborne, H.Q.
19.9.1956. Retired.

P.C. 88 Phillip Richard Martin Scantlebury
An 18 year old single waiter from Menheniott.
Appointed: 15.9.1914.
Promotion: 1.4.1939 Sergeant.
Stationed at: Bodmin 22.12.1914.
13.1.1916 Joined the army for war service.
Reappointed: 18.7.1919
Stationed at: Camborne 21.7.1919. Truro 17.2.1921. Also Bodmin, Fowey, St Just, Truro.
30.5.1945 The County emergency Committee placed on record their appreciation of Sergeant Scantelbury's devotion to duty at all times during his secondment to the Civil Defence.
31.4.1946. Retired.

P.C. 207 Thomas Henry Jose
A 20 year old tin smelter from Illogan, Redruth. 7.11.1914 Married Ada Goldsworthy of Treskillard at Illogan Parish Church.
Appointed: 15.9.1914.
Stationed at: Launceston 14.1.1915. Bodmin 24.6.1915.
2.10.1915 P.C. Thomas H.Jose was warned for being absent from his conference point on the night of the 13th/14th ult., and making false entries in his journal.
29.10.1915 The same Constable was again dealt with for similar offences on the nights of the 22/23rd of October. The Constable was deprived of one months seniority for one year, but at his own request was allowed to resign.
31.10.1915 Resigned.

P.C. 18 Alfred Charles Coombe
A labourer from St Austell, aged 22 years.
5.9.1918 Married Emily Roseveor of Bugle.
Appointed: 16.9.1914.
Stationed at: Launceston 14.1.1915.
23.3.1916 joined the army for war service.
Reappointed: 21.8.1919 as P.C. 7.
Stationed at: Launceston 19.9.1919. Liskeard 7.11.1919. Also Launceston, Camelford, Polruan, St Neot, Troon, Camborne.
31.1.1941 Retired.

P.C. 50 Thomas Henry Landrey
A 19 year old single Porter from Camelford.
Appointed: 1.12.1914.
Stationed at: Bodmin, 1.6.1915.
29.2.1916 Resigned through ill-health.

P.C. 4 Francis Henry Miners
A labourer from Ruan Lanihorne, aged 20 years. 28.11.1917 married Kathleen Mutton of Port Isaac.
Appointed: 1.12.1914.
Stationed at: Bodmin 18.3.1915.
12.12.1915. Joined the army for war service. Awarded the Military Medal for Distinguished Service in France.
Reappointed: 20.1.1919
Stationed at: Bodmin, St Austell, Fowey, Padstow, St Austell, Lostwithiel, Fowey, Hessenford.
31.8.1931 Resigned.

P.C. 131 John Henry Thomas
A 24 year old single miner from Crowan.
Public Service: 4th Batt., D.C.L.I. For three years.
Appointed: 1.12.1914.
Stationed at: Liskeard 1.9.1915.
17.2.1917 joined the army for war service.
Reappointed: 1.9.1920 as P.C. 182.
Stationed at: Camborne 4.9.1920. Torpoint, Saltash, Camborne.
29.9.1921 Resigned.

P.C. 134 John Henry Tucker
A miner from Liskeard aged 19 years single.
Appointed: 4.1.1915.
10.12.1915 Joined the army for war service. Awarded the Military Medal for distinguished service in France.
Reappointed: 1.2.1919.

P.C. 207 (Promotion)
Promotion: 1.3.1932 to Sergeant.
1.10.1939 to Inspector.
Stationed at: Liskeard, Bodmin, Saltash, Lanreath, Rilla Mill. St Mellion, Stoke Climsland, Liskeard, Wadebridge.
30.9.1945 Retired

P.C. 190 Stephen Cortis
An 18 year old miner from Gwennap.
25.5.1918 Married Miss M. Crowle of St Breward.
Appointed: 1.3.1915.
29.2.1916 joined the army for war service.
Reappointed: 25.3.1918
6.2.1919 Died from Consumption. Police Pensions Act 1916 It was resolved that a pension of £26.0.0. Per annum be paid to the widow of the late Police Constable Cortis Dated 30.6.1919.

P.C. 195 George Henry Laity
A single miner from Redruth aged 23 years.
Public Service: 10th., Batt., D.C.L.I. For two years and six months.,
Appointed: 1.12.1918.
Stationed at: Launceston 1.12.1918.
Liskeard 7.5.1919. Launceston 3.7.1919.
30.9.1919 Resigned.

P.C. 208 Thomas Morcumb
A married farmer from St Merryn, aged 20 years.
Appointed: 1.12.1918.
Promotion: 1.7.1931 to Sergeant. 1.7.1936 to Detective Inspector. 1.7.1941 to Superintendent.
Stationed at: Bodmin , Blisland, Bodmin, Charlestown, Camborne, Bodmin, Falmouth.
30.9.1947 Retired.

P.C. 198 George Warne
A single stone mason from Tavistock, aged 20 years. **Public Service:** Royal Navy H.M. Troopship Aquitania for two years 8 months.
Appointed: 20.1.1919.
Promotion: 13.4.1931 to Sergeant. 1.7.1939 to Inspector. 1.10.1947 to Superintendent.
Stationed at: Launceston 1.3.1919. Liskeard 3.7.1919. Stratton, Torpoint, Anthony , Callington, Torpoint, Tywardreath, Falmouth, Chyandour, Camborne, Falmouth.
1.4.1958 Retired.

P.C. 201 John Bennett
A 25 year old single printer from St Austell.
Public Service. 7th., Batt., D.C.L.I. For four years and four months.
Appointed: 1.3.1919.
Stationed at: Falmouth 14.4.1919. Also Cury, Breage, Porthleven, Helston, Chyandour, Penryn.
28.2.1949. Retired.

P.C. 26 William Tamblin
A 26 year old single mining fitter from Deal, Kent. **Public Service:** 1st Garrison Batt., Royal Worcester Reg., for nine months.
Appointed: 1.3.1919.
Stationed at: Camborne. 14.4.1919.
Falmouth 1,4,1920. Also St Mabyn, Wadebridge, Torpoint, Polruan, Saltash.
30.6.1944 Retired. 29.9.1957 Died.

P.C. 205 Samuel Pearce
A married engine driver aged 24 years from Gerrans. Public Service: Royal Garrison Artillery for six years and ten months.
Appointed: 1.3.1919.
Stationed at: Falmouth, Penryn, Porkellis, Porthleven, Camborne, Port Isaac.
29.8.1936 Granted a Favourable Record for brave conduct at Trequeens Cliff, Breage, on the 8.7.1936 when he at great personal risk descended the cliff and assisted in the rescue of Thomas Dudley who had been cut off by the tide.
30.9.1945 Retired 25.12.1951 Died.

P.C. 54 Samuel John Penhaligan
A gardener from Perranporth, single aged 21 years.
Public Service: Royal Garrison Artillery for two years and nine months.
Appointed: 1.3.1919.
Promotion: 1.4.1934 to Sergeant.
Stationed at: Bodmin 3.5.1919.
Padstow, Lostwithiel, St Just.
31.1.1947 Retired.   23.3.1957 Died.

P.C. 196 Walter Henry Dymond
From Liskeard a single butcher aged 19 years. Public Service: H.M. Navy in H.M.S. *Cicero* for one year and nine months.
Appointed: 1.3.1919.
Stationed at: Launceston 7.5.1919. Falmouth 8.11.1920. Also Launceston, Bodmin, Falmouth, Porkellis, Helston, Mawnan Smith.
1.2.1931 Retired.

P.C. 168 Albert Carlyon
A 22 year old single gardener from Liskeard. Public Service. 2nd Batt., D.C.L.I. For four years and five months.
Appointed: 1.3.1919.
Stationed at: Liskeard 8.4.1919. Torpoint, Millbrook,
31.1.1924 Resigned.

P.C. 113 John Charles Mallett
A farm labourer from Lanivet, aged 22 years single.
Appointed: 1.4.1919
Stationed at: Falmouth 4.6.1919. Penryn, St Keverne, The Lizard, Constantine.
28.2.1934 Resigned.

P.C. 117 John Henry Menear
A 23 year old single baker from St Just in Roseland. Public Service: 16th Rifle Brigade for four years and five months.
Appointed: 1.4.1919.
Stationed at: Camborne 4.6.1919. Bodmin 4.2.1921. Also Redruth, Bodmin, Helston.
13.11.1922 Resigned.

P.C. 89 Frank Barnes
A 25 year old mason from Paul, Penzance. 28.8.1919. Married Elsie Waters at The Weslyan Chapel, Mousehole. Public Service: Royal Garrison Artillery for seven years and one month.
Appointed: 1.4.1919.
Stationed at: Falmouth 4.6.1919. Launceston 30.12.1920. Also Helston, Cury, Whitstone,

Lezant, St Cleer, Lostwithiel, St Columb.
31.12.1945 Retired.

P.C. 164 Daniel Straughn Miller
A 21 year old single man from St Columb. Public Service: H.M. Navy H.M.S. **Centurion** for two years and six months.
Appointed: 1.4.1919.
Stationed at: Liskeard 4.6.1919. Also Saltash, Hessenford, Falmouth, Helston, Five Lanes and Grampound.
30.4.1936 Retired.

P.C. 92 Frederick Horniman Trerise
A 23 year old married painter from Falmouth. Public Service: H.Q. Corps for six years.
Appointed: 1.4.1919.
Stationed at: Camborne 4.6.1919. Falmouth 9.10.1920. Also Camborne, Flushing, Falmouth, Truro, Falmouth.
31.12.1945 Retired.

P.C. 207 William Dawe
From Lifton a 24 year old married farm Labourer. Public Service: Royal Marine Artillery land battery for 3 years and two days.
Appointed: 1.5.1919.
Stationed at: Bodmin 26.6.1919. Camborne 17.11.1920. Also Bodmin, Goldsithney, Redruth, St Buryan, Whitstone.
28.2.1937 Retired. 26.2.1946 Died.

P.C. 77 William Thomas Carlyon
A 24 year old single postman from Liskeard. Public Service: 2/4th., D.C.L.I. For four years and four months.
Appointed: 1.5.1919.
Promotion: 1.7.1941 to Sergeant.
Stationed at: Camborne 1.7.1919. Hayle, Lanner, Tywardreath,
18.11.1949 Retired.

P.C. 153 Edward Stewart Arnall
A clerk from Bodmin, aged 22 years, single.
Appointed: 1.5.1919.
Stationed at: Falmouth 1.7.1919. Also Helston, Tregoney, Chacewater, Truro, Launceston, Stratton, Helston, Fowey, Camborne, Porkellis, Portscatho.
28.5.1949 Retired.

P.C. 190 Bertie Edward Carhart
A linen machinist from Westminster, aged 21 years married. Public Service: 1st/4th., D.C.L.I. For four years and six months.
Appointed: 1.5.1919.
Stationed at: Camborne 1.7.1919.
30.11.1919 Resigned.

P.C. 203 Frank Pooley
A 22 year old farm labourer from Lifton, single. Public Service; Royal Engineers for four years and six months,
Appointed: 1.5.1919.
Stationed at: Falmouth 1.7.1919.
Truro 3.1.1921. Also Falmouth, Tregoney, St Ives, Camborne, Truro, Bodinnick, St Ives, St Just, St Ives, Penryn, Mawnan Smith, Penryn, Blisland, Bodmin.
31.1.1947 Retired.

P.C. 163 Wilfred Thomas Hoskin
A 20 year old farm labourer from St Germans, single. Public Service; Royal Berkshire Regt., for four years.
Appointed: 1.6.1919.
Stationed at: Truro 2.8.1919. Camborne 16.8.1919. Also Newquay, Redruth, Lerryn, Camborne, St Ives.
31.7.1929 Resigned through ill-health.

P.C. 154 John Harold Pomeroy
A 24 year old married grocers assistant, from Sheerness, Kent. Public Service; D.C.L.I. For six years.
Appointed: 1.6.1919.
Stationed at: Liskeard 14.10.1919. Also Calstock, Copperhouse, Duloe, Halworthy, St Columb Minor, Trispen ,Camborne.
14.3.1939 Retired.

P.C. 24 John William Pratley
A farm labourer from Gloucestershire. Public Service; 3rd., Batt., Royal Worcestershire Regd., four years and six months.
Appointed: 1.6.1919.
Stationed at: Falmouth 2.8.1919.
28.2.1921 Resigned.

P.C. 138 Bertie Hancock
A 21 year old single farm labourer from Liskeard. Public Service; Royal Garrison Artillery for four years.
Appointed: 1.6.1919.
Stationed at: Falmouth 2.8.1919. Also Penryn, Mawnan Smith, Penryn, St Ives, St Just, Golsithney, Connor Downs, Pool, St Breward.
27.7.1952 Retired.

P.C. 127 Charles Avent
A 23 year old single farmer from Anthony. Public Service: 2nd/4th., D.C.L.I. Machine Gun Corps for four years six months.
Appointed: 1.6.1919.
Promotion: 1.8.1933 to Sergeant
Stationed at: Bodmin 30.10.1919. Also St Austell, Mevagissey, Bude, Lewannick, Week St Mary, Stratton.
31.12.1945 Retired.

P.C. 32 Percival James Pearce
A 22 year old single motor engineer from St Columb Minor. Public Service: R.A.S.C. (M.T.) 2 years and 293 days.
Appointed: 1.7.1919.
Stationed at: Chief Constables Chauffeur.
7.6.1952 Retired.

P.C. 72 Harry Hambly
A 20 year old single farm labourer from St Mabyn. Public Service: H.M. Navy on H.M.S. *Royal Sovereign* for two years and nine months.
Appointed: 7.7.1919.
Stationed at: Truro 5.11.1919. Bodmin 30.12.1920. Also Truro, Tregoney, Tywardreath. Camelford, South Petherwin, Sticker, Wadebridge, Portscatho, Menheniott, Pensilva.
8.9.1953 Retired.

P.C. 53 **Richard Woolcock**
A 23 year old mason from Penzance.
Public Service: Royal Garrison Artillery for 5
years and ten months. 15.10.1919 Married
Elizabeth Rowe from St Just in Penwith.
Appointed: 12.7.1919.
Promotion: 1.3.1936 to Sergeant.
Stationed at: Bodmin 5.11.1919. Also
Padstow, Duloe, St Columb Major,
Lostwithiel, Hayle.
11.7.1948 Retired.

P.C. 165 **Stanley Richard Masters**
A labourer from Roche, aged 23 years single.
Public Service: Royal Garrison Artillery for
one year and six months.
Appointed: 1.10.1919.
Stationed at: Bodmin 30.1.1920. Camborne
4.2.1921. Also Bodmin, Redruth,
Camborne, Praze, Rilla Mill, Torpoint,
Pensilva.
1.8.1921 Granted a Favourable Record for
stopping a runaway horse in Fore Street,
Redruth on 21.7.1921 at great personal
risk.
20.12.1942 Died.

P.C. 185 **Sidney Beswetherick**
A 22 year old single labourer from St
Winnow. Public Service: H.M. Navy for five
years.
Appointed: 1.10.1919.
Stationed at: Camborne 10.1.1920. Truro
5.5.1920. Also St Erth, Crowlas.
No further information.

P.C. 41 **Alfred James Tamblyn**
A 21 year old single farmer from Cubert,
Newquay. Public Service: D.C.L.I. Machine
Gun Corps for two years and ten months.
Appointed: 1.11.1919.
Stationed at: Bodmin 1.4.1920. Falmouth
27.4.1920. Also Wadebridge, Falmouth,
Mawnan Smith, Helston, Porkellis,
Charlestown, Bugle.
31.1.1948 Retired.

P.C. 96 **Sidney Leach**
A 20 year old clerk from Honiton, Single.
Public Service: Royal Garrison Artillery for
five years and twenty days.
Appointed: 1.11.1919.
Promotion: 1.12.1934 to Sergeant.
1.10.1939 to Inspector. 1.6.1946 to
Superintendent.
Stationed at: Bodmin 4.2.1920. Also Fowey,
Lostwithiel, Padstow, Camborne, Lerryn,
Gunnislake, West Looe, Saltash, Liskeard,
Callington, Falmouth Truro, Camborne.
27.8.1920 Granted a Favourable Record for
brave conduct at Fowey when he on hearing
cries for help ran to the spot, jumped into
the harbour and swam to the aid of a drowning boy aged 11 years. Just as the Constable
reached the boy a boat arrived and took
both of them out of the water.
8.11.1955 Retired.

P.C. 121 **Joseph Edwin Mitchell**
A 27 year old single shop assistant from St
Austell. Public Service: Royal Garrison
Artillery for eight years and six months.

Appointed: 1.11.1919.
Stationed at: Camborne 30.1.1920.
Also St Just, St Ives, Camborne, Halworthy,
Stratton, Launceston, Halworthy, Tintagel,
Lezant , Week St Mary.
31.3.1946 Retired.

P.C. 142 **Reginald Ivey**
A single motor mechanic from Madron aged
21. Public Service: RAF & R.A.S.C. 28th.,
Wing three years and seven months.
Appointed: 1.11.1919.
Promotion: 1.11.1934 to Sergeant.
1.4.1939 to Inspector. 1.7.1944 to
Superintendent.
Stationed at: Falmouth 30.1.1920. Also
Helston, Falmouth, Liskeard, Polperro, St
Germans, Slades, St Austell, Camborne, St
Austell, H.Q., Truro.
4.1.1944 Awarded the British Empire
Medal for duties with the civil defence in the
New Years Honours 1944.
30.5.1945 County Emergency Committee
placed on record their appreciation of
T/Superintendent R.B.Ivey's devotion to duty
at all times during his work with the Civil
Defence.
31.12.1945 Retired.

P.C. 161 **John Julyan**
A printer from Luxulyan, aged 22 single.
Public Service: Royal Garrison Artillery for
five years and seven months.
Appointed: 1.11.1919.
Stationed at: Camborne 30.1.1920.
St Ives 31.3.1921.
Resigned through ill-health.

P.C. 195 **William John Gaved**
A 23 year old single clay worker from St Ewe.
Public Service: 3rd., Batt., D.C.L.I. For one
year and twenty nine days.
Appointed: 1.11.1919.
Stationed at: Liskeard 30.1.1920.
31.7.1922 Resigned through ill-health.

P.C. 79 **William Herbert Doble**
A 20 year old single motor driver from
Maker, Plymouth. Public Service. Royal
Warwickshire Regt., for two years and six
months
Appointed: 1.11.1919.
Stationed at: Camborne 4.2.1920. Also
Tywardreath, Lezant, Five Lanes, Bude,
Kilkhamton, Egloskerry.
11.2.1950 Retired.

P.C. 190 **Edward Pengelly**
A clay worker from St Martin by Looe, single
aged 23 years. Public Service: 1st/4th., Batt.,
D.C.L.I. For four years and eight months.
Appointed: 1.11.1919.
Stationed at: Bodmin 4.2.1920.
30.4.1920 Resigned.

P.C. 122 **William Francis Bartlett**
A 19 year old single wireless operator from
Whitstone. Public Service: Royal Navy,
H.M.S. *Chester* for two years.
Appointed: 1.12.1919.
15.7.1920 Resigned.

P.C. 139 **Frank Richards**
A 21 year old single carpenter from Paul,
Penzance. Public Service: Royal Field
Artillery for four years and six months.
Appointed: 1.12.1919.
Promotion: 1.1.1934 to Sergeant. 1.5.1940
to Inspector.
Stationed at: Falmouth 15.3.1920. Also St
Minver, Falmouth, Lelant, Pelynt, West Looe,
Callington, Chyandour, Launceston,
Callington.
1.11.1924 Granted a Favourable Record for
conspicuous bravery at Falmouth on the
20.10.1924 when he attempted to stop a
runaway horse attached to a van where by
he was knocked down and received injuries.
31.12.1950 Retired.

P.C. 69 **John Henry Cobbledick**
A 24 year old single labourer from
Whitstone. Public Service: The Devon Regt.,
for three years and six months.
Appointed: 1.1.1920.
Promotion: 1.10.1931 to Sergeant.
1.10.1937 to Inspector. 1.1.1944 to
Superintendent.
Stationed at: Camborne 1.4.1920. Also
Troon, Newlyn, Falmouth, Tregoney,
Launceston, Truro, Stratton, Launceston, St
Austell, Truro.
31.5.1946 Died.

P.C. 50 **William Charles Hill**
A 22 year old single cooper from St Austell
Public Service: Royal Navy H.M.S. Liverpool
for two years.
Appointed: 1.1.1920.
Stationed at: Falmouth 1.4.1920. Also
Helston, St Minver, Mevagissey, Veryan,
Devoran and Perranporth.
31.10.1949. Retired.

P.C. 162 **Leslie Percy Blewett**
A 20 year old single clerk from Newlyn.
Public Service: 1st Artists Rifles, for one year
seven months.
Appointed: 1.6.1920.
Promotion: 1.7.1933 to Sergeant./ Clerk.
1.4.1939 to Inspector /Chief Clerk. 1.1.1944
to Superintendent / Chief Clerk. 1.7.1958 to
Superintendent First Class.
Stationed at: Chief Constables Office, H.Q.
27.6.1957 Awarded the Queens Police
Medal for distinguished service presented at
the Centenary Parade by the Lord
Lieutenant at the D.C.L.I. Barracks, Bodmin,
on 2.7.1957
12.8.1959 Retired.

P.C. 173 **Reginald John Vanstone**
A 25 year old single labourer from Plymouth.
Public Service: 1st., Batt., D.C.L.I. For one
year and six months.
Appointed: 1.2.1920.
Promotion: 1.7.1936 to Sergeant.
Stationed at: Liskeard 5.3.1920.
Also Callington, Bodinnick, Egloskerry,
Stratton, Boscastle, Chacewater.
28.2.1947 Retired.

P.C. 40 **Horace John Trewella**
A 25 year old married shaft timber man

(South Crofty) from Redruth.
Appointed: 4.2.1920.
Promotion: 1.10.1936 to Sergeant.
1.3.1940 to Inspector.
Stationed at: Truro 5.5.1920. Also St Wenn, Perranporth, Saltash, Camelford. H.Q. CID, Newquay, Truro.
2.7.1931. Granted a Favourable Record for descending a very dangerous mine shaft at Bissoe Pool, Kenwyn, on the 23.6.1931 and rescuing a dog which had fallen in.
1.1.1936 At Tavistock Police Court on the 23.12.1935 complimented by the Justices for good Police work in connection with a case of larceny of fowls at Bere Alston as the result of which four men were detected and convicted.
29.2.1948 Retired.

P.C. 176 George Mallett
A single farm labourer from Lanivet, Bodmin aged 21 years. **Public Service:** 2nd/5th., Batt., Gloucestershire Regt., for 20 months.
Appointed: 5.2.1920.
Stationed at: Launceston 6.5.1920. Also Bude, Launceston, St Mellion, Rilla Mill, 19.8.1932 Resigned.

P.C. 180 William Hugh Garnet Basset
A 24 year old single mechanic from Stratton. Public Service: Royal Garrison Artillery for one year and nine months.
Appointed: 1.3.1920.
Stationed at: Truro 1.7.1920. Camborne 14.10.1920. Also Newquay, Camborne, Truro, Duloe, Camborne.
12.2.1949 Retired.

P.C. 115 Richard Osborne
A 21 year old single draper from Lanivet. Public Service: RAF For two years and four months.
Appointed: 1.3.1920.
Stationed at: Falmouth 14.10.1920. Also Penryn, Truro, Mawgan-in-Pydar, Padstow, Falmouth, East Looe, Torpoint, Liskeard, Polperro , Penzance.
1.11.1953 Retired.

P.C. 48 William Dyer
A clay labourer from Mevagissey aged 26 years, single. Public Service: 2nd/4th., D.C.L.I. For five years and three months.
Appointed: 1.4.1920.
Stationed at: Camborne 1.10.1920. Also Millbrook, Bodinnick, St Wenn, St Columb, St Mellion and Landrake.
2.9.1936 Resigned.

P.C. 131 John Weekley Mutton
A 23 year old single mason from St Stephens by Saltash. Public Service: 100th., Field Comp., Royal Engineers for three years and five months.
Appointed: 19.4.1920.
Stationed at: Bodmin 2.10.1920. Also St Austell, Mevagissey, Probus, St Agnes and Praze.
29.11.1932 Favourable Record at Gullen Cove Portreath on the 30.10.1932. When he at great personal risk descended the cliff and assisted in the rescue of the crew of the

schooner Sarah Evans which had been driven ashore.
3.3.1933 Awarded the Royal Humane Societies Testimonial on Vellum for courage and humanity and having assisted to save life on 30.10.1932 in the rescue of the crew of the Sarah Evans at Gullen Cove Portreath.
30.6.1947 Retired.

P.C. 190 Arthur Fenwick Richards
A warehouse man from Paul, Penzance, aged 24 years and single. Public Service: Royal Garrison Artillery for three years and seven months.
Appointed: 1.5.1920.
Promotion: 1.4.1939 to Sergeant.
Stationed at: Truro 4.9.1920. Also Newquay, Truro, Portscatho, Truro, Lezant, Launceston, Newquay.
20.1.1951 Retired.

P.C. 42 Arthur George Ellicot
A 34 year old married Police Constable from Plumstead, London. Public Service: Royal Navy for seven years and ten months. Metropolitan Police from 13.5.1912. To 31 5. 1920.
Appointed: 1.6.1920.
Stationed at: Liskeard 28.6.1920. Also Bude, Mevagissey, Foxhole,
31.1.1936 Resigned due to ill-health.

P.C. 99 Albert Victor Clark
A 22 year old single motor mechanic from Devonport. Public Service: Royal Garrison Artillery for four years and two months.
Appointed: 1.9.1920.
Promotion: 1.7.1941 to Sergeant.
Stationed at: Camborne 3.1.1921. Also St Kew Highway, Bodmin Road, Bodmin, Falmouth, Redruth, Looe.
No further record.

P.C. 122 Horace Osborne
An iron mongers assistant, single, aged 21 years from Bodmin. Public Service: Norfolk Reg., of Army Ordinance Corps., for three years.
Appointed: 1.9.1920.
Promotion: 1.12.1931 to Sergeant. 1.7.1939 to Inspector. 1.11.1948 to Superintendent.
Stationed at: Falmouth 3.1.1921 Also Comford, Lewannick, St Agnes, Chacewater, St Ives, Redruth, St Austell, Liskeard.
1.8.1929 Favourable Record for brave conduct at Pole Hill Quay, St Agnes, on 21 6.1929 when he at great personal risk descended a disused mine shaft and rescued a dog which had fallen in.
1.10.1929 A favourable Record for descending a very dangerous mine shaft on the 8.8.1929 at Blue Hills, St Agnes and rescuing an Alsatian dog which had been there for several days but which was still alive.
14.2.1929 Awarded the King's Police Medal for conspicuous Gallantry when the S.S. *Alba* was wrecked off the Island, St Ives, on the night of the 31.1.1938. Awarded the Gold Cross of Merit by his Serene Highness the Prince Regent of Hungary and the silver medal and bar by the R.S.P.C.A.
2.11.1952 Died.

P.C. 99 Albert Victor Clark
Born 16.1.1898.
Appointed: 1.9.1920.
Promotion: 1.7.1941 to Sergeant.
Stationed at: Camborne, St Kew Highway, Bodmin Road, Bodmin, HQ., Falmouth, HQ., Redruth, Looe.
15.1.1953 Retired.

P.C. 152 Elford Neil Hoskin
Born 12.4.1901.
Appointed: 1.10.1920.
Promotion: 1.4.1939 to Sergeant.
Stationed at: Truro, Tregoney, St Columb Minor, St Blazey, Redruth Highway, Redruth, Camborne.
28.5.1949 Retired.

P.C. 76 George Alby Stone
Born 1.4.1899.
Appointed: 1.10.1920.
Transferred from the City of London Police.
Promotion: 1.1.1935 to Sergeant.
Stationed at: Saltash, Camborne, Newlyn West, Lostwithiel, Hayle, Camborne, Mawnan in Meneage, Helston, Looe.
31.3.1954 Retired.

P.C. 178 Charles Horace Llewelyn Magor
Born 12.12.1898.
Appointed: 1.11.1920.
Stationed at: Camborne, Veryan, Newlyn East, Kingsand, St Germans.
18.1.1934 At Newquay Police Court on this date was complimented by the Chairman of the Bench for the satisfactory and quick following of clues which resulted in John Henry Summers, aged 25 years, being committed for trial at the Assize, on three charges of burglary and one charge of having in his possession a certain firearm other than for a lawful object.
11.12.1953 Retired.

P.C. 215 Albert Harvey Langdon
Born 5.5.1899.
Appointed: 1.11.1920.
Stationed at: St Ives, Torpoint, Whitstone.
20.5.1929 Resigned.

P.C. 149 William Charles Ryder
Born 5.11.1899.
Appointed: 1.11.1920.
Stationed at: Fowey, Mevagissey, Foxhole, Bugle.
26.7.1935 Resigned.

P.C. 140 Albert Weary
Born 10.3.1895.
Appointed: 1.11.1920.
Stationed at: St Austell, Blisland, Bude, Canworthy Water, Boscastle, Pool, Connor Downs, Goldsithney, Nancledra.
1.4.1929 Granted a Favourable Record for brave conduct at Rose-Mergay, Morvah, on 7.12.1928 when he at great personal risk descended a disused mine shaft and rescued a dog which had fallen in.
31.10.1946 Retired.

P.C. 217 William Stanley Currow
Born 6.12.1898

Appointed: 10.11.1920.
23.12.1920 Resigned.

P.C. 216 David William Grubb
Born 11.6.1900.
Appointed: 15.11.1920.
Promotion: 1.2.1937 to Sergeant.
Stationed at: Launceston, Bude, Halworthy, Lanivet, Cargreen, Egloshayle, Truro.
14.11.1946 Retired.

P.C. 29 Robert Joshua Snell
Born 17.11.1896.
Appointed: 1.12.1920.
Promotion: 1.10.1935 to Sergeant.
1.9.1950 to Inspector.
Stationed at: Truro, Blisland, Bodmin, Newquay., St Germans, Saltash, Callington , Bodmin.
18.1.1934 At Newquay Police Court was complimented by the Chairman of the Bench for the satisfactory and quick following of clues which resulted in John Henry Summers, aged 25 years, being committed for trial at the Assize on three charges of burglary and one charge of having in his possession a certain firearm other than for a lawful object.
14.8.1954 Retired. 4.6.1969 Died.

P.C. 218 Wilfred John Hill
Born 21.4.1898.
Appointed: 1.12.1920.
Stationed at: Helston, Lanreath, Bodinnick, Callington.
31.3.1925 Resigned through ill-health.

P.C. 217 Reginald Richard Tabb
Born 18.2.1897.
Appointed: 1.1.1921.
Promotion: 1.2.1933 to Sergeant. 1.8.1940 to Inspector. 1.9.1950 to Chief Inspector.
Stationed at: Newquay, Saltash, Troon, Heamoor, Egloshayle, Fowey, Callington, Truro.
29.2.1952 Retired.

P.C. 44 George Penwarden Boundy
Born 18.6.1897.
Appointed: 1.1.1921.
Stationed at: Liskeard, Gunnislake, Pelynt, Polruan, Torpoint, St Agnes.
31.5.1951 Retired.

P.C. 19 John Coppin Wherry
Born 7.3.1901.
Appointed: 1.2.1921.
Stationed at: Bodmin, St Ives, Nancledra, Crowlas, Copperhouse.
6.3.1956 Retired.

P.C. 95 Cecil Stanley Rowling
Born 25.5.1894.
Appointed: 1.2.1921.
Stationed at: Redruth, Padstow, St Minver, Bugle, Lezant, Launceston, Lezant , Launceston.
29.2.1948 Retired 9.11.1951 Died.

P.C. 24 Wilfred Bullock
Born 15.12.1895.
Appointed: 1.3.1921.
Promotion: 1.4.1939 to Sergeant

Stationed at: Launceston, Egolskerry, Stratton, Kingsand, Newquay, Falmouth, St Columb.
30.5.1945 The County Emergency Committee placed on record their appreciation of Sergeant W.Bullock's devotion to duty at all times during his secondment with the Civil Defence.
28.2.1951 Retired.

Sergeant Eddy Capell
Born 26.12.1877.
Appointed: to Truro City Police on 2.5.1900 and transferred to the Cornwall Constabulary upon amalgamation on 1.3.1921.
Stationed at: Truro.
28.12.1903. Commended by the Watch Committee of Truro City Police for efficiency in arresting thieves.
28.6.1911 Commended by the Watch Committee of Truro City Police for stopping runaway horses in Truro.
31.5.1926. Retired.

P.C. 143 William John Coad
Born 19.9.1896.
Appointed: 1.3.1921.
Stationed at: Camborne, St Austell, Menheniot,
31.1.1932 Resigned through ill-health.

P.C. 219 Tom Julyan
Born 21.8.1872.
Appointed: to Truro City Police on 10.11.1900 and transferred to the Cornwall Constabulary upon amalgamation on 1.3.1921.
Stationed at: Truro.
24.4.1907 Commended by the Watch Committee of Truro City for stopping a runaway horse.
30.11.1926 Retired.

P.C. 224 Walter Moon
Born 14.12.1893.
Appointed: to Truro City Police on 26.6.1914 and transferred to the Cornwall Constabulary upon amalgamation on 1.3.1921.
Stationed at: Truro.
30.11.1944 Retired.

P.C. 222 William John Sercombe
Born 8.11.1886.
Appointed: to Truro City Police on 17.5.1913 and transferred to the Cornwall Constabulary upon amalgamation on 1.3.1921.
Stationed at: Truro, St Columb Major, North Hill, St Neot.
13.3.1937 Retired.

P.C. 75 Samuel Humphrey Westlake
Born 21.4.1897.
Appointed: 1.3.1921.
Stationed at: Liskeard, Falmouth, Newtown, Falmouth, Helston, Penryn, Trispen, Newquay, St Kew Highway, Redruth, Saltash.
26.10.1946 Retired.

Sergeant Ernest Warne
Born 17.9.1879.

Appointed: to Truro City Police on 28.10.1901 and transferred to the Cornwall Constabulary upon amalgamation on 1.3.1921.
Promotion: 16.1.1927 to Inspector.
Stationed at: Truro, Penryn, Redruth.
29.3.1903 Commended for stopping a runaway horse.
13.1.1909. Commended by the Watch Committee for Truro City Police for detection of crimes.
13.10.1913 Complimented by the Magistrates for obtaining evidence.
8.2.1936 Retired.

P.C. 221 Frank Sloman
Born 16.4.1891.
Appointed: to Truro City Police on 23.8.1911 and transferred to the Cornwall Constabulary upon amalgamation on 1.3.1921.
Promotion: 1.3.1925 to Sergeant.
1.12.1930 to Inspector.
1.10.1937 to Superintendent.
Stationed at: Truro, Camborne, Helston, Launceston, Liskeard.
Commended by the Watch Committee of the Truro City Police in dealing with an outbreak of fire.
15.4.1951 Retired.

P.C. 161 Frank Redvers Ebbett
Born 27.5.1900.
Appointed: 1.4.1921
Promotion: 1.8.1937 to Sergeant.
1.1.1944 to Inspector.
Stationed at: Truro, Tregoney, Newquay, Falmouth, Newtown, Helston, Boscastle, Delabole, St Austell, Redruth, Callington.
30.1.1936 Granted a Favourable Record for promptness and tact shown by him at a fire at the Co-operative Stores Camelford on the night of the 5.1.1936 when at considerable risk he entered the building and assisted in the recovery of business books which would have otherwise been destroyed.
29.6.1937 Granted a favourable record for brave conduct at Tregardock, St Teath, when on the 9.6.1937 when he at great personal risk descended the cliff and entered the sea and assisted in the recovery of the body of Mrs Lillie A. Woollett.
23.4.1940 Presented with a medal and bar of the R.S.P.C.A. As the result of his action in recovering two dogs, one a sheep dog, which had fallen down a disused shaft at Trenance Downs on the 2.7.1939 and secondly the rescue of a dog from Buckey Pit Reservoir on the 21.8.1939.
30.10.1943 With acting.D.C. 150 G.T.G. Harry, a Favourable Record for zeal and efficiency displayed in connection with a series of crimes committed in the Bodmin Police Division, which resulted in the final clearing up of thirteen serious cases, a number of which had been outstanding since the latter part of 1942.
3.6.1948 Retired.

P.C. 10 Alfred James
Born 20.3.1895.
Appointed: 1.7.1921.

Stationed at: Bodmin
30.4.1922 Resigned.
P.C. 3 George Thorn Robins
Born 9.8.1895.
Appointed: 1.8.1921.
Promotion: 1.10.1937 to Sergeant. 1.7.1941 to Inspector. 1.9.1950 to Chief Inspector.
Stationed at: St Austell, Lostwithiel, Mawgan, Devoran, Heamoor, Tywardreath, Bodmin, Wadebridge, Camborne.
8.8.1955 Retired.

P.C. 104 Charles Harris Truscott
Born 1.5.1896
Appointed: 1.10.1921.
Promotion: 1.6.1941 to Sergeant.
Stationed at: Newquay, Falmouth, St Germans, Polperro, Callington, Roche, Egloshayle, St Austell.
1.12.1933 Granted a Favourable Record for courage , energy and initiative, shown at Polperro in the case of an attempted murder of Mr. Greves and the suicide of a Mr.Scott.
30.9.1946 Retired. 28.2.1963 Died.

P.C. 182 Richard James Drew
Born 16.7.1897.
Appointed: 1.10.1921
Stationed at: Falmouth, Newquay, Falmouth, Newtown.
30/6/1943 Resigned.

P.C. 98 Ernest Charles Menear
Born 13.1.1898.
Appointed: 1.11.1921.
Promotion: 1.5.1940 to Sergeant.
Stationed at: Bodmin, Padstow, Blisland, Camborne, Gargreen, Lanivet, Padstow, Callington, Camborne, Saltash.
31.10.1946. Retired.

P.C. 177 Arthur Howard Stephens
Born 17.12.1900.
Appointed: 1.12.1921.
Stationed at: St Austell, Mevagissey, St Austell, St Buryan.
4.2.1931 Resigned.

P.C. 141 William Edward Sambells
Born 30.6.1900
Appointed: 1.12.1921.
Promotion: 1.4.1938 to Sergeant.
Stationed at:, Camborne, St Ives, Sennen, Newlyn West, Constantine, Tregoney, Truro.
31.3.1953 Retired.

P.C. 82 Erwin French
Born 8.6.1901.
Appointed: 1.1.1922.
Stationed at: Redruth, Blisland, Bodmin, Anthony, Lerryn, St Stephens.
31.7.1952 Retired.

P.C. 169 Henry Edward Brooks
Born 26.1.1901.
Appointed: 1.1.1922.
Stationed at: St Austell, Mevagissey, Bude, Launceston, St Austell, Newlyn, Sennen, Redruth, Pool, Mawgan-in-Pydar, Blue Anchor.
31.12.1950 Retired.

P.C. 155 William Wreford Thomas
Born 25.5.1899.
Appointed: 1.1.1922.
Stationed at: Fowey, Launceston
31.1.1924 Resigned.

P.C. 56 Henry Reginald James Bennetts
Born 1.11.1903.
Appointed: 1.1.1922.
Promotion: 1.7.1038 to Sergeant. 1.11.1944 to Inspector. 1.11.1948 to Superintendent. 2.2.1955 to Superintendent Grade 1,
Stationed at: Bodmin, Fowey, Newquay, Truro, Heamoor, Looe.
31.8.1961 Retired.

P.C. 30 Ronald Edwin Pearce
Born 21.11.1901.
Appointed: 1.10.1922.
Stationed at: Torpoint, Newquay, Fowey, Bodmin, The Lizard, St Keverne, Troon.
4.5.1946. Awarded the R.S.P.C.A. Certificate of Merit for the rescue of a dog from a mine shaft at Troon on 10.1.1946.
29.2.1954 Retired.

P.C. 10 Alfred George Botterall
Bude 21.9.1899.
Appointed: 1.10.1922.
Stationed at: Redruth, Camborne,
28.2.1930 Resigned.

P.C. 36 Cedric Tippett
Born 3.8.1904.
Appointed: 1.11.1922.
Promotion: 1.10.1950 to Sergeant.
Stationed at: Fowey, Newquay, Torpoint, Saltash, Torpoint, Millbrook, East Looe, Wadebridge, St Blazey, Roche.
Retired.

P.C. 43 John Miller
Born 23.2.1900.
Appointed: 1.11.1922.
Promotion: 1.7.1939 to Sergeant.
Stationed at: Chyandour, St Just, Breage, St Day, Pool, St Austell, Liskeard, Callington.
13.1.1951 Retired.

P.C. 12 Charles Leslie Teague
Born 30.4.1900.
Appointed: 1.12.1922.
Stationed at: Falmouth , Gwennap, Helston, Penryn, Boscaswell, Goldsithney, Redruth Highway, Redruth.
Retired.

P.C. 93 Ernest Arthur Allen
Born 25.12.1903.
Appointed: 1.12.1922.
Stationed at: Falmouth, Newquay, Duloe, Saltash, Perranporth, Sennen, Marazion.
31.1.1953 Retired.

P.C. 125 Arthur Dines
Born 14.12.1903.
Appointed: 1.1.1923.
Promotion: 1.10.1939 to Sergeant.
Stationed at: Redruth, Newquay, Chyandour, Newquay, Falmouth, Bodmin Road, St Kew Highway, Roche, Marazion, Liskeard, St Austell.
31.12.1948 Retired through ill-health.

P.C. 137 Albert Stanley Dyer
Born 22.10.1898,
Appointed: 1.1.1923.
Promotion: 1.8.1938 to Sergeant.
Stationed at: Bodmin, Lanivet, Bugle, Falmouth, Camborne, St Ives.
1.12.1923 Granted a Favourable Record for brave conduct at Bodmin on 12.10.1923 when he at great personal risk stopped a runaway horse attached to a trap thereby preventing what might have been a serious accident.
31.5.1924 Granted a Favourable Record for brave conduct at Bodmin on the 14.4.1924 when he at great personal risk stopped two runaway horses attached to a wagon thereby preventing what might have been a serious accident.
31.1.1948 Retired through ill-health.

P.C. 117 Donald Endean
Born 4.8.1904.
Appointed: 1.1.1923.
Promotion: 1.4.1939 to Sergeant.
Stationed at: St Ives, Sennen, St Ives, Camborne, Port Isaac, Bodmin, St Austell, Falmouth, St Ives.
6/8/1949 Retired.

P.C. 80 William Roy Hawken
Born 10.5.1901.
Appointed: 1.2.1923.
Promotion: 1.7.1939 to Sergeant.
Stationed at: Torpoint, Anthony, Menheniot, Bodmin, Lostwithiel. Meneage, Fowey, Mawgan-in-Meneage.
31.10.1953 Retired.

P.C. 52 Harold Clemens Jenkin
Born 10.7.1903.
Appointed: 1.4.1923.
Promotion: 1.8.1943 to Sergeant/.
Stationed at: Falmouth, Perranwell, Falmouth., Callington, Launceston.
30.4.1955 Retired.

P.C. 114 Douglas Ivanhoe Keast
Born 9.5.1903.
Appointed: 1.4.1923.
Stationed at: Redruth , St Ives, Truro, Anthony, St Germans.
25.9.1948 Retired.

P.C. 14 William Lewis Vanson
Born 7.9.1901.
Appointed: 1.4.1923.
Stationed at: H.Q.
30.6.1923 Resigned.

P.C. 6 William James Whitford
Born 10.7.1900.
Appointed: 1.4.1923.
Stationed at: Truro
31.5.1924 Resigned through ill-health.

P.C. 78 Alfred William Wherry
Born 24.9.1903.
Appointed: 7.5.1923.
Stationed at: Bodmin, Truro, Newquay, Truro.
10.7.1929 Killed in a motor cycle accident.

P.C. 220 Herbert Percival Hambly
Born 25.12.1901.
Appointed: 7.5.1923.

Stationed at: Bodmin, Torpoint, Liskeard.
30.4.1925 Resigned.

P.C. 16 Edward Bowden Squance
Born 21.7.1903.
Appointed: 1.7.1923.
Stationed at: Bodmin, Millbrook, Calstock, Stoke Climsland.
30.6.1952 Retired.

P.C. 14 Albert Edwards William Lloyd Annis
Born 17.7.1904.
Appointed: 1.7.1923.
Stationed at: Newquay, Falmouth, Newtown, Falmouth, Veryan, Probus, Trispen, Newquay, Camborne.
31.12.1949 Retired.
P.C. 101 George William Harris
Born 7.7.1901.
Appointed: 1.7.1923.
Promotion: 1.11.1938 to Sergeant.
Stationed at: Padstow, Lostwithiel, St Breward, Kilkhamton, Bude, St Columb, Fowey, Redruth, St Just.
7/12/1953 Retired through ill-health.

P.C. 1 William James Martin Lamerton
Born 10.10.1902.
Appointed: 1.10.1923.
Promotion: 1.4.1939 to Sergeant. 1.1.1946 to Inspector.
Stationed at: Falmouth, Nancledra, Heamoor, Chyandour, Helston, Tywardreath, St Columb, Chyandour, St Ives.
30.6.1952 Retired. 27.5.1970 Died.

P.C. 34 Cecil Fred Menear
Born 23.12.1902.
Appointed: 1.11.1923.
Stationed at: Launceston, Truro, Nancledra, Lelant.
28.2.1940 Presented with an illuminated Certificate by the R.S.P.C.A. In recognition of his rescue of a dog from a disused mine shaft at Carbis Bay on 31.10.1939.
30.3.1942 Died. Involved in an accident on duty.

P.C. 70 Thomas Henry Wiley
Born 15.3.1905.
Appointed: 1.1.1924.
Stationed at: Truro, Camborne, St Ives, Bodinnick, Lanreath, Padstow, St Minver, Luxulyan, St Austell, St Dennis.
29.3.1952 Retired.

P.C. 91 Victor Scantlebury
Born 12.3.1902.
Appointed: 1.1.1924.
Stationed at: Launceston, Halworthy, Camborne, Porthleven, Hessenford, Duloe.
30.9.1950 Retired.

P.C. 100 Herbert Edgar Jones
Born 16.10,1905.
Appointed: 1.2.1924.
Promotion: 1.8.1940 to Sergeant.
Stationed at: Truro, Newquay, Truro, St Columb, Calstock, Falmouth.
2.12.1946
Appointed: P.S.O. 3 in the Special Police

Corps., of the Control Commission for Germany and Austria under the Police (Overseas) Service in 1945 and Regulations made there under.
31.10.1950 Retired.

P.C. 103 Bertie Johns
Born 21.6.1902.
Appointed: 1.2.1924.
Promotion: 1.4.1939 to Sergeant. 1.6.1946 to Inspector. 1.6.1949 to Superintendent. 1.3.1953 to Superintendent Grade 1.
Stationed at: Bodmin, St Breward, Port Isaac, Padstow, St Germans, Newquay, Falmouth, Newquay, Launceston, St Austell, Liskeard.
31.3.1957 Retired.

P.C. 86 Joseph Havelock Green
Born 8.8.1899.
Appointed: 1.2.1924
Stationed at: Falmouth, Pipers Pool, Sithians, Saltash, St Cleer.
30.10.1931. Granted a Favourable Record for efficiency and promptness and skill displayed in dealing with two persons seriously injured in a Road Traffic Accident on the 13.10.1931 which in the Medical Officers opinion materially assisted in both these lives being saved.
9.1.1941 Resigned.

P.C. 84 William Henry Juliff
Born 14.12.1900.
Appointed: 1.2.1924.
Promotion: 1.7.1939 to Sergeant. 4.6.1948 to Inspector.
Stationed at: Falmouth, Helston, Saltash, Jacobstow, Lewannick, Tintagel, Looe , Callington, Launceston.
31.10.1952 Retired.

P.C. 108 William James Scantlebury
Born 29.1.1905.
Appointed: 1.4.1924.
Promotion: 1.9.1950 to Sergeant.
Stationed at: St Austell, Newquay, St Austell, Blisland, Foxhole, Mevagissey, Padstow.
30.9.1954 Retired.

P.C. 110 Ernest Leonard Jewells
Born 11.8.1903.
Appointed: 1.5.1924.
Promotion: 1.10.1950 to Sergeant.
Stationed at: St Austell, Bodmin, Redruth, Newquay, Bodmin, Falmouth, St Austell, Hessenford, Lostwithiel, Mawnan Smith, Mullion, Helston.
10.8.1958 Retired.

P.C. 6 William Giles Matthews
Born 12.4.1903.
Appointed: 1.6.1924.
Stationed at: Camborne, Bodmin, Luxulyan, Anthony, Truro, Veryan.
2.12.1950 Retired. 21.2.1957 Died.

P.C. 136 Stanley John Wherry
Born 16.11.1905.
Appointed: 1.6.1924.
Promotion: 1.7.1939 to Sergeant 1.6.1946 to Inspector.

1.3.1953 to Superintendent.
Stationed at: Bodmin, Falmouth, Penryn, Helston, Falmouth, Bude, St Issey, St Stephens, Falmouth, Isles of Scilly, H.Q. Traffic., St Austell, Liskeard.
31.5.1959 Retired. 11.1.1960 Died.

P.C. 90 Kenneth James Dunstan
Born 8.2.1902
Appointed: 1.7.1924
Stationed at: Camborne, St Just, St Ives, Redruth, St Just, Camelford, Luxulyan, St Minver, Falmouth.
30.1.1936 Granted a Favourable Record for promptness and tact shown by him at a fire at the Co-operative Stores, Camelford, on the night of 5.1.1936 when at great personal risk he entered the building and assisted in the rescue of a dog which would have otherwise been burned to death.
7.2.1957 Retired.

P.C. 251 Leslie Thomas Davis
Born 6.4.1901.
Appointed: 12.7.1924
Retired 15.11.1952.

P.C. 109 John Charles Deacon
Born 5.4.1904.
Appointed: 15.8.1924.
Promotion: 1.4.1939 to Sergeant. 1.10.1947 to Inspector. 1.3.1952 to Chief Inspector.
Stationed at: Callington, Saltash, East Looe, Liskeard, Pelynt, Gunnislake, Truro, Wadebridge, St Austell, Truro.
29.11.1938 Granted a Favourable Record for his prompt and efficient action at Gunnislake on the 30.10.1938 in effecting the early apprehension of Norman Frederick Jury who at the Devon Assize on the 7.11.1938 was convicted and sentenced for the following offences
Demanding money with menaces and being in possession of an imitation firearm, at the time of committing the first offence.
27.2.1939 Granted a Favourable Record for vigilance displayed by him and attention to duty in detecting a case of larceny of a motor car at 3.am on the 15.2.1939.
29.7.1944 Granted a Favourable Record for keenness persistence and ability displayed in the detection of cases of larceny of coal and embezzlement resulting in the conviction of seven offenders in Truro City Police Court. on the 29.6.1944. The enquiry being a difficult one with the methods employed and the deeply involved nature of the transactions.
31.8.1963 Retired.

P.C. 144 Samuel Lobb Kent
Born 4.7.1903.
Appointed: 1.10.1924.
Stationed at: Falmouth, Liskeard, Miilbrook, Lanreath
Resigned 31.7.1933.
Died 4.12.1952.

P.C. 116 Ewart Claud Pearce
Born 9.4.1898.
Appointed: 1.11.1924.
Stationed at: Falmouth, Newtown, Helston,

Newtown, St Just, Chyandour, St Ives, Camborne, Rilla Mill,
Hessenford, Constantine, St Austell, Sticker.
Awarded the Military Medal for Devotion to duty on 21, 22, & 23rd., of July 1918 in Russia when he continually drove his military vehicle picking up working parties and tools for sixty hours as well as assisting in the fighting.
18.4.1953 Retired.

P.C. 57 Samuel John Oatey
Born 31.8.1903.
Appointed: 1.2.1925.
Stationed at: Bodmin, Camborne, Bodmin, Truro, St Columb Major,
31.1.1955 Retired.

P.C. 148 Evan Barrett
Born 25.1.1905.
Appointed: 1.4.1925.
Stationed at: Truro, Penryn, The Lizard, Goldsithney, Connor Downs, Hayle, Truro.
31.3.1955 Retired.

P.C. 129 Ernest Carlyon
Born 13.11.1905.
Appointed: 1.4.1925.
Promotion: 1.9.1950 to Sergeant/Clerk.
Stationed at: Truro, Chyandour, Goldsithney, Camborne, Falmouth.
29.5.1954 Retired.

P.C. 146 John Ernest Portsmouth
Born 11.8.1903.
Appointed: 1.4.1925.
Promotion: 1.7.1939 to Sergeant.
1.10.1950 to Inspector.
Stationed at: St Austell, Mevagissey, Jacobstow. Camelford, Stratton, Polperro, St Ives. Camborne, Truro, Stratton.
31.3.1955 Retired.

P.C. 155 Peter Oatey
Born 30.7.1905
Appointed: 1.4.1925.
Promotion: 1.11.1948 to Sergeant.
Stationed at: Bodmin, Truro, South Petherwin, Launceston, Jacobstow, Stratton, Camelford, Bodmin, Camborne, Foxhole, St Austell.
31.5.1955 Retired.

P.C. 6 Walter William Hancock
Born 18.1.1901.
Appointed: 13.4.1925.
From Penzance Borough Police.
Promotion: 28.8.1939 to Sergeant.
Stationed at: Penzance.
28.5.1955 Retired.

P.C. 151 Francis Henry Irish
Born 5.4.1905.
Appointed: 20.4.1925.
Promotion: 1.9.1950 to Sergeant/Clerk.
Stationed at: Launceston, South Petherwin, Pipers Pool, Launceston, Bodmin, A.R.P. Centre, Truro.
30.6.1958 Retired.

P.C. 124 Arthur Charles James
Born 27.9.1903.
Appointed: 17.8.1925.
Promotion: 1.9.1941 to Sergeant.

Stationed at: Torpoint, Portscatho, St Agnes, St Germans, Saltash.
15.3.1952 Retired.

P.C. 181 Richard Anthony Soloman
Born 23.5.1906.
Appointed: 17.8.1925.
Stationed at: St Ives, Redruth, Calstock, Landrake, St Germans, St Cleer, St Ives,
16.8.1952 Retired.

P.C. 168 John Henry Smith Thomas
Born 14.2.1905.
Appointed: 17.8.1925.
Stationed at: St Austell, Truro, Veryan, Probus, Truro, Bodmin, Charlestown.
16.8.1950. Retired.

P.C. 73 Charles Donald Dunstan
Born 23.10.1905.
Appointed: 17.8.1925.
31.8.1925 Resigned.

P.C. 182 Reginald Terrill Darlington
Born 27.6.1905.
Appointed: 24.8.1925.
Stationed at: Bodmin, Falmouth, Bude, Lostwithiel, St Mawes, Mawgan-in-Pydar, Pool.
2.10.1954 Retired.

P.C. 73 John Norman Harvey
Born 2.1.1906.
Appointed: 1.9.1925.
Stationed at: Falmouth,
30.11.1927 Resigned through ill-health.

P.C. 194 Andrew Angwin French
Born 30,8.1905.
Appointed: 1.10.1925.
Promotion: 1.7.1939 to Sergeant.
Stationed at: Camborne, St Ives, Camborne, Redruth, Bude, Camelford. St Austell, Wadebridge, Redruth, Mawgan-in-Meneage, Mullion,
30.9.1950 Retired.

P.C. 195 Clifton Theodore Wills
Born 2.4.1903.
Appointed: 1.11.1925.
Promotion: 1.7.1939 to Sergeant.
Stationed at: St Austell, Newquay, St Austell, Falmouth, St Neot, West Looe. Camelford, Liskeard.
13.5.1954 Retired.

P.C. 218 Frederick John Harding
Born 2.3.1907.
Appointed: 1.12.1925.
Stationed at: Falmouth, Padstow, Bude, Lostwithiel, St Cleer, Gunnislake, Dobwalls.
31.11.1939 Awarded a Silver Medal by the R.S.P.C.A. In recognition of his gallant conduct in rescuing a dog from a disused mine shaft at Greenhill, Gunnislake, on 24.8.1939.
21.12.1942 Resigned.

P.C. 220 Frederick Henry Williams
Born 22.9.1906.
Appointed: 1.12.1925
Stationed at: Camborne, Bude, Falmouth,
28.2.1931 Resigned.

P.C. 107 Frank Martyn Dyer
Born 1.7.1903.
Appointed: 1.2.1926.
Stationed at: Truro, St Columb, St Kew Highway, Newlyn East, St Mawes.
7.11.1954 Died.

P.C. 94 Arthur George Passmore
Born 23.5.1908
Appointed: 1.2.1926.
Stationed at: Redruth Fowey, Bodmin, Whitstone, St Buryan,
30.5.1935 Granted a Favourable Record for gallant conduct at Carn Silver, Tregithian Cliff, St Buryan, on the night of the 13.5.1935 when he at great personal risk descended the cliff and with the assistance of civilians rescued Richard Henry Andrews who had fallen over. Awarded the Royal Humane's Society's Bronze Medal and certificate.
30.6.1941 Retired 16.2.1945 Died.

P.C. 111 John Charles Dale
Born 11.11.1904.
Appointed: 1.4.1926
Stationed at: St Austell, Fowey, Bodmin, Fowey, Redruth, St Austell, St Merryn , Bodmin Fowey, Nancledra, Illogan, St Day.
July 1949 Awarded the R.S.P.C.A. Framed certificate of Merit for the rescue of a dog from a disused mine shaft at Tresaddern Farm, St Day, on 13.9.1948.
30.6.1955 Retired.

P.C. 147 Wesley Arthur Hedley Pollard
Born 8.7.1907
Appointed: 1.4.1926.
Promotion: 1.11.1946 to Sergeant.
Stationed at: Falmouth, Newquay, St Austell, Truro, St Columb Major, St Germans, Looe, Polperro Pelynt, Menheniot, St Columb Minor, Penryn, Newquay.
Granted a Favourable Record with P.C. 76 Pill for prompt action taken in connection with a case of housebreaking at Newquay resulting in the arrest of the offenders, which was favourably commended on by the Chairman of the Pydar Bench, of Morris Cousins and Rosie Kate King for trial at the Cornwall Assize, when the former was sentenced to 15 months imprisonment and the latter bound over in £5.0.0. for two years under the supervision of the probation officer.
31.3.1953. Retired.

P.C. 133 George Wilfred Kersey
Born 29.3.1907.
Appointed: 15.5.1926.
Stationed at: Launceston, Redruth, Camborne, St Ives, Camborne, Mousehole, Boscaswell, St Day, Illogan, Camborne.
25.7.1946 Granted a Favourable Record for persistency and zeal displayed in connection with crimes of housebreaking, store breaking and larceny in his locality which resulted in the arrest of Joseph Henry Smith and Harold Kenneth Tippett who were dealt with at the Cornwall Quarter Sessions on 2.7.1946 and sentenced to six months imprisonment concurrent on each charge.
14.5.1956 Retired.

P.C. 66 Walter Welby Wright
Born 31.5.1899.
Appointed: 1.7.1926.
Stationed at: St Ives, Nancledra, St Ives, Mullion, Mevagissey.
31.5.1954 Retired.

P.C. 23 Cornelius Joseph John Carridick
Born 30.7.1906.
Appointed: 17.7.1926.
Stationed at: Bodmin, Falmouth.
20.12.1929 Resigned.

P.C. 62 Gerald Arthur Clark
Born 13.11.1905.
Appointed: 1.10.1926.
Stationed at: Bodmin, St Austell, Bude, Redruth, Camborne, St Ives, Camborne, Hayle, St Mawes, St Ives and Mawgan-in-Meneage.
Retired.

P.C. 17 Arthur John Metherall
Born 15.6.1905.
Appointed: 1.11.1926.
Stationed at: Truro, Newquay, Mawgan-in-Pydar, Highertown, St Austell.
31.10.1951 Retired.

P.C. 166 Edward John Osborne
Born 28.11.1902.
Appointed: 1.1.1927.
Stationed at: Bodmin, Falmouth, Truro, Torpoint, Lanreath, Troon, St Keverne, Breage, Porkellis.
31.3.1957 Retired.

P.C. 65 Edgar John Roberts
Born 15.8.1908.
Appointed: 1.2.1927.
Promotion: 8.4.1939 to Sergeant/Clerk.
1.5.1951 to Inspector /Clerk.
Stationed at: Camborne, H.Q. , Liskeard, Chief Constables Office, Liskeard.
1.8.1928 Granted a Favourable Record for brave conduct at Gwithian on 24.6.1928 when at great personal risk he swam in heavy seas in an attempt to rescue a drowning man Awarded the Royal Humane Society's Medal and Certificate and a £10.0.0 grant from the Carnegie Hero Fund Trust and a silver watch
28.2.1955 Retired.

P.C. 187 John Michael Archibald Barnicoat
Born 29.4.1904.
Appointed: 15.2.1927.
13.3.1927 Died from an appendix operation.

P.C. 197 Richard James Kersey
Born 9.5.1904.
Appointed: 16.2.1927.
Stationed at: Camborne, Mawgan, Grampound, Heamoor, Sennen, Heamoor.
31.3.1958 Retired.

P.C. 187 Ronald Francis Andrew Rogers
Born 22.9.1907.
Appointed: 1.4.1927.
Promotion: 1.9.1939 to Sergeant.
1.11.1948 to Inspector.
Stationed at: Redruth, St Neot. Burraton,

Bude, Penryn, Redruth.
1944 Awarded the R.S.P.C.A. Bronze medal and certificate for courage and humanity shown in rescuing a dog from a disused mine shaft at Twelve Heads on 19.7.1944.
31.12.1958 Retired
16.2.1963 Died.

P.C. 33 Christopher James
Born 18.4.1906.
Appointed: 16.5.1927.
9.2.1928 Resigned.

P.C. 102 Richard Henry Richards
Born 6.1.1906.
Appointed: 15.6.1927
1.4.1934 Transferred to Penzance Borough Police as P.C. 11
1.4.1947 On amalgamation became P.C. 253
Stationed at: Falmouth, Camborne, St Ives, Redruth, Mousehole , Heamoor, Penryn.
2.3.1959 Retired.

P.C. 2 James Herbert Elliott
Born 5.7.1906.
Appointed: 1.12.1927.
Stationed at: Falmouth, Newtown, Helston, Falmouth, Newquay, St Ives, St Neot, Dobwalls, Gunnislake.
1.1.1960. Retired.

P.C. 135 Leslie Warne
Born 8.12.1906.
Appointed: 1.12.1927.
Stationed at: Newquay, Bude, Blisland, Tywardreath, Foxhole, Stratton, Launceston, Week St Mary, Camelford.
14.1.1956 Retired.

P.C. 46 Charles Edwin Pearn
Born 11.7.1908.
Appointed: 1.12.1927.
Stationed at: Helston, Falmouth, Penryn, St Ives, Camborne, St Ives, Sennen.
29.8.1936 Granted a Favourable Record for brave conduct at Pednevounder Cove, St Leven, on 3.8.1936 when he at great personal risk descended the cliff and recovered the body of Frank Morrison Cross from the sea.
20.12.1957 Retired.

P.C. 150 Edward Reynolds
Born 12.8.1908.
Appointed: 1.12.1927.
Stationed at: H.Q.
31.1.1928 Resigned

P.C. 73 Horace Sidney Hawke
Born 14.9.1908
Appointed: 1.2.1928.
Promotion: 1.7.1939 to Sergeant.
1.9.1950 to Inspector.
Stationed at: Launceston, Stratton, Chief Constables Office, Camborne.
27.3.1957 Retired through ill-health.

P.C. 33 Thomas John Nicholls
Born 29.9.1906.
Appointed: 1.3.1928.
Stationed at: Bodmin, Fowey, Liskeard,

Launceston, Camborne, Launceston, Boscaswell, Meheniot, Pelynt, Sticker, St Austell.
1939 Awarded the R.S.P.C.A. Silver Medal for the rescue of two goats from the cliff at Pendeen on 29.8.1939.
30.6.1954 Retired.

P.C. 150 Elijah Joseph Grenville Harry
Born 6.9.1904/.
Appointed: 1.6.1928.
Promotion: 1.5.1951 to Detective Sergeant.
Stationed at: Falmouth, Slades, St Austell CID
30.10.1943 With Sergeant F.R.Ebbett awarded a Favourable Record for zeal and efficiency displayed in connection with a series of crimes committed in the Bodmin Police Division which resulted in the final clearing up of thirteen serious crimes, a number of which had been outstanding since the latter part of 1942.
3.10.1958 Retired.

P.C. 39 Francis Arthur Holman
Born 8.9.1907.
Appointed: 15.8.1928.
Stationed at: Bodmin., Torpoint, Millbrook, Cargreen Liskeard, Truro, Liskeard Pelynt, Saltash, Polruan, Millbrook.
14.10.1953 Retired.

P.C. 9 Edgar Brooker
Born 10.7.1904.
Appointed: 1.9.1928.
Promotion: 2.1.1951 to Sergeant.
Stationed at: Falmouth, Newquay, St Columb, Millbrook, Calstock, Camelford.
2.2.1958 Retired.

P.C. 219 John Henry Williams
Born 2.5.1907.
Appointed: 15.10.1928.
Stationed at: Falmouth, St Austell, Stratton, Truro, Perranporth, Truro, Blisland, St Austell, Chyandour.
28.2.1941 Retired.

P.C. 61 Ira Barrett
Born 15.5.1906.
Appointed: 1.2.1929.
Stationed at: Falmouth, Sithians, Newquay, Perranwell, Falmouth, Truro, St Columb Major, Falmouth
31.1.1955 Retired.

P.C. 21 Luke Raymond Prynn
Born 29.3.1910.
Appointed: 1.5.1929.
Stationed at: Truro.
29.2.1932.
Take up appointment in the Straits Settlement Police.

P.C. 215 Douglas Bassett
Born 18.3.1909.
Appointed: 1.6.1929.
Promotion: 1.11.1946 to Sergeant.
1.2.1955 to Inspector.
Stationed at: Bodmin, Camborne, St Ives, Chyandour, Redruth, Camborne, Nancledra, Camborne, Lanner Camborne.
31.5.1959 Retired.

P.C. 202 William John Hawkey
Born 4.4.1908.
Appointed: 1.6.1929.
30.6.1929 Resigned. 1.11.1930
Reappointed: as P.C. 213.
31.12.1930 Resigned.

P.C. 221 William George Behenna. Born 23.8.1907.
Appointed: 1.7.1929.
Stationed at: Camborne,
30.4.1930 Resigned.

P.C. 202 William Frederick Timmins
Born 25.10.1909.
Appointed: 1.7.1929.
16.6.1929 Transferred from Metropolitan Police.
Promotion: 1.7.1948 to Sergeant.
Stationed at: Newquay , Truro, St Ives, St Just, Tywardreath, Lanlivet, Bodmin, St Merryn, Hayle.
11.8.1954 Retired.

P.C. 163 Charles Henry Brown
Born 5.5.1908.
Appointed: 1.8.1929
Promotion: 1.4.1940 to Sergeant. 1.3.1948 to Inspector 1.5.1951 to Chief Inspector. 9.11.1955 to Superintendent. 1.9.1961 to Superintendent Grade 1.
Stationed at: Bodmin, Liskeard, Bodmin, Newquay, Launceston, Delabole, Launceston, Torpoint, Redruth, Penzance Camborne, Truro, Falmouth.
18.1.1934 Newquay Police Court. Complimented by the Chairman of the Bench for such a satisfactory and quick following of clues which resulted in John Henry Summers, aged 25 years, being committed for trial at the Assize, on three charges of burglary and having in his possession a firearm.
29.2.1964 Retired.

P.C. 78 Arthur James Kent
Born 26.4.1906
Appointed: 1.8.1929.
Stationed at: Falmouth,
30.4.1931 Resigned.

P.C. 204 William Henry Grenville Tripp
Born 24.4.1909.
Appointed: 1.8.1929.
Promotion: 1.4.1949 to Detective Sergeant. 9.11.1955 to Inspector.
Stationed at: Camborne, Callington, Liskeard, Launceston, Whitstone, Truro, Liskeard, Launceston, Wadebridge,
29.7.1944 Granted a Favourable Record for keenness, persistence and ability displayed in the detection in cases of larceny of coal and embezzlement, resulting in the conviction of seven offenders at Truro City Police Court on 29.6.1944. The enquiry being difficult and transactions involved.
31.8.1959 Retired.

P.C. 59 William Roy Chellew
Born 31.7.1906.
Appointed: 1.10.1929.
Promotion: 5.7.1940 to Sergeant. 1.11.1948 to Inspector.
Stationed at: Bodmin, St Austell, H.Q. CID,

Wadebridge, St Austell.
Granted a Favourable Record for perseverance and hours worked in effecting the arrest of Peter John Lumbly who was dealt with at the Cornwall Assize 12.6.1946 for breaking and entering the head Post Office at Bodmin.
31.1.1955 Retired

P.C. 23 Reginald Silas Firbank
Born 2.7.1911.
Appointed: 1.1.1930.
Promotion: 1.1.1934 to Sergeant.
Stationed at: Truro, Falmouth, Penryn, Perranporth, Egloshayle, Chacewater, Perranporth, Penzance.
1.1.1960. Retired.

P.C. 233 Leslie John Sidney Jones
Born 2.3.1911.
Appointed: 1.1.1930
Promotion: 1.1.1946 to Sergeant.
Stationed at: Camborne, St Ives, The Lizard, Launceston, Lanlivet.
14.2.1939 Awarded the Kings Police Medal for conspicuous gallantry when the S.S. *Alba* was wrecked off the Island St Ives on the night of 31.1.1938.
12.7.1947 Resigned.

P.C. 10 William Henry Treloar
Born 17.1.1911.
Appointed: 1.3.1930.
Stationed at: Launceston, Liskeard, Callington, East Looe, St Issey, Wadebridge, Chacewater, Perranporth.
Retired.19.4.1960

P.C. 221 Bate Burge-Davies
Born 30.1.1906.
Appointed: 1.5.1930.
Promotion: 1.3.1940 to Sergeant.
Stationed at: Bodmin, Newquay, Bodmin, Falmouth.
30.4.1955 Retired

P.C. 120 Frank Lobb
Born 7.8.1909.
Appointed: 1.5.1930.
1.5.1942 to Sergeant.
17.1.1950 to Inspector.
Stationed at: Bodmin, Fowey, Bodmin, East Looe, Cremyl, Saltash, Cargreen , Hatt, Penryn, Mawnan Smith, Launceston, Stratton, Falmouth, St Germans.
7.5.1957 Retired.

P.C. 15 William Douglas Gill
Born 26.1.1907.
Appointed: 1.7.1930.
Stationed at: Bodmin, Redruth, Constantine, St Ives.
31.5.1946 Resigned.

P.C. 188 Joseph Henry Rogers
Born 26.7.1906
Appointed: 1.8.1930.
Stationed at: St Austell, Padstow, St Merryn, Bugle, St Austell.
28.2.1936 Granted a Favourable Record for brave conduct at Credit Farm, Padstow, on 14.2.1936.., when he at great personal risk descended 90 feet into a disused mine shaft

and rescued a Spaniel dog which had fallen down the shaft the previous day.
28.4.1940 Died.

P.C. 8 Richard Arthur Tregaskis
Born 28.7.1911.
Appointed: 1.8.1930.
Promotion: 1.6.1946 to Sergeant.
Stationed at: Bodmin, Falmouth, Launceston, Stratton, Bodmin, Millbrook, Hatt, Burraton, Bude, Falmouth, Camborne.
30.9.1959 Retired

P.C. 174 Kenneth George Julian
Born 20.8.1910.
Appointed: 1.10.1920.
Promotion: 1.3.1940 to Detective Sergeant. 1.2.1946 to Detective Inspector. 1.3.1949 to Detective Superintendent. 8.10.1956 to Assistant Chief Constable.
Stationed at: Liskeard, Saltash, Cargreen, St Columb Major, Foxhole, Tywardreath, Bodmin H.Q. CID
1960 Awarded the Queens Police Medal for Distinguished Service.
31.10.1965 Retired.

P.C. 191 Francis Henry Organ
Born 28.4.1910.
Appointed: 1.11.1930.
Promotion: 1.11.1946 to Sergeant.
Stationed at: Bodmin, St Ives, Truro, Falmouth Helston, Wadebridge, St Austell, St Germans, Wadebridge.
31.3.1955 Retired

P.C. 214 George Edgar Appleton
Born 9.5.1912.
Appointed: 1.12.1930.
Stationed at: Camborne, Redruth, St Ives, Veryan.
14.2.1939 Awarded the Kings Police Medal for conspicuous gallantry when the S.S. *Alba* was wrecked off the Island, St Ives , on the night of 31.1.1938.
Awarded the Silver Cross of Merit by his Serene Highness the Regent of the Kingdom of Hungary
5.12.1939 Died.

P.C. 213 William Francis Crocker
Born 13.6.1910.
Appointed: 1.1.1931
Promotion: 19.11.1949 to Sergeant.
Stationed at: Truro, Chacewater, Truro, Tywardreath, Helston, St Austell..
17.1.1934 Truro City Police Court. Complimented by the Chairman for his alertness in detecting a man stealing coal and his promptitude in arresting the offender.
30.11.1964 Retired.

P.C. 177 Percival George Martin
Born 13.11.1911.
Appointed: 1.2.1931.
Promotion: 5.7.1914 to Sergeant. 1.6.1949 to Inspector. 4.4.1957 to Detective Inspector. 12.8.1959 to Chief Inspector.
Stationed at: H.Q., Falmouth, Newquay, St Austell, Liskeard, Camborne.
31.3.1963 Retired.

P.C. 196 Alfred George Jago
Born 24.11.1910.
Appointed: 5.2.1931
Promotion: 1.9.1950 to Sergeant.
Stationed at: Liskeard, Saltash, Cargreen, St Columb, Foxhole, Tywardreath, Bodmin, H.Q.Admin, Truro.
12.9.1959 Retired.

P.C. 211 Horace Rees
Born 15.4.1911.
Appointed: 1.3.1931.
Promotion: 1.11.1948 to Sergeant.
Stationed at: Launceston, Falmouth, Camelford, Tintagel, St Austell, Bude,
30.9.1963 Retired.

P.C. 123 Sidney Knapman Keast
Born 30.6.1910.
Appointed: 1.3.1931.
Promotion: 1.2.1947 to Sergeant.
1.1.1951 to Inspector.
9.11.1955 to Chief Inspector.
1.6.1959 to Superintendent.
1.4.1964 to Superintendent Grade 1.
Stationed at: Redruth , Camborne, St Ives, Chacewater, Torpoint, Falmouth, St Germans, Falmouth, Newquay, Penzance, Liskeard, Chyandour, Truro.
July 1943 Granted a Favourable Record for zeal and efficiency displayed with a series of larcenies committed at Millpool in the Parishes of St Hilary and Germoe which resulted in the clearing up of a number of crimes and the conviction of ten persons.
June 1947 Granted a Favourable Record for zeal and efficiency shown in investigations in R- v -Rust and also for alertness and attention to duty in cases in Police v Jobbing and Endean and Police v Gilpin.

P.C. 220 Claude Henry John Ackers
Born 1.3.1912.
Appointed: 1.3.1931.
Stationed at: Falmouth , Newquay, Falmouth, Camborne, St Ives, Bodmin, Bude, Five Lanes.
31.7.1938 Resigned.

P.C. 198 Horace John Hyde
Born 25.11.1910
Appointed: 13.4.1931.
Promotion: 1.3.1948 to Sergeant.
1.3.1955 to Inspector/Clerk.
Stationed at: Bodmin, Fowey, Jacobstow, Launceston, Liskeard, H.Q. CID, H.Q. Traffic, Fowey, Liskeard.
23.11.1963 Retired.

P.C. 78 Harry Alfred Elgey Worboys
Born 28.8.1912.
Appointed: 18.5.1931
Stationed at: Camborne, Falmouth, Launceston.
17.2.1936 Resigned.

P.C. 298 Wesley Thomas Prince
Born 10.5.1911,
Appointed: 1.7.1931.
Stationed at: Falmouth, Stratton, Launceston, Five Lanes, Halworthy, Camelford, Whitstone, Launceston, H.Q.

Traffic.
30.6.1959 Retired.

P.C. 4 George Edwin Glover
Born 13.4.1907.
Appointed: 1.9.1931.
Promotion: 1.2.1947 to Sergeant. 1.10.1950 to Inspector. 9.8.1955 to Chief Inspector. 2.4.1958 to Superintendent. 1.6.1959 to Superintendent Grade 1.
Stationed at: St Austell, Mevagissey, Lostwithiel, Padstow, Mevagissey, St Just-in-Penwith, Helston, Penryn, Camborne, Truro, Liskeard.
28.2.1941 Granted a Favourable Record for promptitude in assisting in the rescue of a soldier who had fallen into the harbour at Padstow on the night of the 18.1.1941.
31.1.1964 Retired.

P.C. 69 Sidney Norman Roberts
Born 8.9.1910.
Appointed: 1.10.1931.
Promotion: 1.2.1947 to Sergeant. 1.1.1951 to Detective Inspector. 8.10.1956 to Detective Superintendent. 12.8.1959 to Superintendent Grade 2.
Stationed at: Camborne, Truro, Camborne, Hayle , Camborne CID, H.Q. CID, Camborne and H.Q. CID
31.7.1963 Awarded the Kings Police Medal for Distinguished Service.
31.3.1965 Retired.

P.C. 122 Harry Webb
Born 15.11.1911.
Appointed: 1.12.1931.
Promotion: 1.2.1947 to Sergeant. 6.8.1956 to Inspector.
Stationed at: Falmouth, Chief Constables Office, H.Q. Traffic, H.Q. Recruitment.
30.9.1964 Retired.

P.C. 64 Joseph Phillips
Born 19.1.1912.
Appointed: 1.1.1932.
Stationed at: Torpoint, Stratton, Jacobstow,
31.8.1945 Resigned.

P.C. 143 Charles Percy Cole
Born 17.1.1913.
Appointed: 1.2.1932.
Promotion: 1.10.1947 to Sergeant.
1.11.1952 to Inspector.
Stationed at: Camborne, Truro, Probus, Camborne, Falmouth, Penzance, Launceston, Newquay, St Austell, Bude.
15.2.1938 Awarded the Kings Police Medal for Gallantry for that he on the 4.9.1937 at great personal risk and in face of unknown danger twice descended the East Shaft, Vean Sett, Stray Park, Camborne, in a gallant attempt to rescue a boy aged 8 years who had fallen into the shaft.
6.5.1965 Retired.

P.C. 21 Albert Mitchell
Born 26.8.1912.
Appointed: 7.3.1932.
Promotion: 1.10.1950 to Sergeant.
Stationed at: Falmouth, St Austell, St Blazey Gate, Whitstone, Delabole, Bude, St Austell.
6.3.1958 Retired.

P.C. 134 Frank Sandercock
Born 19.7.1902.
Appointed: 1.6.1932.
Stationed at: Bodmin, Helston, Falmouth, Helston, Porthleven.
18.7.1957 Retired.

P.C. 60 Roy Charles Dustow
Born 9.2.1911.
Appointed: 1.7.1932.
Stationed at: Falmouth , Penryn, Stratton.
31.12.1939 Resigned.

P.C. 176 Garnet Harris
Born 24.6.1910.
Appointed: 1.9.1932.
Stationed at: Camborne, Lanreath, Padstow, Launceston, Camelford, Stratton, Hayle, St Buryan, Trispen, Redruth Highway.
4.12.1960 Retired.

P.C. 31 Frederick Merryfield
Born 25.1.1914.
Appointed: 1.11.1932.
Stationed at: St Austell, Padstow,
28.2.1938 Resigned.

P.C. 171 Francis Courtney Rosevear
Born 2.6.1913.
Appointed: 1.4.1933.
Promotion: 1.1.1946 to Sergeant. 1.4.1949 to Detective Inspector.
Stationed at: Chief Constables Office , H.Q. Emergency Department, H.Q. CID And Admin.
7.11.1959 Retired.

P.C. 47 Eric Botheras
Born 10.9.1913.
Appointed: 1.6.1933.
Stationed at: Truro, Newquay, St Columb Major, Lewannick, St Erth, Redruth, Camborne.
28.2.1961 Retired.

P.C. 162 Arthur Enos Davies
Born 3.5.1913.
Appointed: 1.7.1933.
Promotion: 1.3.1955 to Sergeant.
Stationed at: Bodmin, Launceston, St Austell, Mevagissey, Delabole, Whitstone, Jacbstow, Egloskerry, Launceston, Fowey, St Austell.
30.12.1935 Granted a Favourable Record for brave conduct on 8.12.1935 at Launceston when he at great personal risk ascended a ladder and rescued a woman kneeling on the windowsill, and in a state of acute delirium.
23.7.1948 Awarded the Kings Police Medal for Gallantry at Widemouth Bay, Poundstock, on 23.7.1948.
31.8.1963 Retired.

P.C. 85 Frank Carpenter
Born 7.5.1913.
Appointed: 1.7.1933.
Stationed at: Torpoint, St Ives, Camborne, Newquay, St Neot.
30.6.1941 Resigned.

P.C. 144 Charles Richards
Born 12.12.1913.
Appointed: 1.8.1933.
Promotion: 1.3.1948 to Sergeant. 9.8.1955 to Inspector. 1.6.1959 to Chief Inspector. 1.2.1954 to Superintendent. 1.2.1966 to Superintendent Grade 1.
Stationed at: Bodmin, St Austell, Truro, H.Q., Truro, St Ives, Camborne, Penryn, Helston, Liskeard, Camborne, Traffic, Liskeard, Camborne.
29.6.1945 Granted a Favourable Record for zeal, efficiency, and perseverance in carrying out his duties in connection with several cases of burglary, house breaking and larceny, which culminated in the conviction at the Assize of Christopher Anthony Hennessey who was sentenced to 12 months consecutively.

P.C. 127 James Andrew O'Shea
Born 17.1.1912.
Appointed: 1.8.1933.
Stationed at: Fowey, Helston, Camborne, Helston, Falmouth, Truro, Mawgan-in-Meneage, Mullion, Pendeen, Falmouth, Mullion, Torpoint.
31.8.1963 Retired.

P.C. 132 William Thomas Gundry Cock
Born 26.7.1912.
Appointed: 1.10.1933.
Promotion: 1.7.1947 to Sergeant. 1.7.1952 to Inspector
Stationed at: Bodmin, Camborne, Bodmin, Newquay, H.Q., Launceston, Penzance, Chyandour, St Ives, Wadebridge.
30.9.1963 Retired.

P.C. 167 William Thomas Walke
Born 17.5.1913.
Appointed: 1.11.1933.
Promotion: 1.7.1947 to Sergeant. 1.3.1952 to Inspector. 2.4.1958 to Chief Inspector. 1.9.1961 to Superintendent. 1.4.1964 to Superintendent Grade 1.
Stationed at: Newquay, Camborne, Newquay, St,Merryn, St Austell, Camelford, Falmouth, Camborne, Wadebridge, Newquay, Penzance, Falmouth, Liskeard.
22.1.1944 Granted a Favourable Record for his action in going to the assistance of an army officer who was in difficulties in the sea in Constantine Bay during a military exercise.
28.10.1953 Granted a Favourable Record with DC 97 Arscott for their prompt an efficient action at Trevose golf club when their attention to duty resulted in the arrest of six men for burglary, who were later committed to the Assize. In addition they were concerned in eleven breaking offences and twelve larcenies.
3.1.1966 Retired.

P.C. 184 Richard Norman Bunney
Born 24.1.1912.
Appointed: 1.12.1933.
Promotion: 5.10.1952 to Sergeant.
Stationed at: Torpoint, Redruth, Nancledra, St Blazey, Falmouth, Tywardreath, Padstow.
30.11.1963 Retired.

P.C. 175 Thomas Owen Stanley Sivell
Born 8.10.1914.
Appointed: 1.12.1933.
Promotion: 1.3.1948 to Sergeant. 13.8.1954 to Inspector. 1.4.1964 to Chief Inspector.
Stationed at: Liskeard, Millbrook, Liskeard, Camborne, Liskeard, Saltash, St Cleer, Saltash, Millbrook, Chacewater, Torpoint, Bodmin, Liskeard. 31.12.1958 Awarded a Vote of Thanks on vellum by the Chapter General of the Order of St John for services to first aid in Cornwall. 1.1.1963 Admitted as Serving Brother of the Order of St John 31.3.1963 Retired

P.C. 139 Rodney Owen Thomas
Born 6.6.1915.
Appointed: 1.12.1933.
Promotion: 1.6.1949 to Sergeant. 1.1.1959 to Inspector.
Stationed at: Bodmin, Newquay, St Austell, Perranwell, Newquay, Mylor, Penryn, Camborne, St Columb, St Germans, Torpoint, Wadebridge.

P.C. 225 Frank Clifford White
Born 2.1.1912.
Appointed: 1.12.1933.
Promotion: 11.5.1950 to Sergeant. 2.4.1958 to Inspector. 1.4.1964 to Chief Inspector.
Stationed at: Bodmin, Newquay, St Germans, Liskeard, Looe CID, Sticker, St Germans, Callington, Hayle, Launceston, Camborne.
29.6.1935 Granted a Favourable Record for brave conduct at Newquay on 18.6.1935 when he at great personal risk recovered the body of Mrs Josephine R. Worsley from the sea. 14.6.1943 At the Cornwall Assize was complimented by Mr Justice Charles on the admirable way he had given his evidence in a civil action Gordon McVittie v W.J.Holman & Sons.
31.12.1965. Retired.

P.C. 113 Wilfred Charles Greet
Born 19.9.1914.
Appointed: 1.3.1934.
Promotion: 1.10.1950 to Sergeant.
Stationed at: Falmouth , Helston, Mevagissey, Week St Mary, Boscastle, Halworthy, Kilkhampton, Falmouth, Looe.
4.4.1959 Retired.

P.C. 254 Frederick William Radford
Born 2.10.1909.
Appointed: 24.3.1934.
Appointed: to Penzance Borough Police 24.9.1931.
Promotion: 2.12.1945 to Sergeant. 1.4.1955 to Inspector.
Stationed at: Penzance Redruth, Camborne, Stratton, Bude, Helston.
25.1.1939 Commended by the Watch Committee for valuable social service rendered during 1936 regarding the reformation of the Newlyn Sea Scouts.
25.1.1941 Commended by the Justices for good Police work in the case of Lt. Redding R.N. In four cases of larceny.
19.3.1941 Commended by the Juvenile Bench for successful work in connection with

juvenile delinquents.
13.10.1941 Commended by Justices on manner on which investigations re Dingy and Brown for gross indecency were carried out.
8.3.1943 Commended by Justice Scobell Armstong for his work in connection with charges against Thackery and Barnes for the illegal use of petrol. Seconded by the Watch Committee on 2.3.1943.
5.6.1944 Commended by the juvenile branch for work in connection with a case of housebreaking and larceny of £1.0.0. And the larceny of garden shears
29.3.1945 Granted a Favourable Record for devotion to duty in the extensive enquiries which were necessary in clearing up 61 cases of larceny brought against Thomas Barrett, resulting in the conviction at Penzance Magistrates Court 20.2.1945.
18.5.1963 Retired.

P.C. 54 Edwin George Hoar
Born 4.2.1912.
Appointed: 1.4.1934.
Stationed at: Bodmin, Fowey, Truro,
11.12.1937 Resigned.

P.C. 55 George Edgar Mitchell
Born 4.11.1915.
Appointed: 1.5.1934.
Promotion: 1.4.1949 to Detective Sergeant. 1.4.1957 to Inspector.
Stationed at: Redruth, Torpoint, Looe, H.Q.C.I.D., Liskeard, Camborne, Penzance, St Ives, St Austell.
March 1957 Awarded the Royal Humane Society's Testimonial on vellum at St Ives Magistrates Court by the Chairman on the 13.3.1957 for his prompt and efficient action at Porthmeor Beach , St Ives on the 28.8.1956 when he rescued two men and a girl from rough seas.
12.9.1959 Retired.

P.C. 142 Frederick Gordon Pollard
Born 25.12.1911.
Appointed: 1.11.1934.
Stationed at: Newquay, Truro, Newquay, St Columb Major, Hessenford, Burraton, Saltash, St Germans, Tintagel, Callington.
31.10.1964 Retired.

P.C. 102 Charles Kendall
Born 8.4.1909.
Appointed: 1.11.1934
Promotion: 1.11.1952 to Sergeant.
Stationed at: Falmouth, Penryn, Porkellis, Lostwithiel, Penzance.
7.2.1960 Retired.

P.C. 266 Leslie Symons
Born 12.8.1910.
Appointed: 31.12.1934
Transferred from Penzance Borough Police
Promotion: 1.3.1953 to Sergeant. 1.6.1959 to Inspector.
Stationed at: Penzance, St Austell, Bude, St Austell,
31.10.1966 Retired.

P.C. 76 James Arthur Henry Pill
Born 27.3.1916.

Appointed: 1.1.1935.
Promotion: 1.4.1949 to Detective Sergeant. 1.5.1951 to Detective Inspector. 1.4.1957 to Chief Inspector. 2.4.1958 to Superintendent. 1.3.1964 to Superintendent Grade 1.
Stationed at: Camborne, St Ives, Camborne CID, Devoran , Newquay, Falmouth, St Austell, Liskeard, Penzance, H.Q. Traffic, Camborne.
Granted a Favourable Record for vigilance displayed in the arrest of Patrick Joseph O'Reilly, in connection with which he was commended by the Bridgend Justices, for initiative displayed in the detection of 18 crimes in Truro between August and September 1945.
Granted a Favourable Record with P.C. 147 Pollard for prompt action taken in connection with a case of housebreaking in Newquay resulting in the arrest of the offender which was favourably commended on by the Chairman of the Pydar Bench after the committal of Morris Cousins and Roaslie Kate King for trial at the Cornwall Assize, when the former was sentenced to 15 months imprisonment and the latter bound over in the sum of £5.0.0. For two years under the supervision of the probation officer.
29.3.1955 Cornwall Quarter Sessions was commended by the Chairman for his efforts in bringing to justice four men charged with housebreaking and larceny at Looe.
Still serving on amalgamation.

P.C. 96 Frederick John Sandy
Born 19.8.1915.
Appointed: 1.1.1935.
Stationed at: Bodmin, St Ives, Camborne, St Just, Sennen, Heamoor, Isles of Scilly, Pool, Truro, Roche.
30.11.1963 Retired.

Major Edgar Hare
Born 30.8.1891.
Appointed: 18.4.1935.
As Chief Constable.
Kings Police Medal
12.10.1953 Lord Lieutenant of Cornwall Lt.Co. Sir Edward Bolitho K.B.E., C.B., D.S.O. Presented Major E.Hare M.C. With the Kings Police Medal and the Fire Services Medal for distinguished service, at the Police H.Q., Bodmin.
30.6.1956 Elected honorary member of the Association of Chief Officers of England and Wales.
29.8.1956 Retired
30.7.1966 Died.

P.C. 71 Thomas Matthew A.T. Osborne
Born 6.8.1914.
Appointed: 1.4.1935.
Stationed at: Bodmin, St Austell. Wadebridge, Liskeard, Callington, Newquay, Falmouth, Helston, Perranwell.
31.3.1946 Resigned.

P.C. 159 Ronald Thomas May
Born 10.11.1914.
Appointed: 1.5.1935
Promotion: 1.10.1950 to Sergeant.
Stationed at: Helston, St Just, Camborne,

Redruth, Chyandour, St Keverne, Falmouth, Truro, St Just.
30.6.1963 Retired.

P.C. 227 Ernest Emmanuel Eva
Born 5.11.1915.
Appointed: 1.6.1935.
Stationed at: Liskeard, Millbrook, Hatt, Torpoint , Millbrook, Blisland, H.Q. Bodmin, H.Q. Information Room.
31.5.1960 Retired.

P.C. 228 Douglas Roy Hugo
Born 1.12.1916.
Appointed: 1.6.1935.
Promotion: 20.12.1950 to Sergeant.
Stationed at: Launceston, Falmouth, St Columb, Newquay, St Austell, Camborne, Penzance, Perranporth.
30.8.1960 Retired.

P.C. 229 Bertram Roy Pearn
Born 29.12.1912.
Appointed: 1.6.1935.
Promotion: 1.9.1950 to Sergeant/Clerk. 1.4.1964 to Inspector/Clerk.
Stationed at: Torpoint, Cremyl, Torpoint, Camborne, Torpoint, East Looe, Liskeard, Tregoney, Truro.
27.6.1957. Carniegie Hero Fund Trust decided to have the names of Sergeant B.R.Pearn and P.C. 285 Hawkins inscribed on their illuminated roll of Heroes in recognition of heroism on 21.3.1952 when they rescued Mr S.J.Besley from a savage attack by a bull. Awarded the Carniegie Hero Fund Trust Honorary Certificate framed in oak.
24.10.1957 Awarded the Queens Commendation for brave conduct in connection with the above.
31.5.1967 Retired.

P.C. 226 Frank Arthur
Born 2.8.1916
Appointed: 1.6.1935.
Stationed at: Newquay, Truro, Falmouth, Stithians, Boscastle.
12.10.1946 Resigned .

P.C. 149 Percival Roy Hawkin
Born 25.9.1926.
Appointed: 12.8.1935.
Promotion: 28.10.1950 to Sergeant. 1.6.1955 to Inspector. 2.4.1958 to Chief Inspector. 12.8.1959 to Superintendent.
Stationed at: Bodmin, Mevagissey, St Kew Highway, Bodmin, Helston, Probus, Newquay, Truro, H.Q., Camborne, H.Q. Admin.
31.8.1965 Retired.

P.C. 29 Richard Henry Nicholls
Born 20.9.1909.
Appointed: 1.10.1935.
Stationed at: Redruth, Burraton, St Neot, Stithians, The Lizard.
30.9.1960 Retired.

P.C. 25 Frank William Floyd
Born 23.11.1916.
Appointed: 1.2.1936
Promotion: 1.1.1951 to Sergeant.
Stationed at: Fowey, St Austell, Padstow,

H.Q. Asst., Chief Constable's Office at Berry Towers, Bodmin.
31.1.1966 Retired.

P.C. 42 William Henry Thomas Stanbury
Born 1.2.1913.
Appointed: 1.2.1936
Stationed at: Falmouth, St Blazey Gate, Fowey, Sticker, Bodmin, St Austell, Penryn.
31.10.1961 Retired.

P.C. 22 William John Boscombe
Born 19.4.1911.
Appointed: 1.3.1936.
Promotion: 4.7.1939 to Sergeant. 9.11.59 to Inspector.
Stationed at: Launceston, Stratton, Lewannick, Five Lanes, Bude , Truro, H.Q., Liskeard.
30.1.1939 Granted a Favourable Record for the manner in which he acted resulting in the arrest of Herbert Leslie Lucy on charges of False Pretences and larceny committed at Bude between in the 8th/12th October 1938, where the offender gave the name of Miles.
28.2.1967 Retired.

P.C. 74 Leonard Cocks
Born 10.4.1916.
Appointed: 1.3.1936.
Promotion: 1.5.1951 to Sergeant.
Stationed at: Liskeard, Torpoint, Millbrook, Chief Constable's Office, Bodmin.
28.2.1966 Retired.

P.C. 78 William John Talbot Lovering
Born 29.11.1912.
Appointed: 1.3.1936.
Promotion: 1.4.1939 to Detective Sergeant.
Stationed at: Saltash, Torpoint, Millbrook, Liskeard CID St Kew Highway, Wadebridge, Newquay, Launceston, St Austell.
27.4.1941 Granted a Favourable Record for zeal efficiency and perseverance in carrying out his duty especially in the cases of Cutler and Wilkey who were sentenced at Cornwall Quarter Sessions 10.4.1945 on charges of shop breaking, housebreaking and larceny.
28.2.1961 Retired.

P.C. 106 Arthur George Luscombe
Born 8.4.1911.
Appointed: 1.3.1936
Promotion: 18.9.1959 to Sergeant.
Stationed at: Bodmin, Callington, Saltash, Liskeard, Callington, Looe, St Germans, Hessenford, Kingsand, Saltash, Newquay, Camborne.
28.2.1966 Retired.

P.C. 157 Percival John Pope
Born 5.5.1914.
Appointed: 1.3.1936.
Promotion: 1.4.1949 to Detective Sergeant.
Stationed at: Falmouth, Mawnan Smith, Falmouth, Truro, H.Q.
Granted a Favourable Record for his strict and courageous attention to duty at Falmouth on 25.10.1941 which culminated in two members of H.M.Navy being commit-

ted for trial at the Assize on a charge of shop breaking.
5.3.1962 Died.

P.C. 53 James Raymond Roberts
Born 23.7.1916
Appointed: 1.5.1936.
Promotion: 1.3.1951 to Sergeant. 8.5.1957 to Inspector. 1.4.1964 to Chief Inspector. 1.11.1965 to Superintendent Grade 1.
Stationed at: Bodmin, Fowey, Launceston, Fowey, Liskeard, Tregoney, Torpoint, St Germans, Redruth, Newquay, Camborne.
31.1.1967 Retired.

P.C. 173 Robert John Stothers
Born 27.4.1912.
Appointed: 1.7.1936.
Stationed at: Fowey, Camborne, Fowey, St Austell, Bugle, St Austell, Bodmin, Looe, Launceston, Information Room.
30.6.1966 Retired.

P.C. 256 John Maddern Green
Born 8.4.1915.
Appointed: 10.8.1936.
Transferred from the Penzance Borough Police 31.3.1947.
Stationed at: Penzance, Mousehole, Penzance.
10.7.1939 Commended by the Penzance Borough Justices for good Police Work in detecting in a case of larceny whilst off duty.
26.2.1940 Commended by the Penzance Juvenile Justices for detection of offenders who stole from Church Offertory boxes
11.7.1950 Awarded the Royal Humane Society's Resuscitation Certificate.

P.C. 257 John Edward Toms
Born 16.2.1916.
Appointed: 10.8.1936
Transferred from Penzance Borough Police.
Promotion: 1.4.1939 to Detective Sergeant.
Stationed at: Penzance, Falmouth, H.Q. CID Callington, Redruth.
1.3.1939. Commended by the Watch Committee for saving a dog from the drain under Penzance Promenade.
17.4.1939 Commended by Penzance Borough Justices for vigilance shown and attention to duty in the case of George Wildman whom he arrested for indecency.
8.7.1941 Commended by the Penzance Borough Justices for good Police work re the detection of A.C. Hancock for indecent assault.
June 1947 Granted a Favourable Record for zeal and efficiency shown in his investigation in the case of Rex v Rust.
February 1957 Awarded the R.S.P.C.A. Framed Certificate of Merit on 9.2.1957 in appreciation of his gallantry in connection with the rescue of a sow from Latchley Consuls mine shaft on 26.3.1956.
9.2.1965 Retired.

P.C. 40 Noel Wilkinson
Born 20.12.1913.
Appointed: 1.10.1936.
Stationed at: Camborne, St Ives, Constantine, Helston.

Awarded the Kings Police Medal when the S.S. *Alba* was wrecked off the Island, St Ives, on the night of 31.1.1938.
31.8.1945 Resigned.

P.C. 48 Thomas Joseph Furse
Born 15.10.1917.
Appointed: 1.10.1936.
Stationed at: Falmouth,
23.9.1938 Resigned.

P.C. 183 Cecil Broadley Collins
Born 2.6.1914.
Appointed: 1.10.1936.
Stationed at: Saltash, Callington, Millbrook
31.7.1939 Resigned.

P.C. 258 Ronald Botheras
Born 21.12.1915.
Appointed: 5.10.1936
Transferred from Penzance Borough Police.
Stationed at: Penzance.
20.9.1937 Commended by the Penzance Borough Justices for observation and attention to duty resulting in the arrest of R. Brown.
25.7.1959 Retired.

P.C. 231 Henry Ronald Morcumb
Born 15.4.1918.
Appointed: 1.1.1937.
Promotion: 8.10.1956 to Detective Sergeant.
Stationed at: St Austell, Wadebridge, Penryn, Boscastle, Launceston, Pool, Camborne, Redruth, Penzance. Liskeard, Truro.
November 1949 Granted a Favourable Record for courage and devotion to duty in rescuing an unknown lad from drowning in the sea at Hayle beach on 24.8.1949.
31.12.1962 Retired.

P.C. 232 Ivor William Osborne
Born 26.8.1917
Appointed: 1.1.1937.
Promotion: 22.1.1951 to Sergeant.
1.9.1963 to Inspector.
Stationed at: Camborne, Hayle, Camborne, H.Q.C.I.D. Calstock, Redruth, Connor Downs, Callington, Hayle, Redruth.
31.12.1966 Retired.

P.C. 234 William Raymond Richards
Born 2.5.1914.
Appointed: 1.1.1937.
Promotion: 1.6.1949 to Sergeant. 8.10.1956 to Detective Inspector. 1.9.1963 to Chief Inspector.
Stationed at: Truro. St Austell, H.Q.C.I.D., Falmouth, Camborne, H.Q.C.I.D, Liskeard, Truro.
31.12.1966 Retired.

P.C. 230 Arthur Jellicoe Bawden
Born 11.11.1914
Appointed: 1.1.1937.
8.2.1937 Resigned.

P.C. 217 James Arthur Pollard Bennett
Born 9.11.1912.
Appointed: 1.1.1937.
Stationed at: Camborne, Truro,
28.2.1938 Resigned.

P.C. 233 Jack Probis
Born 5.7.1916
Appointed: 1.1.1937.
Stationed at: H.Q.,
15.1.1937 Resigned.

P.C. 216 Frederick Richard Roberts
Born 25.11.1915.
Appointed: 1.2.1937.
Stationed at: Falmouth. Lerryn, Pelynt, Lerryn, St Austell, St Merryn, Truro, Falmouth.
31.8.1963 Retired.

P.C. 233 Albert John Pellow
Born 23.1.1918.
Appointed: 1.2.1937.
Stationed at: Saltash, Torpoint,
14.6.1938 Resigned.

P.C. 207 Joseph May
Born 20.3.1917.
Appointed: 1.3.1937.
15.3.1947 Resigned
Reappointed: 29.6.1947 as P.C. 51
Stationed at: Bodmin, Padstow, St Austell, Falmouth, Bude, Kilkhampton, Camborne, St Columb.
No retirement date.

P.C. 230 Charles Edward LeWarne
Born 11.2.1916.
Appointed: 1.3.1937.
Stationed at: Launceston, Bude, Launceston, Clerk to the Liaison Office 8th., Corps., Redruth, Launceston Divisional Clerk.
11.4.1948 Transferred to Somerset Police.

P.C. 222 Bernard John Colwill
Born 19.3.1915.
Appointed: 1.4.1937.
Promotion: 9.8.1955 to Sergeant.
Stationed at: Bodmin, Stratton Launceston, Five Lanes, Launceston, Bude, Stratton, Pensilva, Looe, Penryn, Fowey
No retirement date.

P.C. 236 Leslie Walter Firth
Born 6.5.1918.
Appointed: 1.4.1937.
Stationed at: Camborne, Redruth, Helston, St Buryan, Chyandour, Hayle, Liskeard, Camborne, Penryn.
31.3.1967 Retired.

P.C. 235 Lawrence Dunn Hunkin
Born 13.7.1917.
Appointed: 1.4.1937.
Stationed at: Camborne, H.Q. Chief Constable Chauffeur.
31.3.1967 Retired.

P.C. 238 William Charles Harris
Born 13.5.1917.
Appointed: 1.4.1937.
Stationed at: Camelford, Launceston, Camelford, Lewannick, Goldsithney, St Agnes, Helston.
31.3.1962 Retired.

P.C. 237 Leonard Arthur Harris
Born 29.3.1917.
Appointed: 1.4.1937.
Promotion: 1.4.1957 to Sergeant.

Stationed at: Helston, Blackwater, Falmouth, Helston, Porkellis, Penryn, Falmouth, Liskeard.
30.9.1963 Retired.

P.C. 239 Frank Snashall
Born 20.11.1913
Appointed: 1.4.1937.
Promotion: 5.1.1951 to Sergeant.
Stationed at: Bodmin , Pool, Dobwalls, Penryn.
6.6.1953 Resigned.

P.C. 158 Austin Kinver Ware
Born 8.8.1917.
Appointed: 1.7.1937.
Stationed at: Launceston, Bude,, St Neot.
10.6.1944 Killed in Action whilst serving in the Royal Artillery in France.

P.C. 3 Garfield Arthur Slade
Born 11.12.1912.
Appointed: 1.10.1937.
Stationed at: St Austell, Truro, Lezant, Bude, Falmouth.
30.4.1964 Retired.

P.C. 259 William Adamson
Born 23.8.1912.
Appointed: 11.10.1937.
Transferred from the Metropolitan Police to Penzance Borough Police.
Transferred to the Cornwall Constabulary on amalgamation.
Promotion: 1.9.1950 to Sergeant.
Stationed at: Penzance, H.Q. Bodmin, Truro.
8.6.1965 Retired.

P.C. 46 Vivian John Symons
Born 31.5.1915.
Appointed: 1.1.1938.
Promotion: 1.8.1953 to Sergeant/ Clerk
Stationed at: Camborne. Hayle, St Ives, Stratton, Launceston, Stratton, Halworthy, Launceston, St Austell, H.Q. Information Room, Traffic.
No Retirement Date

P.C. 54 Harold Ollerearnshaw
Born 14.4.1914.
Appointed: 1.1.1938.
Stationed at: Fowey, Redruth, Camborne, St Austell, St Mellion, Truro, Devoran, Veryan.
No retirement date.

P.C. 25 Ernest James Jackson
Born 14.1.1914.
Appointed: 28.1.1938.
Promotion: 17.10.1951 to Sergeant/Clerk.
Stationed at: Penzance, St Austell, Penryn, Falmouth,
31.10.1963 Retired.

P.C. 249 Edwin Arthur Tapping
Born 29.5.1917.
Appointed: 3.2.1938.
31.3.1947 Transferred from Penzance Borough.
Stationed at: Penzance, Mousehole.
September 1951 Awarded the Royal Humane Society's resuscitation certificate.
No retirement date.

P.C. 31 Walter George Bunney
Born 29.5.1916.
Appointed: 1.3.1938.
Stationed at: Falmouth, Wadebridge, Redruth, Camelford, Liskeard, Blue Anchor, St Neot, St Austell.
No retirement date.

P.C. 45 Tom Fox
Born 23.3.1915.
Appointed: 1.3.1938.
Promotion: 17.1.1954 to Sergeant.
Stationed at: Newquay, Redruth, Chyandour, Penzance
31.8.1964 Retired.

P.C. 217 Frederick Gordon Trevor Lewis
Born 19.9.1918.
Appointed: 1.3.1938.
Promotion: 16.1.1953 to Sergeant. 2.4.1958 to Inspector. 8.4.1963 to Chief Inspector.
Stationed at: Bodmin, Fowey, St Austell CID, Duloe, St Germans , Anthony, Torpoint CID Looe, H.Q., St Ives, Liskeard, Falmouth.
No retirement date.

P.C. 5 Ronald John Howard Billinger
Born 17.2.1919.
Appointed: 1.3.1938.
Stationed at: Newquay.
15.11.1939 Resigned.

P.C. 87 Kenneth William Harmour-Knight
Born 9.1.1919.
Appointed: 1.3.1938.
Stationed at: Looe,
26.9.1938 Resigned.

P.C. 141 Matthew Henry Trelease
Born 27.12.1916.
Appointed: 1.4.1938.
Stationed at: St Ives, Camborne, Torpoint, Liskeard.
18.1.1947 Resigned.

P.C. 189 William John Roberts
Born 29.9.1914.
Appointed: 1.5.1938.
Stationed at: Falmouth, Saltash, Looe CID, Liskeard CID, Truro, Newlyn East, Redruth.
29.2.1964 Retired.

P.C. 126 George Smitheram
Born 29.12.1914.
Appointed: 1.6.1938.
Stationed at: Bodmin, Torpoint, Bodmin, Fowey, St Austell, Redruth, Isles of Scilly, Camborne.
Injured in German air raid on Plymouth whilst stationed at at Torpoint.
3.6.1966 Died.

P.C. 193 Philip John Hutchings
Born 4.10.1915.
Appointed: 1.7.1938
Promotion: 1.4.1939 to Sergeant. 28.3.1952 to Inspector.
Stationed at: Saltash, Torpoint, H.Q., Bodmin, Camborne.
No retirement date.

P.C. 56 Richard Henry Furse
Born 12.7.1914.
Appointed: 1.7.1938.
Promotion: 16.3.1952 to Sergeant. 1.4.1967 to Inspector
Stationed at: Falmouth, Camborne, Pool, Isles of Scilly, Falmouth, Saltash, Truro, Launceston.
No Retirement date.

P.C. 27 Harry Frost
Born 3.6.1914.
Appointed: 1.7.1938.
Stationed at: Falmouth, Redruth, Pelynt, Lerryn.
12.8.1943 Retired due to ill-health.

P.C. 233 Albert Edward John Lee
Born 25.7.1915.
Appointed: 1.7.1938.
19.4.1947 Resigned.

P.C. 220 Arthur James Lobb
Born 14.6.1919.
Appointed: 1.8.1938.
Promotion:
1.2.1955 to Sergeant. 1.6.1959 to Inspector. 1.4.1965 to Chief Inspector.
1.3.1967 to Superintendent.
Stationed at: Camborne, Sennen, St Just, Chyandour, Fowey, Stratton, CID, Torpoint, Camborne, Falmouth, H.Q. CID, Newquay.
No retirement date.

P.C. 137 Douglas Garnet Searle
Born 22.3.1918.
Appointed: 1.8.1938.
Stationed at: Torpoint, Liskeard, Millbrook, Saltash, Callington.
26.10.1946 Resigned.

P.C. 48 Gerald Redvers Goodfire
Born 22.4.1920.
Appointed: 1.10.1938.
Stationed at: Helston
31.3.1946 Resigned.

P.C. 35 Richard James Beswetherick
Born 29.9.1914.
Appointed: 1.10.1938.
Stationed at: Launceston, Stratton, Launceston.
31.12.1945 Resigned.

P.C. 170 John Osborne
Born 18.11.1918.
Appointed: 1.10.1938.
Promotion: 1.4.1953 to Sergeant. 1.9.1949 to Inspector. 1.1.1957 to Chief Inspector.
Stationed at: Truro, Burraton, Truro CID, Newquay, Truro, Torpoint. Newquay, Falmouth, Camborne, Truro.
No retirement date.

P.C. 49 Roy Grigg
Born 26.11.1918.
Appointed: 1.10.1938.
Promotion: 30.5.1954 to Sergeant /Clerk.
Stationed at: Camborne, Chief Constable's Office, Redruth, Truro, Stithians, Penryn, Falmouth, H.Q. Information Room.
31.7.1966 Retired.

P.C. 87 Victor George Marshall
Born 20.7.1919.
Appointed: 1.10.1938.
Stationed at: Liskeard, Torpoint,
8.5.1940 Resigned.

P.C. 192 Ernest Henry Guy Hugo
Born 3.11.1915.
Appointed: 1.11.1938.
Stationed at: St Austell, Camborne, Stratton,
Camborne, Devoran, Truro, Higher town, St
Austell.
19.7.1956 Died.

P.C. 240 Lionel Howard Lakeman
Born 9.6.1917.
Appointed: 1.11.1938.
Stationed at: Liskeard, Looe, Liskeard, Looe,
St Neot.
29.11.1947 resigned.

P.C. 241 Jack Pomery
Born 1.7.,1918.
Appointed: 1.11.1938.
Stationed at: Truro, Perranporth, Falmouth,
St Ives, Truro, St Austell, Foxhole, Mevagissey,
Rilla Mill, Truro.
No retirement date.

P.C. 161 Charles Arthur Howard
Born 7.1.1918.
Appointed: 1.11.1938.
Stationed at: Newquay, Veryan, Newquay
28.6.1947 resigned.

P.C. 242 Ronald Rowe
Born 23.7.1919.
Appointed: 1..11.1938.
Stationed at: Camborne, Chief Constable's
Office, Camborne, St Just.
14.10.1947 Retired through ill-health.

P.C. 101 Jack Biddlecombe
Born 19.6.1917.
Appointed: 1.11.1938.
Stationed at: Falmouth, Newquay.
30.3.1946 Resigned.

P.C. 243 Stuart Rutherford Surrey
Born 3.10.1917
Appointed: 1.11.1938.
Stationed at: Saltash.
7.6.1939 Resigned.

P.C. 13 Harold George Bunney
Born 27.2.1916.
Appointed: 1.1.1939.
Stationed at: Newquay, Saltash, Connor
Downs, Penzance Connor Downs, Isles of
Scilly, Pool, St Ives.
No retirement date.

P.C. 199 Albert Edward Hobbs
Born 22.4.1920.
Appointed: 1.1.1939
Promotion: 1.4.1955 to Sergeant. 24.11.1953
to Inspector. 1.6.1967 to Chief Inspector.
Stationed at: Camborne, Isles of Scilly, Truro,
Looe, Launceston, Stratton, Launceston,
Penzance, Redruth, Bodmin, H.Q. Training,
H.Q. Admin.
No Retirement date.

P.C. 1 John James Cock
Born 21.6.1914,
Appointed: 1.3.1939.
Stationed at: Saltash, Fowey, Duloe, St
Merryn, St Austell, Blisland.
29.2.1964 Retired.

P.C. 24 Maxwell Wallace Mutton
Born 24.11.1919. 1
Appointed: 1.3.1939.
Promotion: 14.4.1954 to Sergeant.
Stationed at: Callington, Looe, Bodmin,
H.Q. CID, Newquay, Camborne.
9.10.1964 Retired.

P.C. 103 Herbert Frank Short
Born 4.12.1915.
Appointed: 1.3.1939.
Promotion: 16.8.1954 to Sergeant.
Stationed at: Launceston, St Buryan. Hayle,
Connor Downs, Newlyn East, St Austell,
Tregoney, St Ives, Penzance.
20.12.1957 Granted a favourable record
with P.C. 324 Broom for prompt action at
Porth Kidney beach, Lelant, on 7.12.1957,
when they rescued a woman from the sea
and successfully applied artificial respiration.
31.12.1958 Awarded the Royal Humane
Society's Resuscitation Certificate for his
action in the resuscitation of a woman
rescued from the sea at Porthmeor, St Ives on
18.8.1958.
No retirement date.

P.C. 109 Raymond Willis Smith
Born 15.1.1920
Appointed: 1.3.1939.
Promotion: 2.5.1954 to Sergeant.
Stationed at: Falmouth, Newquay, Truro,
Mawgan-in-Pydar, Perranporth. Liskeard , St
Just.
29.2.1964 Retired.

P.C. 117 Percy John Tamblin
Born 22.3.1920.
Appointed: 1.3.1939.
Stationed at: Penryn, Nancledra, Jacobstow,
Camelford, Falmouth, Pendeen.
29.2.1964 Retired.

P.C. 190 Joseph Archibald Trerise
Born 4.3.1920
Appointed: 1.3.1939.
Stationed at: Newquay, St Ives, Falmouth,
Stithians, Falmouth, Chacewater.
31.3.1964 Retired.

**P.C. 152 Leonard Theodore Noel
Trethewey**
Born 25.12.1919.
Appointed: 1.3.1939.
Promotion: 1.9.1959 to Sergeant.
Stationed at: Truro. Tywardreath, Five Lanes,
Dobwalls, Mevagissey, Launceston, Penzance.
No Retirement date.

P.C. 88 William Stanley Pascoe
Born 18.4.1920.
Appointed: 1.3.1939.
Stationed at: Redruth, Camborne, St Austell,
Falmouth,
26.10.1946 Resigned.

P.C. 20 Charles Garfield Clymow
Born 29.1.1920
Appointed: 1.4.1939.
Stationed at: Liskeard, Wadebridge,
Newquay,
October 1948. Granted a commendation
with P.C. 59 Huby and P.C. 131 Holsgrove
granted a Favourable Record for their perseverance and devotion to duty in obtaining
evidence which resulted in the detection of
an offender in a case of shop breaking at
Wadebridge and the clearing up of eight
other offences.
31.3.1954. Resigned.

P.C. 65 William Frederick Claude Davey
Born 7.2.1915
Appointed: 1.4.1939.
Stationed at: St Austell, Week St Mary,
Devoran, Newlyn East, Five Lanes, Lerryn,
Looe.
Awarded the R.S.P.C.A Certificate of Merit
for the rescue of a cat on 18.5.1950.
31.10.1964 Retired.

P.C. 68 Robert Edward Bowen Eden
Born 3.8.1915
Appointed: 1.4.1939.
Promotion: 1.3.1953 to Detective Sergeant.
2.4.1958 to Detective Inspector.
1.4.1954 to Chief Inspector.
1.6.1967 to Detective Superintendent.
Stationed at: Falmouth, Mylor, Falmouth,
H.Q., Falmouth, Liskeard, Falmouth,
Camborne, St Austell, H.Q. CID
26.4.1950 Granted a Favourable Record
with P.C. 99 Cox for the very zealous and
able manner with which they dealt with 23
cases of larceny, 10 cases of receiving and
one case of store breaking at Falmouth which
resulted in eight juveniles and four adults
being convicted at Falmouth Magistrates
Court.

P.C. 179 Douglas James Firbank
Born 13.3.1919.
Appointed: 1.4.1939.
Stationed at: Truro, Torpoint, St Austell, St
Mawes, Pool, Penryn
No retirement date.

P.C. 186 William James Grenville Peters
Born 2.12.1919.
Appointed: 1.4.1939.
Stationed at: Camborne, St Ives, Newquay,
St Ives, Heamoor, Sennen.
16.7.1949 Resigned.

P.C. 244 Cyril John Petherick
Born 31.8.1916
Appointed: 1.4.1939.
Promotion: 28.3.1957 To Sergeant.
Stationed at: Liskeard, Torpoint, Liskeard,
Torpoint, Pensilva, Bodmin, Redruth.
28.10.1946
Appointed: as PSO 111 in the Special
Police Corps in the Control Commission for
Germany and Austria under the Police
Overseas Service Act, 1945
1.11.1948 Returned to duty.
31.12.1964 Retired.

P.C. 195 Rodney Job Frank Pethick
Born 28.5.1918.
Appointed: 1.6.1939.
Stationed at: Launceston, Callington, Looe, Launceston, Halworthy, Pelynt, Portscatho, Five Lanes.
January 1961 Granted a Favourable Record with DC 79 Radford for persistence in difficult cases of sheep and fowl stealing resulting in the arrest and conviction of four offenders. No retirement date.

P.C. 43 Owen George Bulford
Born 25.4.1919.
Appointed: 1.6.1939.
Stationed at: Newquay, Falmouth, Penryn, Stithians, Wadebridge, Hessenford, Isles of Scilly, Camborne, Newlyn.
October 1964 Granted a Favourable Record for zeal and attention to duty which resulted in the detection of Les Downing charged with offences of Larceny at Newlyn. No retirement date.

P.C. 73 John Bertram Bennett
Born 21.11.1920.
Appointed: 1.6.1939.
Promotion: 18.8.1954 to Sergeant. 18.9.1959 to Inspector. 1.3.1967 to Chief Inspector.
Stationed at: St Austell, Falmouth, Helston, Callington, H.Q. CID, Penzance, Wadebridge, Falmouth, Liskeard.

P.C. 246 Thomas Henry Ivor Thomas
Born 6.10.1917.
Appointed: 1.6.1939.
Stationed at: Torpoint, Falmouth, Grampound, Newlyn East,
30.9.1950 Retired through ill-health.

P.C. 84 Ivan Morley Harper
Born 14.2.1920.
Appointed: 1.6.1939.
Stationed at: H.Q.,
31.12.1946 resigned.

P.C. 80 Charlie Couch
Born 30.6.1914
Appointed: 1.6.1939.
Stationed at: Camelford, Lostwithiel, St Blazey Gate.
8.6.1942 resigned.

P.C. 136 Harvey Bryan Hillier
Born 26.1.1921.
Appointed: 1.6.1939.
Stationed at: Liskeard, Looe, Polperro,
3.5.1940 Resigned.

P.C. 146 William Grerson Moffat
Born 19.12.1919.
Appointed: 1.6.1939
Stationed at: Penryn, Falmouth, Penryn, Falmouth.
19.10.1941 resigned.

P.C. 194 Cyril Douglas Mitchell
Born 5.3.1920
Appointed: 1.6.1939.
Stationed at: Helston, Falmouth, Liskeard, Torpoint Truro, Perranwell,
28.12.1946 resigned.

P.C. 243 John Harris Pomeroy
Born 3.10.1920.
Appointed: 1.6.1939.
Stationed at:
Padstow, Fowey, Stratton, Launceston, Stratton, Week St Mary, Launceston, H.Q. Admin.
18.7.1966 Retired.

P.C. 245 Harold Parken
Born 4.8.1917.
Appointed: 1.6.1939.
Promotion: 2.4.1958 to Sergeant
Stationed at: Truro, Saltash, Liskeard, Launceston, H.Q.Traffic, Camborne Traffic.
15.8.1964 Retired..

P.C. 128 Philip James Bennett
Born 31.1.1917.
Appointed: 1.7.1939.
Stationed at: Bodmin, Padstow, St Merryn, St Austell, Bodmin, St Austell, H.Q. Traffic. No retirement date.

P.C. 247 Charles Stephens Gill
Born 25.1.1917.
Appointed: 1.7.1939.
Stationed at: Camborne, St Austell, Connor Downs,
12.10.1946 resigned.

P.C. 223 Samuel Charles Richards
Born 31.12.1916
Appointed: 1.9.1939.
Promotion: 1.5.1955 to Sergeant.
Stationed at: Truro. Falmouth, Perranwell, Launceston, Looe, Callington.
No retirement date.

P.C. 187 William Horace Smith
Born 12.2.1915.
Appointed: 1.9.1939.
Stationed at: H.Q., Bodmin, Five Lanes,
28.2.1948 Resigned.

P.C. 81 Edwin Maurice Thomas
Born 15.4.1917
Appointed: 1.9.1939.
Promotion: 7.3.1958 to Sergeant.
Stationed at: Newquay, Lanivet, Port Isaac, Fowey, St Austell, Launceston, Newquay, Bude, Newquay.
No retirement date.

P.C. 183 Thomas Collins
Born 10.5.1916.
Appointed: 1.9.1939.
Stationed at: Camborne,
24.8.1943 Missing presumed killed on flying ops.

P.C. 125 Daniel Edwards
Born 12.1.1918.
Appointed: 1.10.1939.
Stationed at: H.Q., Redruth.
8.10.1944 Reported killed in action serving with the Hampshire Regt, in Italy.

P.C. 206 Norman Roy Hooper
Born 19.3.1916.
Appointed: 1.10.1939.
Stationed at: St Austell, Fowey, Padstow,

Wadebridge, St Erth.
26.10.1946 resigned.

P.C. 200 Kenneth Albert William Tozer
Born 12.3.1917.
Appointed: 1.10.1939.
Promotion: 1.6.1959 to Sergeant.
Stationed at: Truro. St Ives, Camborne, Helston, Penzance, Newlyn, Padstow, St Austell.
30.12.1941 Granted a Favourable Record for zeal and efficiency in making enquiries re a case of larceny which resulted in his arresting the offender.
31.3.1966 retired.

P.C. 86 William Henry Jago
Born 25.9.1920.
Appointed: 1.2.1941.
Stationed at: Chief Constables' Office, Bodmin, St Austell, Falmouth, Grampound, Camborne, Launceston.
No retirement date.

P.C. 5 Norman Kingdom Dewings
Born 12.8.1921.
Appointed: 1.5.1941.
Promotion: 1.6.1955 to Sergeant. 8.4.1963 to Inspector. 1.4.1965 to Chief Inspector.
Stationed at: Newquay, Liskeard, Nancledra, Chyandour, Falmouth, St Austell, Helston, St Ives, Penzance.
No retirement date.

P.C. 7 William Henry Dyer
Born 31.3.1922.
Appointed: 1.5.1941.
Promotion: 1.5.1955 to Sergeant.
Stationed at: Falmouth, St Austell, St Blazey, Port Isaac, Lostwithiel, Falmouth, Launceston.
No retirement date.

P.C. 18 William Charles Rowe
Born 8.5.1921.
Appointed: 1.5.1941.
21.6.1941 Left to join the RAF

P.C. 11 Kenneth Reginald George Rawlings
Born 2.2.1922.
Appointed: 1.5.1941.
Stationed at: Torpoint, Callington.
30.4.1942 Resigned.

P.C. 51 Richard John Woolcock
Born 8.9.1921.
Appointed: 1.5.1941.
Stationed at: Falmouth, Penryn, Launceston, Stratton,
28.12.1946 Resigned.

P.C. 60 William Howard Denver Bennett
Born 4.5.1922.
Appointed: 1.7.1941.
Stationed at: Liskeard, Wadebridge, Torpoint, Launceston, Boscastle.
30.7.1949 Resigned.

P.C. 63 Christopher John Carlyon Harris
Born 23.7.1921.
Appointed: 1.7.1941.
Promotion: 1.6.1955 to Sergeant.
Stationed at: Camborne, Liskeard, Newquay,

Tregoney,
No retirement date.

P.C. 67 Alfred Trahair Jenkin
Born 9.2.1922.
Appointed: 1.7.1941.
Promotion: 9.11.1955 to Sergeant.
12.8.1959 to Detective Inspector. 1.9.1951
to Chief Inspector. 1.4.1955 to
Superintendent. 1.6.1967 to Chief
Superintendent.
Stationed at: Falmouth, St Ives, St Erth,
Sennen, Penzance, Newquay, Launceston
CID, Penzance, H.Q. CID.
No retirement date.

P.C. 18 Joseph Eric Johns
Born 12.3.1922.
Appointed: 1.7.1941.
30.11.1949 Retired through ill health.
16.9.1951 Rejoined as P.C. 36.
Stationed at: Launceston, St Just, Pendeen,
Redruth, Wadebridge.
No retirement date.

P.C. 248 Christopher James
Born 1906
Appointed: 16.10.1941.
Stationed at: Penzance.
17.4.1961 Retired.

P.C. 35 Lawrence Richard Maidman
Born 1.10.1919.
Appointed: 1.2.1946.
Stationed at: Looe, Torpoint, St Keverne,
Crowlas, Torpoint, Mullion.
No retirement date.

P.C. 37 Victor Charles Magor
Born 18.4.1920.
Appointed: 1.2.1946.
Stationed at: Falmouth, St Austell, Lelant, St
Buryan
7.6.1952 resigned.

P.C. 26 Eric Alfred Doughty
Born 30.11.1919.
Appointed: 1.2.1946.
Stationed at: St Austell, Falmouth, Truro,
Rilla Mill, Fowey, Dobwalls, Liskeard.
No Retirement date.

P.C. 23 Douglas Roger Hocking
Born 28.4.1918.
Appointed: 1.2.1946.
Stationed at: Fowey, St Buryan, Charlestown,
Marazion, Bugle.
No retirement date.

P.C. 27 Eric Edward Clark
Born 14.3.1920.
Appointed: 1.2.1946.
Stationed at: Falmouth.
31.7.1946 Resigned.

P.C. 34 Ronald Edgar Bolton
Born 9.1.1923.
Appointed: 1.2.1946.
Stationed at: St Ives
8.3.1947 Resigned.

P.C. 11 Peter Noall Francis Xavier Re-Foy
Born 23.12.1921.
Appointed: 1.2.1946.
Stationed at: Launceston, Menheniot.
13.11.1948 Resigned.

P.C. 38 Donald Leslie Waters
Born 1.3.1918
Appointed: 1.2.1946
Stationed at: Penzance, Redruth Highway,
Newlyn, Pendeen, Slades, St Austell,
Tywardreath, Redruth.

P.C. 28 Emrys Davies
Born 22.11.1917
Appointed: 1.2.1946.
Stationed at: Newquay
28.9.1946 Resigned.

P.C. 64 John Hoare
Born 3.5.1923
Appointed: 1.3.1946.
Stationed at: Redruth, St Ives.
19.7.1947 Resigned.

P.C. 80 Wilfred James Bottle
Born 4.4.1920.
Appointed: 1.3.1946.
27.4.1936 Resigned.

P.C. 59 John Charles Reginald Tucker
Born 19.9.1920.
Appointed: 1.3.1946.
Stationed at: H.Q.
16.3.1946 Resigned on medical grounds.

P.C. 77 Dennis Edward Richard Troke
Born 15.11.1918.
Appointed: 1.3.1946.
Stationed at: Looe.
12.10.1946 Resigned.

P.C. 52 Foster Owen Thomas
Born 20.8.1924.
Appointed: 1.3.1946.
Stationed at: Bude, Launceston, St Neot,
Kingsand, Lostwithiel, Looe.

P.C. 87 William James Langthorne Davis
Born 29.10.1923.
Appointed: 1.3.1946.
Stationed at: H.Q.
8.3.1947 Resigned.

P.C. 40 George Alan Goodman
Born 2.10.1919.
Appointed: 1.3.1946.
Promotion: 22.7.1954 to Sergeant.
1.4.1964 to Inspector.
Stationed at: Truro. Lanivet, Isles of Scilly, St
Blazey, Looe, Torpoint, Bodmin, H.Q.

P.C. 89 William James Arnold Harvey
Born 31.5.1919.
Appointed: 24.3.1946.
Stationed at: Camborne
31.8.1946 Resigned.

P.C. 85 George Kelynack Richards
Born 17.8.1925.
Appointed: 24.3.1946
Promotion: 1.6.1955 to Sergeant. 1.9.1961

to Inspector. 1.9.1965 to Superintendent.
Stationed at: Truro, Bugle, Penzance, H.Q.
Training, Bodmin.

P.C. 83 Arnold Floyd
Born 11.10.1925
Appointed: 24.3.1946.
Promotion: 1.9.1963 to Sergeant. 1.3.1967
to Inspector.
Stationed at: Wadebridge, St Austell.
Penzance, St Minver, H.Q. Traffic, Newquay,
Liskeard.
October 1943 Awarded the R.S.P.C.A.
Framed certificate of merit for rescuing a dog
from a 50 foot disused mine shaft at
Carclaze, St Austell, on 7.9.1943 whilst
employed as a Cadet.

P.C. 98 Rupert Eton Jones
Born 9.11.1920.
Appointed: 31.3.1946.
Stationed at: Bodmin, St Austell,
Tywardreath, Probus.
27.11.1954 Resigned.

P.C. 100 Arnold Fairhurst
Born 22.5.1922.
Appointed: 31.3.1946.
Stationed at: Falmouth, Polruan, Blue
Anchor, Camborne, H.Q. CID.

P.C. 94 John Patrick Doherty
Born 19.12.1918.
Appointed: 31.3.1946.
Promotion: 19.2.1958 to Sergeant.
Stationed at: Penzance , H.Q., Truro,
Camelford, Falmouth.
27.9.1958 Granted a Favourable Record
with P.C. 116 Gibbs for vigilance displayed
at Truro on 25.8.1956 resulting in the arrest
of John Christopher Brown convicted on
charges of larceny and obtaining money by
forged instrument and credit by fraud

P.C. 92 Joseph Rowe
Born 1.6.1926
Appointed: 31.3.1946.
Stationed at: Launceston, Pelynt,
Launceston, Penzance.
18.9.1958 Died.

P.C. 97 Norman John Arscott
Born 4.4.1918.
Appointed: 31.3.1946.
Promotion: 2.4.1958 to Sergeant.
Stationed at: Falmouth, Blisland ,
Wadebridge, Newquay, Falmouth.
1.3.1953 Granted a Favourable Record with
Inspector W.T.Walke for their competent and
efficient action at Trevose Golf Club where
their alertness and attention to duty resulted
in the arrest of six men for burglary who
were committed to Cornwall Assize for
eleven breaks and twelve larcenies.

P.C. 124 Stanley Herbert Morgan
Born 27.8.1920.
Appointed: 1.5.1946.
Stationed at: Falmouth.
28.9 1946 Resigned

P.C. 105 Frederick Welch
Born 3.5.1917
Appointed: 1.5.1946.
Stationed at: H.Q.
9.7.1946 Resigned.

P.C. 104 Charles Lionel Clark
Born 7.10.1921.
Appointed: 1.5.1946.
Stationed at: Wadebridge, Torpoint, Burraton, Delabole, Stoke Climsland, St Austell.

P.C. 99 Thomas Charles Arthur Cox
Born 2.4.1922.
Appointed: 1.5.1946
Promotion: 1.9.1961 to Sergeant,
Stationed at: Falmouth, Seaton, Camborne.
26.4.1950 Granted a Favourable Record with P.C. 68 Eden for the very zealous and able manner in which they dealt with 23 cases of larceny, 7 cases of receiving and one case of store breaking at Falmouth which resulted in eight juveniles and four adults being convicted at Falmouth Magistrates Court on 21.4.1950.

P.C. 120 Douglas Ivan Jory
Born 4.3.1919.
Appointed: 1.5.1946.
Stationed at: Newquay, St Neot, St Austell, Mevagissey.

P.C. 112 Douglas Richard LeWarne
Born 19.3.1918.
Appointed: 1.5.1946.
Stationed at: Falmouth, St Columb Minor, St Austell, Bodmin, Launceston,
30.11.1961 With P.C. 185 Hancock granted a Favourable Record for keen observation and attention to duty resulting in the conviction of two persons on charges of larceny and receiving stolen petrol
28.2.1963 Resigned.

P.C. 121 Norman George Rundle
Born 18.6.1918.
Appointed: 1.5.1946.
Stationed at: Looe, Lostwithiel,
4.9.1948 Resigned.

P.C. 101 Alfred John Stevens
Born 15.2.1924
Appointed: 1.5.1946.
Stationed at: Torpoint, Information Room, Liskeard.

P.C. 118 Joseph Henry Blatchford
Born 31.3.1925.
Appointed: 1.5.1946
Promotion: 18.9.1955 to Sergeant.
1.10.1964 to Detective Inspector. 1.6.1967 to Chief Inspector.
Stationed at: St Ives, Pendeen, Falmouth, Torpoint, Newquay, H.Q. CID, Truro.

P.C. 160 Henry Frederick Charles Bulley
Born 16.5.1921.
Appointed: 17.6.1946
Promotion: 25.8.1858 to Sergeant.
Stationed at: Falmouth, Liskeard, St Austell, Camborne, Truro, H.Q.Traffic, Tywardreath, H.Q. Information Room.

P.C. 146 John Thomas Jackson
Born 29.9.1924
Appointed: 1.6.1946
Stationed at: Callington, Falmouth, St Columb Minor, Chacewater, Newlyn East, Launceston, St Blazey, Liskeard, Wadebridge.

P.C. 130 Norman Gordon Kohler
Born 1.1.1919.
Appointed: 1.6.1946.
Stationed at: Penzance
1.5.1948 Resigned.

P.C. 136 Robert Thomas Martin
Born 2.9.1920.
Appointed: 1.6.1946.
Stationed at: H.Q.
27.7.1946 Resigned.

P.C. 125 Bruce Shaw
Born 14.12.1922.
Appointed: 1.6.1946.
Stationed at: H.Q.
19.10.1946 Resigned.

P.C. 145 Frederick Godfrey Tregonning
Born 17.6.1920.
Appointed: 4.6.1946.
Stationed at: Falmouth.
6.9.1947 Resigned.

P.C. 165 Richard Norman Davis
Born 16.12.1922.
Appointed: 17.6.1946.
Stationed at: Wadebridge.
9.8.1947 Resigned.

P.C. 158 Frederick Walter Davies
Born 26.7.1922.
Appointed: 17.6.1946.
Stationed at: Bodmin.
29.3.1947. Resigned.

P.C. 156 Ronald Samson
Born 10.3.1922.
Appointed: 17.6.1946.
Stationed at: Bude.
30.9.1950 Resigned.

P.C. 164 Leslie James Mayne
Born 13.8.1920.
Appointed: 20.6.1946.
Stationed at: Truro, Menheniot, Callington, Newquay, Bodmin, Perranporth

P.C. 163 Leslie Dobson
Born 1.3.1920.
Appointed: 20.6.1946.
Promotion: 30.9.1954 to Sergeant.
1.4.1965 to Inspector.
Stationed at: Saltash, Tintagel, Padstow, Penryn, Bodmin,
3.7.1953 Awarded the Royal Humane Society's Bronze medal and certificate for the part he played in an attempt rescue from drowning at Trebarwith Strand, Tintagel, when he was lowered over a cliff on three separate occasions.

P.C. 174 Douglas Roy Whetter
Born 9.4.1919.
Appointed: 1.8.1946.
Promotion: 1.1.1959 to Sergeant.

1.4.1965 to Inspector.
Stationed at: Falmouth, Mylor, Falmouth, St Columb, Saltash, St Ives.
30.4.1960. Granted a Favourable Record with P.C. 136 Todd for zeal and devotion to duty which resulted in three persons being convicted on a number of charges of larceny and shop breaking in various parts of Cornwall.

P.C. 171 Sidney Bright
Born 29,9.1921.
Appointed: 1.8.1946.
Stationed at: Wadebridge.
30.9.1947 Resigned.

P.C. 183 Dennis James Davey
Born 20.4.1922.
Appointed: 1.8.1946.
Stationed at: Tregoney
12.4.1947 Resigned.

P.C. 172 Arthur Robert John Rowse
Born 8.12.1926
Appointed: 1.8.1946.
Stationed at: Falmouth
Granted a Favourable Record for his promptitude , pluck, and devotion to duty on attempting to stop a runaway horse on 18.1.1947.
12.7.1947 Resigned.

P.C. 177 Arthur William Bray
Born 13.5.1921.
Appointed: 1.8.1946.
Stationed at: Newquay, Camborne, Newlyn, Higher Town, Truro,
27.9.1950 Granted a Favourable Record for vigilance displayed at Penzance on 4.8.1956 when off duty and in plain clothes he followed a man and woman and saw them steal from Messrs Woolworth's stores. He arrested them and they were convicted of larceny from shops at Penzance Borough Magistrates Court on 27.8.1956.

P.C. 188 Norman Henry Poynton
Born 27.12.1922.
Appointed: 2.8.1946.
Stationed at: Penryn
26.6.1948 Resigned.

P.C. 205 Richard John Dunn
Born 9.1.1924.
Appointed: 6.8.1946.
Promotion: 27.7.1958 to Sergeant.
20.5.1953 to Inspector. 1.11.1965 to Chief Inspector.
Stationed at: Helston. Polperro, Launceston, Saltash, Helston, St Austell.

P.C. 167 Leonard Victor Bullock
Born 1.9.1899.
Appointed: 31.8.1946.
Stationed at: Falmouth.

P.C. 218 John Edward Bennett
Born 31.10.1920.
Appointed: 2.9.1946.
Stationed at: Newquay.
6.9.1947 Resigned.

P.C. 209 Hugh Godfrey Reginald Pill
Born 26.7.1925
Appointed: 2.9.1946.
Stationed at: Truro, Launceston,
27.8.1948. Resigned.

P.C. 214 Thomas Victor Cullum
Born 20.9.1918.
Appointed: 2.9.1946.
Stationed at: Bodmin, Lostwithiel, St Austell,
Bude, St Austell.
20.1.1964 Resigned.

P.C. 210 Richard Henry Wells
Born 15.1.1920.
Appointed: 4.9.1946
Stationed at: Camborne
28.8.1948 Resigned.

P.C. 219 Keith Edwin Charles Hatcher
Born 16.11.1919.
Appointed: 16.9.1946.
Stationed at: Fowey, St Austell, St Just,
Lanivet.

P.C. 8 Edmund Walter Whitmore
Born 29.4.1923.
Appointed: 16.9.1946.
Stationed at: Redruth
29.11.1947 Resigned.

P.C. 221 Maurice Palmer
Born 16.11.1921
Appointed: 16.9.1946.
Stationed at: Truro., Lanner, Bude, Liskeard,
Torpoint

P.C. 224 Arthur Ronald Searson
Born 16.,12.1921.
Appointed: 16.9.1946.
Stationed at: Penryn, St Blazey
8.3.1943 Resigned.

P.C. 15 Desmond Walter Barnes
Born 8.2.1926.
Appointed: 16.9.1946.
Stationed at: Camborne
4.10.1947 Resigned.

P.C. 27 Samuel John Masters
Born 12.3.1925.
Appointed: 16.9.1946.
Stationed at: St Austell.
25.12.1948 Resigned.

P.C. 48 Douglas Laity
Born 16.1.1922.
Appointed: 1.10.1946.
Promotion: 8.5.1957 to Detective Sergeant.
Stationed at: Truro, Lanivet, Bodmin, Truro,
Camborne.
May 1948   Granted a Favourable Record
for his keenness and devotion to duty at
Truro on 8.3.1948 which culminated in
three youths being charged at Truro City
Court on 6.4.1948 for office breaking and
store breaking. They were ordered to attend
an approved school
June 1949 Granted a Favourable Record for
his keenness and devotion to duty at Truro
on the 18.3.1949 which culminated in
Arthur Jones a disqualified driver of all motor
vehicles being convicted at Truro Magistrates

court on 28.3.1949. under three sections of
the Road Traffic Act, 1930.
26.9.1957 Granted a Favourable Record
together with W.P.S. Adcock for their visit in
connection with Registered Clubs

P.C. 58 Brendon White
Born 3.4.1924.
Appointed: 1.10.1946.
Promotion: 1.3.1963 to Sergeant.
Stationed at: Liskeard, Falmouth, Penryn,
Falmouth, Mawnan Smith, Truro, H.Q.
Information Room, Bodmin.
28.10.1953 Granted a Favourable Record
with DC 97 Arscott for their prompt and
efficient action at Trevose Golf Club, when
their attention to duty resulted in the arrest
of six men for burglary who were later
committed to the Assize. In addition they
were concerned in eleven breaking offences
and twelve larcenies.

P.C. 71 Redvers Jack Hill
Born 24.11.1924
Appointed: 1.11.1946.
Stationed at: Fowey, Lerryn, Fowey, Rilla
Mill, Looe and St Erth.

P.C. 59 Thomas Huby   Born 3.1.1923.
Appointed: 1.11.1946.
Stationed at: Wadebridge, St Austell, Hayle,
Penzance Camborne, Bude.
October 1948.   Granted a Favourable
Record with DC 20 Clymo and DC 131
Holsgrave for their perseverance and devo-
tion to duty in obtaining evidence which
resulted in the detection of the offender in a
case of shop breaking at Wadebridge and
clearing up eight other offences.

P.C. 77 Kenneth Howard Etheridge
Born 15.4.1926.
Appointed: 11.11.1946.
Stationed at: St Austell, Wadebridge,
9.10.1949 Transferred to the Metropolitan
Police.

P.C. 105 Phillip Ricketts
Born 12.1.1925.
Appointed: 1.12.1946.
Stationed at: Callington
31.7.1948 Resigned.

P.C. 88 Leonard Albert Rumbalow
Born 3.8.1920
Appointed: 1.12.1946.
Stationed at: Bodmin, Constantine, Penryn,
Chacewater.

P.C. 80 Arthur Robert Harcourt Stilliard
Born 17.6.1918.
Appointed: 1.12.1946.
Stationed at: Fowey,
5.7.1947. Resigned.

P.C. 89 Richard George Trewella
Born 3.2.1921.
Appointed: 1.12.1946.
Promotion: 13.4.1962 to Sergeant.
Stationed at: Redruth, Porkellis, St Austell,
Penzance, H.Q. Information Room,
Falmouth.

P.C. 124 Kenneth John Roberts
Born 4.1.1926.
Appointed: 1.12.1946.
Stationed at: Launceston.
29.2.1947 Resigned.

P.C. 137 Edward Pryce Hamer
Born 25.2.1924
Appointed: 23.12.1946.
Promotion: 5.4.1959 to Sergeant.
Stationed at: Newquay, Truro,
St Mellyn, Calstock, Millbrook,
Wadebridge, Looe,
St Just, Penzance.

P.C. 140 William George Hains
Born 1.7.1925.
Appointed: 23.12.1946.
Stationed at: Falmouth
4.2.1950 Resigned.

P.C. 125 Howard Edward Nevill
Born 8.6.1920.
Appointed: 23.12.1946.
Stationed at: Truro, Grampound.
27.5.1950 Resigned.

P.C. 206 Robert Howell Burnett
Born 1.7.1924.
Appointed: 30.12.1946.
Stationed at: Falmouth
10.7.1948 Resigned during probation.

P.C. 212 James Edward Martin
Born 11.1.1923.
Appointed: 30.12.1946.
Stationed at: Truro, Portscatho.
30.11.1950 Transferred to Leicestershire.

P.C. 215 Edward James Rogers
Born 12.12.1927
Appointed: 30.12.1946.
Stationed at: Liskeard
27.12.1947 Resigned

P.C. 226 Kenneth Charles Bates
Born 11.1.1923.
Appointed: 30.12.1946.
Promotion: 1.3.1964 to Sergeant.
Stationed at: Launceston, Boscastle, St
Merryn, Looe.

P.C. 247 Ronald Victor Hunt
Born 28.9.1921.
Appointed: 1.1.1947.
Stationed at: St Ives.
8.11.1947 Resigned

P.C. 75 Charles Eldred Stanley Chapman
Born 7.2.1927.
Appointed: 13.1.1947.
Promotion: 1.7.1963 to Sergeant.
Stationed at: Newquay, Halworthy,
St Minver, Looe, Liskeard.

P.C. 191 Vaskaby Lester
Born 24.5.1919.
Appointed: 13.1.1947.
Stationed at: Tregoney Bodmin, Newquay,
Menheniot.
31.8.1959 Granted a Favourable Record
with DC 80 Bayliss for keenness and devo-
tion to duty resulting in the arrest of Stanley

Haw at Newquay for larceny of a motor car in Hampshire

P.C. 136 Leslie Samuel Todd
Born 7.11.1919.
Appointed: 13.1.1947.
Stationed at: Looe , Anthony, St Columb.
30.7.1960 Granted a favourable Record with Sgt Whetter for zeal and devotion to duty which resulted in three persons convicted of a number of charges of shop breaking

P.C. 28 John William Steven Thomas
Born 20.3.1925.
Appointed: 13.1.1947.
Stationed at: Bodmin,
30.10.1948 Resigned.

P.C. 51 Albert George Lawrence
Born 21.5.1922.
Appointed: 13.1.1947.
Stationed at: Hayle.
24.5.1947 Resigned.

P.C. 4 Samuel Alfred Goldsworthy
Born 11.3.1923
Appointed: 17.2.1947.
Promotion: 2.4.1958 to Sergeant.
Stationed at: Stratton, St Erth, Chyandour, Callington, Looe.

P.C. 69 Frederick John Michael White
Born 29.9.1922.
Appointed: 21.2.1947.
Stationed at: Looe, St Cleer, Bude, Falmouth.
27.6.1957. Granted a Favourable Record for his initiative and tenacity of purpose displayed in effecting the arrest of James Stanley Wheatley Robinson at Bude on 15.5.1957 for garage breaking. At Manchester Assize on 5.6.1957 was sentenced to ten years preventative detention. Judge Sir Basil Meild commended the P.C. For arresting a very dangerous criminal 24.10.1927 Awarded the Queens Commendation for brave conduct in connection with this arrest.
4.11.1957 Seconded to Cyprus.

P.C. 122 Henry Ingwold Craig
Born 27.9.1916
Appointed: 3.3.1947.
Transferred from the Police at Durham
Promotion: 1.3.1952 to Sergeant.
Stationed at: Penryn, Falmouth, Wadebridge, Camborne, H.Q.Traffic, Newquay.
8.2.1964 Retired.

P.C. 123 William Charles Hockley
Born 12.4.1924
Appointed: 20.3.1947.
Stationed at: Launceston
27.12.1947 Resigned.

P.C. 34 Jack Snell
Born 1.5.1927.
Appointed: 20.3.1947.
Stationed at: Camborne, Newquay, Helston, St Keverne
30.9.1954 Resigned.

P.C. 141 John Raymond Tamblin
Born 4.6.1919.
Appointed: 20.3.1947.
Stationed at: Camborne, Nancledra, Hayle, Truro.
21.11.1956 Granted a Favourable Record for keenness and observation resulting in the conviction of Charles Hutchinson Anderson for larceny of animal foodstuffs value £42.1.6.
31.8.1965 Granted a Favourable Record for zeal and attention to duty which resulted in the conviction of William Desmond Roger Brooking on charges of indecent exposure , indecent assault and larceny.

P.C. 203 Roy Davenport
Born 24.8.1926.
Appointed: 20.3.1947.
Stationed at: Hayle
23.8.1947 Resigned.

P.C. 194 Robert Raymond Jennings
Born 23.10.1925.
Appointed: 20.3.1947.
Stationed at: Liskeard, Lezant, Stoke Climsland, Bodmin.
2.2.1959 Resigned.

P.C. 7 George Brown
Born 23.9.1909. 14.10.1939 to 31.3.1947 Penzance Borough Police
Promotion: 28.1.1939 to Sergeant. 7.8.1940 to Inspector. 1.5.1951 to Chief Inspector. 1.4.1957 to Superintendent. 1.4.1964 to Superintendent Grade 1.
Stationed at: Penzance , Falmouth, Liskeard, St Austell.

P.C. 124 Theodore Leslie Sandercock
Born 21.1.1927.
Appointed: 1.4.1947.
Stationed at: Truro, Tregoney, Jacobstow, Helston, Camborne.

P.C. 87 David John Giles
Born 17.11.1922.
Appointed: 17.4.1947.
Stationed at: Bude.
19.2.1949 Resigned.

P.C. 84 Henry Orchard
Born 25.3.1922.
Appointed: 17.4.1947.
Stationed at: Falmouth.
23.8.1947 Resigned.

P.C. 183 Reginald Arthur Bruce
Born 6.5.1926.
Appointed: 21.5.1947.
Stationed at: Falmouth.
19.3.1949 Resigned.

P.C. 207 Horace Franklin Laity
Born 19.11.1924
Appointed: 21.5.1947.
Stationed at: Hayle, Isles of Scilly, Redruth, Hayle , Truro, H.Q.C.I.D. Camborne.
December 1947 Granted a Favourable Record for devotion to duty at Hayle on 10.9.1947 for which he was commended by Mr. Justice Lewis at the Assize on 1.11.1947

when Arthur William Blackwell was sentenced to three years Penal Servitude and twelve months imprisonment concurrent for unlawful wounding and twelve months imprisonment concurrent for assaulting a Police Office in the execution of his duty with the intent to resist lawful arrest.

P.C. 158 Peter Lawrey
Born 19.12.1924.
Appointed: 21.5.1947.
Stationed at: Falmouth, St Minver, St Germans.
25.5.1949 Granted a Favourable Record for his courage and devotion to duty in rescuing Donald Pascoe, aged 4 years, of 26 Greenbank Terrace, Falmouth, from drowning in the sea near Greenbank Pier, Falmouth, on 29.1.1949.
12.8, 1949 Presented with the Royal Humane's Society's Testimonial on vellum.
14.10.1957 Transferred to Plymouth City Police.

P.C. 119 Samuel John Oliver
Born 4.1.1927.
Appointed: 30.6.1947.
Stationed at: Callington, Liskeard, Halworthy, Blisland.
15.5.1954 Resigned.

P.C. 131 Howard Ernest Holsgrove
Born 9.2.1922.
Appointed: 21.7.1947.
Stationed at: Wadebridge.
October 1948 With DC 20 Clymo and P.C. 59 Thomas Huby Granted a Favourable Record for their perseverance and devotion to duty in obtaining evidence which resulted in the detection of the offender in a case of shop breaking at Wadebridge and clearing eight other offences.
29.1.1949 Resigned.

P.C. 80 Joseph Hunt
Born 4.9.1918.
Appointed: 21.7.1947.
Stationed at: St Ives
8.11.1947 Resigned.

Ernest Victor Thomas
Worcestershire Constabulary from 5.8.1947 to 13.2.1966
Transferred to the Cornwall Constabulary as Superintendent at H.Q. Traffic

W.P.C. 2 Anne Miller Westcott
Born 5.9.1921.
Appointed: 18.8.1947
Stationed at: Truro
30.7.1949 Resigned.

W.P.C. 1 Margaret McRae Bulley Nee Lacey
Born 20.8.1919.
Appointed: 18.8.1947
Stationed at: Falmouth. St Austell. Camborne, Truro.
26.1.1957 Resigned.

P.C. 84 **Lewis Behenna**
Born 11.5.1923.
Appointed: 25.8.1947.
Stationed at: St Austell, Bodmin.
25.10.1952 Resigned.

P.C. 233 **Robert Ernest Morgan**
Born 13.11.1921
Appointed: 25.8.1947.
Stationed at: Truro, Falmouth, Penryn,
Stithians, Camborne, St Minver.

P.C. 203 **Kenneth Godfrey Penhaligan**
Born 31.5.1923.
Appointed: 25.8.1947.
Stationed at: St Just.

P.C. 172 **Cyril Gordon Leach**
Born 7.3.1900.
Appointed: 31.8.1947
Stationed at: Penzance.
10.3.1955 Resigned.

P.C. 161 **Albert Collins**
Born 24.7.1906.
Appointed: 31.8.1947.
Stationed at: Carbis Bay.
Awarded the R.S.P.C.A. Bronze Medal and
Certificate for the rescue of a dog from a
mine shaft at Lelant Downs
13.9.1960 Died..

P.C. 64 **Isaac Glasson**
Born 23.12.1906.
Appointed: 31.8.1947.
Stationed at: Falmouth, Praze.
30.9.1963 Retired.

P.C. 132 **Edward Randolf Perry**
Born 4.6.1902.
Appointed: 31.8.1947.
30.8.1947 War Reserve.
Stationed at: Helston
3.6.1959 Retired.

P.C. 165 **Percival Franklin White**
Born 31.8.1902.
Appointed: 31.8.1947.
War Reservist
Stationed at: Perranporth
23.7.1960 Retired.

P.C. 167 **Leonard Victor Bullock**
Born 1.9.1899.
Appointed: 31.8.1947.
War Reservist
Stationed at: Falmouth
31.8.1954 Retired.

P.C. 145 **John William James King**
Born 12.10.1923
Appointed: 8.9.1947.
Promotion: 1.6.1967 to Sergeant.
Stationed at: Redruth, Isles of Scilly,
Wadebridge, Goldsithney, Carbis Bay, St
Austell.

P.C. 218 **John James Arnold**
Born 7.8.1923
Appointed: 22.9.1947.
Stationed at: Fowey, Truro, Chacewater,
31.12.1955 Resigned.

P.C. 171 **Horace George Mark Webber**
Born 11.5.1927.
Appointed: 22.9.1947.
Stationed at: Launceston, Delabole, Burraton,
Looe, Pensilva.

P.C. 260 **Sidney Edward Crick**
Born 20.4.1906.
Appointed: 28.9.1947.
7.10.1940 to 27.9.1947 Served as Police
War Reserve
Stationed at: Newquay.
19.4.1965 Retired

P.C. 262 **Albert Edward Harry Peck**
Born 15.6.1926.
Appointed: 6.10.1947.
Stationed at: St Ives, St Just, St Ives , Sennen.
23.3.1952 Resigned,

P.C. 143 **George Henry Skellham**
Born 31.12.1921.
Appointed: 6.10.1947.
Stationed at: Truro, Duloe, Kingsand,
Liskeard, Isles of Scilly, St Austell.

P.C. 15 **Dennis Frederick Wynch**
Born 22.4.1927
Appointed: 6.10.1947.
Stationed at: Falmouth, H.Q.Traffic, Bugle ,
St Agnes, Padstow,

P.C. 261 **Peter Donald Ward**
Born 19.6.1925
Appointed: 6.10.1947.
Promotion: 1.6.1967 to Sergeant.
Stationed at: Stratton, St Columb Minor,
Penzance, Pool, Isles of Scilly, St Ives, Hayle.
31.7.1964 Granted a Favourable Record for
his zeal and attention to duty which resulted
in the arrest of George Hughes and Roger
Stevens on charges of larceny of cash and
receiving committed in Liverpool.

P.C. 80 **William Solin Bayliss**
Born 15.1.1923.
Appointed: 17.11.1947.
Promotion: 18.9.1959 to Sergeant. 1.4.1964
to Detective Inspector. 1.4.1967 to Chief
Inspector.
Stationed at: Falmouth, Mawnan Smith,
Torpoint, Newquay, Penzance, St Austell.
31.8.1959 Granted a Favourable Record
with P.C. 191 Lester for keenness and devo-
tion to duty resulting in the arrest of Stanley
Maw at Newquay for larceny of a motor car
from Hampshire.

P.C. 263 **Ernest Albert Cock**
Born 30.5.1925.
Appointed: 17.11.1947.
Stationed at: Falmouth
28.5.1949 Resigned.

P.C. 264 **Oswold George Gilbert**
Born 10.11.1926.
Appointed: 17.11.1947.
Stationed at: St Austell, Launceston, Bude,
Newlyn East, Newquay, Pelynt.

P.C. 247 **William John Robins**
Born 11.8.1925.
Appointed: 17.11.1947.

Promotion: 9.11.1959 to Sergeant.
Stationed at: St Austell, Falmouth,
Tywardreath, Polruan, Illogan, Truro.

P.C. 242 **Bernard Harry Smith**
Born 27.1.1923.
Appointed: 17.11.1947.
Stationed at:,
Newquay, Camborne
12.6.1948 Resigned.

P.C. 265 **John Ernest Martyn Lamerton**
Born 19.5.1925.
Appointed: 18,11.1947.
Transferred from Somerset Police.
Stationed at: Launceston, Camelford, Week
St Mary, St Buryan, St Austell.
20.1.1964 Resigned.

W.P.C. 3 **Jean Ruby Betty Geddes**
Born 15.4.1920.
Appointed: 18.11.1947.
Stationed at: Camborne, Penzance,
10.3.1951 Resigned.

P.C. 267 **John Bernhard Johanson**
Born 22.2.1925
Appointed: 15.12.1947.
Stationed at: Truro, Newquay.
2.4.1949 Resigned.

P.C. 240 **Gordon Phillips**
Born 25.8.1925
Appointed: 1 5.12.1947.
Promotion: 18.9.1959 to Sergeant.
Stationed at: Newquay, Truro, Tregony,
Hessenford , Stratton, Bude, H.Q.
Information Room, Liskeard.
11.3.1966 Commended by the Chairman
of Liskeard Magistrates Court together with
P.C. 111 Emmett for efficiency and observa-
tion leading to the arrest of Douglas Gosling,
Andrew Ian Boyle and Rodney William Cecil,
on charges of Larceny.

P.C. 8 **Kenneth William Whillock**
Born 22.9.1925.
Appointed: 15.12.1947.
Stationed at: Padstow, Roche,
10.1.1957 Transferred to Lincoln City Police.

P.C. 123 **William John Williams**
Born 4.8.1926.
Appointed: 5.1.1948.
Promotion: 1.6.1959 to Detective Sergeant.
1.4.1964 to Detective Inspector.
Stationed at: H.Q.C.I.D., H.Q. Information
Room, Penzance, Liskeard, Truro
21.10.1966 Commended by the Director of
Public Prosecutions for the efficient manner
in which he investigated the cases of fraud
against Edward and Mary Griffith.

P.C. 215 **Alderman Walford Tucker**
Born 5.4.1926.
Appointed: 5.1.1948.
Stationed at: Newquay.
4.6.1949 Resigned.

P.C. 268 **Wilfred Leslie George Sleep**
Born 2.5.1926
Appointed: 12.1.1948.

Stationed at: Torpoint.
19.3.1949   Resigned.

P.C. 270 Wallace Peter Davey
Born 25.8.1925.
Appointed: 19.1.1948.
Stationed at: St Ives.
14.1.1950   Resigned.

P.C. 269 Eric Lionel James
Born 16.7.1926.
Appointed: 19.1.1948.
Stationed at: Falmouth.
29.1.1949   Resigned.

P.C. 41 Kenneth Charles Gilbert
Born 10.10.1926.
Appointed: 16.2.1948.
Stationed at: St Ives, St Just.
23.10.1948   Resigned.

P.C. 271 William Arthur Pankhurst
Born 15.4.1924.
Appointed: 16.2.1948.
Stationed at: Penzance, Veryan, Trispen,
Helston,

P.C. 144 William Frederick Randolf Fulford
Born 26.2.1923
Appointed: 15.3.1948.
Promotion: 1.4.1965 to Sergeant.
Stationed at: Penzance, Blue Anchor,
Charlestown, St Austell, Falmouth, Praze,
Saltash.

P.C. 187 Richard Desmond Green
Born 14.11.1925.
Appointed: 15.3.1948.
Stationed at: Wadebridge. Five Lanes.
31.12.1952   Resigned.

P.C. 95 Anthony Leon Moate
Born 25.3.1927.
Appointed: 15.3.1948.
Stationed at: Liskeard.
30.10.1948   Resigned.

P.C. 198 John Pearlman Hocking
Born 11.8.1924
Appointed: 19.4.1948.
Stationed at: Camborne, St Mellion, Blue
Anchor, Newquay, Perranporth St Just, Pool.

P.C. 175 Francis Owen Ead
Born. 23.3.1923/.
Appointed: 19.4.1948.
Stationed at: Bodmin
9.4.1949   Resigned.

P.C. 230 William Francis Hoare
Born 26.7.1925.
Appointed: 19.4.1948.
Stationed at: Helston, Trispen, Truro,
Torpoint.

P.C. 272 William Henry Knight
Born 27.12.1927.
Appointed: 3.5.1948.
Stationed at: Launceston
31.12.1954   Resigned.

P.C. 130 Bryce Ward
Born 25.5.1927.
Appointed: 3.5.1948.
Promotion: 1.3.1964 to Sergeant.
Stationed at: Fowey, St Dennis, Newquay,
Penzance.

P.C. 273 John Fenwick Richards
Born 25.7.1927.
Appointed: 10.5.1948.
Promotion: 4.10.1958 to Sergeant.
1.11.1965 to Inspector.
Stationed at: Callington, Liskeard, Looe,
Lerryn, Looe, St Austell, Helston.

P.C. 274 Douglas Francis Smith
Born 27.1.1923.
Appointed: 10.5.1948.
Stationed at: Camborne, Sennen,
Camborne, Penzance.
25.4.1953 Resigned.
Reappointed: as P.C. 46

P.C. 275 George Henry Laity
Born 19.9.1922.
Appointed: 24.5.1948.
Stationed at: Truro, Mawan-in-Pydar, Bude,
Roche, Falmouth.

P.C. 276 Cyril Alan Osborne
Born 13.7.1927.
Appointed: 24.5.1948.
Stationed at: Saltash, Liskeard.
10.9.1949   Resigned.

P.C. 277 Arnold Royston Morgan Bradley
Born 7.2.1927.
Appointed: 24.5.1948.
Promotion: 1.4.1959 to Sergeant.
Stationed at: Bude, Kilkhampton, Duloe,
H.Q. Information Room, Perranporth.

P.C. 279 Albert Edward Truscott
Born 12.12.1927.
Appointed: 14.6.1948.
Promotion: 1.1.1960 to Sergeant. 6.5.1965
to Inspector.
Stationed at: Redruth, Camborne, Redruth,
Truro, Penzance, Newquay, Bude, St Austell.

P.C. 242 Thomas Patrick Fowley
Born 17.7.1921.
Appointed: 14.6.1948.
Stationed at: Camborne.
18.3.1950   Resigned.

P.C. 278 Ernest Norman Haddy
Born 4.9.1925.
Appointed: 14.6.1948.
Stationed at: Hayle.
9.7.1949   Resigned.

P.C. 254 Kenneth Broad Hughes
Born 25.8.1927
Appointed: 14.6.1948.
Stationed at: Camborne, Stratton, Bodmin,
Pelynt, Newquay.
Granted a Favourable Record for courage
and devotion to duty in rescuing an
unknown man from drowning in the sea at
Hayle Towans on 13.8.1949.
1960   Granted a Favourable Record for the

arrest of Robin David Taylor who was wanted
for house breaking at Blanford Dorset.

P.C. 280 Dennis Harry May
Born 29.1.1930.
Appointed: 14.6.1948.
Promotion: 10.10.1964 to Sergeant.
Stationed at: Liskeard, Bodmin, Falmouth,
Slades, Camborne.

P.C. 188 Alan Charles Bennett
Born 25.7.1927.
Appointed: 28.6.1948.
Stationed at: Saltash, Newquay.
11.2.1950   Resigned.

P.C. 281 John Alfred Spencer
Born 5.7.1927.
Appointed: 28.6.1948.
Stationed at: Bodmin
19.3.1949   Resigned.

P.C. 202 Joseph Charles Burnell Bennett
Born 22.5.1927.
Appointed: 5.7.1948.
Stationed at: Falmouth.
26.2.1949   Resigned.

P.C. 285 Douglas Stanley Fitze
Born 21.2.1923.
Appointed: 12.7.1948
Stationed at: Lostwithiel, Wadebridge.
29.4.1950   Resigned.

P.C. 284 James Thomas Gynn
Born 21.8.1927.
Appointed: 12.7.1948.
Stationed at: Torpoint.
11.7.1950   Resigned

P.C. 282 Alfred William Henderson McGill
Born 4.3.1923.
Appointed: 12.7.1948.
Promotion: 8.2.1960 to Sergeant.
Stationed at: St Ives, Hayle, Bodmin, HQ
CID, Penzance , Truro, St Ives.

P.C. 283 Dennis Cyril Rogers
Born 15.8.1926.
Appointed: 12.7.1948.
Stationed at: Millbrook,
20.8.1949   Resigned.

P.C. 286 John Christopher McGuiness
Born 12.12.1921.
Appointed: 2.8.1948
Stationed at: Helston, Bodmin HQ.
24.9.1964   Died.

P.C. 206 Reginald Derek Tabb
Born 4.12.1927.
Appointed: 2.8.1948.
Stationed at: Falmouth, HQ Admin,
Bodmin.
22.4.1957   Resigned.

P.C. 105 Sidney Adam Penpraze
Born 24.9.1927.
Appointed: 9.8.1948.
Stationed at: St Columb Major, Whitstone, St
Germans, Calstock, Lostwithiel, St Austell.
6.7.1956 Commended by Mr. K.A.Hendry

the Chairman of East Powder Magistrates Court for his keen devotion and persistence resulting in the conviction of Still , Rescorl and Wilson on charges of store breaking and larceny.

26.7.1956 Granted a Favourable Record for resourcefulness displayed when he fought a fire single handed which he discovered in an occupied dwelling house at Baytrees, Albaston, at 5.50.am on the 8.5.1956.

P.C. 287 David Bryan Watmore
Born 16.2.1925.
Appointed: 23.8.1948.
Promotion: 1.6.1967   to Sergeant.
Stationed at: Camborne, Launceston, Newquay, Penzance.

P.C. 210 Colin George Allsop
Born 12.1.1928.
Appointed: 13.9.1948.
Stationed at: St Austell.
17.4.1950   Resigned.

P.C. 209 John Henry Frank Ashwood
Born 30.1.1928.
Appointed: 13.9.1948.
Stationed at: St Austell
11.6.1949   Resigned.

P.C. 288 Harold Arthur Thompson
Born 31.12.1921.
Appointed: 4.10.1948.
Stationed at: Saltash, St Stephens, St Austell, Penzance.

P.C. 121 Wilfred Roy Tabb
Born 2.6.1928.
Appointed: 4.10.1948.
Promotion: 1.12.1964 to Sergeant
Stationed at:,
St Austell, St Breward, Bude, St Agnes, St Austell.

P.C. 114 Arthur Roy Sheppee
Born 4.1.1924
Appointed: 4.10.1948.
Promotion:
1.4.1965 to Sergeant.
Stationed at: St Austell, Padstow, Lezant, Delabole, Wadebridge.

P.C. 289 William George Chapman
Born 21.11.1927.
Appointed: 11.10.1948.
Stationed at: Falmouth
29.4.1950   Resigned.

P.C. 290 John Bray
Born 16.5.1927.
Appointed: 18.10.1948.
Stationed at: Redruth, Penzance.
19.8.1950 Resigned.

P.C. 291 William James Kent
Born   6.12.1921.
Appointed: 18.10.1948.
Stationed at: Truro, Mylor, Troon, Mylor Bridge, Redruth.

P.C. 292 Ronald Henry Peters
Born   7.3.1927

Appointed: 18.10.1948.
Promotion: 1.3.1966 to Sergeant.
Stationed at: Wadebridge, Isles of Scilly, Newquay, Camborne, Falmouth, Truro, HQ Information Room, Looe, Bude, Camborne.
5.4.1955   Commended by the Pydar Justices on the manner in which he investigated the cases against Smith, Hayward, & Turner, convicted of larceny of cable and cellulose at St Mawgan

P.C. 293 Charles Walter Scott Mac Redstone
Born 28.3.1922.
Appointed: 18.10.1948.
Stationed at: Falmouth
31.3.1951 Resigned.

P.C. 294 Alan Charles Tilley
Born 19.4.1926.
Appointed: 18.10.1948
Promotion: 1.4.1959 to Sergeant. 1.10.1964 to Inspector. 1.6.1967 to Chief Inspector.
Stationed at:,
Liskeard, Callington, Kingsand, Duloe, HQ Traffic, HQ Information Room, Helston HQ Traffic

P.C. 28 Kenneth Alfred Peters
Born 3.3.1927.
Appointed: 1.11.1948.
Stationed at: Helston, Bodmin, Redruth.

P.C. 41 Edwin Henry Stephens
Born 4.10.1924.
Appointed: 1.11.1948.
Promotion: 20.5.1963 to Sergeant.
Stationed at: Fowey, Truro, St Agnes, St Columb, Newquay.
28.3.1951 Awarded the Royal Lifesaving Society's award of Merit.

P.C. 95 William Ronald Fisher
Born 18.5.1928
Appointed: 1.11.1948.
Stationed at: Newquay, Truro, Wadebridge, St Buryan, Penzance.

W.P.C. 4 Ruby Jeanne Ford
Born 10.7.1924.
Appointed: 15.11.1948.
Stationed at: Falmouth.
1.10.1949 Resigned.

P.C. 147 Reginald Douglas Berry
Born 25.6.1927.
Appointed: 15.11.1948.
Stationed at: Bodmin, Boscastle.

P.C. 155 David Anthony Robert Jack Whitehead
Born 20.10.1923.
Appointed: 15.11.1948.
Stationed at: Truro
25.8.1951 Resigned.

P.C. 11 Kenneth Godfrey Axworthy
Born 23.9.1926.
Appointed: 22.11.1948.
Stationed at: Torpoint.
16.5.1955 Resigned.

P.C. 201 Gordon Harrison
Born 23.3.1925.
Appointed: 22.11.1948.
Promotion: 25.1.1957 to Sergeant. 1.9.1965 to Inspector.
Stationed at: Truro, Newquay, Tywardreath, St Merryn, HQ Traffic, HQ Training, Bodmin, St Austell.
August 1949 Awarded the Royal Society's Testimonial on vellum
Granted a Favourable Record for courage and devotion to duty on 23.7.1950 which resulted in two persons being convicted of larceny and one of assaulting a Constable.

P.C. 296 Ernest Frank Tidball
Born 8.6.1916.
Appointed: 29.11.1948.
Transferred from the Metropolitan Police.
Stationed at: Truro, Chacewater, Truro, Launceston, St Austell.
8.9.1963 Retired.

P.C. 295 Walter Moffat Swan
Born 22.8.1922.
Appointed: 29.11.1948.
Stationed at: Liskeard
25.9.1955 Transferred to Plymouth City Police.

P.C. 299 Dennis James Berryman Corbett
Born 16.11.1926.
Appointed: 28.12.1948.
Stationed at: St Ives
21.1.1950. Resigned

P.C. 211 William Gerald Kent
Born 2.10.1927.
Appointed: 28.12.1948.
Stationed at: Saltash, HQ Admin, Truro Highertown.
3.1.1959 Resigned.

P.C. 298 Kenneth John May
Born 19.7.1925
Appointed: 28.12.1948.
Stationed at: Newquay
19.11.1949 Resigned.

P.C. 300 Douglas James Powell
Born 15.11.1926.
Appointed: 28.12.1948.
Transferred from the Metropolitan Police.
Promotion: 1.1.1965 to Sergeant.
Stationed at: Launceston, Bude, HQ Information Room, Bodmin, Kingsand, Redruth.

P.C. 297 Arthur Symons Ruberry
Born 20.10.1923.
Appointed: 28.12.1948.
Promotion: 1.6.1967 to Sergeant.
Stationed at: Falmouth, Penryn, St Erth, Copperhouse, St Ives.
31.12.1965 Granted a Favourable Record for his observation and his attention to duty which resulted in the arrest of John Robert Barber and Colin Roy Nauman for their subsequent conviction at the Assize for robbery with violence.

P.C. 27 Hugh Hill
Born 28.8.1926.

Appointed: 2.12.1948.
Stationed at: Falmouth, Sticker, Pendeen, Truro.

P.C. 301 Edward Cecil Mansergh
Born 27.7.1917.
Appointed: 17.1.1949.
16.1.1949 Transferred from Hampshire Constabulary.
Stationed at: Penzance, St Germans.

P.C. 302 William John James
Born 11.2.1928.
Appointed: 31.1.1949.
Stationed at: Falmouth, Penzance, HQ Traffic, Bodmin, Looe, Camborne.

P.C. 131 Clifford Henry Davey
Born 3.8.1926.
Appointed: 31.1.1949.
Stationed at: Bude , Launceston, Liskeard.
3.6.1954 Resigned

P.C. 307 Raymond Witts
Born 4.10.1928.
Appointed: 31.1.1949.
Stationed at: St Columb, Isles of Scilly, Truro, Duloe, Kilkhampton, Falmouth, Wadebridge.

P.C. 303 Jack Blewett James
Born 3.1.1926.
Appointed: 31.1.1949.
Stationed at: Redruth, St Just, Sennen, St Columb, Constantine, Camborne.

P.C. 304 William Arthur Desmond Phillips
Born 27.4.1928.
Appointed: 31.1.1949.
Promotion: 1.9.1965 to Sergeant.
Stationed at: Newquay, Porkellis, St Keverne, St Day, Tywardreath, St Austell.

P.C. 269 James Gordon Lother
Born 9.5.1926.
Appointed: 31.1.1949.
Stationed at: Looe.
1.10.1949 Resigned.

P.C. 305 William Howard Tonkin
Born 2.6.1925.
Appointed: 31.1.1949.
Stationed at: Truro
20.5.1950 Resigned.

P.C. 180 John Francis Stephen Maddern
Born 18.8.1927.
Appointed: 2.3.1949.
Stationed at: St Ives.
9.6.1953 Resigned

P.C. 202 Stanley Paul
Born 23.1.1923.
Appointed: 2.3.1949.
Stationed at: Falmouth.
25.2.1950 Resigned.

P.C. 308 Stanley Edgar Winchester
Born 14.5.1927.
Appointed: 2.3.1949.
Stationed at: Newquay, Whitstone
28.5.1955 Resigned.

P.C. 87 Rex Eric Butson
Born 10.10.1926,
Appointed: 2.3.1949.

Stationed at: Falmouth, St Austell, Polperro, Saltash.

P.C. 268 Cedric Gordon Hooper
Born 11.4.1924
Appointed: 28.3.1949.
Promotion: 20.4.1960 to Sergeant.
Stationed at: St Ives , Truro, Redruth, Camborne.
December 1964 Granted a Favourable Record together with DC 2 Furnell and DC 167 Davidson for zeal and attention to duty in making enquiries which resulted in the charging of Owen Davey with receiving , also commended by his Honour H.Aide. Sheppard Q.C. At Cornwall Quarter Sessions 12.11.1964.

P.C. 154 Arthur Stanley Pardon
Born 27.8.1922.
Appointed: 28.3.1949.
Stationed at: Wadebridge, St Austell,
27.7.1957 Resigned.

P.C. 183 David Lower Harding
Born 1.5.1928.
Appointed: 28.3.1949.
Stationed at: Launceston, Tywardreath, Polruan.
2.2.1959 Resigned.

P.C. 306 Delmas Harry Willcocks
Born 16.1.1927.
Appointed: 31.3.1949.
Promotion: 1.6.1967 to Sergeant.
Stationed at: Bodmin, Wadebridge, St Austell, Hessenford, Calstock, St Germans, Bodmin, Truro, Penryn, Tywardtreath.

P.C. 257 Joseph William Murley Clemow
Born 8.11.1927.
Stationed at: Newquay, Truro, Tregoney, St Austell, Newquay, Wadebridge.

P.C. 267 Bryan Anthony Rex Williams
Born 14.6.1925.
Appointed: 2.5.1949.
Promotion: 16.8.1964 to Sergeant.
Stationed at: Redruth, Illogan, Camborne, HQ Admin, Redruth.

P.C. 281 Alfred Thomas Pittam
Born 10.7.1924
Appointed: 2.5.1949.
Transferred from the Metropolitan Police.
Promotion: 1.4.1966 to Sergeant.
Stationed at: Looe, Downderry, Falmouth, Penzance, St Ives.
30.9.1965 Granted a Favourable Record for his observation and attention to duty in checking the movements of suspicious characters at night which lead to the arrest of Frederick John Pope on a charge of wounding with intent to murder at Truro on 31.8.1965

P.C. 193 Arthur Stanley Webber
Born 15.1.1929.
Appointed: 2.5.1949.
Stationed at: Bude.
11.8.1951 Resigned.

P.C. 55 Eric Powell
Born 4.8.1912.
Appointed: 8.5.1949
Transferred from Lancashire Police.
Stationed at: Falmouth
12.6.1949 Resigned.

W.P.C. 5 Clarice May Hannaford
Born 24.6.1924.
Appointed: 13.6.1949.
Stationed at: Looe, Liskeard, Looe
30.9.1950 Resigned.

P.C. 139 William Blakley Battersby
Born 24.12.1924.
Appointed: 25.7.1949.
Stationed at: Helston, Marazion.
27.2.1960 Resigned.

P.C. 78 Herbert Glynn Hodge
Born 24.1.1926.
Appointed: 25.7.1949.
Stationed at: Callington, Lanner, Camborne, Launceston, Fowey.

P.C. 55 Richard Owen Williams
Born 20.4.1924
Appointed: 25.7.1949,
Stationed at: Liskeard, Connor Downs, Blue Anchor, Heamoor, Newlyn.
22.7.1964 Resigned.

P.C. 76 Terrance Ivor Richards
Born 13.1.1928.
Appointed: 25.7.1949.
Promotion: 24.11.1963 to Sergeant.
Stationed at: Millbrook, Torpoint, Millbrook, Bude, Pelynt, Bodmin, HQ Information Room, Bodmin Kingsand, Redruth.

P.C. 153 William Stuart Lean
Born 12.6.1929.
Appointed: 22.8.1949.
Stationed at: Redruth
19.8.1951 Resigned.

P.C. 209 Leo James Hooper Hagelstein
Born 12.10.1923.
Appointed: 3.10.1949.
Stationed at: Truro
Resigned.

P.C. 186 Kenneth William Frederick Lang
Born 26.7.1927.
Appointed: 3.10.1949.
Stationed at:, Redruth Blisland, Lanivet, St Just.
30.4.1958 Granted a Favourable Record for his alertness persistence, and brave conduct on the 5.4.1958 when , with the assistance of P.C. 156 Ham, he arrested A.J.M.Downing a certified homicidal patient who had escaped from St Lawrences Hospital.
30.6.1964 Resigned.

P.C. 60 Charles Samuel Logg
Born 2.5.1926.

Appointed: 3.10.1949.
Stationed at: Bude
21.4.1951 Resigned

P.C. 175 Donald Brian Crabbe
Born 18.11.1927.
Appointed: 3.10.1949.
Promotion: 1.4.1964 to Detective Sergeant.
Stationed at: Torpoint. Liskeard, Falmouth,
Torpoint, Truro, Liskeard.
September 1966. Commended by the
Chairman of Pydar, Magistrates Court at St
Columb on 9.9.1966 for his work in connec-
tion with charges against Redman and
Twomey, committed to Quarter Sessions for
shop lifting and larceny.

P.C. 215 Geoffrey Oatey
Born 5.9.1929.
Appointed: 3.10.1949.
Stationed at: Camborne, Falmouth Newlyn
East, Torpoint.

P.C. 204 Desmond Reginald Rogers
Born 27.6.1929.
Appointed: 3.10.1949.
Promotion: 1.3.1961 to Sergeant.
Stationed at: St Austell, Falmouth, Camborne,
Looe, Helston, HQ Traffic, Bodmin.

P.C. 234 Harold Hall
Born 5.1.1929.
Appointed: 31.10.1949.
Transferred from Blackburn Police.
Stationed at: Bodmin, St Cleer,
14.5.1955 Resigned.

P.C. 263 Eric Denton Hodgson
Born 28.11.1925.
Appointed: 31.10.1949.
Stationed at: Looe, Halworthy, Stratton
6.5.1964 Resigned.

P.C. 276 Frederick Gordon Ivor Fox
Born 28.3.1929.
Appointed: 31.10.1949.
Promotion: 1.9.1963 to Sergeant.
Stationed at: Falmouth, St Austell, Foxhole,
Pendeen, Falmouth, Bodmin, Camelford

P.C. 123 Hugh Barriemore Ollerearnshaw
Born 1.4.1929.
Appointed: 31.10.1949.
Stationed at: St Ives, Chacewater,

P.C. 278 Jack Holmes
Born 20.9.1927.
Appointed: 31.10.1949.
Stationed at: Truro, St Breward, St Kew,
Callington, Constantine.

P.C. 213 Norman Jack Pawley
Born 22.4.1922.
Appointed: 21.11.1949
Transferred from the Metropolitan Police.
Stationed at: Fowey, Porthleven.

P.C. 50 Thomas David Charles
Born 11.3.1928.
Appointed: 28.11.1949.
Stationed at: Liskeard, Torpoint, St Mellion,
Penzance.

P.C. 283 Alan Bennett Williams
Born 22.2.1928.
Appointed: 28.11.1949.
Stationed at: Liskeard, Menheniott, Redruth.

P.C. 77 John James Rogers
Born 8.8.1922.
Appointed: 28.11.1949.
Stationed at: Camborne.
25.11.1950 Resigned.

P.C. 298 Rodney James Allen
Born 12.1.1930.
Appointed: 28.11.1949.
Promotion: 1.4.1964 to Detective Sergeant.
Stationed at: St Austell, HQ CID, Falmouth,
Helston, HQ Information room, Penzance, St
Austell.

W.P.C. 2 Joan Evelyn Garrett
Born 11.3.1924
Appointed: 1.1.1950.
Stationed at: Falmouth
23.2.1952 Resigned.

P.C. 269 Derek David Baldwin
Born 10.7. 1927.
Appointed: 2.1.1950.
Stationed at: Hayle, Newquay.
24.9.1955 Resigned.

P.C. 18 Cyril Crowle
Born 11.12.1923.
Appointed: 2.1.1950.
Stationed at: Lostwithiel, Liskeard,
Callington.
14.9.1958 Resigned.

P.C. 14 Leslie Corin
Born 8.6.1926.
Appointed: 2.1.1950.
Stationed at: Falmouth, Camelford, St
Austell, Pool.
25.4.1957 Granted a Favourable Record
for zeal and devotion to duty which resulted
in the conviction of Cecelia Irene Harris, at
Lesnoweth Magistrates Court on 5.4.1957 on
three charges of larceny from dance halls and
eighteen offences taken into consideration.
30.6.1960 Granted a favourable Record for
keen observation and devotion to duty which
resulted in four persons being convicted on
charges of larceny of coal from the clay dries
in the St Austell area.

P.C. 22 John Derek Cornwall
Born 14.3.1930.
Appointed: 6.2.1950.
Promotion: 1.4.1959 to Sergeant.
1.10.1963 to Inspector.
Stationed at: Falmouth, Camborne, HQ
Information Room, HQ CID Torpoint

P.C. 188 Gerald Wearne Noye
Born 9.3.1927.
Appointed: 27.2.1950.
Stationed at: Newquay.
26.7.1952 Resigned.

P.C. 140 Denis Leighton Dyer
Born 29.9.1925.
Appointed: 27.2.1950.

Stationed at: Torpoint
27.9.1950 Resigned.

P.C. 79 John Bellingham
Born 13.12.1928.
Appointed: 27.2.1950.
Stationed at: Truro
27.1.1951 Resigned.

P.C. 210 James Henry Brian Lord
Born 26.3.1929.
Appointed: 3.4.1950.
Stationed at: Camborne, St Just.
30.1.1952 Resigned.

P.C. 242 Leonard Oatey
Born 8.3.1930.
Appointed: 3.4.1950.
Promotion: 25.8.1958 to Sergeant.
Stationed at: Truro, Isles of Scilly, Troon,
Bodmin, Helston, Liskeard.
4.8.1966 Transferred to Wiltshire
Constabulary.

P.C. 202 Ronald Edward Warren
Born 22.8.1928. **Appointed:** 3.4.1950.
Promotion: 1.11.1963 to Sergeant.
Stationed at: Liskeard, Torpoint, Bude, St
Austell, Bodmin.

P.C. 270 Percy Gordon Lundy
Born 2.10.1926.
Appointed: 23.4.1950
Stationed at: Penzance.
16.1.1954 Resigned.

P.C. 225 Gareth James May
Born 13.3.1929.
Appointed: 28.5.1950.
Stationed at:,
Launceston, Falmouth.
28.3.1953 Transferred to Somerset Police.

P.C. 285 Sidney James Rule
Born 9.1.1924.
Appointed: 28.5.1950.
Stationed at: Truro.
29.9.1951 Resigned.

P.C. 313 Roger Merrit Harper
Born 10.7.1927.
Appointed: 3.7.1950.
Stationed at: Redruth, Isles of Scilly, Redruth.
18.7.1956 Resigned.

P.C. 311 William John Sharp
Born 26.1.1930.
Appointed: 3.7.1950.
Stationed at: Bude.
14.8.1951 Resigned.

P.C. 312 Peter Pascoe
Born 15.7.1930.
Appointed: 3.7.1950.
Promotion: 31.8.1960 to Sergeant. 1.1.1967
to Inspector.
Stationed at: Penryn, Breage, H.Q.
Information Room, Hayle, Redruth.

P.C. 309 William John Chapman
Born 10.8.1930.
Appointed: 3.7.1950.
Promotion: 1.4.1965 to Detective Sergeant.

Stationed at: Camborne, Redruth, Illogan, Redruth, St Austell, Truro.

P.C. 289 Maurice Garland Collings
Born 17.1.1928.
Appointed: 3.7.1950.
Stationed at: Newquay, St Columb Major, Pool, St Kew Highway, St Austell.

P.C. 310 Henry Andrew Deal
Born 23.4.1927.
Appointed: 3.7.1950
Stationed at: Padstow, Newlyn, Lostwithiel.

P.C. 125 Clement James Alexander Lang
Born 25.9.1924
Appointed: 3.7.1950.
Stationed at: Truro, Egloskerry, Pensilva, Looe.

P.C. 299 Leslie Martin Pedlar
Born 25.4.1930.
Appointed: 3.7.1950.
Stationed at: Falmouth, Mullion, Falmouth, St Austell, Launceston.
31.10.1960 Awarded a special commendation for outstanding courage in attempting to arrest two men one of who was armed with an iron bar who had broken into a garage and forced open a safe at 3.30.am on 4.8.1960.

P.C. 305 Peter Gladstone Terry
Born 20.8.1926
Appointed: 3.7.1950.
Stationed at: Bude, Launceston, Truro. Constantine, St Columb, Truro.

P.C. 315 Robert Hamilton Burrow
Born 14.10.1924
Appointed: 31.7.1950.
Stationed at: Penzance.
27.9.1951 Awarded a Favourable Record for courage and devotion to duty at Penzance on 19.8.1951 in effecting the arrest of William Scheidweiler for larceny and an assault on the Constable.
29.8.1953 Resigned.

P.C. 314 John Herbert Rees
Born 22.7.1926.
Appointed: 31.7.1950.
Stationed at: HQ.
18.11.1950 Resigned.

P.C. 284 Russell James Miners
Born 2.9.1926.
Appointed: 31.7.1950.
Stationed at: Redruth, Troon, St Ives, Rame.
31.10.1962 Granted a Favourable Record for zeal and devotion to duty which resulted in the arrest of Albert Graham charged with shop breaking and larceny at St Ives.

P.C. 140 Cyril Gilbert Snell
Born 9.8.1928.
Appointed: 31.7.1950.
Stationed at: Looe, Probus, Mevagissey, St Merryn, Camborne.

P.C. 168 Ernest George Edwards
Born 1.2.1926

Appointed: 28.8.1950.
Stationed at: Wadebridge
30.10.1954 Resigned.

P.C. 316 Maxwell Claude Martin
Born 14.5.1927
Appointed: 28.8.1950.
Stationed at: Camborne
29.3.1952 Resigned.

P.C. 290 David Edwards
Born 9.12.1926.
Appointed: 28.8.1950.
Promotion: 6.5.1965 to Sergeant.
Stationed at: St Ives, Goldsithney, Isles of Scilly. Liskeard, HQ Information Room.

P.C. 113 Neville Maurice Gladstone
Born 16.9.1928.
Appointed: 2.10.1950.
Stationed at: HQ
11.8.1951 Resigned.

P.C. 36 Kenneth Robert Jackson
Born 8.8.1925.
Appointed: 2.10.1950.
Stationed at: HQ
31.3.1951 Resigned.

P.C. 21 Frederick Ivor Timmins
Born 15.2.1930.
Appointed:. 2.10.1950.
Stationed at: Falmouth, Saltash
12.7.1952 Resigned.

P.C. 129 Howard Davey
Born 1.4.1926.
Appointed: 2.10.1950.
Promotion: 1.1.1967 to Sergeant.
Stationed at: St Ives, Blisland, Carbis Bay, Penryn.
February 1965. Granted a Favourable Record for initiative and attention to duty which resulted in the arrest of James Patrick McArthy and Michael George Hall on a charge of ware house breaking and larceny at Gulval. Also commended by the Chairman of Penzance Borough Magistrates Court on 1.1.1965.

P.C. 108 Frank Pellow
Born 26.3.1930.
Appointed: 2.10.1950.
Promotion: 1.8.1966 to Sergeant.
Stationed at: Truro, St Mawes, Truro, Wadebridge, Bodmin, Liskeard , HQ Information Room
7.3.1964 Awarded a Special Commendation for bravery and initiative in the arrest of man who had committed murder who stated he was armed with a gun. The Constable was commended by the Judge at the Assize.

P.C. 110 Charles John Burley
Born 16.1.1929.
Appointed: 2.10.1950.
Stationed at: Camborne, Penzance, Penryn, Blisland.

P.C. 151 Douglas Frederick Simmonds
Born 25.1.1930.

Appointed: 30.10.1950.
Stationed at: Liskeard, Bude, Camborne, St Ives, Hayle, Whitstone.
January 1961. Granted a Favourable Record with P.C. 282 Phillips in the action they took on the 15.10.1960 at Camborne Railway Station which resulted in the arrest and conviction of four prisoners for safe breaking.

P.C. 91 Edgar Burnard Trounce
Born 22.10.1930.
Appointed: 30.10.1950.
Stationed at: Camborne.
3.5.1952 Resigned.

P.C. 149 Brian Neil Combe
Born 9.6.1930
Appointed: 27.11.1950.
Promotion: 8.4.1963 to Sergeant. 1.1.1967 to Inspector.
Stationed at: Liskeard, Bodmin Information Room, Truro, Bude.

P.C. 6 George Henry Trewella
Born 19.8.1925.
Appointed: 15.12.1950.
Stationed at: Penzance
7.6.1952 Resigned.

P.C. 229 Alfred John Jennings
Born 20.2.1930.
Appointed: 1.1.1951.
Stationed at: HQ .
27.1.1951 Resigned.

P.C. 25 Daniel Richard Portlock
Born 14.9.1926.
Appointed: 1.1.1951.
Stationed at: HQ
14.7.1951 Resigned.

W.P.C. 4 Rosemary Elizabeth Palmer nee Johns.
Born 2.6.1927.
Appointed: 1.1.1951.
Stationed at: Truro
20.8.1955 Resigned.

P.C. 159 Brian Thomas Burrow
Born 10.4.1926.
Appointed: 1.1.1951.
Stationed at: Liskeard.
29.3.1952 Resigned

P.C. 156 Albert Ivor Christophers
Born 2.1.1927.
Appointed: 2.1.1951.
Stationed at: Camborne.
4.11.1952 Resigned.

P.C. 232 Stanley Joseph Grose
Born 19.5.1928.
Appointed: 29.1.1951.
Stationed at: HQ
24.2.1951.

P.C. 229 Alfred Keith Hosking
Born 20.2.1929.
Appointed: 29.1.1951
Stationed at: Falmouth, Callington.
6.12.1952 Resigned.

P.C. 9 Bertram Frederick George Porter
Born   25.5.1927.
Appointed: 29.1.1951.
Stationed at: HQ
24.2.1951   Resigned.

P.C. 169 Douglas Norman Shearn
Born   7.6.1926.
Appointed: 25.2.1951.
Stationed at: Penzance
23.2.1952   Transferred to the Metropolitan Police.

P.C. 9 Maurice John Hancock
Born   19.9.1927.
Appointed: 26.2.1951.
Stationed at: Looe, Halworthy, Chacewater, Blackwater
31.5.1961   Resigned.

P.C. 246 Eric Webber
Born   16.4.1927.
Appointed: 28.5.1951.
Stationed at: Launceston,
28.6.1953   Died.

P.C. 250 Austin Nelson Reed
Born   21.1.1931.
Appointed: 28.5.1951.
Stationed at: Falmouth
31.5.1952   Resigned.

W.P.C. 5 Frances Madge Hoskin
Born   31.12.1928.
Appointed: 2.7.1951.
Stationed at: St Austell, Penzance
12.3.1955   Resigned.

P.C. 259 Albert Donald Langdon
Born   27.1.1931.
Appointed: 2.7.1951.
Stationed at: Bude, St Ives , Goldsithney, HQ Admin, Anthony.
31.8.1959   Granted a Favourable Record for keenness and devotion to duty in effecting the arrest of Harold Warmington and causing the arrest of Trevor Hilton on charges of larceny.
1.7.1963   Granted a Favourable Record for keenness and devotion to duty when off duty, on 29.5.1963, arrested Percival James Phillipson on a charge of larceny at Exeter

P.C. 314 Alan William Thompson
Born   1.2.1931.
Appointed: 30.7.1951.
Stationed at: Truro,
31.5.1952   Resigned.

P.C. 293 Alfred Victor May
Born   25.6.1927.
Appointed: 30.7.1951.
Stationed at: Truro, Stithians, Newquay, St Kew.

P.C. 196 Jack Dodd
Born   21.5.1931.
Appointed: 30.9.1951.
Promotion: 1.9.1964 to Sergeant
Stationed at: Newquay, Penzance, St Ives, Camelford and Truro

P.C. 25 Roy Glover
Born   2.2.1925.
Appointed: 29.10.1951.
Promotion: 1.6.1967 to Sergeant.
Stationed at: Truro, St Columb, Sennen.

P.C. 239 Ivor William Crabb
Born   10.10.1930.
Appointed: 10.12.1951
Stationed at: Fowey
31.12.1953   Resigned.

P.C. 150 Philip Tom Leonard
Born   28.10.1926
Appointed: 10.12.1951
Promotion: 1.10.1963 to Detective Sergeant.
1.1.1967 to Detective Inspector.
Stationed at: Torpoint, Probus, Camborne. Newquay, Camborne.
23.2.1955   Granted a Favourable Record for vigilance displayed at Torpoint on 22.12.1954 resulting in the conviction of Henry Phillip Baker on a charge of larceny and for which the Constable was commended by the Chairman of the Cornwall Quarter Sessions on the 14.2.1955.

P.C. 74 Norman George
Born   12.3.1930.
Appointed: 10.12.1951.
Promotion: 1.4.1964   to Sergeant.
Stationed at: Camborne, Redruth, Camborne, Penzance, Torpoint.

P.C. 77 Marshall Eric Gilbert
Born   12.5.1931.
Appointed: 10.12.1951.
Stationed at: Truro, Grampound, Saltash, Newquay,
28.2.1966   Granted a Favourable Record for vigilance and attention to duty which resulted in the arrest and subsequent conviction of Arthur John Stanford and Jacqueline Stanford on charges of housebreaking and larceny at Newquay.

P.C. 53 Ivor James Wakely
Born   9.6.1928.
Appointed: 10.12.1951.
Stationed at: Bude, Callington, Lezant, Pool, Falmouth.

P.C. 228 Frank Caddy
Born   17.5.1929.
Appointed: 17.12.1951.
Stationed at: Newquay, Tregoney, Truro, Stithians, Penryn.

P.C. 212 Cecil Williams
Born   14.8.1931.
Appointed: 17.12.1951.
Stationed at: Newquay, Tregoney, Perranporth, Tregoney, Newquay, Stratton, Bude.

W.P.C. 3 Elizabeth Summers
Born   6.6.1924.
Appointed: 27.1.1952
Stationed at:,
St Austell, Falmouth
19.12.1953   Resigned.

P.C. 44 Brian Christopher Foster
Born   19.6.1930
Appointed: 28.1.1952.
Stationed at: Wadebridge
Resigned.

P.C. 113 Royden Percy Frank Mills
Born   27.1.1928.
Appointed: 28.1.1952.
Stationed at: Newquay, HQ CID, Penzance, Camborne.
31.5.1963   Resigned.

P.C. 79 Kenneth John Radford
Born   26.8.1931.
Appointed: 28.1.1952.
Promotion: 1.10.1963 to Detective Sergeant
1.3.1967 to Inspector
Stationed at: Saltash, St Austell, Launceston, HQ CID
January 1961   Granted a Favourable Record with P.C. 195 Pethick for persistence and devotion to duty with difficult cases of sheep and fowl stealing which resulted in the arrest and conviction of four offenders.

P.C. 60 Alfred Charles Ross
Born   9.12.1927.
Appointed: 28.1.1952.
Promotion: 1.6.1967   to Sergeant.
Stationed at: Bude, Redruth, Perranwell, Truro, Falmouth.

P.C. 232 Sidney Maurice Bearne
Born   11.12.1930.
Appointed: 2.1.1952.
Stationed at: Wadebridge, Port Isaac, Looe, Tywardreath.

P.C. 209 Lawrence James Connibeer
Born   14.2.1926.
Appointed: 25.2.1952.
Stationed at: Liskeard
30.8.1952   Resigned.

P.C. 210 Arthur McCall
Born   31.7.1926.
Appointed: 25.2.1952.
Stationed at: Helston, Penryn, Saltash, Week St Mary, Whitstone, Newquay,
24.8.1955   Granted a Favourable Record for the capable and efficient way he applied artificial respiration to a boy named Toms, who had come into contact with high voltage electricity wire at Penryn on 7.7.1955. And was in the word of the house surgeon at Falmouth Hospital, the means of saving the boys life. The Constable was also commended by Penryn Borough Council.
21.12.1955   Awarded the resuscitation certificate of the Royal Humane Society,

P.C. 252 Thomas Lloyd
Born   18.10.1931.
Appointed: 25.2.1952.
Stationed at: Bude
25.4.1953   Resigned.

P.C. 155 James Reid
Born   5.3.1929.
Appointed: 25.2.1952

Stationed at: Penzance.
12.5.1955   Resigned.

P.C. 153 Ernest Ashley Tabb
Born 15.6.1928.
Appointed: 25.2.1952.
Stationed at: Camborne, Hayle,
2.1.1957   Resigned.

P.C. 285 Reginald John Hawkins
Born   2.3.1927.
Appointed: 10.3.1952.
Transferred from the Metropolitan Police.
Stationed at: HQ, Truro, St Columb Major,
Newquay, St Cleer.
4.11.1957   Seconded to Cyprus as a Sergeant.
7.9.1959   Returned
Stationed at: St Cleer, Newquay.
27.6.1957   Carneigie Hero Trust Fund
decided to have the names of Sergeant
B.R.Pearn and P.C. 285 Hawkins inscribed
on their illuminated Roll of Heroes in recognition of heroism on 21.3.1957 when they
rescued Mr S.J. Besley from a savage attack
by a bull.
Awarded the Carneigie Trust Fund Certificate
framed in oak
24.10.1957   Awarded the Queens commendation for brave conduct in connection with
the above.
30.6.1962   Resigned.

P.C. 193 Alfred Bruce Atkinson
Born 19.1.1928.
Appointed: 1.4.1952.
Stationed at: Truro
25.4.1953   Resigned.

P.C. 17 James Edward Goulding
Born 16.12.1928.
Appointed: 1.4.1952.
Stationed at: Newquay, Isles of Scilly.
22.12.1955   Resigned.

P.C. 311 George Alfred Chappell
Born 26.12.1931.
Appointed: 21.4.1952.
Promotion: 1.1.1965 to Sergeant.
Stationed at: Falmouth, Torpoint ,
Camborne, Bude.
25.11.1954   Granted a Favourable Record
for the manner in which he carried out his
duties during a disturbance at Falmouth on
11.9.1954.

P.C. 169 Ronald Peter Clive Pearce
Born 21.11.1931.
Appointed: 28.4.1952.
Stationed at: St Ives.
19.3.1955   Resigned

P.C. 262 Reginald James Gaved
Born 13.9.1927
Appointed: 28.4.1952
Stationed at: Saltash, Penryn, Devoran, St
Austell.

P.C. 70 Richard Noall Peters
Born 3.12.1930.
Appointed: 28.4.1952.
Stationed at: Saltash.
27.3.1954   Resigned.

P.C. 122 Hugh David Petrie
Born 2.4.1927.
Appointed: 28.4.1952.
Stationed at: Truro.
6.6.1953   Resigned.

P.C. 159 Roger Michael Wonnacott
Born 5.10.1931.
Appointed: 28.4.1952.
Stationed at: Truro, Newquay, Perranporth,
Tregoney, Liskeard, Launceston.
28.2.1961   Granted a Favourable Record for
keen observation and attention to duty which
resulted in the conviction of an offender in a
case of larceny.

P.C. 56 Frederick William Gillson
Born 6.7.1926.
Appointed: 5.5.1952
No Stations listed
13.2.1954   Resigned.

P.C. 91 David Gordon Burbidge
Born 13.1.1932
Appointed: 26.5.1952.
Stationed at: Truro
8.8.1953   Resigned.

P.C. 32 Derek Ian Crawley
Born 12.10.1928
Appointed: 16.6.1952.
Stationed at: Camborne
29.8.1953   Resigned.

P.C. 6 Maurice Elliott
Born 3.9.1931.
Appointed: 16.6.1952.
Stationed at: Liskeard, Whitstone, St
Keverne, Truro.

P.C. 185 Raymond George Hancock
Born 11.12.1928.
Appointed: 16.6.1952.
Promotion: 1.1.1967 to Sergeant.
Stationed at: Callington, Launceston, Indian
Queens, Hayle
30.11.1961   Granted a Favourable Record
with P.C. 112 LeWarne for keen observation
and attention to duty resulted in the conviction of two persons on charges of larceny
and receiving stolen petrol.

P.C. 250 Peter Oliver Richards
Born 31.7.1928.
Appointed: 16.6.1952.
Stationed at: Penzance, Liskeard, St
Germans, Truro, Bude.

W.P.C. 2 Phyllis Victoria Margarita Standen
Born 11.2.1924.
Appointed: 16.6.1952.
Stationed at: St Austell, Falmouth, St Austell.

P.C. 316 Albert Charles Hammill
Born 19.5.1928.
Appointed: 28.7.1952.
Stationed at: Penzance.
14.11.1954   Transferred to Leeds City
Police.

P.C. 314 David John Boyling
Born 11.3.1932.

Appointed: 28.7.1952.
Stationed at: Camborne, Isles of Scilly,
Redruth, Bodmin, Foxhole, Bude
30.11.1960   Awarded a Favourable Record
with P.C. 138 Pedlar for zeal and devotion
to duty on 1.11.1960 which resulted in the
arrest of two men on charges of burglary and
house breaking in the Metropolitan Police
District and Devon. And the tracing of two
girls missing from home.

P.C. 10 Raymond John Radmore
Born 19.11.1929.
Appointed: 4.8.1952.
Transferred from the Metropolitan Police.
Stationed at: HQ, Padstow, Newquay,
Bodmin, Camborne.

P.C. 21 Maurice Harry Ferrer
Born 15.11.1928.
Appointed: 15.9.1952.
Stationed at: Bude, Truro, Portscatho,
Penzance.

P.C. 16 Thomas Percy Arnold Day
Born 3.8.1931
Appointed: 15.9.1952.
Stationed at: Truro.
6.6.1953   Resigned.

P.C. 37 Brian Joseph Harry
Born 26.7.1930.
Appointed: 15.9.1952.
Promotion: 4.8.1966 to Sergeant.
Stationed at:
Redruth, HQ Traffic, HQ Information Room,
Camborne, Truro.
7.3.1964   Granted a Favourable Record for
zeal and attention to duty which resulted in the
arrest of Derek Hollow of Camborne on
charges of burglary, house breaking and larceny.

P.C. 82 Harold John Gilbert
Born 10.12.1930.
Appointed: 29.9.1952.
Stationed at: Newquay, Falmouth, Liskeard,
Tregoney, Newquay, Tregoney, Bodmin,
Millbrook, Bodmin.

P.C. 138 Norman Brian Pedlar
Born 1.5.1932.
Appointed: 29.9.1952.
Stationed at: Bude, Stratton, Falmouth.
3.11.1950   Granted a Favourable Record
with P.C. 314 Boyling for zeal and devotion
to duty on 1.11.1950 which resulted n the
arrest of two men on charges of burglary and
house breaking in the Metropolitan Police
District and Devon and the tracing of two
girls missing from home.
30.6.1958   Awarded the Royal Humane
Society's Testimonial on vellum with P.C.
172 Hoatson for brave conduct on 7.4.1958
when they twice made hazardous 150 foot
descents with ropes down the cliffs at Bude
to rescue four boys who had been trapped
for nine hours.
3.10.1958.   Granted a Favourable Record
for his brave conduct when he crossed a
swollen river to ascertain that the residents
there were in no danger.
29.2 . 1964   Resigned.

P.C. 181 **Edward John Burgess**
Born 31.10.1929.
Appointed: 29.9.1952.
Promotion: 1.5.1963 to Sergeant.
Stationed at: St Ives, St Keverne, Falmouth.
Bodmin, Helston.

P.C. 209 **Desmond Leyland Tiltman Barrett**
Born 1.11.1926.
Appointed: 24.11.1952.
Stationed at: Newquay, St Austell, Torpoint.

P.C. 188 **Briar James Watters**
Born 20.10.1929.
Appointed: 24.11.1952.
Stationed at:,
Helston, St Mawgan, St Austell, Launceston.

P.C. 84 **Michael William Beresford**
Born 12.7.1932
Appointed: 8.12.1952.
Promotion: 1.4.1965 to Sergeant.
Stationed at: Bude, St Breward, Hayle,
Penryn, Truro.

P.C. 184 **Arnold Edward Heathcote**
Born 18.3.1925.
Appointed: 15.12.1952.
Stationed at: Falmouth, HQ CID
15.1.1966 Transferred to Blackpool
Borough Police.

W.P.C. 6 **Sheila Dorothy Hockley**
Born 2.3.1932.
Appointed: 15.12.1952.
Stationed at: St Austell.
15.12.1956 Resigned.

P.C. 102 **Peter Clifton White**
Born 3.1.1932.
Appointed: 15.12.1952.
Stationed at: Truro.
16.1.1954 Resigned.

P.C. 12 **Ronald Robert Ingerson**
Born 9.6.1929
Appointed: 26.1.1953.
Stationed at: St Just.
13.8.1955 Resigned.

P.C. 251 **Harry Victor George Hawkes**
Born 8.7.1929.
Appointed: 26.1.1953.
Stationed at: Bodmin, Torpoint, Seaton, St
Agnes.

P.C. 156 **William Walter Smith**
Born 5.2.1931.
Appointed: 29.1.1953.
Promotion: 1.6.1967 to Sergeant.
Stationed at: St Ives, Connor Downs,
Nancledra, Bodmin.

P.C. 68 **William Howard Blewett**
Born 25.4.1928.
Appointed: 16.3.1953.
Stationed at: HQ, Falmouth.
3.4.1954. Resigned.

P.C. 266 **Russell Gummow**
Born 4.12.1929.
Appointed: 16.3.1953.

Stationed at: Launceston
29.8.1953 Resigned.

P.C. 93 **Alan Smith**
Born 23.4.1932.
Appointed: 16.3.1953.
Stationed at: Bude, Penzance.
19.12.1953 Resigned.

P.C. 317 **William Godfrey Edward
Matthews**
Born 21.6.1930.
Appointed: 16.3.1953.
Promotion: 3.5.1966 to Sergeant.
Stationed at: St Just, Penzance, Cyprus.
Wadebridge, Bodmin, Penzance. Millbrook,
St Agnes, St Austell.
26.1.1955. Awarded the British Empire
Medal (Civil) for brave conduct at St Just on
the 9.8.1954 when he descended a sheer
cliff to rescue the body of a man who had
fallen from the cliff.
31.8.1965 Granted a Favourable Record
with DC 167 Davidson, DC 268 Partridge,
P.C. 291 Kent, P.C. 102 Rogers, for zeal and
initiative shown in conducting enquiries
resulting in the detection of 63 crimes at
Camborne and Truro Divisions and the
successful prosecution of fifteen person for
offences of warehouse breaking, office
breaking, canteen breaking, store breaking
and larceny. Also complimented by the
Chairman of East Penwith Magistrates Court
on 12.8.1965.

P.C. 187 **William Maurice Eva**
Born 19.5.1928.
Appointed: 16.3.1953.
Stationed at: Truro, Marazion.

P.C. 225 **Pelham Harry Godfrey Morcomb**
Born 19.11.1932.
Appointed: 16.3.1953.
Stationed at: Truro, St Columb, Egloskerry,
Launceston, Camborne.

P.C. 217 **Thomas Maxwell Hancock**
Born 7.5.1932.
Appointed: 23.3.1953.
Stationed at: Looe.
19.3.1955 Resigned.

P.C. 225 **John Charles Beard**
Born 6.7.1932.
Appointed: 27.4.1953.
Stationed at: Truro, Newquay.
28.4.1955 Resigned.

P.C. 170 **John Borlase**
Born 20.6.1930.
Appointed: 27.4.1953.
Stationed at: Truro, Falmouth, Launceston.

P.C. 193 **Brian Malcolm Davis**
Born 3.12.1929.
Appointed: 27.4.1953.
Stationed at: St Austell, Bodmin, HQ
Information Room, Bodmin , Nancledra.

P.C. 116 **John Stewart Gibbs**
Born 21.1.1929.
Appointed:. 27.4.1953.
Stationed at: Padstow, Truro, Fowey, St

Austell.
27.9.1956 Granted a Favourable Record
with DC 94 Doherty for vigilance displayed
at Truro on 25 8.1956 resulting in the arrest
of John Christopher Brown on charges of
larceny, credit by fraud and obtaining money
by forged instrument.

P.C. 252 **Donald Leonard Webb**
Born 2.12.1931.
Appointed: 11.5.1953.
Transferred from the Metropolitan Police
District.
Stationed at: Falmouth.
19.10.1957 Resigned.

P.C. 274 **Stanley Edward Wilton**
Born 28.4.1930
Appointed: 15.6.1953
Stationed at: Bude , St Columb, Calstock,
Fowey.
30.4.1967. Resigned.

P.C. 16 **Percy Ramsden**
Born 30.11.1909.
Appointed: 13.7.1953.
Transferred from Birmingham City Police,
where he was a Sergeant. Reverted to P.C.
On transfer.
Stationed at: Perranporth.
31.1.1956 Retired to Pension.

P.C. 180 **Richard Antonio Southern**
Born. 14.5.1933.
Appointed: 27.7.1953.
Promotion: 9.6.1965 to Sergeant.
Stationed at: Truro, Chacewater, Bodmin,
Blackwater, Truro, HQ Training.

P.C. 122 **Bernard John Waters**
Born 20.4.1933.
Appointed: 27.7.1953.
Stationed at: Redruth, Isles of Scilly,
Camborne, Hayle, St Breward, St Austell.

P.C. 91 **Clifford Maurice Coffin**
Born 3.12.1932.
Appointed: 14.9.1953.
Stationed at: Bodmin, St Austell.
30.7.1958 Resigned.

P.C. 246 **William Charles Terrance Paul**
Born 16.5.1927.
Appointed: 14.9.1953.
Stationed at: Penzance.
8.10.1955 Resigned.

P.C. 32 **Wilburn James Sweet**
Born 2.9.1928.
Appointed: 14.9.1953.
Stationed at: Penzance, St Erth, Lerryn.
30.6.1954 Granted a Favourable Record for
zeal and attention to duty which resulted in
the arrest of Robert Lyons for attempted shop
breaking and Mervyn Reade Legassick ,
friend, and Dennis Frederick Clark, friend,
being charged with aiding and abetting.

P.C. 39 **Jack Buzza**
Born 31.7.1932.
Appointed: 26.10.1953.
Stationed at: Callington , Falmouth, Bude.

30.6.1958 Granted a Favourable Record for brave conduct on 21.5.1958 when he was lowered approx., 100 feet, down a dangerous cliff face at Bude and rescued R.Larkin, aged 31 years, who had been trapped there for four hours.
17.1.1960 Resigned.

P.C. 266 Martin Clive Holmes
Born 13.4.1926.
Appointed: 26.10.1953.
Stationed at: Liskeard.
27.8.1955 Resigned.

P.C. 72 Kenneth John Pinder
Born 23.3.1931.
Appointed: 26.10.1953.
Promotion:
1.11.1965 to Sergeant.
Stationed at: Torpoint, Kingsand, St Ives, Truro, St Austell.

P.C. 315 Richard Thomas Gerald Tremelling. Born 5.2.1928.
Appointed: 26.10.1953.
Promotion: 1.9.1963 to Sergeant.
Stationed at: Fowey, Constantine, St Ives, St Austell, Falmouth.
2.9.1964 Awarded the Testimonial on vellum combined with a resuscitation certificate by the Royal Humane Society for his rescue from drowning of a student at Gyllynvase Beach, Falmouth, on 25.6.1964.

P.C. 318 Bryan Gordon Howell
Born 27.9.1931.
Appointed: 26.10.1953.
Stationed at: Wadebridge, Newlyn, Newquay, Whitstone.

P.C. 115 Cyril Derek Anstis
Born 7.4.1931.
Appointed: 14.12.1953.
Stationed at: Truro.
31.3.1959 Resigned.

P.C. 320 Percival Lionel Williams
Born 19.1.1929.
Appointed: 14.12.1953.
Stationed at: Falmouth, Tywardreath, St Ives.

P.C. 321 Dennis James Jordan
Born 1.7.1926.
Appointed: 14.12.1953.
Stationed at: Launceston.
26.3.1955 Transferred to Hereford Police

P.C. 178 David Richard Edwin Whithurst
Born 1.6.1932.
Appointed: 14.12.1953.
Stationed at: Saltash, Kilkhampton, Wadebridge, St Ives.
26.7.1965 Resigned.

P.C. 319 Douglas Wesson
Born 7.6.1928.
Appointed: 14.12.1953.
Stationed at: Falmouth, St Just, Helston.
28.7.1965 Resigned.

P.C. 322 Peter Royston Belk Hagland
Born 19.10.1928.

Appointed: 14.12.1953.
6.3.1954 Resigned.

P.C. 324 Terrance Sidney Dyer
Born 7.4.1928.
Appointed: 25.1.1954.
Stationed at: HQ
20.2.1954 Resigned.

P.C. 93 Graham Roy Hooper
Born 1.9.1933.
Appointed: 25.1.1954.
Promotion: 19.10.1966 to Sergeant.
Stationed at: Bodmin, HQ CID, Bodmin, Hayle, Helston, Hayle, Newquay.

P.C. 270 Thomas James Martin
Born 11.8.1928.
Appointed: 25.1.1954.
Stationed at: Redruth, Camborne, Redruth, Fowey, Trispen, Falmouth.

P.C. 325 Derek Frances Philp
Born 6.12.1932.
Appointed: 25.1.1954.
Stationed at: Launceston, Grampound, Probus.

P.C. 102 Glenville Courtney Gray Rogers
Born 12.9.1933.
Appointed: 25.1.1954.
Stationed at: Newquay, Truro, Perranwell, Illogan, Camborne.
31.8.1965 Granted a Favourable Record with DC 167 Davidson, P.C. 268 Partridge, P.C. 291 Kent, P.C. 317 Matthews for zeal and initiative in conducting enquiries resulting in the detection of 53 crimes in Camborne and Truro Divisions and the successful prosecution of 15 persons for offences of warehouse breaking, office breaking, canteen breaking, store breaking and larceny. Also complimented by the Chairman of East Penwith Magistrates Court on 12.8.1965.
1.8.1966 Granted a Favourable Record for observation and attention to duty which resulted in the conviction of Anthony Glenwood Harry on charges of office breaking, Larceny and burglary.

P.C. 239 Cedric Stanley Vokes
Born 25.1.1933.
Appointed: 25.1.1954.
Stationed at: Launceston, Polperro, Newquay, Ladycross.

P.C. 45 Kenneth Roger John Wilcox
Born 11.6.1928.
Appointed: 25.1.1954.
Stationed at: Falmouth, St Neot.

W.P.C. 3 June Coe Nee Ede
Born 21.6.1933.
Appointed: 1.2.1954
Stationed at: St Austell, Newquay, Camborne, Truro.
30.4.1958 Resigned.

P.C. 326 Glynn Morris
Born 21.9.1926.
Appointed: 1.2.1954.

Stationed at: St Austell, Burraton, Falmouth, Liskeard.

P.C. 56 Arthur John Brown
Born 11.11.1928.
Appointed: 15.3.1954.
Stationed at: Looe, Liskeard
18.5.1957 Resigned.

P.C. 30 Anthony Charles Walter Oliver
Born 25.1.1931.
Appointed: 15.3.1954.
Stationed at: Millbrook.
31.7.1954 Resigned.

P.C. 323 John Allan Wilson
Born 20.10.1931.
Appointed: 15.3.1954.
Promotion: 1.5.1966 to Sergeant.
Stationed at: Falmouth, Stratton, Bude, Looe, St Mellion, Liskeard.
March 1963. Awarded a Special Commendation for Bravery and devotion to duty on 27.2.1963 when a man jumped from Looe Bridge into the water and Constable Wilson dived into the water and swam across the harbour and supported the man until a boat arrived Without doubt he saved the mans life.
30.6.1964 Granted a Favourable Record for zeal and attention to duty in the detection of offences at Looe resulting in the arrest of Peter Robert Pratt and the detection of a juvenile offender

P.C. 324 Gordon Broom
Born 5.9.1932.
Appointed: 15.3.1954.
Stationed at: St Ives, Millbrook, Truro, Camelford.
20.12.1957 Granted a Favourable Record with Sergeant Short for prompt action at Porth Kidney Beach, Lelant, on 7.12.1957, when they rescued a woman from the sea and successfully applied artificial respiration.

P.C. 322 Richard Clifford Mitchell
Born 20.1.1929.
Appointed: 15.3.1954.
Stationed at: Newquay, Padstow, Penzance, Padstow.

P.C. 70 Kenneth Andrew
Born 1.2.1934
Appointed: 12.4.1954
Stationed at: St Austell, Mevagissey, St Austell, St Columb, Saltash, St Austell.
17.2.1959 Died.

P.C. 20 Malcom Stuart Dann
Born 3.9.1933
Appointed: 26.4.1954.
Stationed at:,
St Columb.
4.3.1957 Transferred to Plymouth City.

P.C. 327 Samuel George Matthews
Born 18.3.1928.
Appointed: 26.4.1954.
Stationed at: Penzance, Falmouth.

P.C. 328 Ernest Francis Reynolds
Born 20.4.1933.
Appointed: 26.4.1954.
Stationed at: Millbrook, Saltash, Millbrook, Looe, Millbrook, Isles of Scilly, Saltash, Jacobstow, Kingsand.

P.C. 68 William Charles Rogers
Born 19.3.1933.
Appointed: 26.4.1954
Stationed at:.
Penryn, Falmouth, Launceston, St Dennis, Penryn.
31.3.1962 Granted a Favourable Record for keen observation and devotion to duty, whilst off duty, which resulted in Perry John Lister being convicted of larceny from shops at Falmouth

P.C. 24 Peter Loadey
Born 1.5.1929.
Appointed: 14.6.1954
Stationed at: Wadebridge, Whitstone, Hayle.
2.9.1964 Granted a Favourable Record for zeal and attention to duty in effecting the arrest of seven youths concerned in the commission of a large number of offences of larceny over a large area.
P.C. 66 Sidney Arthur Semmens
Born 31.1.1932.
Appointed: 6.7.1954.
Stationed at: Truro, Gunnislake,

P.C. 49 Ronald Leslie Berryman
Born 14.6.1933
Appointed: 26.7.1954.
Stationed at: St Austell.
27.9.1955 Resigned

P.C. 119 Ronald Juleff
Born 17.8.1933
Appointed: 13.9.1954.
Stationed at: Truro, St Ives, Isles of Scilly.
11.5.1958 Transferred to the Surrey Constabulary.

P.C. 216 Peter Glyn Thompson
Born 14.2.1934.
Appointed: 13.9.1954.
Stationed at: Camborne, Falmouth, Newquay, Camborne.
31.12.1965 Retired through ill-health.,

P.C. 30 Bryan Hendra Brabyn
Born 12.6.1931.
Appointed: 13.9.1954.
Promotion: 1.12.1963 to Sergeant.
Stationed at: Newquay, St Austell, Falmouth, Newquay.

P.C. 131 Arthur John Passmore
Born 16.7.1934.
Appointed: 13.9.1954
Promotion: 1.6.1967 to Sergeant.
Stationed at: Newquay, Launceston, St Mellion, St Ives, Launceston.
26.9.1957. Granted a Favourable Record for his courage and devotion to duty at Newquay on 6.9.1957 when he boarded a moving coach and subsequently arrested two RAF Personnel from St Eval who were convicted for taking a motor vehicle without

the owners consent and other traffic offences.

P.C. 73 Kenneth Edwin Appleton
Born 23.11.1930.
Appointed: 13.9.1954.
Stationed at: Launceston, Looe, Callington, Troon.
27.1.1966 East Middle Callington Magistrates Court, commended by the Chairman for the action taken regarding the larceny of petrol by seven youths.

P.C. 33 Ronald James Bray
Born 18.6.1934
Appointed: 13.9.1954
Stationed at:,
Truro, St Austell, Chyandour.

P.C. 109 Sidney Howard Davey
Born 13.9.1931.
Appointed: 13.9.1954
Stationed at: Padstow, Fowey, Padstow, St Stephens.

P.C. 103 Dennis Alcock
Born 30.5.1931.
Appointed: 25.10.1954.
Stationed at: Looe.
30.8.1956 Resigned.

P.C. 34 Anthony Ricardo Pearce
Born 29.8.1934
Appointed: 25.10.1954.
Promotion: 1.2.1967 to Detective Sergeant.
Stationed at: Truro, Penzance, and Bristol Forensic Science Laboratory.

P.C. 40 John Gilbert Arthur
Born 25.8.1934
Appointed: 25.10.1954.
Stationed at: Redruth, Isles of Scilly, Falmouth, Mullion, Falmouth.

P.C. 163 Courtney Downing
Born 13.5.1929.
Appointed: 22.11.1954.
Stationed at: HQ.,
15.1.1955 Resigned.

P.C. 168 Morley Desmond Jenkin
Born 5.1.1934
Appointed: 20.12.1954.
Stationed at: Falmouth, Helston, Hayle,
21.6.1958 Seconded to Cyprus as Sergeant. Returned to Bodmin.
14.1.1962 Resigned.

P.C. 182 Donald James Whatmore
Born 14.12.1933.
Appointed: 20.12.1954.
Stationed at: Saltash, Ashton, Falmouth.
10.8.1966 Resigned.

P.C. 167 Robert Lambie Davidson
Born 22.10.1932.
Appointed: 20.12.1954.
Promotion: 7.3.1966 to Sergeant
Stationed at: Falmouth, Hayle, St Austell. Redruth, Penzance.
2.1.1964 Granted a Favourable Record for zeal and attention to duty resulting in the

detection of 43 crimes and the conviction of the offenders.
3.11.1964 Granted a Favourable record with DC 2 Furnell, Sergeant G.S.Hooper, for zeal and attention to duty in making enquiries which resulted in the charging of Owen Davey with receiving. Also commended by the Chairman, His Honour H. Aide Sheppard Q.C. At the Cornwall Quarter Session on 12.11.1964
31.8.1965 Granted a Favourable Record with DC 268 Partridge, P.C. 291 Kent, DC 102 Rogers and P.C. 317 Matthews for zeal and initiative in conducting enquiries resulting in the detection of 63 crimes in the Camborne and Truro Divisions and successfully prosecuting 15 persons for offences of ware house breaking, office breaking, canteen breaking, store breaking, and larceny. Was complimented by the Chairman of East Penwith Magistrates Court

P.C. 272 Bernard John Seabourne
Born 25.11.1932.
Appointed: 2.1.1955.
Stationed at: Redruth, Penzance, Troon Padstow.

P.C. 107 Trevor Edwin Tamblin
Born 30.1.1929.
Appointed: 24.1.1955.
Stationed at: Redruth, Lezant, Camelford, Egloskerry, Kilkhampton.

P.C. 98 Peter George Crick
Born 28.10.1933.
Appointed: 24.1.1955.
Stationed at: Camborne
25.8.1956 Resigned.

P.C. 57 William Robert Pascoe
Born 7.11.1934.
Appointed: 21.3.1955.
Stationed at: St Ives, Duloe.
31.1.1960 Resigned.

P.C. 61 Charles Reginald Truscott
Born 11.5.1934.
Appointed: 25.3.1955.
Stationed at: Penzance.
2.11.1956 Resigned.

P.C. 220 Colin Channon
Born 6.5.1933.
Appointed: 25.4.1955.
Stationed at: Liskeard,
23.11.1956 Resigned.

P.C. 309 Dennis John Kellow
Born 28.5.1932.
Appointed: 25.4.1955.
Stationed at: Camborne.
11.7.1956 Resigned.

P.C. 148 Stanley Riches
Born 8.12.1931.
Appointed: 25.4.1955.
Stationed at: Camborne.
28.4.1956 Resigned.

P.C. 163 Kenneth Ivan Craddick
Born 5.12.1933

Appointed: 25.4.1955.
Stationed at: St Just, St Ives, Padstow, Tywardreath.
31.10.1960 Granted a Favourable Record for zeal and devotion to duty on 6.5.1960 which resulted in the arrest and conviction of five persons on charges of store breaking and larceny, a total of 19 offences being cleared up

P.C. 172 David Michael Hoatson
Born   30.1.1934
Appointed: 25.4.1955.
Stationed at: Bude, Probus, Tregoney.
30.6.1958 Awarded the Royal Humane Society's Testimonial on vellum for brave conduct with P.C. 138 Pedlar when they twice made a hazardous 150 foot descent with ropes down cliffs at Bude to rescue four boys who had been trapped for nine hours.

P.C. 162 Richard Sidney Osborne
Born   26.11.1934
Appointed: 25.4.1955.
Stationed at: Hayle, Callington, Kingsand , Helston, Falmouth.
30.11.1959. Granted a Favourable Record for keenness and devotion to duty resulting in Ronald M.Robothan being convicted on charges of house breaking and larceny.

P.C. 169 Robert Percy Matthews
Born   9.4.1930.
Appointed: 25.4.1955.
Stationed at: Bodmin, Blue Anchor, Newlyn.

W.P.C. Dorothy Miles Nee Barber
Born   21.7.1933.
Appointed: 2.5.1955.
Stationed at:.
Falmouth, Penzance.
28.3.1957. Commended by the Penzance Borough Magistrates for her highly meritorious act in arresting and conveying R.E.Warburton to Penzance Police Station having found him drunk in charge of a motor vehicle.
29.8.1958 Resigned.

P.C. 7 Wlliam John Howard
Born 16.5.1930.
Appointed: 5.7.1955.
Stationed at: Liskeard, St Austell, Pool, Truro.

P.C. 5 James Arthur Coad
Born 17.5.1935.
Appointed: 25.7.1955.
Stationed at:,
Falmouth, Helston, Falmouth, Wadebridge, Bodmin.

P.C. 11 Peter Pentreath
Born 13.11.1934.
Appointed: 25.7.1955.
Promotion: 1.6.1967 to Sergeant.
Stationed at: Redruth, Goldsithney.

P.C. 199 Reginald Douglas Middleton
Born 11.9.1930.
Appointed: 2.8.1955.
Stationed at: St Austell, Camelford, Coads Green, Newquay.

Granted a Favourable Record for keenness and devotion to duty at 1.am. on the 13.8.1958 resulting in Kenneth Gordon Wright and John Leonard Hewing being successfully prosecuted on a joint charge of larceny of petrol from unattended motor vehicle in a St Austell car park.

W.P.C. 4 Joyce Hutchings
Born 14.4.1935.
Appointed: 29.8.1955.
Stationed at: St Austell, Newquay, Camborne.
31.5.1958 Granted a favourable Record for her persistence, keenness and devotion to duty resulting in the arrest of Violet White on 19.4.1958, for stealing a pound note from a handbag in a ladies cloakroom during a dance in the Launceston Town Hall. Three other similar charges admitted by White.
2.9.1960 Resigned.

P.C. 12 Theodore Samuel Kemp
Born 7.5.1931.
Appointed: 19.9.1955.
Stationed at: HQ.
20.9.1955 Resigned.

P.C. 12 William John Best
Born 28.6.1935.
Appointed: 24.10.1955.
Stationed at: Newquay, St Columb.
18.12.1958 Resigned.

P.C. 111 James Emmett
Born 5.12.1930.
Appointed: 24.10.1955.
Promotion: 1.6.1967 to Sergeant.
Stationed at: Bodmin, Liskeard.
7.3.1966 Commended by the Chairman of Liskeard Magistrates Court together with Detective Sergeant Phillips for efficiency and observation leading to the arrest of Douglas Godling, Andrew Ian Woodall and Rodney William Cecil on charges of larceny.

P.C. 63 Grenville John Harry
Born 20.5.1934.
Appointed: 24.10.1955.
Stationed at: Torpoint, Liskeard, Saltash. Isles of Scilly, Foxhole, St Stephens

P.C. 85 Clarence Edward Peters
Born 22.3.1935.
Appointed: 24.10.1955.
Stationed at: Callington, Liskeard, Saltash, St Merryn

P.C. 157 Anthony Charles Ham
Born 24.9.1935.
Appointed: 21.11.1955.
Stationed at: Wadebridge, Bodmin Bude, Perranporth, Newquay, Truro.
29.2.1964 Resigned.

P.C. 155 David Coe
Born 12.4.1932.
Appointed: 21.11.1955.
Stationed at: Newquay, Camborne, Truro, Foxhole, Mawgan-in-Meneage, Newquay.

P.C. 222 Ernest James Broderick
Born 11.9.1932.
Appointed: 19.12.1955.
Stationed at: St Ives.
12.4.1957 Resigned.

P.C. 67 John James Brian Miles
Born 25.7.1933.
Appointed: 19.12.1955
Stationed at: Penzance, Polruan, Looe.

P.C. 217 Henry Robert George Brunsden
Born 11.5.1927
Appointed: 6.2.1956.
5.2.1956 Transferred from the Metropolitan Police.
Stationed at: Penzance Egolskerry, Falmouth, Seaton.
7.3.1962 Commended for alertness in a case of housebreaking.
13.3.1963 Commended for ability and determination in effecting the arrest of four dangerous and violent criminals.

P.C. 184 Idris Ronald Davies
Born 21.4.1932.
Appointed: 20.2.1956.
Stationed at: Looe, Torpoint , St Columb, Newquay, St Columb, Newquay, Camelford, Camborne.

P.C. 223 Donald Roose
Born 7.10.1933.
Appointed: 20.2.1956.
Stationed at:, Callington, St Ives, Looe, Launceston.
17.2.1958 Resigned.

P.C. 218 Gerald Tregunna
Born 20.1.1935.
Appointed: 20.2.1956.
Promotion: 1.3.1967 to Sergeant.
Stationed at: Truro, Camborne, Millbrook, Truro, St Blazey, St Austell.

P.C. 225 Redvers Harry Angwin
Born 25.3.1933.
Appointed: 20.2.1956.
Stationed at:
Fowey, St Just, Redruth.

P.C. 17 Leslie Royston Pearce
Born 5.12.1935.
Appointed: 29.2.1956.
Promotion: 1.6.1967 to Sergeant.
Stationed at: Wadebridge, Newquay, Traffic Bodmin, Mawgan-in- Pydar, Truro.

P.C. 269 Phillip Charles Tregunna
Born 9.5.1931.
Appointed: 3.4.1956.
Stationed at: Camborne, Redruth, St Ives. Bodmin, St Mellion, Bude.

P.C. 295 John Maxwell Gilbert Tripp
Born 8.2.1935.
Appointed: 23.4.1956.
Stationed at: Redruth, Falmouth, Perranwell, Penryn.

P.C. 255 John Ellidge Duckworth
Born 31.10.1935.

Appointed: 23.4.1956.
Stationed at: Looe, Liskeard, St Breward.

P.C. 246 William Arthur George Cowling
Born 18.8.1931.
Appointed: 23.4.1956.
Promotion: 1.10.1962 to Sergeant.
Stationed at: St Austell, Tywardreath, Wadebridge, Helston.

P.C. 234 Keith Bullen
Born 11.3.1935.
Appointed: 23.4.1956.
Stationed at: Newquay,
27.10.1956 Resigned.

P.C. 266 Phillip Sedgeman Symons
Born 5.10.1935.
Appointed: 23.4.1956.
Stationed at: Penzance, St Columb, Falmouth, Bude, Devoran.
Granted a Favourable Record with P.C. 158 Curnow for keenness and devotion to duty at 1.10.am on 26.9.1958 whilst off duty in Falmouth, resulting in Ray David Peterson Scott-Holte being convicted on charges of shop breaking and larceny.

P.C. 16 Archibald George Fisher Clark
Born 21.11.1932.
Appointed: 18.6.1956.
Stationed at: St Just.
15.12.1956 Resigned.

P.C. 148 Denis Stephen Jago
Born 18.1.1935.
Appointed: 18.6.1956.
Stationed at: HQ. Penzance
1.1.1961 Transferred to Plymouth City Police.

P.C. 19 Reginald Thomas Aunger
Born 7.3.1932.
Appointed: 18.6.1956.
Stationed at: Launceston, Falmouth, Newquay, Camelford.

P.C. 135 Michael Ronald James
Born 2.5.1934.
Appointed: 18.6.1956.
Transferred from Plymouth City Police.
Stationed at: Redruth, Calstock, Drakewalls, Bude.

P.C. 133 John Godman Rowe
Born 15.3.1936.
Appointed: 20.8.1956.
Stationed at: Newquay, Perranporth, Tregoney, Probus, Newquay.

P.C. 313 Brian Juliff
Born 17.6.1933.
Appointed: 20.8.1956.
Stationed at: Falmouth,
31.7.1958 Resigned.

P.C. 308 Roger Ollerearnshaw
Born 8.9.1931.
Appointed: 20.8.1956.
Stationed at: Truro.
5.1.1957. Resigned.

P.C. 321 James Henry Vosper Swiggs
Born 9.6.1935.
Appointed: 20.8.1956
Stationed at: Bodmin
30.3.1957 Resigned

***Chief Constable* Richard Bonar Matthews**
Born 18.12.1915.
Appointed: 1.9.1956.
9.3.1936 to 19.9.1954 Metropolitan Police.
20.9.1954 to 31.8.1956 East Sussex Constabulary
31.3.1964 To Warwickshire Constabulary.

P.C. 316 Albert George Ley
Born 28.5.1925.
Appointed: 3.9.1956.
2.9.1956 Transferred from City of London Police.
Stationed at: Perranporth, Newquay, Halworthy, Padstow, Helston.

P.C. 192 Derick Joseph Harry
Born 17.9.1935.
Appointed: 17.9.1956.
Stationed at: St Ives.
28.6.1958 Resigned.

P.C. 103 John Henry Owen Williams
Born 28.8.1932
Appointed: 17.9.1956.
Stationed at: Liskeard.
26.1.1957 Resigned.

P.C. 49 Dennis Richard Harry
Born 17.9.1935.
Appointed: 17.9.1956
Stationed at: Camborne, Liskeard, St Mawes, St Germans, Helston.

P.C. 329 John Edward Chambers
Born 22.6.1936.
Appointed: 29.10.1956.
Promotion: 1.6.1967 to Sergeant.
Stationed at: Camborne, Gunnislake, Drakewalls, Perranporth.

P.C. 61 Kenneth Gerald Harvey
Born 12.4.1936.
Appointed: 19.11.1956.
Stationed at: Newquay.
14.2.1959 Resigned.

P.C. 330 Roy Angove
Born 28,4.1932.
Appointed: 19.11.1956
Stationed at: Camborne, St Ives, Camborne, Mawnan Smith, St Ives.

P.C. 331 Alan Hughes
Born 2.10.1931
Appointed: 19.11.1956.
Stationed at: Truro, Duloe, St Day.

P.C. 332 Anthony George Isaacs
Born 16.7.1932.
Appointed: 19.11.1956.
Stationed at: St Austell, St Just.

P.C. 231 John Michael Sampson
Born 2.10.1932.

Appointed: 19.11.1956.
Stationed at: Redruth, Tintagel, St Ives.

P.C. 8 John Brian Matthews
Born 21.9.1936.
Appointed: 28.1.1957.
Stationed at: Newquay, Bodmin, Egolskerry, St Buryan.
31.10.1963 Resigned.

P.C. 16 Michael Albert Matthews
Born 16.11.1936.
Appointed: 28.1.1957.
Stationed at: Penzance, Penryn, Ashton, Liskeard.

P.C. 44 David Charles Wadd
Born 6.9.1935.
Appointed: 28.1.1957.
Stationed at: Falmouth, Redruth, Penzance , Crowlas.

P.C. 98 Alan Cooper
Born 2.4.1932.
Appointed: 25.2.1957.
30.11.1957 Transferred to Southend Borough Police.

P.C. 103 John Williams
Born 22.2.1934.
Appointed: 25.2.1957.
Promotion: 1.3.1967 to Sergeant.
Stationed at: Redruth, St Austell, Newquay.

***W.P. Sergeant* Elizabeth Ann Adcock**
Born 5.10.1925.
Appointed: 18.3.1957.
Transferred from Kent County Constabulary as Sergeant.
Stationed at: H.Q., Truro.
26.9.1957 Granted a Favourable Record together with Detective Sergeant Laity for her work in connection with Registered Clubs.

P.C. 234 Martyn Henry Colwill
Born 19.12.1931.
Appointed: 25.3.1957.
Stationed at: Saltash.
17.3.1958 Transferred to Barnsley Borough Police.

P.C. 308 John Radley
Born 1.11.1934.
Appointed: 25.3.1957.
Promotion: 19.9.1964 to Sergeant.
Stationed at: Launceston.
31.12.1964 Transferred to Warwickshire Police.

P.C. 220 Leonard Dudley Brokenshire
Born 25.12.1933.
Appointed: 25.3.1957.
Stationed at: Camborne, St Germans, Penryn.

P.C. 90 David John Clifford Doyle
Born 11.1.1932.
Appointed: 29.4.1957.
Stationed at: Helston, St Just, Falmouth.

P.C. 153 Richard Charles Nankervis
Born 29.1.1934.

Appointed: 29.4.1957.
Stationed at: Helston, Wadebridge, St Austell, Helston, Regional Crime Squad.

P.C. 20 Frederick Thomas Rodda
Born 31.12.1933.
Appointed: 29.4.1957.
Stationed at: Torpoint, Falmouth, The Lizard, Redruth.

W.P.C. 1 Winifred Miriam Wakeham
Born 10.3.1937.
Appointed: 6.5.1957.
Stationed at: Truro, St Austell, Liskeard.
30.11.1959 Granted a Favourable Record with P.C. 140 Snell for the exemplary manner which observations were carried out on a licensed premises , resulting in a number of persons being convicted on charges under the licensing laws.
29.12.1963 Resigned.

P.C. 166 Leslie Owen Morcumb
Born 5.9.1936.
Appointed: 27.5.1957.
Stationed at: Truro,
28.3.1959 Resigned.

P.C. 201 Leonard Stanley Yeatman
Born 28.5.1932.
Appointed: 27.5.1957.
11.7.1957 Resigned.

P.C. 48 John Arthur Allen
Born 15.4.1936.
Appointed: 24.6.1957.
1.6.1967 to Sergeant.
Stationed at: Camborne, Mawgan-in-Pydar, Camborne, St Ives.
August 1962 Granted a Favourable Record for initiative and attention to duty which resulted in the arrest of Frederick William Joyce wanted on warrant for larceny of motor vehicles in Scotland.

P.C 56 Clive Mitchell
Born 16.10.1934
Appointed: 24.6.1957.
Stationed at: Bodmin, Wadebridge, Heamoor, Torpoint

P.C. 222 David Matthews
Born 31,3,1936.
Appointed: 29.7.1957.
Stationed at: Falmouth , Padstow, Tintagel.

P.C. 206 William Maurice Tonkin
Born 3.2.1933.
Appointed: 29.7.1957.
Stationed at: Launceston, Bodmin, Carbis Bay.

P.C. 134 Joseph Vivian Colliver
Born 25.7.1932.
Appointed: 26.8.1957.
Stationed at: Falmouth, Truro, Mevagissey.

P.C. 154 Frederick John Clemente Hall
Born 22,2.1935.
Appointed: 26.8.1957.
Stationed at: Wadebridge, Tywardreath, St Austell, Polperro, Callington.

P.C. 201 Lional Rodney Matthews
Born 25.1.1938
Appointed: 26.8.1957.
Stationed at: Falmouth, Camelford, St Germans, St Mawes, Penryn.

P.C. 237 Ronald James Moore
Born 3.11.1934.
Appointed: 26.8.1957.
Stationed at: Bude, Launceston Liskeard, St Germans.

P.C. 244 John Hendy
Born 27.4.1935.
Appointed: 23.9.1957.
Stationed at: Liskeard, Bodmin, St Austell.

P.C. 321 Brian Herbert Lawry
Born 24.7.1934.
Appointed: 23.9.1957.
Stationed at: Newquay, Truro, Coads Green.

P.C. 333 Eric Benjamin Franklin
Born 17.10.1928.
Appointed: 3.11.1957.
Transferred from Bristol City Police.
Stationed at: Liskeard, Bodmin.
P.C. 334 John Harrison
Born 19.3.1935.
Appointed:. 25.11.1957.
Stationed at: St Ives, Padstow, Wadebridge, Jacobstow.
31.5.1967 Reigned.

P.C. 335 Cyril Richards
Born 13.6.1937
Appointed: 25.11.1957.
Stationed at: St Ives, Redruth.
4.5.1959 Resigned.

P.C. 158 Brian William James Curnow
Born 18.10.1935
Appointed: 25.11.1957.
Stationed at: Falmouth, Truro.
26.9.1958 Granted a Favourable Record with P.C. 266 Symons for keenness and devotion to duty at 1.10 am on 26.9.1958, whilst off duty at Falmouth, resulting in Ray David Peterson Scott-Holte, being convicted on charges of shop breaking and larceny.

P.C. 252 Howard Lee
Born 14.10.1934.
Appointed: 23.12.1957
Stationed at:
Penzance, Dobwalls.

P.C. 98 Paul Stockbridge
Born 23.2.1933.
Appointed: 1.1.1958.
Stationed at: Penzance.
6.10.1958 Transferred to the Metropolitan Police.

P.C. 234 Graham Lester Williams
Born 5.8.1932.
Appointed: 24.3.1958.
Stationed at: Helston, Mawnan Smith,
1.6.1964 Transferred to Plymouth City Police.

P.C. 223 Frederick Michael Leslie Collins
Born 7.10.1936.
Appointed: 24.3.1958.
Stationed at: Looe, Isles of Scilly, Truro, Port Isaac.

P.C. 94 Dennis Henry Stone
Born 30.6.1937.
Appointed: 24.3.1958.
Stationed at: Falmouth, Camborne, Bodmin, Probus.

P.C. 81 Roy Tossell
Born 4.1.1934.
Appointed: 24.3.1958.
Stationed at: Torpoint, Burraton, Newquay.

P.C. 97 Gordon David Stewart Maddock
Born 5.5.1936.
Appointed: 28.4.1958.
27.4.1958 Transferred from the Metropolitan Police.
Stationed at: Falmouth, Helston.
11.8.1965 Transferred to the Wiltshire Police as Sergeant.

W.P.C. 3 Sylvia Vivian James
Born 16.11.1932.
Appointed: 28.4.1958.
Stationed at: Truro, Penzance, Liskeard.

P.C. 4 Kenneth Russell Searle
Born 11.8.1937.
Appointed: 28.4.1958.
Stationed at: Penzance, Egloskerry, Saltash, Pool.

P.C. 245 Derek Clive Gregor
Born 29.1.1934.
Appointed: 28.4.1958.
Stationed at:.
Truro.
28.2.1959. Granted a Favourable Record for his keenness to duty which resulted in Christopher Helps being summoned under Section 10 Larceny Act 1916.

P.C. 197 Dennis Roy George Taylor
Born 18.7.1930.
Appointed: 1.5.1958.
Stationed at: Bodmin,
29.12.1958 Transferred to the Metropolitan Police.

P.C. 17 Brian Richards.
Born 9.6.1933.
Appointed: 27.5.1958.
Stationed at: Launceston, St Buryan.

P.C. 205 Neil Michael Bodman
Born 3.8.1931.
Appointed: 28.7.1958.
Stationed at: Redruth, Looe, Lostwithiel.

P.C. 192 Ivan Pollard
Born 25.5.1935.
Appointed: 28.7.1958.
Stationed at: St Austell, Truro.

P.C. 119 Alan Roy Sanders
Born 30.11.1937.
Appointed: 28.7.1958.

Stationed at: Camborne, Bude, Bodmin, Kilkhampton, Newquay.

P.C. 91 Nigel Graham Pocknell
Born 20.5.1939.
Appointed: 25.8.1958.
Stationed at: Bodmin.
2.7.1959 Resigned.

P.C. 313 Martin John Cox
Born 7.11.1938.
Appointed: 27.10.1958.
Stationed at: Newquay
1.2.1963 Transferred to Plymouth City Police.

P.C. 242 Brian Gray
Born 18.7.1939.
Appointed: 27.10.1958
Stationed at: Liskeard
2.1.1960 Resigned.

P.C. 92 Ralph Paddon
Born 6.4.1934.
Appointed: 27.10.1958.
Stationed at: HQ.
31.10.1962 Resigned.

P.C. 18 Gilbert Charles Pollard
Born 17.9.1939.
Appointed: 27.10.1958.
Stationed at: Falmouth, Launceston.
30.6.1959 Granted a Favourable Record for persistance and devotion to duty on the 14.5.1959 at Falmouth when Joseph Patrick Cullen and Hugh Mulholland were arrested for shop breaking, larceny and assault on Police

P.C. 273 Peter Frederick Harris
Born 2.11.1939.
Appointed: 24.11.1958.
Stationed at: St Ives, Redruth, Launceston.
20.6.1963 Resigned

P.C. 98 Arthur David John Pascoe
Born 6.2.1938.
Appointed: 24.11.1958.
Stationed at: Newquay.
31.5.1960 Resigned

P.C. 336 Christopher Warren Brown
Born 12.7.1934.
Appointed: 24.11.1958
Stationed at: Redruth, Bodmin.

P.C. 337 Maurice Anthony Wilkins
Born 20.1.1938.
Appointed: 24.11.1958.
Stationed at: Launceston, Falmouth, Liskeard, Newlyn East, Newquay.
31.7.1963 Granted a Favourable Record for zeal and attention to duty in effecting the arrest of Michael John Dann at Liskeard on 9.7.1963 whilst attempting to steal cable from a S.W.E.B. Compound.

P.C. 339 Alwyne Ernest William Henry Earl
Born 2.1.1933.
Appointed: 22.12.1958.
Stationed at: Truro, Sticker, Looe.

P.C. 338 Roger Frederick Pimley
Born 19.1.1937.
Appointed: 22.12.1958.
Stationed at: Truro, Perranporth, Isles of Scilly, Launceston, Roche.

P.C. 12 Jack Worth
Born 25.5.1933.
Appointed: 22.12.1958.
Stationed at: Truro, Penzance, Gunnislake.

P.C. 174 Anthony Michael Lake
Born 21.1.1940
Appointed: 26.1.1959.
Stationed at: Falmouth, Camelford, Duloe, Newquay.

P.C. 197 William Ronald Brenton
Born 4.6.1938.
Appointed: 23.2.1959.
Stationed at: Falmouth, Saltash, Newquay.

P.C. 253 Trevor Hill
Born 15.3.1934.
Appointed: 23.3.1959.
Stationed at: Falmouth, Helston, Bodmin.

P.C. 211 Michael Edward Carne
Born 15.12.1934.
Appointed: 23.3.1959.
Stationed at: Falmouth, Bodmin, Mylor, St Ives.

W.P.C. 5 Maureen Daphne Yelland
Born 12.7.1933.
Appointed: 23.3.1959.
Stationed at: Truro, St Austell.
10.11.1961 Resigned.

P.C. 22 Roger Harvey
Born 14.4.1940.
Appointed: 27.4.1959.
Stationed at:
Newquay, Wadebridge, Stratton.

P.C. 61 Malcolm Gordon Perry
Born 1.4.1940.
Appointed: 27.4.1959.
Stationed at: Penzance , Launceston, Bodmin.

W.P.C. 6 Marie Elizabeth Appelton
Born 29.11.1935
Appointed: 4.5.1959.
Stationed at: Truro.
16.1.1960 Resigned.

P.C. 137 Gerald Goodman
Born 4.10.1937.
Appointed: 25.5.1959.
7.11.1959 Resigned.

P.C. 70 John D'Arcy Roberts
Born 4.5.1935.
Appointed: 25.5.1959.
Stationed at: St Austell, Redruth, Penzance.

P.C. 123 Roger Alan Wilson
Born 12.4.1940.
Appointed: 27.7.1959.
Stationed at: Camborne
16.8.1960 Resigned.

P.C. 200 Richard Anthony Dawe
Born 6.7.1940.
Appointed: 27.7.1959.
Stationed at: Falmouth, Bude, Newquay, St Mellion, Camelford.

P.C. 166 Trevor Thomas Hattam
Born 26.7.1940.
Appointed: 27.7.1959.
Stationed at: Liskeard, Saltash, Falmouth.

P.C. 294 Brian Smith
Born 23.6.1935.
Appointed: 1.8.1959.
Transferred from the Gloucester Police 31.7.1959.
Promotion: 16.3.1966 to Sergeant.
Stationed at: Penzance, St Ives, Camborne.

P.C. 277 James Torquil Stone
Born 28.1.1940.
Appointed: 10.8.1959
Transferred from the Metropolitan Police.
Stationed at: HQ., Liskeard.
9.4.1962 Resigned.

P.C. 183 John Henry Carter
Born 17.8.1937.
Appointed: 24.8.1959.
Stationed at: Penzance, Newquay Scenes of Crime.

P.C. 132 Alfred Henry Gilmore Waddell
Born 25.6.1940.
Appointed: 21.9.1959.
Stationed at: HQ.,
1.12.1959 Resigned.

P.C. 115 Eric Edward Dinnis
Born 30.6.1936.
Appointed: 21.9.1959.
Stationed at: Truro, Indian Queens.

P.C. 208 Peter James Telling
Born 11.9.1940
Appointed: 21.9.1959.
Stationed at: Liskeard, Fowey, Mawnan Smith.

P.C. 235 Thomas Deryck Chappell
Born 27.9.1933.
Appointed: 16.11.1959.
Transferred from the Metropolitan Police.
Stationed at: Redruth, Bodmin, Stoke Climsland.
31.8.1960 Awarded a Favourable Record for keenness and devotion to duty which resulted in the arrest of Richard Charles Mounce at Redruth on 12.7.1960 on a charge of office breaking.

P.C. 91 Michael Harold Reeve
Born 22.11.1940
Appointed: 23.11.1959.
Stationed at: Falmouth, Bodmin.
6.7.1963 Resigned.

P.C. 247 Spencer Joseph Turley
Born 13.4.1936.
Appointed: 23.11.1959.
Stationed at: Camborne.
30.1.1961 Resigned.

P.C. 80 Thomas John Couch
Born 16.11.1934.
Appointed: 23.11.1959.
Stationed at: Redruth, Camelford,
Perranporth, Launceston

P.C. 152 Wilfred Robert Warne
Born 15.3.1939.
Appointed: 23.11.1959.
Stationed at: Falmouth, Camborne, Bodmin,
St Germans.

P.C. 137 Barry John Doney
Born 7.7.1940
Appointed: 21.12.1959.
Stationed at: Falmouth.
13.11.1960 Resigned.

P.C. 240 Peter Leslie Brew
Born 15.1.1941.
Appointed: 18.1.1960.
Stationed at: Bodmin, Penzance, Truro,
Fowey.

P.C. 118 James Wilfred Timms
Born 12.12.1939.
Appointed: 25.1.1960.
Stationed at: Camborne, Perranporth,
Launceston, Isles of Scilly, Camborne..

P.C. 279 Brian Green Ward
Born 16.11.1936.
Appointed: 25.1.1960.
Stationed at: Camborne, The Lizard.

P.C. 106 Peter Rosevear
Born 14.3.1940
Appointed: 26.1.1960.
Stationed at: Truro
19.2.1961 Resigned.

P.C. 282 Richard George Phillips
Born 5.2.1941
Appointed: 25.2.1960.
Stationed at: Penzance, Portscatho,
Camborne, Pool.
Jan 1961 Granted a Favourable Record with
P.C. 151 Simmons for the action they took on
the night of the 15.10.1960 at Camborne
Railway Station which resulted in the arrest
and conviction of four persistent safe breakers.

W.P.C. 6 Ann Moyle Nee Hobbs
Born 11.11.1936
Appointed: 29.2.1960.
Stationed at: Truro. Camborne.

P.C. 39 Brian Harold Ivor Pascoe
Born 27.5.1937.
Appointed: 25.4.1960.
Stationed at: Camborne, Heamoor,
Penzance.
Granted a Favourable Record for persistence
and attention to duty resulting in the arrest
and conviction of Malcolm Crossley Jones,
on charges of assault, malicious wounding
and house breaking at Penzance and
Hampshire.
8.8.1966 Commended by the Chairman,
Mr Thurston T. Lane, of Penzance Borough
Magistrates Court on 8.8.1966 for his obser-
vation, together with DC 123 Stephens in the

detection of Jeffrey Collins and Peter James
Clarke on charges of larceny.

P.C. 2 Alton Keith Vincent
Born 24.3.1937.
Appointed: 25.4.1960.
Stationed at: St Austell.
4.10.1960 Resigned.

P.C. 57 Neville Rex Brewer
Born 14.4.1935.
Appointed: 8.5.1960.
Transferred from Somerset Constabulary.
Stationed at: Liskeard, Truro, Launceston.
24.10.1964. Resigned.

P.C. 132 Graham Anthony Young
Born 17.12.1940.
Appointed: 9.5.1960.
Stationed at: Falmouth.
30.11.1960 Resigned.

P.C. 139 John Rodney Dakin
Born 1.11.1940.
Appointed: 6.6.1960.
Transferred from the Metropolitan Police.
Stationed at: Penzance.
4.3.1963 Transferred to Metropolitan
Police.

P.C. 242 Thomas David Scott
Born 10.6.1941.
Appointed: 20.6.1960.
Stationed at: Falmouth, Liskeard, St Austell.
31.1.1966 Transferred to Nottingham City
Police.

P.C. 258 Arthur Francis Aitken
Born 23.8.1940.
Appointed: 22.8.1960.
Stationed at: Falmouth, Camborne, Pool.
31.8.1964 Died.

P.C. 227 Richard Barry George
Born 17.5.1936.
Appointed: 22.8.1960.
Stationed at: Redruth Burraton, Hayle.

P.C. 268 Frank Partridge
Born 22.11.1940.
Appointed: 22.8.1960.
Stationed at: Newquay, Millbrook, Redruth.
31.8.1965 Granted a Favourable Record
with DC 167 Davidson, P.C. 291 Kent, P.C.
162 Rogers and P.C. 317 Matthews for zeal
and initiative in conducting the enquiries
resulting in the detection of 63 crimes in the
Camborne and Truro Divisions and the
successful prosecution of five persons for
offences of warehouse breaking, office
breaking, canteen breaking, store breaking
and larceny. Also commended by the chairman of the East Penwith Magistrates Court on
the 12.8.1965.

P.C. 123 John Ralph Stephens
Born 18.7.1941.
Appointed: 22.8.1960.
Stationed at: Falmouth, Penzance.
Granted a Favourable Record for observation
and devotion to duty resulting in the arrest
and conviction of four men of store breaking

and larceny at Falmouth.
8.8.1966 Commended by the Chairman
Mr.T.T.Lane of Penzance Borough Magistrates
Court for his observation, together with DC
39 Pascoe in the detection of Jeffrey Collins
and Peter Lanes Clarke on charges of larceny.

P.C. 98 Lionel Reginald Wood
Born 12.5.1941.
Appointed: 22.8.1960.
Stationed at: Camborne, Isles of Scilly,
Camborne.
7.3.1964 Granted a Favourable Record for
zeal and attention to duty which resulted in
the arrest of Geoffrey Leon Watts and
Reginald Arthur Keen on charges of office
breaking and larceny.

P.C. 165 Harold Walter Preece
Born 25.11.1936.
Appointed: 19.9.1960.
Stationed at: Liskeard
8.2.1964 Resigned.

P.C. 2 Maurice Eric Furnell
Born 14.6.1933.
Appointed: 10.10.1960.
Transferred from the Metropolitan Police.
Stationed at: Redruth, St Ives.
3.12.1964 Granted a Favourable Record
with Sergeant C.G.Hooper and DC 167
Davidson for zeal for attention to duty which
resulting in the charging of Owen Davey with
receiving.
Also commended by his Honour
H.A.D.Shepherd Q.C. At Cornwall Quarter
Sessions 12.1.1964.
21.6.1965 Resigned.

P.C. 312 Michael William Murphy
Born 12.1.1940.
Appointed: 24.10.1960.
Stationed at: Helston.
16.6.1962. Resigned.

P.C. 29 Jeffrey Tony Bolt
Born 14.4.1938
Appointed: 24.10.1960.
Stationed at: Camborne, Pool, Callington

P.C. 340 Roger Maddern
Born 7.7.1938.
Appointed: 24.10.1960.
Stationed at: Camborne, Isles of Scilly.

P.C. 161 Douglas Roger Graham Wipp
Born 23.2.1941.
Appointed: 24.10.1960.
Stationed at: Newquay, Looe.

P.C. 132 Jeffrey John Gendall
Born 5.2.1936.
Appointed: 21.11.1960.
Stationed at: St Ives.
10.6.1961 Resigned.

**W.P.C. 4 Janet Rosemary Augusta Jones
Nee Curtis**
Born 27.5.1933
Appointed: 21.11.1960.
Transferred from the Devon Constabulary.
Stationed at: Truro, Falmouth.

P.C. 137 Graham Morton Parkin
Born   22.7.1941.
Appointed: 21.11.1960.
Stationed at: St Austell, Helston.
6.10.1963 Resigned.

P.C. 341 Roger John Kinsman
Born   2.10.1940.
Appointed: 19.12.1960.
Stationed at: Truro, Polperro, Mousehole.
15.8.1966   Transferred to Bristol City
Police.

P.C. 342 Arthur James Shelcott Parsons
Born   15.3.1937
Appointed: 19.12.1960.
Stationed at: Liskeard, Slades.

P.C. 176 Malcolm George Bull
Born   1.2.1937.
Appointed: 30.1.1961.
Transferred from Stockport Borough Police.
Stationed at: Redruth
18.1.1961 Letter from Stockport Borough
Police that P.C. Bull was to receive a Chief
Constables recommendation for when he
arrested a man tearing sheet lead from a
store roof, the man being subsequently
convicted.
12.10.1961 Resigned.

P.C. 106 Brian Read
Born   7.3.1939.
Appointed: 20.3.1961.
Stationed at: St Ives, Penzance.
26.7.1965   Resigned.

P.C. 47 Leslie Bruce Mayne Roberts
Born 5.10.1936.
Appointed: 20.3.1961.
Stationed at: Looe, St Columb Minor.

P.C. 62 Alan Remick Brokenshire
Born   8.3.1942
Appointed: 22.5.1961.
Stationed at: Camborne, Camelford, Bude,
Torpoint, Helston.

P.C. 148 Keith Shelley Soloman
Born 31.9.1937
Appointed: 19.6.1961.
Stationed at: Falmouth, Liskeard.

P.C. 204 Barry Cutler
Born 13.5.1937.
Appointed: 17.7.1961.
Promotion: 1.6.1967   to Sergeant.
Stationed at: Camborne, Isles of Scilly.

P.C. 247 Anthony Arthur Wood
Born   22.9.1938.
Appointed: 24.7.1961.
Stationed at: Redruth.
31.5.1965   Resigned.

P.C. 248 Denys Victor Trudgeon
Born   1.7.1934
Appointed: 18.9.1961.
Stationed at: Bodmin, Millbrook, Torpoint.

P.C. 9 Cyril John Hocking
Born 5.9.1942.

Appointed: 23.10.1961.
Stationed at: Newquay, Saltash, Burraton,
Saltash.
31.10.1963   Granted a Favourable Record
for zeal and attention to duty resulting in the
detection of eight offences of shop breaking
and store breaking at Newquay and the
arrest of the offenders

P.C. 99 David Norman Baber
Born 7.10.1942.
Appointed: 20.11.1961.
Stationed at: Falmouth, St Blazey.

W.P.C. 5 Sheila Patricia Dawe Nee Angove
Born 19.1.1937.
Appointed: 8.1.1962.
Stationed at: Truro, Newquay.
31.12.1963   Resigned.

P.C. 132 Desmond Morley Rescorla
Born 8.12.1941.
Appointed: 22.1.1962.
Stationed at: Falmouth, Bude, Newquay.

P.C. 238 William Robert Ellam
Born   8.12.1942.
Appointed: 24.4.1962.
Stationed at: Newquay.
23.4.1964   Resigned.

P.C. 42 William George Laws
Born   10.4.1943.
Appointed: 24.4.1962.
Stationed at: Falmouth, Helston, Falmouth,
Penzance.
5.9.1966   Killed whilst on motor cycle
patrol.

P.C. 168 Roger Garfield Doble
Born 21.3.1943.
Appointed: 24.4.1962.
Stationed at: Falmouth, St Austell,
Tywardreath, Praze.

P.C. 176 Franklin Roy Grigg
Born   3.1.1943.
Appointed: 24.4.1962.
Stationed at: St Austell, Bude, St Austell,
Newquay.

P.C. 277 Michael James Chadwick
Born 10.7.1942.
Appointed: 14.5.1962.
Stationed at: Liskeard, Launceston.

P.C. 89 Peter Sampson Moyle
Born 14.9.1942.
Appointed: 21.5.1962.
Stationed at: Newquay, Looe, Camborne.

P.C. 312 Michael John Rogers
Born 19.7.1943.
Appointed: 23.7.1962
Stationed at: Falmouth, Wadebridge.

P.C. 343 Michael John Rowe
Born 12.7.1942.
Appointed: 23.7.1962.
Stationed at: Falmouth, Truro, Duloe,
Bodmin.

P.C. 285 Edmund Robert Hallett
Born 24.2.1943
Appointed: 20.8.1962.
Stationed at: Falmouth, Bodmin Launceston,
St Austell, Liskeard.

P.C. 344 Norman John Williams
Born 22.6.1938.
Appointed: 22.10.1962.
Stationed at: Redruth
18.8.1963   Resigned.

P.C. 92 Christopher Leonard Jewels
Born 6.12. 1943.
Appointed: 6.12.1962.
Stationed at: St Austell, Looe.

P.C. 345 Peter John Simpson Robinson
Born 10.7.1943.
Appointed: 21.1.1963.
Stationed at: Falmouth, Helston, Liskeard.

P.C. 313 David Walter John Carne
Born 22.2.1943
Appointed: 18.2.1963.
Stationed at: HQ.,
26.4.1963   Resigned.

P.C. 224 Brian Norman Henry Nicholls
Born 14.7.1943.
Appointed: 18.3.1963.
Stationed at: Camborne, Launceston, Bude.

P.C. 112 John Gerald Nott
Born 22.7.1943.
Appointed: 18.3.1963.
Stationed at:
Newquay, Penzance.

P.C. 139 William John Brett Harvey
Born 29.2.1944.
Appointed: 22.4.1963.
Stationed at: Truro, Helston, Penzance,
Helston, Penzance.

P.C. 181 Robert George Curnow
Born 18.10.1943.
Appointed: 17.6.1963.
Stationed at: Redruth, Liskeard, Mylor
Bridge.

P.C. 58 Clive John Wooders
Born 10.5.1944.
Appointed: 17.6.1963.
Stationed at: Newquay.
16.5.1964   Resigned.

P.C. 75 David James Goodman
Born 21.7.1944.
Appointed: 22.7.1963.
Stationed at: Newquay, St Austell, Bodmin.

P.C. 313 Michael John Keat
Born 16.6.1939.
Appointed: 22.7.1963.
Stationed at: Falmouth, Perranporth,
Mawgan-in-Pydar.

P.C. 41 William Patrick Walker
Born 24.8.1936.
Appointed: 22.7.1963.
Stationed at: Truro, Praze.

14.3.1966 Transferred to Manchester City Police.

P.C. 113 Michael Dawson Colgan
Born 20.4.1940.
Appointed: 2.9.1963.
Transferred from the Metropolitan Police.
Stationed at: Launceston, Blackwater.

P.C. 273 Brian Richards
Born 27.9.1944.
Appointed: 16.9.1963.
Stationed at: Falmouth.
19.2.1965 Resigned.

P.C. 83 Clive Anthony Rowe
Born 3.9.1944.
Appointed: 16.9.1963.
Stationed at: Falmouth, Saltash.

P.C. 91 Roger William Jacob
Born 21.9.1944.
Appointed: 16.9.1963.
Stationed at: Penzance, Camborne, Isles of Scilly, Camborne, Liskeard

P.C. 149 Ian Kennerley Haspell
Born 6.12.1939
Appointed: 16.9.1963
Stationed at: Camborne, Ponsanoooth.

P.C. 276 Trevor George Hignet
Born 19.3.1940.
Appointed: 21.10.1963.
Stationed at: Falmouth, Truro.

P.C. 137 Colin James Harris Ivey
Born 5.5.1944.
Appointed: 21.10.1963.
Stationed at: Falmouth, Bude, Launceston.

P.C. 296 Andrew John Pethick
Born 25.4.1944.
Appointed: 21.10.1963.
Stationed at: Liskeard, Looe.

P.C. 64 Malcolm James Quick
Born 26.3.1943.
Appointed: 21.10.1963.
Stationed at: Falmouth, Helston.

P.C. 150 Peter Anthony Batson
Born 30.6.1944.
Appointed: 18.11.1963.
Stationed at: Redruth, Ponsanooth.

P.C. 315 Malcolm Lester Bullock
Born 25.3.1944.
Appointed: 18.11.1963.
Stationed at: Liskeard, Bude.

P.C. 79 Barry George Toms
Born 7.1.1942.
Appointed: 18.11.1963.
Stationed at: Truro, St Keverne.

P.C. 246 Douglas Alan Trethowan
Born 8.12.1944.
Appointed: 16.12.1963.
Stationed at: Truro, Camborne.
1.6.1965 Granted a Favourable Record for zeal and attention to duty in taking action

leading to the arrest of Thomas Molam escapee from Bellis River Prison, Westmorland.

P.C. 76 Henry Richard Hosking
Born 3.9.1940.
Appointed: 16.12.1963.
Stationed at: Truro, Falmouth.

P.C. 202 John Roger Haine
Born 6.5.1943.
Appointed: 20.1.1964.
Stationed at: Penzance
16.9.1964 Resigned.

P.C. 8 Gordon Roy Stevens
Born 18.1.1945.
Appointed: 20.1.1964.
Stationed at: St Austell.
28.8.1965 Resigned.

P.C. 96 Allen Keith Lancaster
Born 22.12.1940.
Appointed: 20.1.1964.
Stationed at: Liskeard, Polperro.

P.C. 30 Nicholas William McMillan
Born 6.2.1945
Appointed: 20.1.1964.
Stationed at: Helston, St Germans, Mousehole.

P.C. 308 Joseph Henry Brokenshire
Born 20.12.1938.
Appointed: 1.2.1964.
Transferred from Gloucestershire Police.
Stationed at: Wadebridge.

W.P.C. 5 Norma Elaine Arscott
Born 15.5.1944.
Appointed: 10.2.1964.
Stationed at: Truro, Newquay.

W.P.C. 1 Juliet Elizabeth Hyam
Born 10.5.1944.
Appointed: 10.2.1964.
Stationed at: Truro, Penzance, St Ives.

P.C. 127 Kenneth John Charman
Born 6.9.1941.
Appointed: 17.2.1964.
Stationed at: Camborne, Looe.

P.C. 138 Andrew Roland Billing
Born 1.2.1944.
Appointed: 16.3.1964.
Stationed at: Newquay, Falmouth.
21.8.1965 Resigned.

P.C. 1 John Charles Burrow
Born 26.9.1944.
Appointed: 16.3.1964.
Stationed at: Newquay, Liskeard, Penzance.

P.C. 157 Nigel Trewern
Born 6.4.1945
Appointed: 20.4.1964.
Stationed at: Liskeard.

P.C. 226 Charles John Dinner
Born 2.11.1944.
Appointed: 20.4.1964.

Stationed at: Camborne, Launceston, Liskeard.

P.C. 175 John Henry Hawkey
Born 15.3.1945.
Appointed: 20.4.1964.
Stationed at: Penzance, Camborne, Torpoint, Liskeard, Torpoint.

P.C. 130 Christopher Reginald Jewell
Born 12.11.1944.
Appointed: 20.4.1964.
Stationed at: Truro. Launceston.

P.C. 298 Richard Harry Newton
Born 25.10.1944.
Appointed: 20.4.1964.
Stationed at: Falmouth, Camborne, Isles of Scilly.

P.C. 189 Bevin Arthur Lawry
Born 7.7.1939.
Appointed: 9.5.1964.
Stationed at: Camborne, Polruan.

P.C. 214 Michael Ollis
Born 18.3.1941.
Appointed: 9.5.1964.
Stationed at: Truro, Ashton.

P.C. 117 Robin Harper
Born 3.12.1943.
Appointed: 19.5.1964.
Stationed at: Falmouth, Bude, Portscatho.

P.C. 265 Dennis Harvey
Born 26.5.1944.
Appointed: 19.5.1964
Stationed at: Camborne
22.5.1965 Resigned.

P.C. 74 Roger Brown
Born 12.1.1942.
Appointed: 25.5.1964.
Transferred from Coventry City Police.
Stationed at: Launceston.
31.1.1965 Resigned.

P.C. 203 Terrance Geoffrey Johns
Born 28.3.1942.
Appointed: 1.6.1964.
Stationed at: Penryn, Falmouth.
Transferred to Plymouth City Police.

P.C. 3 Peter Dudley Williams
Born 30.5.1945.
Appointed: 15.6.1964.
Stationed at: Falmouth, Bude.

Chief Constable Kenneth Mortimer Wherly
Born 30.7.1912.
Appointed: 7.7.1964.
5.1.1933 to 12.1.1958 Plymouth City Police
13.1.1958 to 10.6.1964 Walsall Borough Police.
5.4.1965 Awarded the Queens Police Medal for distinguished service.

P.C. 238 Alan Michael Veale
Born 2.10.1940.
Appointed: 20.7.1964

Stationed at: Truro.
30.4.1965 Resigned.

P.C. 165 Derek Nicholas
Born 10.11.1944.
Appointed: 17.8.1964.
Stationed at: Camborne, Penzance.
30.4.1966 Resigned.

P.C. 186 Michael Thomas Gill
Born 12.9.1939.
Appointed: 17.8.1964.
Stationed at: Penzance, Fowey
24.10.1966 Resigned

P.C. 190 Brian John Priest
Born 11.1.1938.
Appointed: 24.8.1964.
Stationed at: Penzance.
13.9.1965 Transferred to the Metropolitan
Police.

P.C. 55 Colin Archer
Born 21.1.1939.
Appointed: 14.9.1964.
Stationed at: Truro.

P.C. 263 David Worthington Crowle
Born 28.6.1942.
Appointed: 19.10.1964.
Stationed at: Camborne, Saltash, Burraton.

P.C. 258 Godfrey Perkins Richards
Born 28.2.1943
Appointed: 19.10.1964.
Stationed at: Penzance, Hayle, Penzance.
3.5.1965 Granted a Favourable Record for
zeal and attention to duty which resulted in
the arrest of John Wisdom on a charge of
larceny of a motor car at Ilford.

P.C. 234 Michael Clarence Waters
Born 5.10.1945.
Appointed: 19.10.1964.
Stationed at: St Austell, Callington.

P.C. 267 Mervyn Gilbert Goode
Born 30.12.1944
Appointed: 16.11.1964.
Stationed at: Newquay
13.4.1965 Resigned.

P.C. 196 Bruce Millington
Born 20.10.1945.
Appointed: 16.11.1964.
Stationed at:
Bodmin, Launceston, Newquay.
24.11.1966 Resigned.

P.C. 286 Albert William Batten
Born 26.2.1938.
Appointed: 16.11.1964.
Stationed at: Truro, Newquay.

P.C. 58 David Ernest Broom
Born 30.3.1940.
Appointed: 16.11.1964.
Stationed at: Redruth, Mawgan-in-Meneage.

P.C. 344 Frederick Alan Reynolds
Born 12.12.1944.

Appointed: 16.11.1964.
Stationed at: Liskeard.

P.C. 308 Barry Leslie Cooper
Born 26.4.1937.
Appointed: 1.12.1964.
Transferred from Nottingham Police.
Stationed at: Bodmin
31.1.1965 Resigned.

P.C. 202 Sidney Brian Roberts
Born 2.8.1939.
Appointed: 7.12.1964.
Transferred from the Metropolitan Police.
Stationed at: Penryn, Helston, Bude,
Camborne.

P.C. 142 Joseph Vivian Hendy
Born 23.11.1945.
Appointed: 14.12.1964.
Stationed at: Truro, Redruth.

P.C. 65 Donald Robin Ellis
Born 15.6.1943.
Appointed: 14.12.1964.
Stationed at: Truro, St Columb.

P.C. 280 Spencer John Webber
Born 20.1.1945.
Appointed: 1.1.1965.
Stationed at: Camborne, Newquay, Truro.

P.C. 300 Thomas Hugh Trevarthan
Born 28.,12.1942.
Appointed: 18.1.1965.
Stationed at: St Ives.

P.C. 121 Michael Andrew Arthur
Born 24.4.1942.
Appointed: 18.1.1965.
Stationed at: Redruth, Penzance.

P.C. 57 David Phillip LeBailley
Born 2.4.1945.
Appointed: 18.1.1965.
Stationed at: Newquay, Saltash.

P.C. 311 Keith Skinner
Born 15.8.1945.
Appointed: 18.1.1965.
Stationed at: Liskeard.

W.P.C. 7 Gillian Davey
Born 28,10.1944.
Appointed: 8.2.1965.
Stationed at: Truro, Penzance.

P.C. 185 Michael Blatchford
Born 1.2.1948.
Appointed: 13.2.1965.
Stationed at: Newquay.

P.C. 74 Roger John Gill
Born 23.1.1946.
Appointed: 15.2.1965.
Stationed at: Newquay.
18.9.1965 Resigned.

P.C. 347 James Barry Old
Born 20.11.1944.
Appointed: 15.2.1965.
Stationed at: Falmouth.

P.C. 194 Derek Ian Hilder Redgewell
Born 10.1.1946.
Appointed: 15.2.1965.
Stationed at: Newquay, Liskeard.

P.C. 346 Michael John James Smart
Born 29.9.1943.
Appointed: 15.2.1965.
Stationed at: Falmouth.

P.C. 348 James Blair Campbell
Born 31.1.1942.
Appointed: 15.3.1965.
Stationed at:.
St Austell, Sticker.

P.C. 349 Dennis John Pascoe
Born 6.5.1938.
Appointed: 15.3.1965.
Stationed at: Redruth, Pendeen.

P.C. 351 James Arthur Reynolds
Born 25.10.1941.
Appointed: 15.3.1965.
Stationed at: Camborne, Truro.

P.C. 260 Christopher Bartlett
Born 10.4.1946.
Appointed: 2.4.1965.
Stationed at: Truro, St Austell.

P.C. 350 Brian William Albert Watson
Born 26.4.1937.
Appointed: 8.4.1965.
Transferred from the Metropolitan Police.
Stationed at: Liskeard, Bodmin.

P.C. 114 David Boyns
Born 16.3.1946
Appointed: 20.4.1965.
Stationed at: St Ives.

P.C. 273 James Anthony Piper
Born 18.4.1942.
Appointed: 20.4.1965.
Stationed at: Truro, Fowey.

P.C. 144 Henry Maxwell Henwood
Born 23.12.1936.
Appointed: 17.5.1965.
Stationed at: Camborne.
4.9.1965 Resigned.

P.C. 84 Duncan Lionel Sadler
Born 24.12.1943.
Appointed: 17.5.1965.
Stationed at: Redruth.
31.12.1965 Resigned.

P.C. 309 Perry James Lobb
Born 11.6.1946.
Appointed: 14.6.1965
Stationed at: St Austell, Liskeard.

P.C. 290 Peter Ross James
Born 3.6.1946.
Appointed: 14.6.1965.
Stationed at: Falmouth.

P.C. 180 Michael Denman Menear
Born 21.4.1945.

Appointed: 14.6.1965.
Stationed at: Camborne, Looe.

P.C. 267 Colville John Rowse
Born   12.6.1946.
Appointed: 19.7.1965.
Stationed at: Falmouth.

P.C. 265 Roger Charles Parker
Born 22.6.1946.
Appointed: 19.7.1965.
Stationed at: Camborne.

P.C. 247 Bernard Hemborough
Born 13.8.1938.
Appointed: 19.7.1965.
Stationed at: Penzance, Hayle.
31.3.1966.   Granted a Favourable Record for keenness and attention to duty which lead to the arrest of Raymond James Lynch, Kevin Andrew Given and Anthony Leo Morgan on charges of house breaking and larceny at Saltash and Plymouth.

P.C. 238 Christopher John Hancock
Born   7.5.1946.
Appointed: 19.7.1965.
Stationed at: Newquay.

P.C. 352 Robert Henry Morcumb
Born   10.12.1943.
Appointed: 26.7.1965.
Transferred from the Metropolitan Police.
Stationed at: Camborne, St Mawes

P.C. 2 Michael Edward Hammett
Born   13.5.1945.
Appointed: 16.8.1965.
Stationed at: Penzance.
6.6.1966   At Penzance Borough Juvenile Court commended by the Chairman for his attention to duty resulting in the detection of six breaking offences and one offence of larceny and five offences of receiving

P.C. 178 Graham Roy Bulford
Born   20.5.1946.
Appointed: 13.9.1965.
Stationed at: Falmouth.

P.C. 319 Robin Neil Houghton
Born   6.9.1946.
Appointed: 13.9.1965.
Stationed at: Redruth, Truro.

P.C. 144 John Morgan
Born   19.11.1944.
Appointed: 18.10.1965.
Stationed at: St Austell, Liskeard.

P.C. 8 Barry John Reginald Norris
Born 8.7.1942
Appointed: 18.10.1965
Transferred from British Transport Police.
Stationed at: Truro.

P.C. 74 Victor Thomas Waters
Born   2.5.1946.
Appointed: 18.10.1965.
Transferred from the Metropolitan Police.
Stationed at: St Austell.

P.C. 190 Patrick John Philp
Born 5.3.1945.
Appointed: 18.10.1965.
Stationed at: Penzance.

P.C. 97 George John Bell
Born 26.9.1937.
Appointed: 15.11.1965.
Stationed at: Liskeard.
25.2.1967   Resigned.

P.C. 138 Alan Richards
Born 30.3.1945.
Appointed: 15.11.1965.
Stationed at: Camborne.
31.8.1966   Resigned.

P.C. 106 Maurice Edward Shaw
Born 14.5.1944.
Appointed: 1.12.1965.
Transferred from the Surrey Police.
Stationed at: Penzance, Heamoor.

P.C. 304 James Michael Doney
Born   7.7.1944.
Appointed: 13.12.1965.
Stationed at: Newquay, Truro.
2.8.1966   Commended by the Chairman, B.H.Phillips Esq., of Pydar Magistrates Court for his tenacity and attention to duty in dealing with five youths at Newquay who were dealt with at the court on charges of receiving and threatening behaviour.

P.C. 353 Alan John Best
Born 5.12.1946.
Appointed: 13.12.1965.
Stationed at: St Austell, Camborne.

P.C. 72 Peter John Jelliss
Born   2.11.1946.
Appointed: 13.12.1965.
Stationed at: Redruth.

P.C. 216 Trevor John Pearce
Born 2.1.1947.
Appointed: 17.1.1966.
Stationed at: Newquay.
31.12.1966.   Resigned.

P.C. 84 Kenneth Davies
Born 16.10.1935
Appointed: 17.1.1966.
Stationed at: Helston.

P.C. 356 Graham Charles Mill
Born 28.11.1946.
Appointed: 17.1.1946.
Stationed at: Truro.

P.C. 354 Rodney Stewart Martin
Born 5,1.1947.
Appointed: 17.1.1966.
Stationed at: Newquay.

P.C. 355 Colin John Trudgeon
Born 26,12.1946.
Appointed: 17.1.1966.
Stationed at: Penzance.

Chief Inspector **Peter Selwyn Hart**
Born 2.3.1934.

Appointed: 1.2.1966.
Transferred from Leicestershire and Rutland Constabulary.
Stationed at:,
Camborne.

P.C. 357 Keith Freemantle
Born 20.11.1947.
Appointed: 14.2.1966.
Stationed at: Truro.

P.C. 242 Stewart James Phillip Lamerton
Born 28.7.1938.
Appointed: 14.2.1966.
Stationed at: Camborne.

P.C. 358 Geoffrey Theopont Provis
Born 23.11.1946.
Appointed: 14.2.1966.
Stationed at: Truro.

P.C. 359 Richard John Rogers
Born   28.12.1946.
Appointed: 14.2.1966.
Stationed at: Falmouth

W.P.C. 8 Judith Hosking
Born 4.12.1945.
Appointed: 14.3.1966.
Stationed at: Truro.
31.3.1967.   Resigned.

P.C. 361 Graham North
Born 2.10.1942.
Appointed: 14.3.1966.
Stationed at: Camborne.

P.C. 41 Clive Edward Polkinghorne
Born 22.7.1947.
Appointed: 14.3.1966.
Stationed at: Falmouth.

P.C. 360 Roger Richard Trevennen
Born 25.3.1937.
Appointed: 14.3.1966.
Stationed at: Penzance.

P.C. 292 Christopher Charles Watters
Born 12.11.1945.
Appointed: 18.4.1966.
Stationed at: Launceston.

P.C. 294 Leonard Edward Roach
Born 15.8.1941.
Appointed: 18.4.1966.
Stationed at: St Austell.

P.C. 167 William Everett Benney
Born   11.8.1936.
Appointed: 23.4.1966.
Transferred from Somerset Police.
Stationed at: Camborne, Illogan.
26.2.1963   Commended by the Chief Constable for initiative and persistance and devotion to duty whilst off duty for the arrest of Avery.

P.C. 237 Noel Jago
Born 25.12.1946.
Appointed: 13.6.1966.
Stationed at: Camborne.

P.C. 126 Spencer Thomas Pritchard
Born   22.6.1947.
Appointed: 6.7.1966.
Stationed at: Truro.

P.C. 165 Darrel Glen Brown
Born   11.7.1947.
Appointed: 18.7.1966.
Stationed at: St Austell.

P.C. 317 William Arthur Tozer
Born   1.8.1947.
Appointed: 15.8.1966.
Stationed at: Camborne, St Ives.

P.C. 323 Terry John Allison
Born   17.2.1947.
Appointed: 12.9.1966.
Stationed at: Newquay.

P.C. 281 David Anthony Duckham
Born 30.7.1942.
Appointed: 12.9.1966.
Stationed at: Falmouth.

P.C. 243 David Langridge
Born   13.3.1946.
Appointed: 12.9.1966.
Stationed at: Penzance, Truro.

P.C. 341 Richard Walker
Born   21.12.1946.
Appointed: 12.9.1966.
Stationed at: Newquay.

P.C. 42 Joseph Terrance Jenkin
Born   12.7.1945.
Appointed: 3.10.1966.
Stationed at: Falmouth.

P.C. 362 Alan William Russell
Born   4.3.1944.
Appointed: 3.10.1966.
Stationed at: Newquay.

P.C. 182 David John Hingston
Born   6.5.1937.
Appointed: 1.10.1966
Transferred from Somerset Police.
Stationed at: Falmouth, Bodmin.
22.6.1962.   Commended by Yeovil
Magistrates Court regarding shop breaking
and other offences.

P.C. 138 Colin Graham Handy
Born   7.4.1946.
Appointed: 17.10.1966.
Stationed at: Camborne.

P.C. 37 Michael Colin Hawke
Born   19.9.1947.
Appointed: 17.10.1966.
Stationed at: Helston.

P.C. 263 Godfrey John Penhaligon
Born   4.10.1947.
Appointed: 17.10.1966.
Stationed at: Newquay.

P.C. 108 Alan Howard Watts
Born   30.9.1947.

Appointed: 17.10.1966.
Stationed at: St Austell.

P.C. 364 John Christopher Russell
Born   8.6.1943.
Appointed: 17.10.1966.
Stationed at: Redruth.

P.C. 186 John Christopher Anthony
Born   6.7.1946.
Appointed: 14.11.1966.
Stationed at: Liskeard.

P.C. 366 David William Berryman
Born   16.8.1941.
Appointed: 14.11.1966.
Stationed at: Penzance.

P.C. 367 Edward John Pearce
Born   9.11.1943.
Appointed: 14.11.1966.
Stationed at: St Austell.

P.C. 369 Michael William Poad
Born   18.11.1945.
Appointed: 12.12.1966.
Stationed at: Liskeard.

P.C. 368 John McDonald
Born   11.12.1946.
Appointed: 12.12.1966.
Stationed at: Newquay.

P.C. 196 Peter John Parnell
Born   24.5.1939.

Appointed: 16.1.1967.
Stationed at: Newquay.

P.C. 216 Gerald David Patterson
Born   30.1.1948.
Appointed: 13.2.1967.
Stationed at: St Ives.

P.C. 34 Dennis John Dale-Green
Born   13.3.1948.
Appointed: 13.3.1967.
Stationed at: Newquay.

P.C. 129 Montague Dudley Lowther
Born 10.4.1947.
Appointed: 13.3.1967.

P.C. 93 Michael Tony Moncini
Born   7.12.1946.
Appointed: 13.3.1967.

P.C. 97 Clement Richard Gage
Born   27.2.1942.
Appointed: 17.4.1967.

P.C. 236 Jeffery Stewart Clements
Born   14.10.1945.
Appointed: 17.4.1967.

P.C. 235 Ian Denton Fox
Born   26.4.1948.
Appointed: 1.5.1967.
Stationed at: HQ.

P.C. 365 Francis Jeffery Lamerton
Born   4.10.1941.
Appointed: 1.5.1967.

P.C. 218 Dennis George Beeching
Born   5.4.1937.
Appointed: 15.5.1967.
Stationed at: HQ.

P.C. 103 Max Raymond Wallace
Born   22.5.1940.
Appointed: 15.5.1967.
Stationed at: HQ.

P.C. 274 David Harry Cann
Born 10.9.1935.
Appointed: 30.5.1967.
Transferred from the Metropolitan Police.
Stationed at: Penryn.